W9-CSY-307

► **Mining eBay Web Services:**
Building Applications with the eBay API

John Paul Mueller

▶ Mining eBay® Web Services:
Building Applications with the eBay API

Sybex

SYBEX

San Francisco · London

Associate Publisher: Joel Fugazzotto
Acquisitions and Developmental Editor: Tom Cirtin
Production Editor: Leslie E.H. Light
Technical Editor: Russ Mullen
Copyeditor: Cheryl Hauser
Compositor: Happenstance Type-O-Rama
Graphic Illustrator: Happenstance Type-O-Rama
Proofreaders: Laurie O'Connell, Nancy Riddiough
Indexer: Lynnzee Elze
Cover Design and Illustration: Richard Miller, Calyx Design

Library of Congress Card Number: 2004104104

ISBN: 0-7821-4339-3

This book is dedicated to Matt Wagner—a source of encouragement in troubled times and a voice of reason when things go wrong, a friend in weather foul and fair.

Acknowledgments

Thanks to my wife, Rebecca, for working with me to get this book completed. I really don't know what I would have done without her help in researching and compiling some of the information that appears in this book. She also did a fine job of proofreading my rough draft and page proofing the result.

Russ Mullen deserves thanks for his technical edit of this book. He greatly added to the accuracy and depth of the material you see here. Russ is always providing me with great URLs for new products and ideas. I also appreciated his hard work in testing endless versions of applications and providing input in my ideas. This book is technically challenging in that it relies on a number of programming languages, new and evolving technology, and several new products. Russ met the challenge with an efficiency that few other people could match.

eBay was very helpful in putting this book together. I don't know everyone from eBay who worked on this book, but I can thank those that I do know by name. Gary Downing made many introductions and acted as eBay's ambassador for the book. Michael Knopp provided a great many helpful comments and personal insights into eBay. I know that the book is much better for all of the help I received from these and other individuals from eBay.

A number of people read all or part of this book to help me refine the approach and to test the examples on a number of systems. These unpaid volunteers helped in ways too numerous to mention here. I especially appreciate the efforts of Eva Beattie who read the entire book and selflessly devoted herself to this project. Mike and Jody Cummings of The Treasure Mill provided me with training on using eBay in a real world business environment, helped me understand some of the nuances of the bidding process, and generally provided their expertise on a decidedly complex environment. Alessandro Vernet provided a variety of helpful tips and hints. Osvaldo Téllez Almirall provided extensive input on international issues, making the book much better suited to international needs as a result. David Clark helped with accessibility, user interface, and PHP development issues.

Matt Wagner, my agent, deserves credit for helping me get the contract in the first place and taking care of all the details that most authors don't really consider. I always appreciate his help. It's good to know that someone wants to help.

Finally, I would like to thank Tom Cirtin, Leslie Light, Cheryl Hauser, and the rest of the editorial and production staff at Sybex for their assistance in bringing this book to print. It's always nice to work with such a great group of professionals and I very much appreciate the friendship we have built over the last three books.

Contents at a Glance

Appendices

Contents

Introduction

You hear the staccato trill of the auctioneer's voice as the buyers motion using any of a number of signals. Bids are accepted as the auctioneer looks for the next better deal. The gavel finally strikes and the sale is made. Would it surprise you to know that eBay doesn't have anything to do with this scenario? Many people think that eBay is an auctioneer. In reality, eBay is a venue for a variety of sales models including auctions, fixed price sales, and even storefronts. This book is your gateway to understanding how the eBay selling model works and how you can use that information to create applications that give you or your clients an edge.

What's in It for Me?

Buying and selling products is an activity that was ancient long ago. Whether the marketplace is physical or electronic, goods change hands in exchange for compensation, usually monetary. The special addition that eBay makes to this age-old activity is speed and audience. Sales occur at lightning speed, so you need to keep track of items, buyers, and sellers if you want to make the best use of eBay as a venue. In addition, your audience is global—sales can and do occur any time day or night. You're open for business 24 hours a day, 7 days a week, 365 days a year. This book helps you understand how eBay Web Services combined with the right application lets you keep track of items without spending your entire life in front of a computer screen.

The essential goal of this book is to show how to use eBay Web Services. In many cases, the tasks are familiar because you perform them all the time. For example, eBay Web Services lets you upload new items for sale and relist items that didn't sell the first time. You can create various kinds of sales depending on how you create your application—Dutch and Chinese auctions are equally easy to create. The end result is the same, but by using eBay Web Services you save considerable time and effort. You can automate some tasks and reduce the time required to perform others. Using eBay Web Services makes it possible to store all of your information locally, rather than online.

The problem with many high-tech solutions is that they're, well, high tech. This book takes a lot of the high tech out of eBay Web Services and makes it accessible to anyone who wants a little more out of their eBay experience. You gain a competitive advantage without a large investment in time and money. Even though I enjoy working with technology a great deal, I know that your time is precious and that you want quick solutions to problems. I wrote this book to open eBay Web Services to anyone who wants to spend a few hours learning about it.

You might be surprised at how many tasks you can perform with eBay Web Services. For example, sellers can learn more about buyers and buyers can learn more about sellers. Good communications help create good feelings after the sale that could translate into more sales later. Knowing more about the people you deal with makes it easier to create deals that appeal to them and translate into sales that keep you in business. This book helps you increase your knowledge of eBay Web Services by showing you how to download and understand buyer and seller statistics.

Some people are nervous about using the Internet as a sales venue because the person on the other end of the line really is a faceless entity that they've never seen (and may never see). Using eBay Web Services makes it possible to automate comparisons of items based on various criteria such as shipping costs and you can automatically correlate this information with the buyer or seller information so you know which deal is best based on statistics you download. All this information is available in seconds rather than hours of intense searching online. Knowledge makes it possible to reduce the risk of a sale while increasing its appeal. The examples in this book help you understand how to put various calls together so you can gain a new perspective of eBay—one that isn't available when you use the manual interface.

It's possible to perform research on eBay within the terms of your licensing agreement. For example, I find that I can search for antiques online and learn about them relatively quickly. The pictures that sellers upload make it easier to identify the antiques and verify that I have the correct listing. The information tells me about the relative value of my antique and tells me about the original maker. Combining information that I gain on eBay with information from searches in other areas of the Internet usually provides a clear picture of the item that I just bought. More importantly, it tells me how much I should insure the piece for and helps me determine whether I want to keep it. Researching this material manually can consume days—doing it with a specially designed application requires minutes. In the end, this book provides you with ideas that you can extend into the perfect eBay application for your needs.

Who Should Read This Book?

I've designed this book to meet the needs of anyone who wants to use eBay Web Services. You might be a corporate developer, a researcher, a college student, or a store owner running a small business who needs an Internet presence. Depending on your needs, you won't use every part of the book; but you'll find that most parts have something to offer. No matter who you are, make sure you read Chapters 1 through 5. Chapter 6 is special in that it provides a gentle introduction to working with eBay Web Services and you can see results more or less instantly so you know that you're working with eBay Web Services correctly. Chapters 7 through 10 are language specific, so choose a language and read the appropriate chapter (more if you're multilingual). Chapter 11 helps anyone who wants to write an application for mobile devices.

Finally, Chapters 12 through 14 will help people who want to go a little further in the development process. Especially important for sellers is Chapter 13 because making things easy for the buyer eventually ends up increasing sales. In short, the book has something for everyone, but you might not need to read everything.

Some people have noted that a one-size-fits-all approach generally doesn't work. I realized this early on and made a few assumptions about your skills. You need to know something about computers—you can't pick up this book as a complete novice and expect to learn something. This book is packed with resources—many of which you'll need to locate on the Internet and read. I've assumed that you're motivated to learn what eBay Web Services can do for you and will use these resources to augment the information that I've provided. That said, all of the examples include complete explanations, so you don't have to worry that this book is incomplete. In fact, you'll find many instances where the information provided doesn't appear anywhere else.

It's possible to use this book without much programming knowledge, but you'll get a lot more out of it if you do know how to program at least a little. I've included a few examples in Chapters 2 and 4 that don't require many programming skills. The examples in Chapter 5 are essential to understanding the eBay authorization and authentication technique. If you really don't want to spend time with complex programming languages, try the JavaScript examples in Chapter 6. The VBA examples in Chapter 7 are very easy and might be the best choice if your programming skills are weak.

You won't find any information on using the programming language of your choice in this book—this book concentrates on eBay Web Services solutions of all types. In fact, I suggest several additional books you might want to try in addition to this book if you don't have the required background. Consequently, you won't want to look at this book until you've already learned to use the programming language of your choice.

Tools Required

There are some assumptions that I've made while writing the application programming examples in this book. During the writing of this book, I used a Windows 2000 server and two Windows XP workstations (along with other devices). I also tested many of the examples using Windows 9x. The test machines included SQL Server and MySQL. I also created Web server setups using Internet Information Server (IIS) and Apache. The test base was as broad as I could make it, but it wasn't possible for me to test every combination of machine and software.

I tested all of the examples in this book using the most current version of the appropriate language product. In most cases, I tell you which language version I used as part of the example description. I don't guarantee that the example will work with any older versions of the product, nor did I test using educational versions of products. I'm reasonably certain that most examples will work with any newer version of the supported language. eBay Web services is more complex than any other Web service I've worked with and I've noted areas where you might have problems getting examples to work as part of the language-specific chapters.

All of the desktop and Web application examples will work on a single machine, but I tested any database application on a two-machine setup, as well, to ensure you could place the database on another machine. The mobile device applications are all tested using an actual device, but I also tested them using an emulator. Chapter 11 tells you how to work with emulators and presents a number of emulators you might try when writing your application.

About the Author

John Mueller is a freelance author and technical editor. He has writing in his blood, having produced 63 books and over 300 articles to date. The topics range from networking to artificial intelligence and from database management to heads down programming. Some of his current books include several C# developer guides, an accessible programming guide, a book on .NET security, and books on both Amazon Web Services and Google Web Services. His technical editing skills have helped over 35 authors refine the content of their manuscripts. John has provided technical editing services to both *Data Based Advisor* and *Coast Compute* magazines. He's also contributed articles to magazines like *InformIT, SQL Server Professional, Visual C++ Developer, Hard Core Visual Basic, asp.netPRO,* and *Visual Basic Developer*. He's currently the editor of the .NET electronic newsletter for Pinnacle Publishing (`http://www.freeenewsletters.com/`).

When John isn't working at the computer, you can find him in his workshop. He's an avid woodworker and candle maker. On any given afternoon, you can find him working at a lathe or putting the finishing touches on a bookcase. He also likes making glycerin soap, which comes in handy for gift baskets. You can reach John on the Internet at `JMueller@mwt.net`. John has a Web site at `http://www.mwt.net/~jmueller/`. Feel free to look and make suggestions on how he can improve it. One of his current projects is creating book FAQ sheets that should help you find the book information you need much faster.

Part I

▶ **Discovering** eBay Web Services

Chapter 1

Discovering the eBay
Web Services

Considering Uses for the
eBay Web Services

▶ Learning about eBay Web Services

Getting and Setting Up
the eBay Web Services Kit

Understanding System
Setup Considerations

One of the most successful online businesses in the world is eBay. With 85.5 million (and growing) users, it's easily the most used Web site anywhere. Given the complex set of rules that many buyers and sellers follow, plus all of the functionality that eBay provides, it's only natural that eBay would eventually come out with a Web services package. Web services can help you automate and reduce the complexity of the tasks you perform with eBay. In short, you become faster and more accurate, while reducing the risk of a missed opportunity.

Web services are very useful, but they can also become quite confusing. In fact, of all the Web services that I've used, eBay Web Services is easily the most complex, yet well thought out, product. Fortunately, eBay understands the problems that developers could face. When other Web services leave you scratching your head trying to figure out what to do next, eBay Web Services does provide some level of help.

This chapter is your introduction to eBay Web Services. It won't show you how to write code, but it will tell you about Web services in general and eBay Web Services in specific. You'll want to read this chapter even if you already have Web services experience because eBay Web Services can be a little overwhelming at first, even with eBay's stellar support system. The documentation you get from eBay doesn't really provide a gentle introduction to the topic—that's what you get from this chapter.

You'll also get a wealth of practical information from this chapter. For example, many of you probably don't know how to set up a development system for maximum flexibility. This chapter tells you how I've set up my system and provides guidelines on how you can set up your system to make it easier to use. After all, no one wants to make the development process difficult. Part of the setup and installation process includes pointers on getting the eBay Web Services Kit and installing it on your machine.

Understanding the eBay Web Services

Whenever a new technology appears on the scene, it's important to compare it with other technologies. The comparison process often helps you decide how this new technology differs from what you used in the past and reduces problems caused by hype. The media might try to convince you that a new product or service is something completely different, when in fact it's merely an update or a new implementation of an existing technology.

Currently, there's a lot of hype about Web services that makes them sound like something new and very complex. This section of the chapter defines Web services generally, examines eBay Web Services specifically, and compares this technology to older technologies. What you'll find might surprise you because Web services are really a new implementation of an old technique.

> ▶ **NOTE**
>
> Don't confuse *new* with *useful*. Web services are very useful because they add new functionality to an existing idea that has worked for a long time. They're also new in that they use a different process from other technologies. However, the technology itself builds on other techniques that you've already used in some way. In sum, the implementation is new, the process is useful, but the technique is the same one you've used in the past.

What Is a Web Service?

You can look at a Web service from a number of perspectives. The easiest way to view a Web service is as a means of obtaining access to information. Essentially, you ask the server for information and the server returns that information in some form. The request and the returned information normally appear in eXtensible Markup Language (XML) form. Using XML preserves the meaning behind the information, regardless of the diversity of the platforms involved, so that you receive not only the information, but understand the context in which the information is used. The "Understanding XML Basics" section of Chapter 4 tells you more about XML. All you need to know now is that you receive information in XML format.

From an eBay Web Services perspective, you request information based on any of a number of search, buy, sell, management, or comment criteria (feedback). Many of your interactions with eBay will begin with some type of search. eBay supports a number of search techniques and not every technique works well for every kind of search. Chapter 2 discusses search techniques in detail. For now, just think of the search criteria as a form of request.

The request defines the kind of information you want to know and how detailed that information will be. eBay Web Services returns the information you request (when available) in a standardized format.

A Web service also performs some type of useful work. The useful work might be something as simple as interpreting your request, calculating the answer, and sending the result back. In the case of eBay Web Services, the Web service accepts your request in the form of a search string, bid for a product, upload of a new product or change to an existing product, account or other configuration, or a comment. The Web service interacts with the database through a search engine to obtain the information you requested and sends the information back to you. The search can take various forms. For example, you don't have to search all product categories—you can concentrate on just one. You might want to look for product pictures rather than text. For that matter, you might have an interest in payment or shipping options rather than a product description at first. The rest of the book shows how to perform all of these tasks. The main idea is that you can submit a variety of search request types—the request type affects the information you receive back from eBay.

The final consideration for a Web service (at least from the Web service user perspective) is that it executes on the remote machine, not on your machine. In short, this means you're using resources on that other machine with the permission of the machine's owner. The remote machine can set requirements for using the Web service, as well as require you to perform specific setup and security checks as part of your request. In the case of eBay Web Services, you need to obtain this permission by requesting a license. You also need to download the eBay Web Services Kit to ensure you follow the terms of the licensing agreement. The "Downloading and Installing the Kit" section of this chapter tells how to obtain the required permission and what this permission means to you.

> ▶ **TIP**
>
> You may find that eBay Web Services is so indispensable that you'll want to work with Web services from other vendors. For example, Microsoft supports the MapPoint Web Service (`http://www.microsoft.com/mappoint/net/`). In time, standards organizations will set up directories of these Web services that you can access with ease. In the meantime, you can search for companies that offer Web services using the Web Services Finder page at `http://www.15seconds.com/WebService/`. Some people have problems using the Web Services Finder; it might produce an error instead of presenting a list of Web services. In some cases, you'll need to use a specialty Web service list such as the one at `http://www.flash-db.com/services/`. The Web services on this site are special because many of them perform one task well, such as providing you with a location based on a domain name.

How Do Web Services Work?

Many people fear new technology because they don't understand how it works, and many of those who do know how it works enjoy the mystique of knowledge too much to share it with anyone else. Web services are actually quite easy to understand if you look at them in a way that relates the task to everyday occurrences. For example, you might compare the operation of a Web service to making a withdrawal at the bank—the process really is the same. The one thing to remember is that the process a Web service uses to perform a task is always the same. No matter what technology you use to make a request or receive a response, the steps are still the same. Here are the steps that most Web services, including eBay Web Services, use to complete a transaction.

1. *The client discovers the Web service.* During the act of discovery, the client might do things like download a file that tells how to interact with the Web service. This step is the same as someone walking into the bank. The person knows the bank exists and the bank teller might have noticed the person. The bank posts the rules for making a withdrawal or the teller might help a first-time customer understand the rules.

2. *The client makes a request based on the rules delivered during the discovery phase.* The rules might specify that the request has to appear in a certain form and the client must provide specific data. This step is the same as the person walking up to the teller's window with a withdrawal request. The request must contain the person's account number, the amount they wish to withdraw, and other identifying information. The bank specifies the format of the request and the information it must contain.

3. *The server might ask the client for credentials depending on the openness of the Web service.* eBay Web Services is public but still requires that you supply a developer license (account) number as identification. This step is the same as the bank teller asking you for a driver's license or other form of identification before honoring your withdrawal request.

4. *The Web service performs the work required to honor your request.* In most cases, the Web service accesses a database for information, it could enter an order, and it might even provide some level of formatting information about the original information (such as the typeface used for a word-processed document). eBay Web Services performs a number of tasks depending on the request you make. The easiest request is a general search, but you can also perform checks such as learning about a buyer or seller. This step equates to the bank teller getting the money from the drawer and counting it.

5. *The Web service sends the data to the client.* The content of the information depends on the Web service. eBay Web Services provides data in a very specific format based on the content of the associated database and the nature of the request. This step equates to the teller handing the person their money. In general, the teller orders the money in a specific way and counts it out to the person, rather than simply handing the money over.

6. *The client logs out of the Web service or the Web service disconnects the client after some period of inactivity.* This step equates to the person leaving the bank, money in hand. If the person doesn't leave the bank (they just hang out in the lobby), you can be sure that someone will ask them to leave.

7. *The client does something with the data it receives.* In many cases, it formats the data and presents it on screen for the user. This step equates to the person spending the money they receive from the bank.

You can add any amount of complexity needed to the individual steps, but these seven steps define the process every Web server follows. When you break a Web service down into these seven steps, the process that used to appear as magic suddenly becomes quite doable. Chapters 6 through 11 are essentially options you can use to perform these seven steps using different technologies. This book explores the seven steps using various languages and platforms—eBay Web Services makes information available to just about anyone who needs it. However, it's important to remember that everything comes down to a client making a request and the Web server returning data.

> ▶ **TIP**

> You don't have to be a programmer to work with eBay Web Services. In fact, Chapters 6 and 7 are specifically designed for people who want to automate tasks without developing extensive programming skills. Of course, you can do a lot more with eBay as you learn some programming techniques.

Considering the Usage Requirements

There's no free lunch. Some people would have you believe that the Web service does everything for you and that the client does nothing at all. However, the client interacts with the Web service, which means the client must possess some intelligence to perform the task. To use a Web service, you must understand the usage requirements.

From a client perspective, the type of device you use to access the Web service (including the connection type and speed it offers) determines the access speed, as well as what you can do with the data once you receive it. Although a PDA such as the Pocket PC can access eBay Web Services just fine, you wouldn't want to use it to perform detailed searches or attempt complex activities such as uploading new products for sale. A PDA or cellular telephone do work well enough to bid on products or check the status of an auction. You could possibly use these devices to check the price of an item as well. (See The Wall Street Journal article at `http://www.sfgate`
`.com/cgi-bin/article.cgi?file=/news/archive/2003/12/08/financial1006EST0033.DTL` for

details about this use of eBay.) On the other hand, a desktop or laptop machine has all of the processing power, screen real estate, and functionality to perform any task. eBay Web Services hasn't changed, but the capability of the client has.

> **▶ NOTE**
>
> This book discusses a number of mobile devices. The Pocket PC provides additional functionality and features that make it a better target for some types of applications than devices such as the Palm. On the other hand, most Palm devices are much easier to carry and cost less than the Pocket PC. This book examines the entire range of mobile devices to ensure you understand the limitations of using a specific device to access eBay Web Services. I'm not saying one device is better than another—simply that one device works better than the other for a given application.

eBay Web Services also has some usage requirements, and these requirements might change the way that you use your client. The limitations on your account depend on the kind of license you purchase from eBay. Most developers will begin with the Individual license that limits you to 50 API calls per day. These limitations assure that the eBay servers won't become overwhelmed with calls. You can learn more about the eBay licensing levels at `http://developer.ebay.com/DevProgram/membership/services.asp`. One of the issues the terms listed on this Web page doesn't make clear is that the 50 API calls apply to work performed with the actual Web service. In addition, even if you exceed the 50 call limit, you can still make listing and relisting calls. You can make up to 5,000 sandbox (test environment) API calls per day (see the "What Is Sandbox Mode?" section for a description of sandbox calls). Since all of your work with eBay is in sandbox mode until you get an application approved, the 50 API call limit shouldn't pose much of a problem.

> **▶ WARNING**
>
> If you violate the licensing terms, eBay Web Services simply denies your request. In addition, you might receive a message from eBay requesting that you adhere to the terms of usage for the Web service.

Often, you can get around the licensing requirements for a Web service by using smart programming techniques. For example, using good caching techniques means that you can create applications that are lightning fast, unless the request is new or the data is too old. Obviously, given the fast-paced nature of eBay auctions, you'll need to weigh the costs of making your application fast and resource friendly against the possibility of losing an auction to a competitor.

What Is Sandbox Mode?

Unlike many Web services on the market, eBay provides access to sensitive data with its Web service. In addition, you wouldn't want just anyone to have access to the various items for auction or to the buyer's personal information. It's also important that eBay maintain the integrity of its servers and ensure that none of the requests cause errors. For all these reasons, your first applications will operate in what eBay calls sandbox mode. Essentially, this is a safe area where you can create your application without working with real eBay data. The initial data won't affect anyone, but will give you useful results that you can use to create your application. Consequently, you can work with eBay Web Services even if you don't really understand what you're doing at first because using the sandbox limits the possibility of error.

Once you feel confident about your programming skills, you can create a better application—one that works with eBay Web Services flawlessly. This application goes through a certification process. The certification process is the time when eBay can discuss any potential application problems with you and help you fix them. After your application is certified (everyone is happy that it works as anticipated), you can begin using it with real eBay data.

The sandbox mode offered by eBay is an important feature that most Web services don't provide. You can experiment and work with data without presenting any kind of problem to other developers and users of eBay. This safety feature means that you can learn to work with eBay without losing sleep at night over potential problems with your application.

Discovering Uses for the eBay Web Services

You can perform any task with eBay Web Services that you can with the manual or eBay.com user interface. However, you can perform these actions significantly faster using the automation that a custom application provides. In addition, you can perform some tasks with eBay Web Services that the manual interface doesn't support. For example, you can search for specific shipping criteria or you can locate products that meet certain conditions, such as antique dishes without nicks. That's the quick overview. However, this short description doesn't even begin to scratch the surface of what you can do with eBay Web Services. The following sections provide a much better overview and the rest of the book provides a wealth of specifics.

> ▶ NOTE
>
> At the time of writing, eBay releases new versions of eBay Web Services every few weeks. These new versions are compatible with the previous versions—they simply add new features. Consequently, when you read this, you might find that eBay has already added new features you can use to make your experience better. Make sure you also read the late-breaking news found in Appendix C.

Buying Products

Most people start learning how to use eBay by buying products. It doesn't take long to learn that you need to maintain a close watch on the bidding process or you'll lose out on whatever product you want. The fact that bidding takes place worldwide doesn't help because you have competitors in other countries in other time zones. In short, you're stuck watching your email or checking out the online service with your browser.

Fortunately, an eBay Web Services application can help you overcome the problem of waiting. You can use eBay Web Services to monitor the items that you want to bid on. Whenever the high bid changes, the application can notify you so that you don't end up waiting for the change to occur (or miss the change completely).

Of course, before you can buy a product, you need to find a product that meets your needs. Locating a product is one area where eBay Web Services has a definite advantage over the manual interface. For example, the online search engine only lets you search for items that you can purchase with PayPal—with eBay Web Services, you can search for other forms of payment such as Cash on Delivery (COD) or American Express. The idea is to find an item that meets your expectations and to ensure you can actually get purchasing terms that you like.

> ▶ **TIP**
>
> If you haven't spent a lot of time working with eBay, you might want to check "The Life Cycle of an Auction on eBay" help topic in the User's Guide section of the eBay SDK Reference. This description is relatively short, yet describes the auction process clearly. More important, you'll learn some eBay jargon that will help you understand the remainder of the eBay SDK Reference.

In many cases, the people who buy products online don't know the seller. Fortunately, using eBay Web Services you can also check on seller statistics without having to jump through a lot of screens. The seller information appears as part of the item statistics, so you can learn about the seller immediately and filter out sellers that don't meet your purchasing criteria.

Selling and Relisting Products

The main reason that some people spend time on eBay is to sell items. Generally, the seller uses a manual interface to define facts about the item, such as an item description and picture. The seller also provides information such as the payment terms and method of shipment. You can automate all of these tasks using eBay Web Services. Any task that you can perform using the manual interface, you can also perform using the automation of eBay Web Services. This includes relisting a product if it doesn't sell the first time.

It might be hard to envision much time savings in using automation to create the product entry—after all, you still need to collect the data and take pictures. The time savings occur when you begin uploading the data. Instead of waiting for the interface to display the next page, you simply press a button and let your application send the data. All of the items still require the same amount of time to upload; the difference is that you don't have to wait for the upload to complete.

Automation also helps when you want to monitor the auction. For example, you can obtain a list of bidders automatically and track the highest bid with ease. The information you receive can also act as input for second chance offers—a method of selling other items to users who didn't win the current auction, but might be interested in another copy of the same item or a similar item you have in stock. In fact, eBay Web Services includes special calls for making the second chance offer, so you can build this functionality directly into your application.

Using eBay Web Services can also help you garner some important security information faster than using the manual interface. For example, you can use special features to authenticate the user you're working with. The eBay SDK Reference discusses this topic in the "User Authentication & Authorization" section of the "Working with Users" part of the Developer's Guide. This help topic also discusses the proper way to perform security-related tasks, such as a Web site logon page redirection. In short, using eBay Web Services can actually improve the security of your online selling experience by providing additional input about the user.

Determining Product Facts

Any piece of information you can learn about a product using the manual interface, you can also learn using eBay Web Services. However, when you use the manual interface, you need to visit each product separately. Sure, you can learn a little about the product by reading the summaries, but if you really want to learn all the facts you have to go farther and select that item. Using eBay Web Services lets you download all the information in the background and review the information you want to see all at one time. The time savings in searching for a particular product can be significant.

You also define the amount of information that eBay sends you for a particular product or search. When using the manual interface, you normally have to wait for all of those graphics to download. Using eBay Web Services, you only download time-consuming items such as graphics when you need them.

The best part about using eBay Web Services is that you can perform product analysis. For example, you might want to create a table comparing various products based on the keywords in their description. You can't perform that task using the manual interface, but you can do it using eBay Web Services. Data mining includes the idea of combining information from various sources to create a better composite image of the product. You could easily combine data from various areas from eBay (or even other Web services) to learn more about a particular product.

Discovering Product Payment and Shipping Methods

The manual interface doesn't allow you to do much in the way of searching for specific product payment and shipping methods. Even when you use the advanced search, you can only specify PayPal as a payment option. You couldn't search for someone selling an item that accepts COD. However, by checking the results you receive using eBay Web Services, you can find items that meet your particular payment and shipping needs.

However, you can go further than simply finding favorable payment and shipping options: you can also perform comparisons between sellers. For example, two sellers might offer acceptable items and a similar price. However, one seller charges a premium for shipping. You'd normally need to tabulate such information using paper and pencil, but an eBay Web Services application can perform this analysis automatically and highlight the better buy.

Giving and Receiving Feedback

Most eBay users know that eBay allows responses to every feedback that someone offers about either a buyer or a seller. The response system ensures that you understand both sides of the issue when viewing feedback. In many cases, one person's negative comment is a positive comment when viewed in another light. For example, using a substantial amount of packing material to protect antique glassware could evoke a negative comment from a buyer who thinks the shipping prices are too high. However, ensuring the antique actually arrives at its destination is the positive side of this particular issue. A conscientious seller who wants to ensure the buyer actually receives the goods purchased will ensure the packing material meets the requirement, even if the cost of shipping is a little higher.

An eBay Web Services application won't significantly reduce the time required to provide feedback for buyers and sellers (automation does help speed downloads and uploads). You still have to create the comment and phrase it in a way that won't be misunderstood online. (Phrasing your comments correctly can prove very time consuming because you can't depend on visual cues such as facial expression or aural cues such as voice inflection to make your point.) This fact points out one of the expectation factors discussed in the "Limitations of the eBay Web Services Output" section of Chapter 2. Fortunately, an eBay Web Services application can help you manage the feedback. For example, it can continuously monitor eBay for new comments and alert you to their arrival. You can also depend on such an application to sort and classify feedback based on content or other criteria.

Learning about a Store

Some sellers use a store-style auction to sell their goods. When you're interested in such as product, you can use special calls to learn more about the store. For example, you can learn the owner's name. You can also obtain any special information that eBay can supply about the store or its owner. In some cases, the store owner also supplies specialized information (departments) that you can retrieve. This information varies by store—it usually provides helpful information that you can use to make a buying decision.

Working with User Information

For the purposes of eBay Web Services, both buyers and sellers are users. Anyone involved in eBay in any way is a user of some sort. You can obtain a wealth of information about eBay users. Some of it's supplied by the user. For example, you can learn about the user by viewing the About Me page the user sets up. You can also let the application scan the user's information for particular keywords and phrases.

User information also includes eBay specifics. For example, you can discover whether the user is in good standing with eBay. Other information includes whether the user is allowed to perform live auctions. All other information, such as the user's seller level or feedback star indicator is also available.

In some cases, you'll also find some localized data. For example, you can learn whether a German user has the Computer Investment Program (CIP) in checkout option—essentially a banking option that isn't available elsewhere.

All of this information allows you to reduce the risks of working with other people through eBay. It's important to understand that the eBay automation isn't always correct or factual because some of it's provided by the user. However, by using multiple Web services (such as eBay Web Services with Google Web Services), you could automatically search for additional details about the person and either confirm or deny much of the information you find on eBay.

Performing Research

Some people assume that eBay is only about buying and selling products. In most cases, that's what happens—a seller offers an item that someone else buys. The buying and selling on eBay does lend itself to other forms of activity. One of the most important alternative activities today is the use of all that data for research purposes. For example, you might want to know how well a particular item retains its value. By comparing the list price, the new selling price, and the prices for items of various ages on eBay, you can learn how well the item retains its value.

Another way to use eBay for research is in the area of collectibles. Even though you can find a lot of books on the market that describe dishes created by various vendors over the years, these books are incomplete. By knowing even a little about a particular dish, you can research it on eBay and find out more about it. This additional information helps you perform extended research using other techniques. In sum, eBay can act as a stepping stone for research where you only have a little information in the beginning. Obviously, this technique can work for any product—dishes to cars.

> ▶ TIP
>
> eBay understands the value of data to many companies and individuals. If you're really interested in using eBay for data mining, you should also check out the eBay Data Licensing Program at `http://developer.ebay.com/devprogram/membership/data.asp`.

Creating an Offline Archive

Generally, you can build an offline archive of data with any Web service. Some Web services restrict the amount of time you can store the data. In most other ways, however, the Web service leaves the details of how you store the data you receive up to you. eBay Web Services go a lot farther by providing integrated database support as part of the library. At the time of this writing, eBay Web Services provides support for both Microsoft Access and Microsoft SQL Server. This support isn't available unless you use eBay Web Services.

An offline archive can help your business become a lot more efficient. Whenever someone requests information, an application can store the data locally. The next time someone requests the information, the application can use the local data store for most of the information, rather than request it from eBay. The response is almost immediate, rather than requiring the user to wait until eBay processes the application request and the application downloads the response.

You can also use an offline data store to provide some fault tolerance in your application. Disruptions of your connection with eBay might not happen very often, but they can be devastating when they do. Using an offline data store allows you to continue working, albeit at a slightly reduced pace. No, the information doesn't magically get updated, but you can still make decisions and upload changes based on the data you had when the connection was severed.

Offline archives are also valuable analysis tools because they show how your company interacts with eBay. You might discover that you're buying an expensive item from a local retail store when you could be buying it for much less on eBay. The database archive can also provide historical information on which products sell best and at what price. If you have more than one employee working with eBay, you could monitor which employees work with which products most often and use that information to build pools of expertise. Individual users could use the same analysis to discover areas of future research and training so that you become better at managing your business.

Downloading and Installing the Kit

Like many Web services, eBay provides an application development kit and means of obtaining a license to use their Web service. You need to spend time getting the license, downloading and installing the kit, and determining specifics of your setup before you begin writing the application. In addition to the normal Web service requirements, eBay also requires that you determine a licensing level—most levels aren't free, but you get quite a bit of support in return. The following sections discuss these elements of the setup process.

> ▶ **NOTE**
>
> The following sections and the rest of the book contain a few URLs that you can't access unless you log in as an eBay member. These URLs generally lead to information that's specific to the developer program. If you can't access a particular URL, please try it again logged on as an eBay member.

Determining Which Licensing Level Is Best

Unlike many Web services, eBay offers their Web service as a free or paid service. If you choose the free option, you'll find that you're limited in what you can do with eBay Web Services, but this is the best option for first time Web service developers. The free option lets you experiment without cost until you're ready to work with eBay on a regular basis. All of the paid options have an annual fee plus a monthly usage charge, which means the clock is ticking from the moment you join the program. You can learn about the various licensing options at `http://developer.ebay.com/DevProgram/membership/services.asp`. As you can see from Figure 1.1, eBay currently offers four programs and you can move from the free option to any of these programs once your project starts to take shape.

You need to consider a few developer program highlights almost immediately. The most important is that you're limited to 50 calls per day. Given the amount of documentation eBay provides, this limit might not be as severe as you think. Most developers can work on a project without running up against this limit, so long as you're not testing your code every five minutes.

FIGURE 1.1:
Determine which
licensing level
best suits your
needs before you
do anything else.

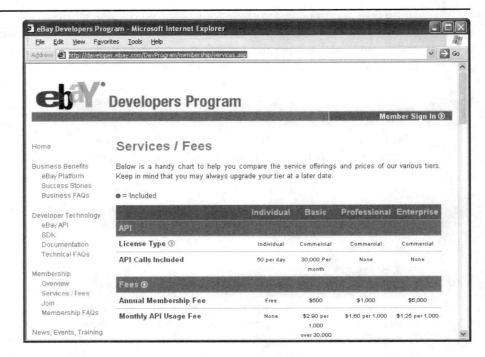

The eBay documentation is truly stellar, but it's not perfect. Unfortunately, if you choose the free option, eBay won't provide any help in using the development kit. However, you can get peer support using the Developer Zone Website and the Member Forums. The free option also affords access to the Developer Newsletter and NewsFlashes. Finally, you have access to all of the tools and notifications supplied to paying members, except for the Platform Notifications feature.

▶ TIP

Make sure you read the Developer Newsletter each time you receive it in your email. The Developer Newsletter contains notification of new features, as well as coding examples and other aids. You'll notice that the developer program currently has several new features underway, including an eBay Developer Conference and Developer Education Services.

Becoming an eBay Developer Program Member

Once you decide on a licensing level, you need to join the eBay Developer Program. You'll find the easy five-step process at `http://developer.ebay.com/DevProgram/membership/join.asp` as shown in Figure 1.2.

> ► **WARNING**
>
> Make sure you enable full cookie and scripting support for the membership process. Otherwise, the process will fail and you'll need to contact eBay support at `developer-relations@ebay.com` for help.

One of the more important steps appears near the bottom of the page. Make sure you have your eBay user identification and password available because you can't join the developer program without joining eBay as a member first. Join eBay by registering at `https://scgi.ebay.com/saw-cgi/eBayISAPI.dll?RegisterEnterInfo&siteid=0`. The developer registration process also assumes that you know how to speak English. If you want to work with the developer program in another language, contact the International Developer Program Team at `http://developer.ebay.com/DevProgram/Userform.asp?contact=intl`.

FIGURE 1.2:

Make sure you join the eBay developer program before you attempt to download the kit.

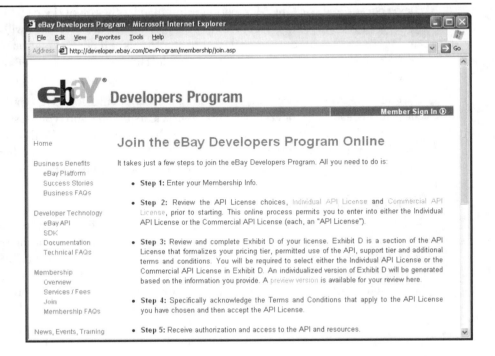

To start the registration process, click the Next link at the very bottom of the page. You'll begin by providing your eBay user identification and selecting a program. Most of the steps are self-explanatory—all you need to do is follow the on-screen prompts and provide the required information. Step 3 requires special consideration. At this point, you'll view a unique part of your license named Exhibit D. This portion of the license is unique, and you should save a copy of it for your records. Appendix B discusses licensing issues in greater detail.

Obtaining Your License

After you complete the initial registration process, you'll receive a confirmation message in your email. This message includes a link you must click to confirm your new account. Clicking this link starts the key generation process. You'll eventually see a Web page containing the three keys that you'll use during the development process. Print out a copy of these keys so that you have them for your records. If you lose the keys, you'll need to contact eBay support (`developer-relations@ebay.com`) to have them clear the old keys (they can't send them to you again) and send you another confirmation process.

Performing the Download

Now that you have an eBay user account and you've obtained your developer license, you can visit the developer area. Go to the developer Web site at `http://developer.ebay.com/DevProgram/` and click the Member Sign In link near the top of the page. Provide your name and password, and then click Sign In. After you sign in, the Web page will change, as shown in Figure 1.3. You'll see various new entries for tools and documentation. Many of these tools appear in other areas of the book. For example, check the "Using the eBay API Tool" section of Chapter 4 for an exciting tool that helps you develop applications faster.

The eBay Web Services Kit, or Software Development Kit (SDK), appears at `http://developer.ebay.com/DevZone/build-test/sdk.asp`. Make sure your system meets the minimum requirements for installation and then click the Download With Installer link. Always use this option for an initial installation of the eBay Web Services Kit. However, you can save time when making an update by using the Download Without Installer link.

Installing the Kit

The Zip file you receive from eBay contains the compressed installation file. If you have Windows XP or a newer version of Windows, you can open the file using the built-in features of the operating system. Otherwise, you'll need a program such as WinZip (`http://www.winzip.com/`) or WinRAR (`http://www.rarlabs.com/`) to decompress the file. Double-click the resulting file and you'll see the installation dialog box. Follow the prompts to accept the licensing agreement and select an installation directory. You can choose between a Typical and a Custom installation. When you choose the Custom installation, you'll see a Custom Setup dialog box like the one shown in Figure 1.4.

FIGURE 1.3:

The initial developer's page provides access to documentation and tools.

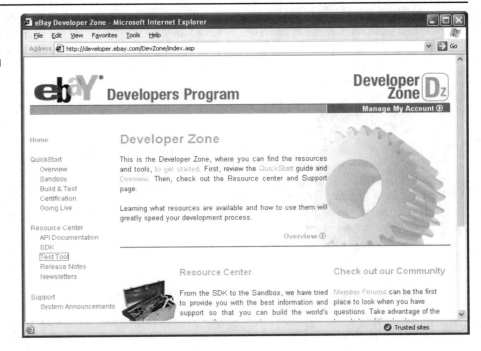

FIGURE 1.4:

Choose the options you want to install to save disk space.

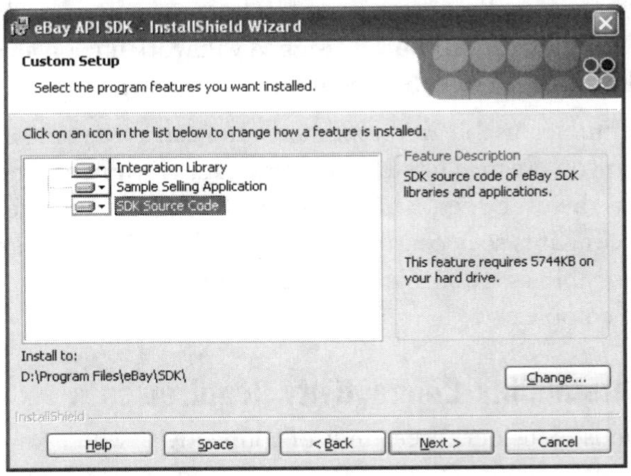

Choose the features you want to install by selecting options from the drop-down list boxes next to the drive icons. In many cases, you can save a little over 5MB of disk space by telling the installer to only install the Sample Selling Application when needed. You could also choose to simply make the feature unavailable. The Integration Library feature is only necessary if you want to perform advanced programming, such as using a database with your eBay application. Likewise, the SDK Source Code is only useful if you want to see how eBay has implemented certain features or if you want to understand errors better when you debug your application. After you choose the features you want, follow the prompts to install the eBay Web Services Kit.

> ▶ NOTE
>
> You can use many of the examples in this book without adding all of the eBay Web Services Kit features. However, I did perform a full installation as part of my setup so that I could demonstrate as many features of the eBay Web Services Kit as possible. You might want to perform a full installation while learning to use eBay Web Services, and then reinstall later with just the features you need. As with most modern installations, you can add and remove features as needed.

System Setup Considerations

Once you obtain the eBay Web Services Kit and a developer license, it's easy to think that you're ready to write your first program. Theoretically, you can do just that. The problem with proceeding at this point though is that you don't know about the viability of your system configuration. For example, if you have a very fast processor and a lot of memory, it's easy to assume that the eBay application you've designed will work fine on all systems. However, once you load the resulting application on someone else's machine, it might not work very quickly (if at all).

Defining a usable development setup can save you considerable time and effort later. When you create a great development environment, you ensure that you'll see the application as the user does, which reduces the potential for deadly errors. Because the eBay Web Services Kit is so accommodating, you'll need to spend a little extra time considering all of the possible usage scenarios. The following sections provide tips you can use to reduce the setup complexity.

Understanding Connectivity Requirements

You must consider three kinds of connectivity when you set up your development system. The first level of connectivity is your own machine. Make sure your machine has a connection to the Internet. Otherwise, any tests you run will fail. Remember that a Web service runs on the remote machine, not your local machine. You're borrowing the resources of that remote machine to perform useful work.

The second level of connectivity is the user's machine. If you create a Web site that simply contains links to eBay's Web site, you can assume the user has a connection, but how fast is that connection? The best Web sites I've seen ask about the user's connection speed. This question allows the application to send the user the level of information that their connection can comfortably support. If you know that most users will rely on a dial-up connection for your Web site, make sure you also use a dial-up connection for testing. This additional step can greatly reduce the chances that you'll make the application too robust. Users who leave your site and don't use your application are users who are probably visiting someone else.

The third level of connectivity is the non-connected mode. You need to consider what happens when the user loses the connection or doesn't have one available. Applications can store static data locally to enable the user to continue using data they have already queried from the Web service. However, you need to observe any refresh requirements and ensure the data retains the same information the user would see online. For example, the local copy of the data must include any required copyright statements or trademarks.

> ▶ NOTE
>
> eBay's licensing terms are flexible in that they allow you to store information as long as that information remains viable to you and you retain your relationship with eBay. This flexibility means you can create user applications that only query eBay when necessary, instead of for each request. It's important to note that any application you create using eBay Web Services will require your license to access the site. Any queries a user makes using your application will count against your licensed access total for the day.

Programming Setups for the Non-Developer

Many of the people reading this book have marginal experience with programming or do it as a hobby. It's true that Web services rely on the resources of the remote machine, but it's also true that the client must perform some work too. If you have a machine that's already marginal—that doesn't run applications well—trying to write a Web service application for it could make matters worse. The local machine must have some resources for using the Web service application. Fortunately, eBay makes the requirements for their Web service clear. You can find these requirements on the developer site at `http://developer.ebay.com/ DevZone/build-test/sdk.asp`. These requirements really are the minimum you can use though, so don't try to squeak by with something less.

> ▶ **NOTE**
>
> This book doesn't teach you how to program, so make sure you spend at least a little time learning one of the programming languages discussed in this book before you begin working with the examples. I do provide good descriptions of the applications, but these descriptions won't be enough if you don't understand basic programming concepts.

Depending on the kind of application you create, you'll also need local resources for the programming environment. For example, VBA users have not only the Office application of choice running, but also the VBA development environment. The addition of the VBA development environment can reduce your system performance to a crawl and give you unrealistic performance for your application.

It's also possible for you to speed things up too much. If the target platform is a 400MHz Pentium and you're using a 3GHz development machine, your application performance will look nothing like the user's performance in most cases. For a Web site, the machine performance differences might not be quite as significant as when you develop applications that run on the desktop.

Considering the User

Depending on how you use the Web application you build, user needs will take on significant importance. Many applications start out as projects that the developer is creating for personal use. Some of the best applications I've written fall into this category. However, taking shortcuts in developing the user interface, even if you're the only user, is never a good idea. At one time, I wrote rough applications that I understood but couldn't use efficiently because they were only for test purposes. After I ended up rewriting a number of the applications because I couldn't figure them out or other people asked me for copies, I began writing every program as if it were for someone else.

The applications you write with eBay Web Services will likely see use from other people, even if you don't know it right now. Consequently, you need to consider what a hypothetical user will need. For example, you might need to include a few special search options. Sure, you could get the same results by typing a little extra text, but adding the functionality directly into your application makes it easier to use (faster, in most cases, as well).

It's also important to consider users with special needs. The "Addressing Users with Special Needs" section of Chapter 13 contains details on this topic, but you might need to perform setups before you even begin coding. For example, if you work on a Windows machine, you'll probably want to set up the Accessibility features (these features normally appear in the Control Panel and within the `Start\Programs\Accessories\Accessibility` folder).

Using Multiple Test Devices

If your application will appear on the Internet, you need to perform testing using multiple devices. It's no longer safe to assume that only desktop users will have any interest in your application. You might attract some Personal Digital Assistant (PDA) and cellular telephone users as well. This is especially true of a Web application that helps users find a particular kind of information quickly. People often rely on these applications when time is tight and they don't have time to look for a product themselves.

> ▶ **NOTE**
>
> Not every developer is concerned about writing applications for every platform—sometimes it's a matter of time; other times it's a matter of skill or perceived need. When an application you write falls into this category, you can still provide a modicum of support for wireless users by directing them to the eBay Anywhere Wireless service at `http://pages.ebay` `.com/anywhere/index.html?ssPageName=STRK:SRVC:009`.

It would be nice if everyone could afford to test every application on every device, but that's not realistic for the developer. Sometimes you need to use an emulator to perform the testing because you don't have the real device handy. Fortunately, you can find a vast array of useful emulators on the Internet—everything from the Pocket PC to cellular telephones of all types. Emulators have limitations, but they do make good test devices in many cases. We'll discuss the advantages and concerns of using emulators in the "Working with Emulators" section of Chapter 11.

Sometimes it also helps to have multiple desktop machine setups. For example, you might need to consider how a Web page looks and acts in Netscape versus Internet Explorer. (Theoretically, you can run both browsers from the same machine, but doing so causes interference problems that some developers find distasteful.) Differences in how the browsers react to specific Web page designs could cause problems in your application. In some cases, you'll need multiple machines to perform this kind of testing. For example, you might need to consider how the application looks on a Macintosh versus a PC if your application has broad enough appeal. Obviously, you can still write eBay Web Services applications if you don't have a multiple machine setup, but having more than one machine does make development tasks a lot easier and less error prone.

Emulating the Real World

Developers often live in a laboratory. In the laboratory, everyone has the proper equipment, fast machines, and an even faster connection. The user never disconnects unexpectedly and always knows how to get the most out of their computer. The problem with the lab is that it doesn't model the real world. In the real world, users get bored, try odd key combinations just to see what they do, don't understand their computer very well, but do know how to complain about the smallest application problems. If you want to avoid problems with the application you develop, you need to create a development environment that models the real world.

It's also easy to get lost in the development environment setup. Make sure you understand the person who uses your application. For example, it's quite possible that only desktop users will have any interest in your site on desktop machine maintenance, but you need to determine that fact in some way (online surveys work well). You also don't want to spend a lot of time testing the application to meet the needs of users who have no use for your product. Again, surveys and newsgroup polls are helpful in determining the real world environment that you must emulate with your system.

Your Call to Action

If you've read the entire chapter, you know what a Web service is, how the eBay Web Services fits within the general definition of a Web service, and what you can use the eBay Web Services to do. You can use this knowledge to create opportunities to exercise eBay as a search engine, a place to buy or sell products, or as a means to perform research. Data mining is increasing in importance as companies strive to gain more from the resources of the Internet—this technique accesses the needed information and discards unneeded information. At this point, you also have a machine that's set up to create a eBay Web Services application of some sort and you have the eBay Web Services Kit installed.

The next step of the process is to evaluate where you're going based on the content of this chapter. You need to consider what you want to do with the information eBay provides, how you plan to present it, your own capabilities, and the capabilities of the person using your application. This may sound like a lot of work, but it's important to create a firm foundation for your application. When you take these preliminary steps, you begin thinking about problems and solutions to those problems.

Chapter 2 builds on the knowledge you gained in this chapter. The emphasis of Chapter 2 is on data mining—the process of using specialized search techniques to whittle search results down to just the information you need. In many cases, you can also access these search techniques using the eBay search page, but the emphasis of data mining is automation. Only by using the eBay Web Services can you automate the search process and then display the results in the form you want, rather than rely on eBay's formatting methodology.

Chapter 2

Understanding How Web
Services Output Data

Getting Your Application
Certified

▶ Using eBay Web Services to Your Advantage

Viewing Some Simple
Examples

Changing the Data to
Meet Specific Needs

Understanding that Web services provide data after you make a request is a good beginning but hardly adequate to work with a Web service. A Web service doesn't view information in the same way that a person views it. A computer has no concept of context and can't derive information from the placement of the data unless you use a special application (and even then, the interpretation is quite limited). Consequently, a Web service needs some type of structure to tell it what the data means and how to handle it. Your request doesn't mean much without this structure.

This chapter helps you understand the structure that a Web service requires. You'll begin seeing some XML in this chapter. Don't worry about the XML too much—Chapter 4 will introduce you to XML. The idea in this chapter is to understand how Web services fit within the grand scheme of things. In short, you'll discover a little more about Web services in general and eBay Web Services in specific.

It's important to test your application with the Web service to ensure it will act as expected. Most Web services leave this testing up to you. However, given the sensitive nature of the data you work with when using eBay Web Services, eBay provides you with tools to verify that your application will work. The first tool ensures your application meets strict requirements (certification). Other tools will appear in other chapters of the book (such as the API Test Tool in Chapter 4).

Rather than spend a lot of time discovering how Web services work from a theoretical perspective, this chapter presents several examples. Each example shows how some aspect of eBay Web Services works. Again, you don't really need to understand the code behind the examples; the chapter concerns itself more with the process involved in working with eBay Web Services. These examples provide hands-on time that you can use to develop an opinion of what makes eBay Web Services useful to you and your organization.

Finally, this chapter begins a discussion on data manipulation. The data you receive from eBay Web Services isn't ready for display. Your program must interpret the data, modify its appearance as needed, and then display it on screen for the user. This last section describes handling and formatting issues you should consider as part of your application design process.

Knowing What to Expect As Output

For many developers, the idea of a Web service is easy to grasp—knowing what to expect from it is hard. The output begins with a certain amount of raw data that you'll receive from the Web service. However, the raw data doesn't really define the Web service output completely. You also need to consider quantifiable components such as the input to the Web service and that data manipulation you'll perform. In addition, there are variant elements to the output, such as the timeliness of the data. Finally, you need to consider the intangible elements. The output has some value to you, but someone else will view the output in another way. Concepts such as relevancy are difficult to quantify or even define.

eBay Web Services is no different from any other Web service when it comes to output. You'll provide input, receive raw data, manipulate that data in some way, and view the output—the result of everything you have done with the Web service. The following sections discuss various elements of Web service output as they relate to eBay Web Services. These sections provide an overview—the book continues to explore the subject in other chapters. However, this is the starting point—the point at which you start to consider what to expect as output from your efforts.

Limitations of eBay Web Services Output

Many developers are used to working with a variety of data types when creating applications. Data types help define the kind of data you're using. For example, if a data element is a number, you might use an integer (a number without a decimal) or real number (Single or Double for Visual Basic developers). A Web service has no concept of data type when it comes to the data itself. Every data transfer is text. The XML used to transfer the data does include type information, but of the sort that's normally associated with database fields, which means you have to know the field names to make an interpretation. (Developers who use the SDK technique don't actually see the XML transferred to eBay Web Services in most cases, but it's important to know how this communication takes place.) For example, you might receive data in a message like the one shown here.

```
<?xml version="1.0" encoding="iso-8859-1" ?>
<eBay>
    <EBayTime>2004-02-10 02:26:35</EBayTime>
    <User>
        <UserIdLastChanged>2004-02-07 22:11:10</UserIdLastChanged>
        <SiteId>0</SiteId>
```

```
            <UserId>
                <![CDATA[ bubbam9999]]>
            </UserId>
            <Status>1</Status>
            <SellerLevel>0</SellerLevel>
            <AboutMe>0</AboutMe>
            <RegDate>2004-02-07 22:10:43</RegDate>
            <CIPBankAccountStored>0</CIPBankAccountStored>
            <AllowPaymentEdit>1</AllowPaymentEdit>
            <IDVerified>1</IDVerified>
            <Star>0</Star>
            <CheckoutEnabled>1</CheckoutEnabled>
            <MerchandisingPref>1</MerchandisingPref>
            <eBayGoodStanding>1</eBayGoodStanding>
            <StoreOwner>0</StoreOwner>
            <IsLAAuthorized>0</IsLAAuthorized>
            <UserIdChanged>0</UserIdChanged>
            <Email>
                <![CDATA[ bubbam9999@yahoo.com]]>
            </Email>
            <NewUser>1</NewUser>
            <Feedback>
                <Score>0</Score>
            </Feedback>
        </User>
    </eBay>
```

You don't need to know anything about XML to see that the XML contains information about the user. For example, the user identification last changed on February 7, 2004. The user's identification is bubbam9999. The XML data also includes information about the user, such as an email address of bubbam9999@yahoo.com. All of the XML entries eBay provides work together to identify this particular user. You'll find this XML file in the \Chapter 2 folder of the source code located on the Sybex Web site as Sample1.XML. You can open this file using a browser such as Internet Explorer. Figure 2.1 shows a typical example of the display you'll see.

▶ NOTE

You'll find the Sybex Web site at http://www.sybex.com/. Simply type the book title in the Search field, click Go, and you'll see a link for this book. The book page contains a link where you can download the code.

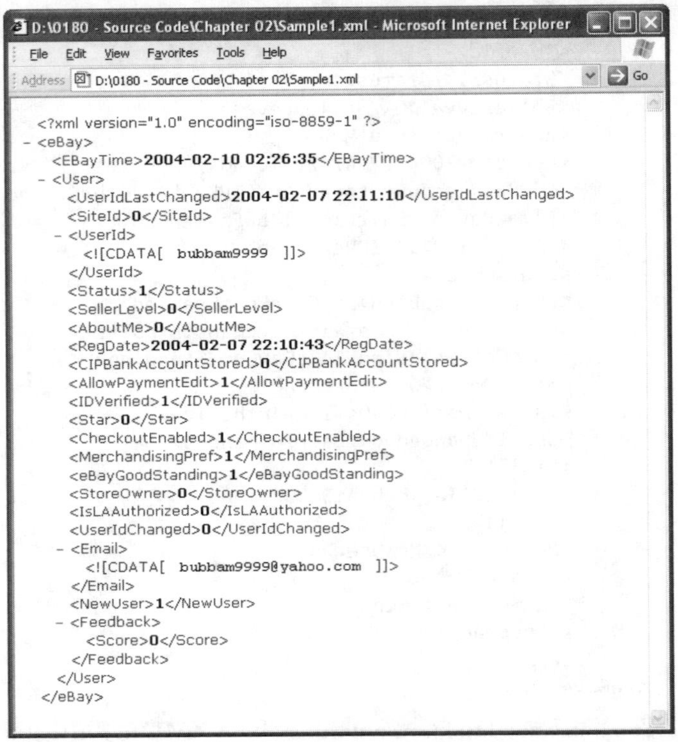

FIGURE 2.1:

You can view XML files using a browser such as Internet Explorer.

```
D:\0180 - Source Code\Chapter 02\Sample1.xml - Microsoft Internet Explorer

 File   Edit   View   Favorites   Tools   Help

 Address    D:\0180 - Source Code\Chapter 02\Sample1.xml                    Go

    <?xml version="1.0" encoding="iso-8859-1" ?>
  - <eBay>
      <EBayTime>2004-02-10 02:26:35</EBayTime>
    - <User>
        <UserIdLastChanged>2004-02-07 22:11:10</UserIdLastChanged>
        <SiteId>0</SiteId>
      - <UserId>
          <![CDATA[ bubbam9999 ]]>
        </UserId>
        <Status>1</Status>
        <SellerLevel>0</SellerLevel>
        <AboutMe>0</AboutMe>
        <RegDate>2004-02-07 22:10:43</RegDate>
        <CIPBankAccountStored>0</CIPBankAccountStored>
        <AllowPaymentEdit>1</AllowPaymentEdit>
        <IDVerified>1</IDVerified>
        <Star>0</Star>
        <CheckoutEnabled>1</CheckoutEnabled>
        <MerchandisingPref>1</MerchandisingPref>
        <eBayGoodStanding>1</eBayGoodStanding>
        <StoreOwner>0</StoreOwner>
        <IsLAAuthorized>0</IsLAAuthorized>
        <UserIdChanged>0</UserIdChanged>
      - <Email>
          <![CDATA[ bubbam9999@yahoo.com ]]>
        </Email>
        <NewUser>1</NewUser>
      - <Feedback>
          <Score>0</Score>
        </Feedback>
      </User>
    </eBay>
```

Your browser is actually very handy for viewing XML data, even if it might not make sense right now. The "Viewing XML Data in Your Browser" section of Chapter 4 discusses in detail how you can use your browser. For right now, all you need to know is that you can look at the various kinds of XML responses by opening the files in your browser.

Figure 2.1 points to another potential problem with Web service output. All of the tags and other information supplied in a request and response consume space. The file is larger than a text file with the same data because of all the tag information required. In addition, it's far more efficient to store many data types in their native format, rather than use characters. Consequently, Web service data suffers from bloat. The data uses more bandwidth than a binary message and, consequently, you could experience performance problems. Because of this issue, you need to create efficient queries for your application that maximize data throughput despite the limitations of the XML format. The "Making Sensible Queries" section of the chapter discusses this issue in detail.

The results you obtain from eBay are largely a matter of the input you provide in the form of a request. For example, when you search for an item online, the results you receive depend on the keywords you provide. Ambiguous input often results in less than useful return values, which means you must make the query again. Every time your application makes a less than useful query, it uses up resources. The value of making good search decisions is important enough that Chapter 3 discusses it in detail.

It's also possible to perform some tasks using more than one technique. For example, you can use more than one method for verifying that an item was added. Using one of the category-specific calls can save resources and help you ensure that you provide all the required data the first time. Again, providing the correct input ensures you obtain the right output and don't need to make the query again. In some cases, using the right technique means interpreting the results of a previous call properly. It's possible to perform an item search and obtain most of the information you need without getting the item as well. However, in other cases, you'll need to make two calls. The examples in this book provide you with the information you need to use eBay Web Services effectively.

Making Sensible Queries

eBay Web Services can help you perform a number of tasks. The problem is that each request and response consumes resources. To get the most from this Web service, you need to optimize the requests and responses so that the value of the information you receive exceeds the cost of transmitting and manipulating the data.

Creating a request and then handling the response has several costs associated with it. Some of the costs are real world in that you must provide the infrastructure required to perform the task. Inefficient queries could mean adding additional bandwidth capacity or providing additional servers (if you make enough queries). Some costs are employee related—inefficient queries mean more waiting time as the computer crunches the data. Finally, inefficient queries can incur intangible costs. For example, people can become frustrated with poor query results, which affects their performance. Some of these costs are impossible to measure accurately, but they're real.

The important issue is to obtain the data you need, but no more than you require for making a good decision. It's helpful to work with eBay Advanced Search (`http://pages .ebay.com/search/items/search_adv.html`), shown in Figure 2.2, to learn which searches work best for your particular needs and how to maximize results by using keywords and special search options. The By Seller (`http://pages.ebay.com/search/items/search_ seller.html`), By Bidder (`http://pages.ebay.com/search/items/search_bidder.html`), and Store (`http://pages.ebay.com/search/items/search_stores.html`) searches are also extremely useful for learning how eBay will react to item search queries.

FIGURE 2.2:

Use the Advanced
Search, By Seller,
By Bidder, and Store
searches to learn
how to define your
requests.

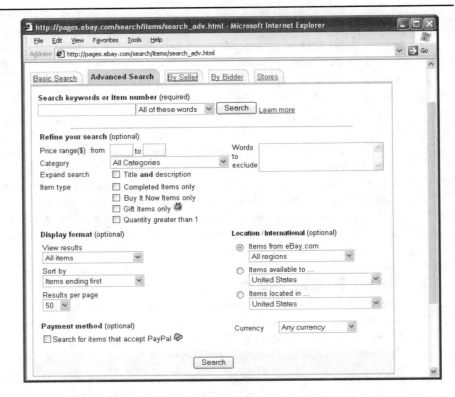

Another way to make good queries is to limit the number of return values. You can define the maximum number of entries you want returned or use other features to ensure you receive just the entries you want. If you really only want the lowest cost entries, then sorting by the price and retrieving just the top two or three items might be the most efficient way to query eBay. Chapter 3 discusses search techniques in greater detail, and the "Using the eBay API Test Tool" section of Chapter 4 shows techniques for using these queries as part of your XML message to eBay.

Defining Static and Dynamic Data

Applications that rely on data from an outside source, such as a Web service, can include the concept of static and dynamic data. Dynamic data is the best type to use for Web services because it reflects changes in the eBay database. An application gains important benefits by using dynamic data. For example, you won't try to purchase a product that eBay no longer carries because the dynamic nature of your application automatically tells you that product is no longer part of the eBay catalog.

Unfortunately, dynamic data can also cause problems. For one thing, you need a connection to the Internet to work with dynamic data. When you use a desktop machine, maintaining a connection usually isn't a problem. However, many third party developers are working on applications where a connection might not be available, such as a user-checking application for a PDA (an application that tells you about buyers or sellers you have dealt with on eBay). You download the information from eBay Web Services and then perform some outside activity—the connection doesn't exist while you're away from the Internet connection so the data is no longer dynamic.

Using the term *dynamic* to refer to application data is also somewhat of a misnomer. Nothing is truly a dynamic data application. The moment the response to your query leaves the eBay server, it begins to age. The data doesn't change once it leaves the eBay server, so in reality it isn't truly dynamic. The only way you can achieve a dynamic presentation of sorts is to make multiple queries. You must define how often is often enough for your needs.

These facts lead into the discussion of static data. Truly static data never changes at all. Most Web sites still rely on static data presentation because the information they display doesn't change often enough to warrant a dynamic presentation. When you make a single query to eBay Web Services, the response you receive is static data. It's a snapshot of that particular part of the database at a specific time. The data won't change unless you make another query.

Understanding the static and dynamic nature of data is important when you design an application that relies on eBay Web Services. Errors creep into the presentation you create as the data from eBay Web Services ages on your system. Part of the design process for your application is to determine how much error you can accept and to ensure you meet the application's minimum update requirements.

Understanding the Certification Requirements

Unlike many Web services, eBay is extremely concerned about the security and privacy of the data in its database, the safety of your application, and the overall protection of everyone who uses eBay. Given the open nature of the Internet and all of the holes that crackers discover regularly, absolute security and reliability is a difficult goal to meet. Because your application is part of the security, privacy, and reliability picture, eBay doesn't let you work with live data until you prove you can do so safely. In short, certification is a process where you work with eBay to create robust applications.

Some people might wonder why eBay goes through all this effort to check your application. Unlike other Web services where you're working with information in the public domain or hand-off transactions to the Web service, with eBay Web Services you're in direct contact with the application user and perform transactions directly. Your application will handle private details, such as the user's address, telephone number, and credit card. The need for certification is valid. Not only does certification ensure that applications meet a high standard, but it also protects you from potential errors in judgment and eBay from lawsuits that arise from a lack of diligence.

This section of the chapter discusses three elements of the certification process. The first is to create a test user. Using a test user ensures that any data you create is fake—that no one's real information is compromised if your application fails. The second element is the sandbox itself. The sandbox doesn't contain any real data, just data created by all of the application developers who use eBay Web services—even so, this data does look like the data you'll see on eBay. The third element is the certification process. Once you know your application works well in sandbox mode, you can ask eBay to look at it and certify it for use with the real database. (eBay will also monitor your application periodically after you begin using it in the production environment to ensure it complies with all the requirements.)

Creating a Test User

Test users let you check the operation of your eBay Web Services application without potentially releasing details of a real user. Each test user requires an email account. You can only create one test user per email account. If you're part of a large organization that has an email server, you could potentially create test email accounts for use in testing. The only problem with this approach is that you're potentially revealing your organization name as part of the email address. A better solution is to use a free email service. One of the better options for this purpose is Yahoo Mail (`http://billing.mail.yahoo.com/bm/MailReg?.v=8`) because you don't need to sign up for a Passport account (as you would for Hotmail) or jump through any other hoops. Because some functions require two interactive users, it's a good idea to create a minimum of two email accounts. For example, you can't create a feedback dialog with only one user—this feature requires at least two users. Likewise, you need two accounts to create a buyer and a seller scenario. More accounts can be helpful, but two accounts will work for all of the examples in this book.

After you create the two test email accounts, you need to register them with eBay. Make sure you go to the sandbox Web site at `http://sandbox.ebay.com`. Simply click the registration link located near the top of the page. The process for creating a test user is the same as the process you followed to create your real account on eBay. The only difference is that this user resides on the sandbox server and not the live eBay server. You also don't need to enter your credit card information for selling privileges—using the `ValidateTestUserRegistration()` call takes care of that need.

Before you begin developing applications around the users you've created, you need to verify that they are registered correctly. You can perform this task in a number of ways. The easiest method is to start one of the sample applications located in the `\Program Files\eBay\ SDK\Samples` folder of your hard drive. I used the application found in the `\C#\SimpleXmlPost` folder, but any of the applications will work fine. Figure 2.3 shows typical correct output for this application. Don't worry too much about the complex-looking XML right now; all you need to verify is that the application returns the current eBay date and time.

An error message is going to look a lot more complex than the XML you see in Figure 2.3. For example, if the user doesn't exist, you'll see a lengthy explanation such as the one shown here.

```xml
<?xml version="1.0" encoding="iso-8859-1"?>
<eBay>
  <EBayTime>2004-02-07 22:03:11</EBayTime>
  <Errors>
    <Error>
      <Code>35</Code>
      <ErrorClass>RequestError</ErrorClass>
      <SeverityCode>1</SeverityCode>
      <Severity>SeriousError</Severity>
      <Line>0</Line>
      <Column>0</Column>
      <ShortMessage>
        <![CDATA[Invalid user name or password.]]>
      </ShortMessage>
      <LongMessage>
        <![CDATA[Invalid user name or password...]]>
      </LongMessage>
    </Error>
  </Errors>
</eBay>
```

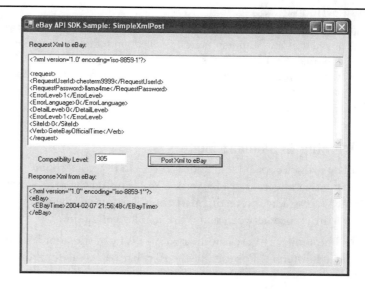

FIGURE 2.3:

Verify that the user is entered into the eBay system correctly by running one of the test applications.

If you see an error message, make sure you've entered all of the test user information correctly and verified the account by checking the test user's email account for a message from eBay and following the instructions. Something else you should notice in Figure 2.3 is that the application displays both the username and the password in plain text. Someone looking over your shoulder could see this information. That's the reason you don't want to use your real account when creating an application—it's too easy to reveal information that you don't want other people to know.

eBay does provide a special way to validate users when working in the sandbox. You must perform this special validation before eBay will allow the user to bid on items or list items for sale. All you need to do is modify the <Verb> tag shown in Figure 2.1 (the action you want eBay to perform) so it looks like this:

```
<Verb>ValidateTestUserRegistration</Verb>
```

When the call returns, you'll see a success message similar to the one shown here:

```
<?xml version="1.0" encoding="iso-8859-1"?>
<eBay>
  <EBayTime>2004-02-07 22:22:28</EBayTime>
  <ValidateTestUserRegistration>
    <ValidateTestUserRegistrationStatus>
      Success
    </ValidateTestUserRegistrationStatus>
  </ValidateTestUserRegistration>
</eBay>
```

▶ TIP

If you don't want to use the C# application that eBay provides with the kit, you can also use the eBay API Test Tool described in the "Using the eBay API Tool" section of Chapter 4. This tool lets you enter a request based on XML input, just as the C# example described in this section does.

Working in Sandbox Mode

eBay provides a sandbox mode so you can test your application in a safe environment—one that won't affect other eBay users. You can find the main sandbox page at http://sandbox .ebay.com. The interesting part about working in the sandbox is that you won't notice much of a difference between it and the standard eBay site.

The similarity between the two sites is by design, but it's important to realize that they are indeed different. For example, a user that you create in the sandbox won't appear in the real eBay and vice versa. This fact means that your eBay account is inaccessible from the sandbox unless you create a new version of that account with the same user identification. The two accounts won't interact in any way—they're separate accounts. Likewise, products you offer for sale in the sandbox won't appear on the real site.

> **▶ TIP**
>
> The user account issue is important because it would be easy to miss it in the heat of writing code—you could supply your personal account information by accident, rather than a test user. The resulting error information might not immediately tell you what's wrong. When in doubt, check your settings to ensure you're using the correct URLs and account information. Make sure you check URLs to verify that they begin with `http://sandbox.ebay.com`.

Because the sandbox is separate from the real eBay, some developers might not treat the sandbox with the same care as they would the real environment. However, because this is your testing ground, you need to use the same procedures and processes as you would in the real environment. For example, if you plan to check all seller information before making a bid in the real world, you need to do the same thing in the sandbox. When listing a product, make sure you include all of the graphics so that you can check issues such as the performance of your application and subtle problems with the graphic upload process. Make sure you maintain your working area as well by cleaning up old materials—just as you would in the real environment.

Getting Your Application Certified

After a lot of testing and tweaking, your application will be ready to use in the production environment. At least, you hope it's ready for use by other people. In some cases, developers will look at the certification process as a nuisance at best and a trial at most. The certification process isn't adversarial—eBay isn't looking for ways to give your application a failing grade. In fact, they want you to succeed. Consequently, you need to look at the certification process as a last look by eBay to ensure your application will work as intended on the first try (which includes meeting security and privacy requirements). It's a partnership between eBay and you to ensure your success.

If your application is for personal use only—the only option available to developers who sign up for the Individual Tier license (the "Determining Which Licensing Level Is Best" section of Chapter 1 discusses this issue), you can self-certify your application. Using this option means that you can't sell or distribute your application to anyone else. You'll pay a licensing fee and adhere to the certification requirements at `http://developer.ebay.com/DevZone/docs/API_Doc/Certification/CertificationRequirements.htm`. When you're ready to begin the self-certification process, go to `http://developer.ebay.com/` `DevZone/launch/SelfCertify.asp` and answer the questions. eBay needs to know about the development environment you use, your operating system and XML parser, and a number of other issues surrounding your application. When your application passes self-certification, you'll receive an email and you can pick up your production keys.

> ▶ **NOTE**
>
> If you live in the United States, United Kingdom, Canada, New Zealand, and Australia, you must pay the licensing fee using PayPal. This requirement means you must set up a PayPal account before you begin the self-certification process.

Standard certification—the level you need to distribute an application—is a lot more intensive than self-certification. If you're at the Individual Tier of licensing, you'll begin by upgrading to the next level. You'll download the API Usage Document located at `http://` `developer.ebay.com/DevZone/Kb_SearchDocs/APIUsage_v2.doc`. This document contains a lot of very detailed questions, so you'll need to set time aside to fill it out. You'll need to answer questions such as precisely which calls you use in your application. The document requires that you assign a type to your application, such as Server-Side/Web-Based Application. You also need to estimate the amount of traffic your application will generate and tell eBay how you plan to meet security and privacy requirements.

> ▶ **NOTE**
>
> The traffic estimate is just that—a guess you make based on current usage statistics. For example, if you currently see 10,000 hits on your Web site each day and estimate that half of those people will use your eBay application, then the traffic estimate would be 5,000 users per day. You would need to multiply this value by the number of calls you expect each user to make. Good sandbox beta testing can help you estimate the calls per user. Make sure you create good user models that simulate the kinds of users you expect to use your application.

Once you submit the API Usage Document, the test team will set up a test plan with you. Your company will actually implement the test plan and generate test logs that eBay will review. In some cases eBay will also set up special test scenarios and ask to see your source code. Only after eBay is satisfied that your application works as intended, meets privacy, security, and efficiency requirements, and adheres to the API Usage Document you submitted will you receive your production keys. In short, the application examination is very thorough, but you'll know that your application meets or exceeds eBay requirements when you're finished.

Working with Some Simple Examples

It's time to look at some simple eBay examples. You don't need to worry about the details of the applications at this point—all you really need to understand is what task the application is performing using eBay Web Services. In other words, the emphasis in this chapter is on the Web services process, rather than the actual code.

> ▶ **NOTE**
>
> The examples in this chapter all include spaces for the keys that eBay provides when you set up an account. To use the examples, you must replace these spaces with the keys you receive from eBay. Simply enter the values when prompted when you start the application. You can also enter your keys permanently by editing the files and recompiling the application as necessary. When working with a text file (such as an HTML page or an eXtensible Stylesheet Language Transformations, XSLT, file), use a pure text editor such as Notepad. See the "Becoming an eBay Developer Program Member" and "Obtaining Your License" sections of Chapter 1 for details on getting keys if you don't have them.

You can look at the source code if desired. You'll find these examples in the \Chapter 02 folder of the source code located on the Sybex Web site.

Understanding the Example Types

I designed most of the examples in this section with eBay Web Services process in mind. This means they aren't always the most realistic examples or that they'll provide results good enough to use for your next application. However, the examples demonstrate principles that make it easier for you to work with eBay Web Services as the book progresses. Most importantly, the examples serve as a basis for learning that Web services aren't difficult.

Many people won't actually build an application to work with eBay. If they do build a simple application, it will be part of a Web page—not part of a Web server setup. The first set of examples demonstrates that this technique is possible, although it has limitations. The Web page approach is quite useful when you want to present someone with options or help them locate information associated with a product. Given the requirements of a standard certification, you probably won't want to use this approach if you plan to distribute or sell your application because it's going to be very difficult to meet the eBay requirements. This technique works best if you want to create a quick application you can use for your own needs.

The second set of examples demonstrates two kinds of applications. The first type is for desktop users. Many people will build applications to make eBay friendlier for environments where desktop applications see greater use, such as in an office. The book discusses a number of applications; this one simply demonstrates how the process works. The second example demonstrates that size is unimportant in many ways. Although you'll find that the Pocket PC does pose some limits on how you interact with eBay, it's quite capable of performing many tasks.

Using a Browser Example

This first browser example simply performs a search. Generally, browser applications provide a good way to experiment with eBay Web Services and provide utility-like applications. One of the best features of a browser application is that it works on a lot of platforms and devices. Unfortunately, the browser needs some type of XML support, so you generally have to provide an XML solution for a particular need. In this case, the browser example relies on a Microsoft XML solution. Figure 2.4 shows how this example looks. You'll find the complete source for this example in the \Chapter 02\SimpleBrowser folder of the source code located on the Sybex Web site.

FIGURE 2.4:

Browser applications offer great flexibility but limited processing.

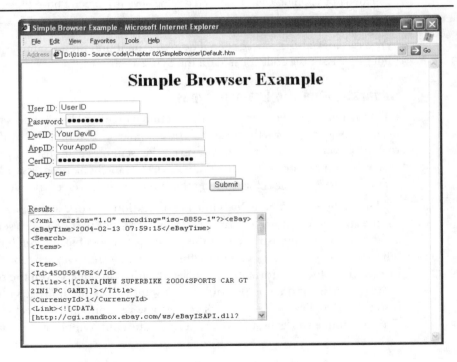

You must provide some input for this example to work. As with all the eBay examples, you must provide five inputs as a minimum:

- Username
- User password
- Developer identifier
- Application identifier
- Certificate identifier

This example provides a single handy output—the raw XML that eBay sends as a response to the request. All of the interactions you have with eBay will involve some type of XML. In some cases, eBay helps hide the XML from view so that you can write code more quickly and worry about fewer details. However, when working with a browser application, you'll always need to consider the XML portion of the communication.

The information in the Results text block isn't formatted perfectly, but it's formatted well enough that you can begin to understand a little of how eBay interacts with your application. You should scroll through the results and pick out the data elements. Again, don't concentrate on the XML—concentrate on the data and the process that has just occurred.

Viewing the XSLT Example

Developers of browser applications don't have to settle for raw XML feedback. The text you see in Figure 2.4 is a little difficult to read and definitely less useful than a similar display on eBay. You can use a number of techniques to make the output more useful. For example, you could manipulate the raw XML programmatically to create the desired output. While this technique works, it's time consuming. Fortunately, a better solution exists—using eXtensible Style Language Transformation (XSLT) changes the XML into a Web page. Figure 2.5 shows typical XSLT output. The example begins with the same input page shown in Figure 2.4, but this time the output is a little more interesting. You'll find the complete source for this example in the \Chapter 02\XSLTBrowser folder of the source code located on the Sybex Web site.

The output is a new page in this case. The input for this new page is the same raw XML shown in Figure 2.4. Notice that XSLT can provide identifying text, structure, and data formatting. It can also help you select just the data you want—the raw XML contains considerably more data than shown here. You could easily change the output by simply changing the XSLT file, which means that a single call to eBay could produce a number of reports.

F I G U R E 2 . 5 :

Using XSLT extends browser functionality, but at the cost of additional programming.

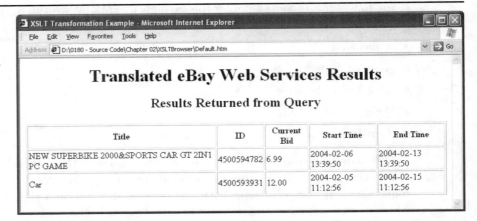

F I G U R E 2 . 5 :
Using XSLT extends browser functionality, but at the cost of additional programming.

Viewing the Desktop Example

Desktop applications form the basis of most of the work that people do with computers today. Yes, many people use browsers to search for data, make purchases, and perform other tasks, but many common tasks such as word processing and manipulating databases remain on the desktop. That's why having a special desktop application to work with eBay can be very appealing. The application reduces the user's learning curve by presenting a familiar interface. A company can customize the appearance of the eBay data to reflect its method of working with eBay. In many cases, it's also easier to integrate the data produced by a desktop application with other applications in use at a particular location. For example, you could send data directly from the custom application to a database or spreadsheet for further manipulation.

Figure 2.6 shows a simple search application written in Visual C#. You'll find the complete source for this example in the \Chapter 02\CSharp_ItemSearch folder of the source code located on the Sybex Web site. I chose this particular example because many people will begin using eBay by looking at what it offers. A customized search application can make that process easier.

Obviously, a search is only the first step in the purchasing process. Once you have the data from a search in a convenient location, such as a database, you can perform analysis on the product price, packaging, payment terms, and other features, and then make a bid on the item that offers the most for your particular needs. The idea is that you can make all of these decisions with the speed that only computer automation can provide.

Desktop applications are platform specific but offer great processing flexibility.

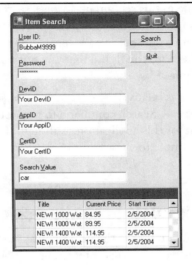

The application also demonstrates the flexibility of eBay Web Services in this case. You could use the same search as a starting point for a number of tasks including buying a product or simply researching product prices based on a set of criteria such as the shipping terms. In other words, you could answer questions such as whether some sellers are able to lower their selling price by increasing their shipping and handling costs. A good deal might not be so good if it doesn't offer favorable payment terms.

The output shown in Figure 2.6 is a very small subset of the information that eBay provides. For example, you'll find that eBay provides a number of product URLs you can use to learn more about the product or download images provided by the seller. You can also drill down through the data to learn more about the item seller. In short, by making this single call you open the door to learning just about everything there is to know about the product. Figure 2.6 simply shows a small sample of the available data.

Viewing the Pocket PC Example

Having eBay in your pocket (so to speak) can help you keep track of auctions while you're out of the office. Nothing works quite so nicely as the Pocket PC in this case because it includes a lot of intelligence that lets you create a robust application. You can also use cellular telephones and devices such as the Palm, but these devices normally require some form of external support such as a Web server. The idea of the Pocket PC example is to let you communicate with eBay with the fewest possible encumbrances. The added intelligence lets you perform some tasks locally, and you can also make use of local storage in a limited way to improve processing speed.

The example in this section performs a search. Figure 2.7 shows the opening display for the example. You'll find the complete source for this example in the \Chapter 02\PocketPC _Search folder of the source code located on the Sybex Web site. Because of the small screen size of a Pocket PC, you'll find that you normally need to use multiple forms to work with your applications.

The example is relatively simple. Once you fill in the details required to make the request, you use the File ➤ Search command to request the information from eBay. Figure 2.8 shows typical output for this application. Although the text is small, it's still readable. You could also extend this example to show additional information or use more detailed forms to show individual items.

Manipulating Data to Meet Specific Needs

At some point, you'll have the data required to make your application functional. The problem is that raw data isn't that interesting, so you need to manipulate it to make it easier to read or provide conclusions based on the facts. The following sections discuss data manipulation needs you should consider for your application and how to use the eBay examples to help you understand some of these data transformation needs.

FIGURE 2.7:

You can take eBay with you on the road using a mobile application.

The details page
shows the information
in tabular format
similar to a desktop
application.

Understanding Data Transformation Requirements

Getting data from eBay often means transforming application data to text. Every input you provide to eBay is text—it doesn't matter how you make the request. This first form of data transition is relatively easy because you can perform most translations quickly. Most languages provide a method for changing a numeric page number to text. When you use a Web page, translation is actually unnecessary because the Web page stores all input data as text.

The difficult data transformations occur when you accept a response from eBay and need to turn it into something your users will need. Not only is the data from eBay somewhat bulky due to the XML storage requirements but you'll also find that little nuances in request strategy can make a big difference in what you receive and how your application reacts to it. For example, some requests won't return data in all fields. When searching for an item, you can't depend on the seller providing an item description. The Description property can be blank, so your application needs a way to detect this fact and handle the property appropriately.

The way you make the request and accept the response is also important. For example, working directly with the XML can provide some benefits, especially when you want to create a browser-based application. Using this technique ensures that you see the raw data without any kind of filtering and that you have better control over the session. However, working with classes in languages such as C# is actually more convenient. The classes hide unnecessary details from view and you can assume that many of the properties have default values so you don't need to fill them in. In addition, you'll find that using the classes does provide some advantages in error handling because you don't have to decipher the meaning behind some of the messages.

Another way to view the XML versus class issue is the manner of presentation the two provide. When you use an XML request and response, all of the data appears to your application as text. However, when you work with classes, the class automatically transforms most data into a more convenient form. For example, when you're working with a .NET application, a date appears as a `System.DateTime` type, rather than a simple string. The manner of presentation doesn't mean that you always want to work with a class; sometimes working directly with XML is still better. (If you want to see a quick example of how this works before you get to the chapters on languages, look at the C# example in the `\Program Files\eBay\SDK\Samples\ C#\SimpleXmlPost folder`.)

Viewing the eBay Examples

eBay provides a number of examples for you to use. The examples don't show how to perform every API task—generally, you'll find one or two examples for each of the languages that eBay supports. The easiest way to locate the samples is to look in Start ➢ Programs ➢ eBay SDK ➢ Sample Code. You can also find the samples in the `\Program Files\eBay\ SDK\Samples` folder of your hard drive. eBay also provides a number of samples on their Web site at `http://developer.ebay.com/DevZone/docs/Samplecode.asp`.

Although these examples aren't all inclusive, you want to look at them for several reasons. First, the examples do explain some basics of working with eBay Web Services in that particular language. The eBay SDK Reference doesn't always make the actual coding sequence clear, so these examples help. Second, the examples demonstrate eBay's coding philosophy. Knowing how eBay writes an example will help you get started with your own application faster. It also ensures you have a better chance of getting your application certified quickly. Third, you might find some helpful code you can use to get your application started. Obviously, these applications are quite generic, but they can give you a starting point for your own code.

Each of the language chapters in this book, Chapters 6 through 11, will examine the eBay examples when available. I'll point out special features or issues that you won't want to miss when working with the code.

Using the PERL Example

This book doesn't have a Practical Extraction and Reporting Language (PERL) chapter. However, I thought it important to discuss the PERL example provided with the eBay Web

Services Kit. You'll find this example in the `\Program Files\eBay\SDK\Samples\Perl\`
`SimpleList` folder of your hard drive. The sample application helps you create a new item
listing on eBay. The item will appear in the sandbox database, so you don't need to worry
about providing less than useful information, but try to make your input as realistic as
possible.

> ▶ **NOTE**
>
> The PERL example isn't very flexible, but it is helpful. You can only run this application in
> Windows using the ActiveState's ActivePerl product. Download this product at `http://www`
> `.activestate.com`. For the purposes of this book, I used version 5.8.3 of the product.
> (Newer versions of the product should work as well.)

To start the sample application, you need to open a command prompt in the example
folder, type **D:\Perl\Bin\Perl5.8.2 SimpleList.pl**, and press Enter. The application will
request your eBay supplied key values, along with a user identifier and password. After you
type these required values, the application will ask for you a number of other inputs, such as
the title of your new listing. After you enter a modicum of information about the product, the
application will tell you that everything is ready to go. All you need to do is press Enter to
add the new item.

At this point, the application uses eBay Web Services to make an item request for your new
item. If the Web service detects an error in your input, such as a missing location or a BuyIt-
Now price that's lower than the initial bidding price, you'll receive an error message back.
Figure 2.9 shows typical output for a successful addition.

FIGURE 2.9:

The PERL example
provided in the eBay
Web Services Kit lets
you add a new item.

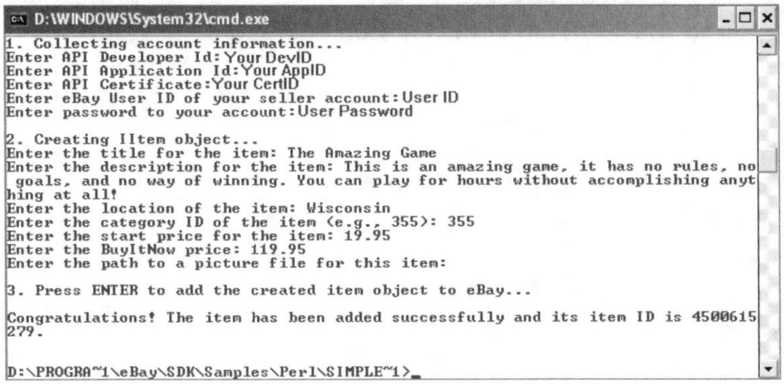

> **▶ NOTE**
>
> Figure 2.9 and some of the other screenshots in the book have been modified to protect my personal information. The output is same output that you'll normally see, as are the data entry steps. The only reason for the changes is to keep the developer keys that eBay provided me private.

Your Call to Action

You now know how to work with eBay Web Services from a user perspective. The examples in the chapter let you see how eBay Web Services can perform useful work for specific needs. In addition, you now know what to expect from the Web service in the way of output and understand the need to modify that information for display. In general, eBay Web Services provides text data with formatting information to make conversion easy, but the data still requires some type of conversion for presentation purposes.

Reading the material in the chapter will help you understand eBay Web Services in theory. However, before you can really understand what's going on, it helps you get some hands-on time. If you haven't tried the examples in the chapter yet, make sure you do. It's also a good idea to try the various examples that come with the eBay Web Services Kit.

Chapter 3 builds on the knowledge you gained in this chapter. The emphasis of Chapter 3 is on data mining—the process of using specialized search techniques to whittle search results down to just the items you need. In many cases, you can also access these search techniques using the eBay search pages, but the emphasis of data mining is automation. Only by using the eBay Web Services can you automate the search process and then display the results in the form you want, rather than rely on eBay's formatting methodology.

Chapter 3

Defining a
Simple Search

Using Search
Conditions

Modifying the
Presentation

Localizing the
Information

Invoking an eBay
Site Search

▶ Defining a Search

The point behind using eBay is to find a good buy (or to sell someone else a good buy). You not only want to locate a product, you want to get it at the lowest possible price. Of course, no matter what price a seller offers, the search isn't any good unless you also get the terms that you want. In short, an eBay search can be as simple as requesting an obscure product using a single keyword or as complex as locating a common item using multiple keywords to ensure you get the right one.

Note that the idea of searching isn't just for buyers. A seller needs to perform searches, as well, to see what other sellers are offering in the way of price, packaging, and payment terms to remain competitive. Looking at what other sellers are doing can also help you create a more compelling presentation for your product. The extremely competitive environment that eBay provides means knowing what others are doing at all times.

A successful eBay search is one in which you obtain the information you need and, hopefully, only that information. An efficient eBay search is one in which you obtain the information during the first few URL clicks. The faster you find the desired product, the more efficient your search becomes. The focus of this chapter is the search techniques you can combine with the automation a Web service provides to get usable results quickly.

The chapter begins with a discussion of typical searches you can perform without expending a lot of energy defining search terms. It moves on to special search arguments you can add to a request that make it more specific. For example, you might want to search for a Stanley No.5 hand plane made around 1975. You could simply start with Stanley bench plane. If that phrase results in too many hits, you could further narrow the search by adding the date or the model number. This section also discusses a number of special searches that eBay provides so that you can narrow your search by using a specialized search page.

The final portions of the chapter discuss special kinds of searches that return a particular result instead of the massive quantity of unfocused results you normally receive. For example, you might not want to pay more than a certain amount for a product, so looking at items outside your price range isn't very efficient. You might also want to limit the number of shipping locations—paying overseas freight charges for a large item could reduce the advantages of getting a good price. The bottom line is that you can use a multitude of ways to search for information, but locating the most efficient and practical way to perform the search is essential.

Performing a Typical Search

The first question most people will have about this section is what constitutes a typical search. A typical search is one that you make without considering any optimization. You just enter some keywords to make the query. I consider this a typical search because most people use this kind of search until they really begin to understand eBay.

You'll normally enter all of the information for a typical search on a single line. Most people begin at their eBay home page, as shown in Figure 3.1. Simply type the keywords you want to use and click Search.

> ▶ NOTE
>
> I've modified some figures, such as Figure 3.1, in this book to hide my personal information. The essential characteristics of the page remain the same, but you'll see additional personal information when you view the page using your browser.

FIGURE 3.1:

A typical search can begin directly from your home page.

Unfortunately, this kind of typical search is extremely limited because eBay doesn't provide an easy method for extending the search. For example, you can't use special terms to tell eBay that you only want to view products within a specific price range. You can use keywords carefully to limit the search results. For example, you can add a model number, release year, or other information to make the search more specific. You can learn more about these search techniques at `http://pages.ebay.com/help/buy/contextual/search_tips.html`.

When you want to perform a more extensive search, use the Basic Search page at `http://pages.ebay.com/search/items/basicsearch.html`. Figure 3.2 shows a typical example of the Basic Search page. Notice that this page provides the means to request a search based on location or price range. eBay also makes this functionality available through a special toolbar you can obtain at `http://pages.ebay.com/ebay_toolbar/` (the toolbar is built using eBay Web Services).

This page has several interesting features that you can also add into your applications. For example, searching for a particular price range is essential because otherwise you'll spend a lot of time looking at products you can't afford or of such quality that you don't want them. However, notice the Words to Exclude field. At first, this field might not attract much attention, but it's an important field to consider. You can control a search better when you provide a basic list of keywords and then tell eBay which words you don't want to see. For example, you might want to buy a car, but not a classic car. Placing the word *classic* in the Words to Exclude field would tend to reduce the number of classic car hits.

FIGURE 3.2:

The eBay home page provides access to a simple search as well as tools and services.

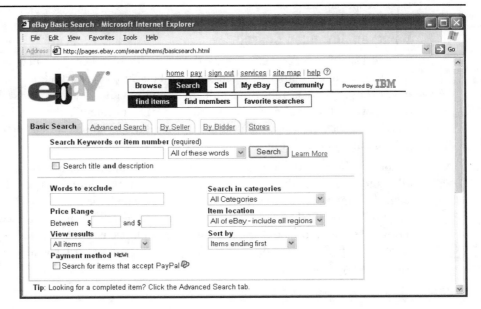

Some businesses will want to make some of the search options on this page required for their custom application. For example, if you're in the business of locating and buying large items on eBay for sale, you might not want to haul them all the way from *San Diego, CA*, when you live in *Buffalo, NY*, so you would set the Item Location field to a specific area. Likewise, you might only be interested in antiques and not the rest of the items that eBay offers. Consequently, you might set the Category field in your application to *Antiques* for all searches. Working with the Basic Search for a while will help you decide which options to use for your customized search to make it easier to use and still effective.

Adding Search Conditions

Every second you spend searching for an item is a second that you aren't bidding on it or using it for research. That second is also lost for other activities, such as helping customers or enjoying time with your family. Consequently, you might find that a basic search isn't as useful as it could be—perhaps you can narrow your search still further in an attempt to find the perfect results with just one or two tries.

Special searches can help define searches in more precise terms. In fact, careful use of search terms can reduce the number of results to the few you need. A perfect search returns just the results you need, but a less optimal result is acceptable in most cases. The idea is to reduce the number of results to a manageable level. The following sections describe various types of special searches.

Using an Advanced Search

A typical search won't meet every need. In fact, the searches many people conduct are less than successful or inefficient when successful because keywords alone usually can't express a query very well. (A search with results that require half a day to process when all you need is one answer is both successful and inefficient.) The problem is that you haven't defined the search criteria completely. You can test most eBay special searches using the Advanced Search Page shown in Figure 3.3.

Look at the issue this way. Let's say that it takes about a minute for you to click a link in eBay and decide whether the item will work or not. (A minute isn't very long when you consider the time required to load the page and actually look at some of the information. A small result set of 60 links requires 60 minutes to search.) Many of the search results we've discussed so far in the book contain hundreds of links. Even if you eliminate many of those links by reading the item titles that eBay provides, you can still spend a lot of time looking for the link you need.

▶ TIP

An interesting exercise is to time how long a typical eBay page takes to load. With all of the graphics and other information that eBay provides, someone using a dial-up connection can spend significantly more than a minute waiting for the page to load completely. This is one reason you want to use efficient searches—the load time can cause significant problems at some point.

Some of the special options shown in Figure 3.3 actually help you extend your search. When you use a Basic Search, eBay assumes that you want to obtain items from your country. However, notice the Items Located In field in Figure 3.3. This field lets you search for an item in other countries. Using this field can help you locate extremely rare items that you might not find in your own country. Of course, once you leave your country, you must begin considering the issue of locale—the rules for that particular area. For example, what currency does the seller want to use to make the transaction? You can limit your search to a particular kind of currency to avoid exchange rate problems.

Notice that this page also includes an interesting feature that you'll always want to include in a custom application—the Results per Page field. Waiting for the Basic Search to present the default number of links is time consuming. You might just want to see the top few items on the list or you might think that you'll have trouble finding the item, so specifying a large number of item links lets you do something else while they load.

It's important to note some of the special searches indicated in Figure 3.3. For example, the Item Type options can help you locate auctions that accommodate special needs. Someone looking for a whole box of sunglasses to sell will want to check the Quantity Greater Than 1 option. Likewise, if you're performing research, you might want to check the Completed Items Only option so that you can see how an auction ended. It doesn't really pay to look at an auction in progress, in most cases, when you're performing research because the information isn't complete.

Using Other Special Search Techniques

eBay provides a number of special search forms. You wouldn't locate an item using these search forms—you would look for something else. For example, if you're a buyer, you might want to use the Seller Search page shown in Figure 3.4.

Notice that you can search for a single seller or a group of sellers. eBay does limit you to searching for 10 sellers at a time. The search form lets you choose some of the data presented, including the list of bidder emails and the completed items for a specific time frame (or none at all).

A seller might want to check out a buyer as well. To perform that task, you'd use the Bidder Search shown in Figure 3.5. As with the Seller Search, you can limit the results of a Bidder Search to a degree. For example, you can tell eBay to only include the items where the bidder is the high bidder on the item.

You'll notice that many of the special eBay searches require unique information you might not have. In many cases, this is a user identifier that you can look up by clicking the Look It Up link on the search page or selecting the Find Members option at the top of the page. In both cases, you'll see a Find Members page similar to the one shown in Figure 3.6.

FIGURE 3.4:

Use the Seller search to locate a specific seller.

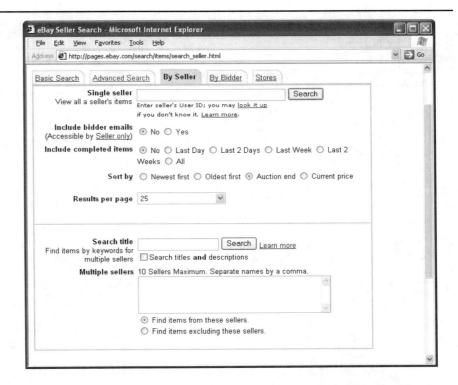

FIGURE 3.5:

The Bidder search helps you locate the people buying products.

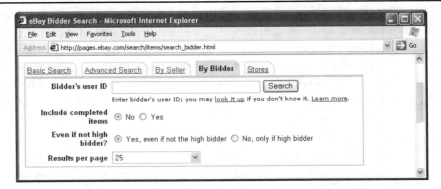

Near the bottom of this Web page, you'll see a Request User ID feature. By providing an email address, you can learn the identification of a user—assuming, of course, that the person is actually an eBay user. eBay provides a special number that you must type in as part of the request for security purposes. Make sure you understand the limitations of this feature—eBay provides them as part of the description in that section. In general, you can only use the feature to obtain the full information of someone that you're currently engaged with in a transaction. There are a few exceptions to this rule where you can obtain partial information. Most of the rules for using this feature are in place to protect other people's privacy—much as you would want your own privacy protected.

This page does have a number of other useful features. For example, it's interesting and educational to read the About Me page for a member that you're working with, because you might find that they have other interests that you share. You can also use this page to obtain feedback about the user, learn the User ID history, and gain contact information (as long as you're engaged in a transaction).

Sometimes you need to perform a special search based on the products carried by a specific store. For example, you might want to get the tools carried by Sears stores such as a Craftsman ratchet or maybe a Lands' End jacket. The idea is to find a specific brand carried by that store. To perform this task, you'd use the Store Search shown in Figure 3.7.

FIGURE 3.7:

Sometimes the Store search can help you locate a business that sells a particular product.

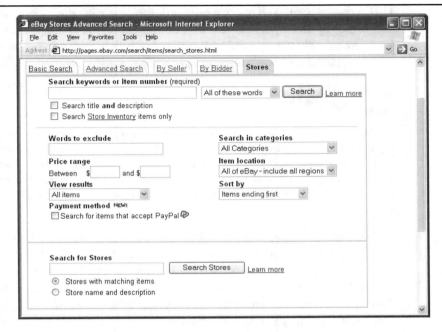

The upper half of the form in Figure 3.7 works just like the Basic Search discussed earlier. The lower half of the form accepts a store name. When you click Search, you'll see eBay sellers that carry a product with that brand. Interestingly enough, when you enter some names, such as Sears, you'll see an actual entry for that store. That's because Sears uses eBay to sell older products, products that weren't popular, or products that they plan to discontinue. In some cases, the products might be returns that they couldn't put back out on the store floor.

Considering the URL Search Form

A few developers might be under the impression that they only have two choices for searching: the manual search and the one eBay Web Services provides. This view isn't entirely correct. You can also create a custom page that assembles a special URL for searching. The result still comes from the eBay site, but you have control over how the search is constructed. Some people might be tempted to use screen scraping techniques to retrieve the resulting data (essentially extracting the data from the resulting page and presenting it in a new form), but the Web service is definitely an easier solution, and one which eBay supports, when you want to control the presentation.

To construct an URL with your search criteria, all you need to know is the base URL and the arguments used to pass the search information to eBay. The base URL for eBay searches is `http://search.ebay.com/search/search.dll?MfcISAPICommand=GetResult`. To this base

URL you add a series of query words with their associated keywords that are separated from each other by an ampersand (&). For example, every search includes a query entry. To search for a 2000 Chevy, you'd provide an URL of `http://search.ebay.com/search/search.dll?MfcISAPICommand=GetResult&query=2000+Chevy`.

▶ NOTE

This book uses the term *query word* to refer to a special word that you use to make an eBay query. You'll discover the query words that eBay currently supports while reading this chapter. For example, category0 is a query word that tells which category an item belongs to. A *keyword* expresses what you want to look for with eBay. For example, when you want to search for candles, you might include the word *votive* as a keyword.

Unfortunately, searching for a 2000 Chevy car retrieves everything from the car, to car covers, to just about anything else you can think of. To further limit the search, you'd need to add the *category0* query word, so the URL looks like this: `http://search.ebay.com/search/search.dll?MfcISAPICommand=GetResult&query=2000+Chevy&category0=6000`. In short, you can create your own query page using nothing more than the correct keywords. This technique doesn't overcome the limitations of a manual search, but you can customize the search page to meet specific needs. Here's a list of common query words.

▶ WARNING

The terms provided in this list could change at any time, as could the values provided. You'll need to test the features out with your custom search page to ensure they work as planned. In addition, you'll want to watch for changes to the eBay setup so you can make appropriate changes to your search page.

search_option This option defines how eBay handles the keywords you provide. A value of 1 tells eBay to look for all of the words. A value of 2 tells eBay to search for any of the words. Finally, a value of 3 tells eBay to perform an exact search.

minPrice and maxPrice Defines the minimum and maximum prices you're willing to pay for a particular item. You don't have to provide both values. For example, you might only be concerned that the item doesn't exceed a certain value.

srchdesc=y, completedOnly=30, itf=2, gift=1, and qty=y These query words are the entries for the five check boxes on the Advanced Search form. In order, they tell eBay to search both the title and the description, search for completed items only, look for BuyIt-Now items only, find gift items only, or locate items that have a quantity greater than one.

exclude   Use this option to exclude keywords from a search. The only items that eBay returns are those that match the keywords you provide but don't match these exclusion terms.

SortProperty   This option defines how eBay sorts the results for you. You can choose items where the auction is ending first (MetaEndSort), new items first (MetaNewSort), the lowest price order (MetaLowestPriceSort), and the highest price order (MetaHighest-PriceSort).

maxRecordsPerPage   Use this option to define the maximum number of entries you want to see per page.

Defining the correct category can be important for limiting your search. As previously mentioned, you use the *category0* query word to perform this task. Here is a list of common categories and their values.

- Antiques—20081
- Art—550
- Automotive-eBay Motors—6000
- Books—267
- Business and Industrial—12576
- Clothing, Shoes, and Accessories—11450
- Coins—11116
- Collectibles—1
- Computers—58058
- Consumer Electronics—293
- Dolls and Bears—237
- Entertainment—45099
- Home—11700
- Jewelry and Watches—281
- Musical Instruments—619
- Pottery and Glass—870
- Real Estate—10542
- Specialty Services—316
- Sports—888

- Stamps—260
- Tickets—1305
- Toys and Hobbies—220
- Travel—3252
- Everything Else—99

Understanding the Developer Search Options

Lest you think that the searches you can perform with eBay Web Services won't resemble the search pages, there are specialized tags for every possible search condition. You don't need to know too much about XML to see how these search criteria in an XML message follow the online search capability.

```xml
<?xml version="1.0" encoding="iso-8859-1"?>
<request xmlns="urn:eBayAPIschema">
    <RequestUserId> </RequestUserId>
    <RequestPassword> </RequestPassword>
    <DetailLevel>0</DetailLevel>
    <ErrorLevel>1</ErrorLevel>
    <Query>toy</Query>
    <SiteId>0</SiteId>
    <Verb>GetSearchResults</Verb>
    <Category></Category>
    <CharityNumber>1</CharityNumber>
    <Currency>1</Currency>
    <HighestPrice></HighestPrice>
    <IncludeSellers></IncludeSellers>
    <ExcludeSellers></ExcludeSellers>
    <LowestPrice></LowestPrice>
    <MaxResults>10</MaxResults>
    <Modifier>ebayavail</Modifier>
    <ModifierCode>0</ModifierCode>
    <Order>MetaEndSort</Order>
    <Region>60</Region>
    <SearchByCharity>1</SearchByCharity>
    <SearchInDescription>1</SearchInDescription>
    <SearchType>0</SearchType>
    <Shortcut>1</Shortcut>
    <Skip></Skip>
    <StoreID></StoreID>
    <StoreName></StoreName>
    <StoreSearch>0</StoreSearch>
</request>
```

The mandatory search items appear in normal text—all of the elements in bold are additional search items. For example, you don't have to provide a sort order as provided by the <Order> tag, but it's one of the options that you can use. Setting the <SearchInDescription> tag to 1 means that eBay will search within the descriptions for the keywords you've provided. You can also perform specialty searches, such as a store search.

The Web services form of the search provides some functionality that you can't get using any of the manual search techniques. For example, you search for specific payment methods. As of this writing, the manual search technique limits you to searching for PayPal. You can also perform a more detailed analysis of the information when using a Web services search. For example, you couldn't create a cross tabulation using the eBay search pages, but you can when working with a custom application.

Changing the Presentation

Presentation is everything when a search is involved. The presentation helps you cut through the clutter and reduce information overload. You might have an interest in a specific detail, so making this detail more prominent is important. The ordering and content of the data is also important because looking through an unordered list is time consuming.

The manual search techniques discussed in this chapter can help you achieve some presentation goals. For example, you can use the various sorting options to sort the data you receive from eBay. However, the sort options are a little limited—you can search by price or the time an auction has left to run. These options might not fulfill every need, but they do help.

In some ways, you can also control the kind of items you'll see. For example, you can choose to display just the items with item numbers when you perform an advanced search. You can also choose to hide the pictures when performing the initial search (just click the Hide link next to the Pictures column). Unfortunately, that's about the only options you have when selecting the actual presentation using a manual search.

One of the most important reasons to use a custom application for searching is to order (show, hide, sort, or present) the data in other ways. Using a Web service, you have full control over the presentation of the data. If you don't want to see the starting date of an auction, you don't have to display it. Likewise, users who don't like waiting for pictures to download don't have to wait—they can display just the text.

A custom application can also offer a level of flexibility not offered by other search methods. You might choose to begin with a short overview of the returned items—checking those off that seem to offer what you need most. It's then possible to expand the information displayed for the selected items without making another query to eBay Web services—this information is already available from the first query, you just didn't display it. This refining process can go on through several iterations until you have just the items you want to bid on. While it might seem like a time-consuming way to perform a search—you can actually perform searches faster in many situations.

Localizing the Information

The concept of localizing information is a little hard to nail down because it depends on where you are and what you need. In general, the manual search techniques do an adequate job if you want to consider the three most important localizing needs when conducting a search: shipping location, payment currency, and language.

Shipping location is important for heavy or delicate items. The farther you ship a heavy item, the more it costs. Likewise, shipping delicate items long distances tends to increase the chance that the item will break. However, shipping location can play a much bigger role when you have to consider transportation from another country. You might need to think about tariffs and shipping regulations. The manual search technique can help you with the first two issues by letting you search for a specific region. However, you'll need a custom application if you want to build intelligence in for overseas shipments or when you want to perform searches from multiple regions simultaneously.

Payment options include the currency you're using for the transaction. You can perform a manual search that looks for the use of specific currencies, but this limits the results you get in unforeseen ways. For example, if the seller allows a credit card transaction, the credit card company will take care of any differences in currency for you automatically. However, you won't know whether the seller allows credit card transactions without viewing each item page individually or performing a search with a custom application.

In short, you can search using the manual techniques and gain a certain level of localization. However, if you find that localization issues become a problem, you'll definitely want to look at the custom search techniques provided in this book.

Your Call to Action

This chapter discusses many ways to search for information—some people are probably yawning at this very moment after several hours of good sleep. Search techniques aren't the most exciting topic, but it's an essential topic for eBay users and eBay Web Services developers. Locating a product isn't hard. All you need is a good keyword. But unless you really like going through millions of hits, you need to find the most efficient way to locate just the information you want.

It's time to try a few of these techniques on your own. One way to try them out is to use the eBay Advanced Search page at `http://pages.ebay.com/search/items/search_adv.html`. Unfortunately, this technique doesn't really tell you how the information will look from a developer perspective. With this in mind, you'll also want to test the search-related sample applications in this book. See how they work with various keyword combinations. Make sure you try a few of the special searches as well—including the filtering and restriction methods. It's also a good idea to try the various examples that come with the eBay Web Services Kit.

Some of the examples in this chapter expose the underlying XML you'll use to interact with eBay Web Services. Chapter 4 goes on to the next step of working with eBay Web Services—actually using XML to perform tasks. Chapter 4 discusses how XML works, shows examples of how various languages use XML, and describes some of the problems you'll encounter when using XML. For example, XML itself isn't secure and it causes privacy issues you'll need to consider. This next step helps you move from merely using the Web service to telling it what information you'd like to request.

Chapter 4

| Discovering XML Basics | Working with Netpadd | Working with XMLwriter 2 | Presenting Information Using XSLT |

▶ Working with Web Service Data

| Working with the eBay Supplied Tools | Working with XML in the eBay API | Understanding the eBay API Structure | Developing with Privacy and Security Issues in Mind |

All Web services rely on some form of eXtensible Markup Language (XML) to receive requests and send information. Web services use XML to transfer data within a specific context, so the meaning of the data isn't lost. This chapter isn't going to drown you in XML terminology, and it certainly won't make you an expert, but it does contain helpful information on using XML with eBay Web Services.

> **▶ NOTE**
>
> eBay currently supports two different programming models. The API uses XML requests and responses. The Software Development Kit (SDK) completely hides the XML from view—the function calls appear much as they would for a local resource. The "Choosing between the API and SDK" section of Chapter 5 discusses the merits of each approach to application development. A third option, Simple Object Access Protocol (SOAP), will eventually appear on the scene as part of the SDK, according to a recent eBay press release. You can learn more about this option in Appendix C and at http://developer.ebay.com/DevZone/ KB_SearchDocs/OReilly_Conference_Release-Final.pdf.

You do need to understand some XML basics to use some features of eBay Web Services. The first section of the chapter helps you understand these basics, including the formats that eBay uses to return data from requests. You'll receive enough information in this section to work with the examples in the book. However, once you start working with XML, you might find that you want to know more, so the section also includes a listing of resources (including tutorials) that you can use to increase your XML knowledge.

XML isn't necessarily easy for the average human to read—it includes text mixed with tags in such a way that you can see the structure if you look hard enough, but the data isn't easy to interpret. The eXtensible Stylesheet Language Transformations (XSLT) technology can transform XML into a readable Web page. Again, this section won't make you an expert, but you'll leave the section with enough information to create basic reports and informational layouts. Like the XML section, this XSLT section contains additional information on where you can learn more about XSLT.

The next few sections describe some eBay-specific issues you need to consider when working with XML. You'll begin by learning how to use an important tool, the eBay API Test Tool. Far from an actual testing feature, this tool can reduce the development time of your project. When you finish these sections, you'll know how to build an XML message for eBay and how to interpret a response.

Finally, this chapter discusses two essential issues. The first is the problem of maintaining privacy with Web service applications. Because you handle user data with your application, you need to consider how best to protect the user's identity, while ensuring transactions occur in the most efficient manner possible. The second is the problem of security. Your application handles sensitive information, so you must consider security measures when building your application.

> ▶ **NOTE**

Many of the examples in this chapter rely on the XML-over-HTTPS method of communicating with eBay. This technique is also known as REpresentational State Transfer (REST) or the API method in eBay terms. Unfortunately, the eBay SDK Reference that comes with the eBay Web Services Kit doesn't tell you anything about this technique, even though it's actually more flexible than using the SDK method. You can learn more about the API using the documentation at `http://developer.ebay.com/DevZone/docs/API_Doc/index.asp`. You can see a number of API examples in Chapter 6.

Understanding XML Basics

Almost everyone has heard about and used XML in some way. If nothing else, you've seen XML extensions on Web pages because many magazines now use XML as a fast way to present highly formatted data online. Even though your browser presents what appears to be a standard Web page, underneath the presentation the page is an XML file. XML sees more use than Web pages and Web services—it's becoming the glue that holds the Internet together. In fact, you'll find XML used for many non-Internet purposes, such as application configuration files.

In many ways, knowing XML is a way to understand the presentation and distribution of information on the Internet today. Presentation is especially important when working with eBay because the wrong presentation can cost time during intense bidding or it can leave the user without enough information to make a good buying decision. For example, you might need some data presented as a table, rather than as running text to help the user make comparisons. Although the following sections provide the information you need to work with eBay Web Services, you'll eventually want to explore this topic further by using the resources in the "Learning More about XML" section.

Defining the Parts of an XML Message

All XML messages consist of three components: elements, attributes, and data. For all of the complexity of the examples in the previous chapters, XML doesn't contain very much in the way of complex information. In addition, XML messages consist entirely of text for the most part. Yes, you can attach encoded data, but the message itself is pure text, which makes XML quite readable. Here's a simple example that shows all three kinds of XML message components. You'll find this example in the \Chapter 04\Sample XML folder of the source code located on the Sybex Web site.

```
<?xml version="1.0" encoding="UTF-8"?>
<Hello xmlns:xsi="http://www.w3.org/2001/XMLSchema-instance">
    <Element1>Some Text 1</Element1>
    <Element2 MyAttribute="SomeValue">Some Text 2</Element2>
    <Element3>
        <![CDATA[Special Text]]>
    </Element3>
</Hello>
```

The first line is an element. It's a special kind of element that every XML file has—the XML heading. The <?xml?> element (or tag, as some books say) defines this file as an XML file of some kind. An element that tells an application how to work with a file is also called a processing instruction. The version attribute further defines the XML file by telling the XML parser that this is a version 1.0 file. The encoding attribute states how the data preparer formed the characters within the file. The two most popular encoding techniques in use are Unicode Transformation Format 8-bit (UTF-8) and UTF-7, however, eBay uses a special encoding called International Standards Organization (ISO) 8859 version 1. This encoding appears as encoding="iso-8859-1" in the eBay XML files. You can learn more about the Unicode Transformation Format (UTF) standard at http://www.ietf.org/rfc/rfc2152.txt and http://www.utf-8.com/. Learn about iso-8859-1 encoding at http://www.bbsinc.com/iso8859.html.

The second line also contains an element. However, notice this element has an opening and a closing tag. The opening <Hello> tag appears first, followed by three child elements, followed by the closing </Hello> tag. Standard elements all require an opening and closing tag unless they're self-contained. You can create a self-contained tag by adding the ending slash as part of the initial tag like this <Hello />. The <Hello> element includes a special namespace attribute. You can detect namespace elements because they normally begin with xmlns, followed by a colon, followed by the name of the namespace (xsi in this case). The namespace normally has an URL attached to it. The page pointed to by the URL contains a description of the elements that the namespace defines. Whenever an XML parser sees a namespace attached to an element, it goes to the URL defined for that namespace to learn how to interpret the element, associated attributes, or data. The <Hello> tag also fulfills another important task—it defines the root node. A node is a specific place in the XML hierarchy. Every XML document contains one root node that acts as a container for all of the other elements.

The <Element1> element is a child of the <Hello> element. Elements can have child/parent relationships. This element doesn't include any attributes, but it does have data in the form of Some Text 1. The value of <Element1> is Some Text 1. The XML Parser links the element to its data.

The <Element2> element is also a child of the <Hello> element and a sibling of <Element1>. This element also includes an attribute. In this case, the attribute is extra data that describes the element in some way. The value of MyAttribute appears in quotes after the attribute. To create an attribute, you must always provide a name, followed by the equals sign and a string value in quotes. An element can contain as many attributes as needed to provide a full description of its functionality.

eBay uses some special formatting displayed as part of <Element3>. The <![CDATA]> or character data element holds special text that could confuse the XML parser. When these characters appear in a <![CDATA]> element, the XML parser ignores them, so there isn't any confusion. You'll normally see a <![CDATA]> element used to store information such as URLs and product descriptions. Any node that could contain confusing information is encased in a <![CDATA]> element.

Viewing XML Data in Your Browser

One of the problems of working with XML data is that it can become quite lengthy. The length of an eBay search result can make it difficult to locate the very information you seek. (Searches are one of the longest responses you receive from eBay—data such as user queries and item listings are much shorter.) Fortunately, you can see the formatted data in a browser such as Internet Explorer. The data contains indentations to show the relationships between parent and child. In addition, you can differentiate between elements, attributes, and data by looking at the colors. Finally, special elements such as processing instructions and the XML header appear in a different color.

Unless you know how a browser displays XML, you might conclude that the indentation and coloration are the only help you receive. However, browsers have a lot more to offer than that in most cases. At the very least, you can expand and collapse various levels of information. Figure 4.1 shows an example of an eBay response to a `GetCategoryListings` request that relies on the ability of the browser to collapse information to present a clearer picture of the response. You'll find this example in the `\Chapter 04\Sample XML` folder of the source code located on the Sybex Web site.

As you can see, the entire response fits within one screen, making it easy to get an overview of the data. Notice the minus (–) sign next to the `<Items>` element. This symbol indicates that you can collapse this level. The plus (+) sign that appears next to each of the `<Item>` elements shows that you can expand the level to show child entries. Clicking either a minus or plus sign performs that task within the browser, so you can display any level of detail desired.

FIGURE 4.1:
Internet Explorer and other browsers can display XML files in a variety of ways.

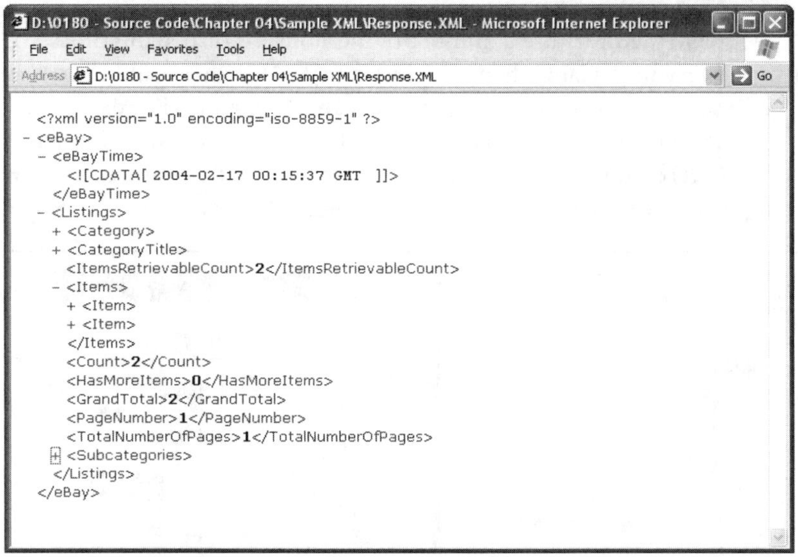

```
D:\0180 - Source Code\Chapter 04\Sample XML\Response.XML - Microsoft Internet Explorer

File   Edit   View   Favorites   Tools   Help

Address  D:\0180 - Source Code\Chapter 04\Sample XML\Response.XML         Go

    <?xml version="1.0" encoding="iso-8859-1" ?>
  - <eBay>
    - <eBayTime>
        <![CDATA[ 2004-02-17 00:15:37 GMT ]]>
      </eBayTime>
    - <Listings>
      + <Category>
      + <CategoryTitle>
        <ItemsRetrievableCount>2</ItemsRetrievableCount>
      - <Items>
        + <Item>
        + <Item>
        </Items>
        <Count>2</Count>
        <HasMoreItems>0</HasMoreItems>
        <GrandTotal>2</GrandTotal>
        <PageNumber>1</PageNumber>
        <TotalNumberOfPages>1</TotalNumberOfPages>
      + <Subcategories>
      </Listings>
    </eBay>
```

Getting XML Data Tools

A browser is a good tool for viewing XML, but you can't modify the XML using it. Because XML is pure text, you can use any editor like Notepad to edit it. However, Notepad isn't optimal because it doesn't display the XML structure. In addition, Notepad lacks tools for making the editing experience better. For example, if you want to add a new element, you must type the tag manually. Manual techniques often leave you open to data errors. Consequently, you need an editor that works well with XML files.

> **▶ NOTE**
>
> Many of the tools mentioned in this book rely on Microsoft XML Core Services (MSXML) 4.0. In addition, some of the coding examples also rely on this library. The latest version at the time of writing is Service Pack (SP) 2, which you can download at http://www.microsoft.com/ downloads/details.aspx?familyid=3144B72B-B4F2-46DA-B4B6-C5D7485F2B42 (MSXML 4.0 is approximately 5MB, so make sure you allocate enough time to download it). Both of the editors in the sections that follow rely on MSXML 4.0. However, Netpadd is perfectly happy using MSXML 5.0, which comes with Microsoft Office 2003. On the other hand, XMLwriter 2 specifically requests MSXML 4.0 every time you start it, even if you have MSXML 5.0 installed. Fortunately, you can install the two versions of MSXML side by side without any ill effects.

XML editors use a number of methods for displaying the XML file. Because presentation is very important when working with XML, you should choose an XML editor that presents the information in a way that you can understand. For example, Figure 4.2 shows the tree view editor used by many XML editors such as XML Notepad and XMLSpy. In addition, XML editors cost differing amounts based on the features they provide. Some editors are very expensive because they provide automated generation features and edit a number of file types.

FIGURE 4.2:

Many XML editors provide a tree view display that experts like.

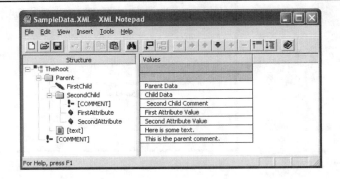

▶ **TIP**

One of the most popular XML editors on the market today is XMLSpy (`http://www.xmlspy`
`.com/`). You can download a limited-time evaluation copy of the product from the Altova Web
site. Once the evaluation period ends, you must either remove XMLSpy from your system or
buy a copy. Another popular choice is XML Notepad—a free download originally provided by
Microsoft. Microsoft doesn't officially support XML Notepad any longer. Consequently, you
can't download it from Microsoft. One alternate download site is WebAttack at `http://`
`www.webattack.com/get/xmlnotepad.shtml` (this site has the 1.5 version). A good free
option is XMLFox (`http://www.xmlfox.com/`). The left side of the XMLFox display is yet
another version of the standard tree display—this one sports special symbols and colors.
The unique feature of this product is that it uses a tabular view of the XML data, which
works pretty well with some types of complex XML files, including those from eBay. All of
these editors provide superior handling of XML files by including special symbols and specific methods for adding data. In addition, XMLSpy works on a number of other file types
and provides task automation that you'll find helpful if you work on XML files frequently.

I chose the two XML editors presented in the sections that follow because they're simple
to use and you can download them free. I'm not endorsing these editors as the only selections
on the market—you should try a number of editors before you settle on one. However,
because these editors provide good functionality and don't provide too many confusing features, you might want to try them as a starting point for your XML learning experience.

▶ **WARNING**

Make sure that you download any required security updates such as the one described in
Microsoft Knowledge Base article KB832414 for MSXML 3.0 (`http://www.microsoft`
`.com/downloads/details.aspx?FamilyID=0031ba5d-7b07-4872-b7a7-6bbd384ba8e9`).
You can find a list of MSXML downloads, including many security updates, at `http://`
`www.microsoft.com/downloads/results.aspx?productID=&freetext=msxml`.

Using Netpadd

Netpadd (`http://www.netpadd.com/`) is a freeware product that has some interesting features,
but is also very simple to use. To write XML using this product, you need to type all of the
information manually. There's little automation in this product, so when you create an opening tag, you must create the closing tag to go with it.

The display, shown in Figure 4.3, is very much like the display you'd see in Notepad, rather than the heavily formatted display provided by products such as XMLSpy that some newer developers find confusing. (You'll find the sample file shown in Figures 4.2 and 4.3 in the \Chapter 04\Sample XML folder of the source code found on the Sybex Web site.) Netpadd does provide keyword highlighting for your XML file, which makes viewing the information a lot easier. Use the Options ➤ Hilite ➤ XML menu options to define which file types receive highlighting.

One of the more interesting features that Netpadd provides for XML developers is multiple data views. For example, you can use the View ➤ XML Tree command to display a tree view like the one shown in Figure 4.4. Other commands let you view the XML in other ways. Use the View ➤ XSL Transformation command to display the information as transformed by an XSL file. This particular view is very helpful when working with eBay Web Services because you can fine-tune your XSL file without making numerous requests to the Web service.

You'll also like the special dialog boxes that Netpadd provides. For example, the View ➤ Special Characters command displays the Special Characters dialog box. Select the character you want to use and click either Paste or Paste as HTML to place the symbol in your document. If you've ever wasted time looking up language codes online, you'll really like the Language Codes dialog box (displayed using the View ➤ Language Codes command). Simply select the language you want to use and click Paste.

FIGURE 4.3:

Netpadd provides an easy to understand display of the XML file.

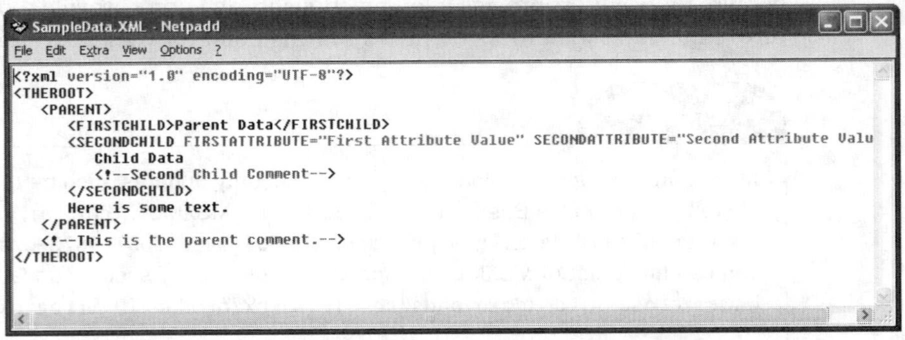

FIGURE 4.4:

View your XML files in various ways using Netpadd's View commands.

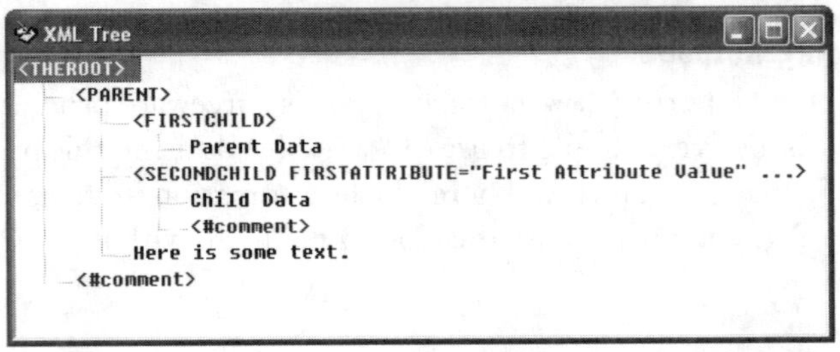

Using XMLwriter 2

XMLwriter 2 (`http://www.xmlwriter.net/`) is a try-before-you-buy product. I won't say that this product is shareware in the strictest sense because the trial period limits use to 30 days. That said, the trial period means you can download the product and try it before making a buying decision, which makes the buying decision easier.

Unlike many other XML editors on the market, XMLwriter 2 also uses a Notepad-style document display for editing as shown in Figure 4.5. This product automatically assumes you want to use color-coding for keywords. You'll also find the use of automation nice. For example, when you type an opening tag, XMLwriter 2 automatically creates a closing tag for you. Load a schema for your XML file and you'll be able to choose tags directly from the TagBar displayed on the left side of the screen. The IDE also features an XML checker. Simply right-click the document and select Validate XML File from the context menu. Any errors appear in a TODO list at the bottom of the IDE.

This product includes a number of features that the serious XML developer will need. For example, you can build projects using XMLwriter 2. Creating a project organizes the files and makes it easier to build the links you need. XMLwriter 2 comes with built-in support for all of the standard files—including XML, XSL, XSLT, HTML, XHTML, CSS, DTD, XSD, and text. In addition, you can open some types of image files, such as the GIF, JPG, and PNG files used by many Web sites. However, the files you can open aren't actually limited to these types. You can add new types to the list, so long as XMLwriter 2 can read them (which means that you can add any text-based file extension).

FIGURE 4.5:
XMLwriter 2 uses a document style editor, but provides many features found in high-end products.

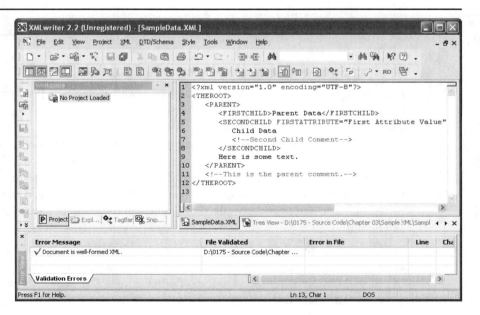

The IDE itself is fully configurable using any of the Options dialog box entries. Fortunately, the default setup is quite usable. For example, the tabbed presentation means you can see multiple versions of your XML file with ease. For example, if you want to see a tree view of your document, simply right-click the document and select View As Tree from the context menu. Figure 4.6 shows a typical example of the tree view. You can also choose a browser view for your document.

FIGURE 4.6:

Select a tree view to see the overall layout of your XML document.

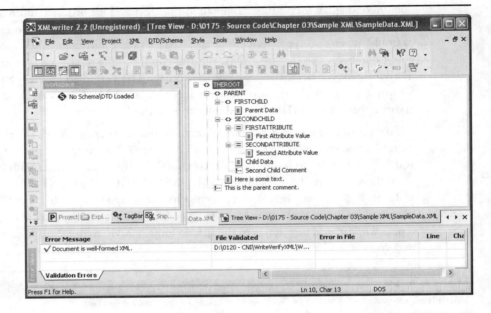

Sending Special Characters Using URL Encoding

For most people, working with Web sites is a unique experience because they encounter unexpected oddities that they haven't had to consider in the past. When you type a space into a word-processed document, nothing odd happens—the computer simply accepts the character. However, look at the word processor again. Notice how the word processor automatically looks at the space and uses it to determine where to split lines of text. The word processor does treat the space differently—it treats it as a delimiter (a fancy term that programmers use to mean a character that has a special meaning). Likewise, when you add a hyphen to a word, the computer could choose to split the sentence in the middle of the word. The hyphen acts as a delimiter.

The Internet also uses delimiters for a number of purposes, including URLs. When a Web server sees a space, it could assume that it has reached the end of the URL or the beginning of a new input parameter (or a number of other things). Consequently, you must replace spaces, question marks, and other characters with other characters that don't work as delimiters. You might have noticed this practice at work when you fill out a form on the Internet. The browser commonly replaces a space between two words with %20 or a plus sign (+). The Web server interprets these special character sequences as a space.

At first, you might think that the character replacement is random, but there's some method to the madness. In fact, it's relatively easy to write a JavaScript function that performs the character replacement so you don't need to worry about it. Listing 4.1 shows this function. You'll find the complete source for this example in the \Chapter 04\URL Encode folder of the source code located on the Sybex Web site. Note that you can write similar functions in other languages; I'm just using this one because most people can run JavaScript using their browsers.

Listing 4.1   **Replacing Characters in a String**

```
function ReplaceCharacter(InputStr, Replace, UseInstead)
{
    // Define the length of the inputs.
    var InputLength = InputStr.length;
    var ReplaceLength = Replace.length;

    // Determine whether either input has a 0 length. If so,
    // the function can't succeed. However, because this is
    // a recursive function, the function does need to return
    // the original string.
    if ((InputLength == 0) || (ReplaceLength == 0))
        return InputStr;

    // Locate the first replacement value.
    var ReplaceIndex = InputStr.indexOf(Replace);

    // If the replacement value doesn't appear within the string,
    // then return. Again, keep the recursive nature of the
    // function in mind.
    if (ReplaceIndex == -1)
        return InputStr;

    // Create a string that includes the first part of the original
    // string and the replacement character, but not the rest of the
    // string.
    var Output = InputStr.substring(0, ReplaceIndex) + UseInstead;

    // Use recursion to process the string again if there is more data
    // to process.
    if (ReplaceIndex + ReplaceLength < InputLength)

        // Keep adding to the output string after each recursion.
        Output += ReplaceCharacter(
```

```
            InputStr.substring(ReplaceIndex + ReplaceLength, InputLength),
            Replace,
            UseInstead);

    // Return the output during each recursion.
    return Output;
}
```

This might look like a lot of very complicated code, but it's actually an easy program. It uses a special technique called recursion to perform its work. In recursion, the programmer writes a program that solves the simplest form of a problem, and then has that program keep calling itself until it achieves that simple form. No matter how complex the input is, the program can solve it (given enough memory and time) because eventually the input will reach this simple solution.

In this instance, the program keeps calling itself until one of several conditions occurs. First, the program could run out of text to process. Second, the program might have some text left, but it might not contain the special character you want to replace (such as a space). If that's the case, then the program has already performed all of the required work, so it can stop.

Once the program determines there's data to process, it uses the substring() function to look for that character in the string. The substring() function returns just the first part of the string—the part that doesn't contain the special character. To this string, the code adds the replacement characters, such as %20 for a space.

It's at this point that the recursion process occurs. The code still has the other part of the string to consider—the last half. The first half of the string is free of the special character, but not the second half. When the code detects that there's still string to process, it calls itself again with the last half of the string. This process continues until the code has processed all of the input string. Figure 4.7 shows typical output from this program.

FIGURE 4.7:

The example program shows how you can perform URL encoding.

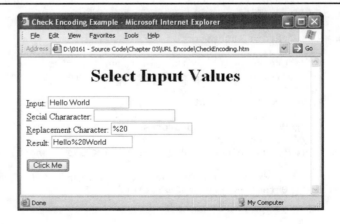

Of course, the problem is figuring out which characters to replace and what numbers to use to replace them. Unfortunately, eBay doesn't publish a list of offending characters, so you'll need to experiment a little with special characters that you want to use. A space never works, and you have to exercise care with both double and single quotes. Determining what number to use is easy. Simply break out a copy of the Character Map utility that comes with Windows and you have everything you need. Figure 4.8 shows what this utility looks like.

Simply select the character you want and look at the number that appears at the bottom of the dialog box. This is the number you should use to replace the character in a string. You can also hover the mouse over the character and the program will display both the character name and the associated number. For example, you replace the quotation mark with %22 in an URL encoded string.

Learning More about XML

Whether you know it or not, you'll run into XML many times during your computer use. The reason is simple—XML makes a great way to exchange data between disparate systems. Fortunately, XML is relatively easy to learn. Visit the W3C Schools site at http://www.w3schools .com/xml/ to find a complete XML tutorial. You might also want to review the namespace tutorial at http://www.zvon.org/index.php?nav_id=172&ns=34.

Unlike many topics discussed in this book, there are multiple versions of XML so you can't rely on just one reference. The most important reference for eBay Web Services appears at http:// www.zvon.org/xxl/xmlSchema2001Reference/Output/index.html. However, make sure you also look at the references at http://www.zvon.org/xxl/xmlSchemaReference/Output/index.html for complete information. The annotated XML reference at http://www.xml.com/axml/axml .html is also handy for seeing the specification and expert commentary side by side.

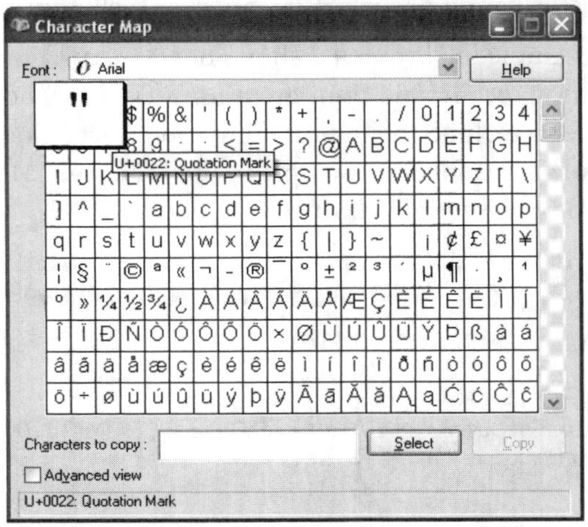

FIGURE 4.8:

Character Map makes it easy to learn the numbers associated with special characters.

You can also find a number of good general-purpose XML sites online. For example, the Microsoft XML Developer Center (`http://msdn.microsoft.com/nhp/default.asp?contentid=28000438`) is a great place to visit if you use Microsoft products.

Using XSLT for Presentation

For many people, reading XML borders on the impossible. Using XSLT can remedy the problem to a great extent, by telling a browser or application how to interpret the information the XML file contains. Presentation can mean everything once you get past the requirements of accurate data. Unfortunately, creating Web pages by hand to achieve a combination of great presentation and accurate data consumes a lot of time, so Webmasters have looked for an easier way to create a presentation online. The combination of XML (data) and XSLT (presentation) has become more than a convenience for many organizations. Using this technique helps companies create accurate presentations with little effort. Because eBay Web Services relies on XML, XSLT also provides one of the best ways for you to create a great presentation. The following sections provide a good overview of XSLT. You'll also find a section with references to other XSLT information sources.

Using a Script to Call an XSLT Page

eBay doesn't know how you want to present the data it provides, so the XML you receive doesn't include any form of XSLT declaration (another kind of processing instruction). This declaration appears as `<?xml-stylesheet type="text/xsl" href="SearchDisplay.xsl"?>` in the XML file. The `href` attribute tells where to find the XSLT file. Without this information, the browser will never display anything but XML on screen. It would seem that the situation is hopeless. However, you have other options, such as writing a script that performs the transformation process using another technique.

The example in Listing 4.2 shows how you can download a response from eBay, store the information locally, and translate it using XSLT. The result is the same as modifying the XML file to include the required linkage information, but far more automatic. You'll find the complete source for this example in the `\Chapter 04\Viewing XSLT` folder of the source code located on the Sybex Web site.

Listing 4.2   **Performing a Transformation in JavaScript**

```
function GetData(XSLFile)
{
    // Call eBay and get the data.
    var TheData = new ActiveXObject("Msxml2.DOMDocument.4.0");
    TheData.async = false;
    TheData = CalleBay();
```

```
   // Check for errors.
   if (TheData == null)
      return;

   // Create an XSLT document and load the transform into it.
   var XSLTData = new ActiveXObject("Msxml2.DOMDocument.4.0");
   XSLTData.async = false;
   XSLTData.load("Default.xsl");

   // Display the output on screen.
   document.write(TheData.transformNode(XSLTData));
}
```

Before the script can do anything, it must obtain the search results from eBay. When working with eBay in a browser environment, you need to use the API technique for obtaining the data. This technique requires that you work directly with XML. Don't worry too much about the intricacies of working with the API now—the "Using JavaScript to Access eBay Web Services" section of Chapter 6 discusses that issue. All you need to know, for the moment, is that the script obtains the query results from eBay using the `CalleBay()` function.

The next step is a little tricky and definitely Windows specific. The code creates an instance of the Microsoft XML component. The `ActiveXObject()` function performs this task. The `Msxml2.DOMDocument.4.0` string identifies the component. You might have to use `Msxml2.DOMDocument.5.0` on newer machines with Microsoft Office 2003 or another new product loaded—the last part of the string identifies the component version number. Setting the `async` property to false is important because you don't want the call to load the XML to return until the browser actually receives this file. The `CalleBay()` function returns the actual XML document used by the example.

▶ NOTE

Most versions of MSXML work fine for this example. However, you'll probably want to get MSXML Version 4.0 from http://msdn.microsoft.com/library/en-us/xmlsdk/htm/sdk_intro_6g53.asp. (MSXML Version 5.0 isn't available for download as of this writing.) The 5.0 version includes a number of features that make working with XML documents a lot easier. In addition, you'll find that the latest versions are slightly faster and contain a number of bug fixes that make your application more reliable.

The code now has a local copy of the data from eBay. This local copy will disappear as soon as the function ends, so you don't have to worry about update requirements, but it's important to understand that the copy resides in memory on your machine somewhere.

At this point, the code has data to work with, but no XSLT file. The next step loads the XSLT file defined by the `XslFile` variable. Notice that the code uses the `XSLTData.load()` function because the XML appears in a file that the application must load into memory. If the code were loading an XML or XSLT file from a Web location using a string, it would use the `loadXML()` function instead.

The coupling between the XML response and the XSLT occurs in the `XMLData.transformNode()` function call. This call produces output that the `document.write()` function then sends to the current page. The result is that you see the transformed XML on screen, as shown in Figure 4.9. Notice that the URL doesn't change, even though the content differs, because you're still theoretically on the same Web page.

Understanding How XSLT Works

Unlike an XML file, an XSLT file generates some type of presentation, using information from the XML file as input. Consequently, XSLT (or simply XSL) files often contain a combination of output text and XML. In fact, all XSLT files begin with the usual header and the special XSLT header shown here.

```
<?xml version="1.0" encoding="UTF-8"?>
<xsl:stylesheet version="1.0"
 xmlns:xsl="http://www.w3.org/1999/XSL/Transform"
 xmlns:fo="http://www.w3.org/1999/XSL/Format">
```

FIGURE 4.9:

The results of using a script to transform XML data received from eBay.

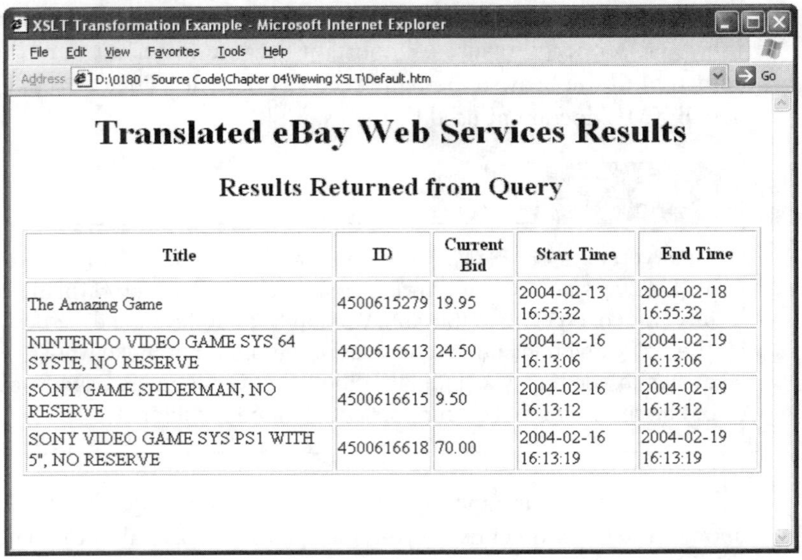

Title	ID	Current Bid	Start Time	End Time
The Amazing Game	4500615279	19.95	2004-02-13 16:55:32	2004-02-18 16:55:32
NINTENDO VIDEO GAME SYS 64 SYSTE, NO RESERVE	4500616613	24.50	2004-02-16 16:13:06	2004-02-19 16:13:06
SONY GAME SPIDERMAN, NO RESERVE	4500616615	9.50	2004-02-16 16:13:12	2004-02-19 16:13:12
SONY VIDEO GAME SYS PS1 WITH 5", NO RESERVE	4500616618	70.00	2004-02-16 16:13:19	2004-02-19 16:13:19

Remember that the `<?xml?>` element tells the XML parser that this is an XML file. The next element is an XSLT processing instruction. It tells the XML parser that this is an XSLT derivative of an XML file and it includes namespace pointers to Web sites that describe how to interpret XSLT. This instruction is important because otherwise the XML parser looks at this file as XML and won't have a clue what to do with all those XSLT instructions it contains.

An XSLT document describes how to transform an XML document into readable form. Therefore, the first thing it must do is tell the XML parser how much of the XML document to use for the transformation. You can choose anything from just one or two lines of the document to the entire document. Normally, XSLT documents are concerned with an entire XML document, so you'll see a line such as `<xsl:template match="/">` somewhere in the document.

It's important, at this point, to stress that XSLT doesn't have to output HTML. You can use XSLT to transform XML into anything you want. For example, I recently read an article in Visual Studio magazine in which the author uses XSLT to transform XML data into program code. (See the article entitled "Generate .NET Code With XSLT" by Kathleen Dollard at `http://www.fawcette.com/vsm/2003_05/magazine/features/dollard/` for details.) That's right—she stores her coding requirements in XML and generates the required code automatically using XSLT.

Once you define a document as XSLT and decide how much of the XML document input you want to process, you begin using a combination of text and XSLT processing instructions to transform the XML into some type of output. The "Writing a Simple XSLT Page" section shows a specific example of this transformation.

In general, XSLT is a programming language. One of the most common programming instructions retrieves a value from the XML file. For example, the instruction `<xsl:value-of select="Title"/>` retrieves the value of the `Title` element. However, XSLT doesn't limit you to simply retrieving data from the XML file. You can also use functions, such as the `count()` function that returns the number of nodes in a result set, to perform data manipulation on the XML input.

You'll also find that XSLT includes a limited number of loop and logic features. For example, you can tell XSLT that you want to perform the same task with every child of the current node using the `<xsl:for-each select="Search/Items/Item">` instruction. In this case, the `select` attribute tells which node to use for processing purposes.

A final consideration for this book is that XSLT also defines something called an axis. An axis defines a way of looking at the data. For example, the at (@) symbol tells XSLT to look at the attributes of a node, rather than the element. Another common axis is `parent`, which tells XSLT to look at the parent of the current element.

Writing a Simple XSLT Page

This section describes the XSLT page used with the transformation described in the "Using a Script to Call an XSLT Page" section (see Listing 4.2). Listing 4.3 shows how to create an XSLT page that outputs HTML code. You could use the same technique to create a report or any other form of output based on the XML input received from eBay. You'll find the complete source for this example in the \Chapter 04\Viewing XSLT folder of the source code located on the Sybex Web site.

Listing 4.3   **Designing an XSLT Page**

```xml
<?xml version="1.0" encoding="UTF-8"?>
<xsl:stylesheet version="1.0"
    xmlns:xsl="http://www.w3.org/1999/XSL/Transform"
    xmlns:fo="http://www.w3.org/1999/XSL/Format">
<xsl:output method="xml" indent="yes"/>
<xsl:template match="/eBay">
<html>
<head>
    <title>XSLT Transformation Example</title>
</head>
<body>
    <!-- Display a heading. -->
    <h1 align="center">Translated eBay Web Services Results</h1>

    <!-- Display the search result values. -->
    <table align="center" border="1" width="100%">
        <caption><h2>Results Returned from Query</h2></caption>
        <tbody>
            <tr>
                <th>Title</th>
                <th>ID</th>
                <th>Current Bid</th>
                <th>Start Time</th>
                <th>End Time</th>
            </tr>
            <xsl:for-each select="Search/Items/Item">
                <tr>
                    <td>
                        <xsl:value-of select="Title"/>
                    </td>
                    <td>
                        <xsl:value-of select="Id"/>
                    </td>
                    <td>
                        <xsl:value-of select="CurrentPrice"/>
                    </td>
                    <td>
                        <xsl:value-of select="StartTime"/>
                    </td>
                    <td>
```

```
                    <xsl:value-of select="EndTime"/>
                </td>
            </tr>
        </xsl:for-each>
      </tbody>
    </table>

  </body>
  </html>
  </xsl:template>
  </xsl:stylesheet>
```

The code begins with the usual declarations. The `<xsl:output method="xml" indent="yes"/>` tag is important because it determines the kind of output the parser creates. You can also choose text as the output method or tell the parser that you don't want the output indented. Notice that the code also matches the eBay element using the `<xsl:template match="/eBay">` tag. All of the data appears within this element, so there isn't a good reason to match the root node of the XML document.

The code then outputs the heading. Notice that this is pure HTML and that the code isn't doing anything but outputting this text. The code moves on to the body where it outputs a heading.

The XSLT-specific code begins when the code outputs the search results. Each return value requires special handling, so the code relies on a table. Notice the head of the table is standard HTML, but that the next selection is an `<xsl:for-each>` element. This statement tells the parser to look at all of the children of the `Search/Items/Item` node. The system will process each `<Item>` element in turn. The next step is to use the `<xsl:value-of>` element to retrieve the name and value attributes of each `<Item>` element. The code ends by completing the HTML page, and then completing both the template and the stylesheet.

Learning More about XSLT

This chapter only skims the surface of what you can do with XSLT. You can perform an incredible number of tasks using this technology. One of the better places to learn about XSLT is `http://www.w3schools.com/xsl/`. You should also view the examples in the XSLT reference at `http://www.zvon.org/xxl/XSLTreference/Output/index.html`. The XSL reference at `http://www.zvon.org/xxl/xslfoReference/Output/index.html` can also come in handy when you begin creating complex XSLT pages. You can also find a good tutorial on the Webmonkey site at `http://hotwired.lycos.com/webmonkey/98/43/index2a.html?tw=authoring`.

Make sure you check out some of the better third party XSLT reference sites. For example, the XSLT.com site at `http://xslt.com/` provides links and resources for XSLT from various vendors (not just Microsoft).

It also helps to have some great books on the topic. Make sure you read books such as *Mastering XSLT* by Chuck White (Sybex, 2002). It also helps to know something about XML schemas, so check out *XML Schemas* by Chelsea Valentine, Lucinda Dykes, and Ed Tittel (Sybex, 2002).

Using the eBay API Test Tool

The eBay API Test Tool is an essential aid to understand how eBay works. In fact, you should probably create a link to this particular site and use it as part of your application development process. This tool helps you build the XML documents required to make an eBay Web Services request. Yes, it's also a test tool, but I've begun looking at it less as a tool for testing and more as a tool for designing. You'll find this tool at `http://developer.ebay.com/DevZone/build-test/test-tool.asp`. Figure 4.10 shows how this page looks when you first open it.

FIGURE 4.10:
Use the eBay API Test Tool to build XML requests for your application.

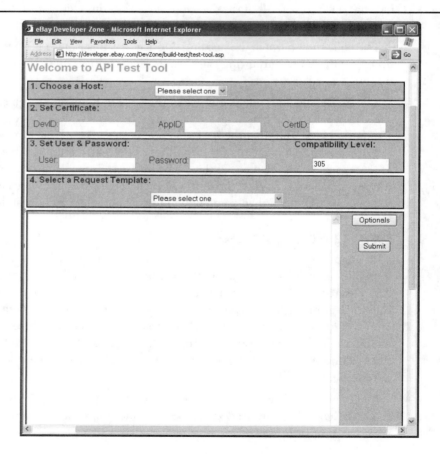

The first step for using this tool is to choose a host. You can use either the SandBox or Production host if you have keys for that host. Generally, most developers will only have access to the SandBox host and that's what all of the examples in this book will use. Notice that you also have to provide the usual information for an eBay application including your developer ID, application ID, certificate ID, username, and password. There probably isn't a good reason to change the Compatibility Level field; although, the compatibility level can affect the output of a particular call (see the API Technical Reference at `http://developer .ebay.com/DevZone/docs/API_Doc/index.asp` for details). The final step is to select one of the API calls, which can be any of the following at the time of writing:

AddItem	GetItem	ReviseCheckoutStatus
AddItem—Motors	GetItemTransactions	ReviseCheckoutTransactionDetails
AddItem—Real Estate Ad-Type	GetLogoURL	ReviseItem
AddItem—Real Estate Sale	GetSearchResults	ReviseItem—Motors
AddItem—Store–Auction	GetSellerEvents	ReviseItem—Real Estate Ad-Type
AddItem—Store–Fixed	GetSellerList	ReviseItem—Real Estate Sale
AddToItemDescription	GetSellerTransactions	ReviseItem—Store–Auction
EndItem	GetStoreDetails	ReviseItem—Store–Fixed
GetAccount	GetUser	SetSellerPaymentAddress
GetBidderList	GetWatchList	ValidateTestUserRegistration
GetCategories	LeaveFeedback	VerifyAddItem
GetCategory2DomainMap	RelistItem	VerifyAddItem—Motors
GetCategoryListings	RelistItem—Motors	VerifyAddItem—Real Estate Ad-Type
GetDomains	RelistItem—Real Estate Ad-Type	VerifyAddItem—Real Estate Sale
GeteBayOfficialTime	RelistItem—Real Estate Sale	VerifyAddItem—Store–Auction
GetFeedback	RelistItem—Store–Auction	VerifyAddItem—Store–Fixed
GetHighBidders	RelistItem—Store–Fixed	

As soon as you select an API call, the tool will generate the minimal XML required to make that call. You can also copy and paste examples from the API Technical Reference into the API Test Tool or create XML requests of your own that you want to try. (The XML appears in the window at the bottom of Figure 4.10.) For example, the GetSearchResults call generates XML that looks like this:

```
<?xml version="1.0" encoding="iso-8859-1"?>
<request xmlns="urn:eBayAPIschema">
<RequestUserId>User Name</RequestUserId>
<RequestPassword>Password</RequestPassword>
<DetailLevel>0</DetailLevel>
<ErrorLevel>1</ErrorLevel>
<Query>toy</Query>
<SiteId>0</SiteId>
<Verb>GetSearchResults</Verb>
</request>
```

You can set the required information at this point. In this case, the only information you'd need to change is the <Query> element. You now have a minimal request put together. However, you don't have to stop here. You can add more information to the request by clicking the Optionals button. The tool displays an index number dialog box that you can safely click OK to close. You'll see a list of optional arguments for the current API call. Figure 4.11 shows a partial list of the optional arguments for the GetSearchResults call.

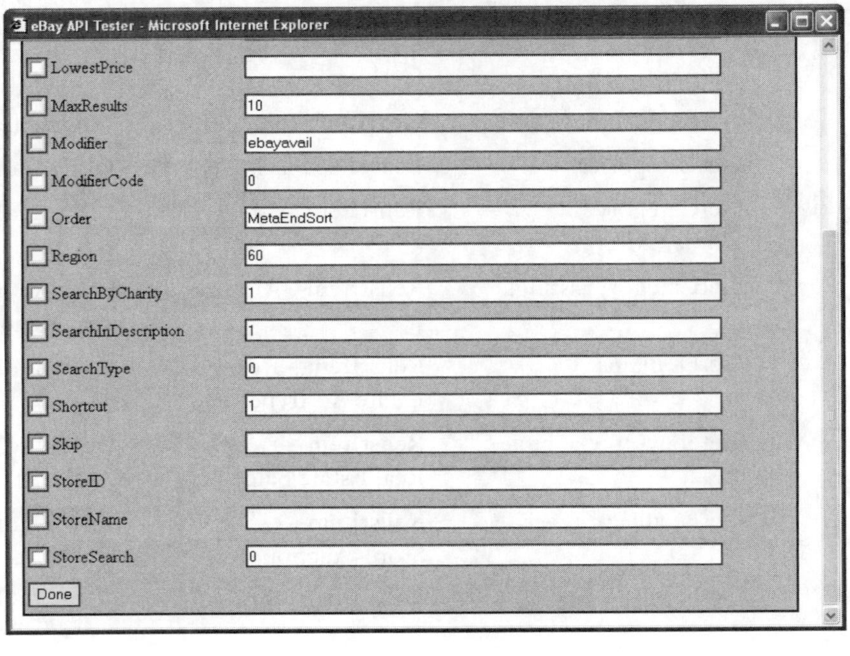

FIGURE 4.11:
Optional arguments make it possible to create a more precise request.

Notice that many of these entries contain the default values for that optional argument. To select one of the optional arguments, check the box next to the argument entry. Fill in a value for that argument (you can change it later). Click Done when you're finished adding optional arguments.

When you finish adding arguments, the XML is finished. You can use this display to create the code for your application. If you want to test the XML to ensure it fulfills the minimum requirements, click Submit. The eBay API Test Tool will make the request and open a new window showing the result. Figure 4.12 shows an example of the output you'll see.

This output information is also very helpful because it tells you how to interact with the XML you receive from eBay as the result of a request. The response helps you understand the structure of the XML and how you'll have to parse it in your application. It also shows the location of various pieces of information. In sum, the entire eBay API Test Tool is a useful design aid.

FIGURE 4.12:

The output provides a view of the XML you'll receive from eBay Web Services.

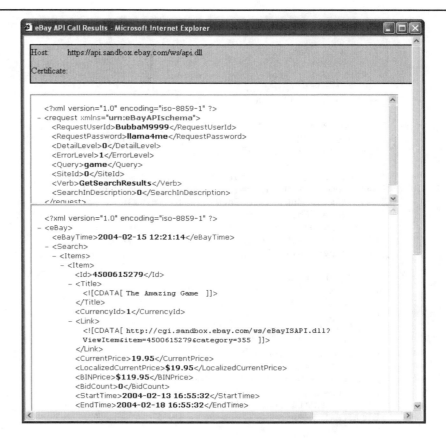

Creating Messages for eBay Using XML

At this point, you know what XML is about and how to use the eBay API Test Tool to reduce your workload. However, you haven't really put everything together to generate messages of your own. The concept of a Web service is that you send a request and the Web service sends a response to that request. As you've seen in the chapter, eBay uses a number of request and response message formats to support the kinds of tasks that most developers will have to include with their applications.

Although this chapter doesn't get into the fine details of application construction, it's possible to look at a very simple example of putting a message together. Listing 4.4 shows just the XML message construction code of an eBay application. In this case, the example relies on JavaScript to perform the task, but the process is essentially the same for every language. You'll find the complete source for this example in the \Chapter 04\Viewing XSLT folder of the source code located on the Sybex Web site.

Listing 4.4   **Creating an XML Message**

```
// Add the XML request header.
var ProcInst =
    XMLData.createProcessingInstruction(
        "xml", "version=\"1.0\"  encoding=\"iso-8859-1\"");
XMLData.appendChild(ProcInst);

// Construct the XML request message.
var Root = XMLData.createElement("request");
Root.setAttribute("xmlns", "urn:eBayAPIschema");

// Add the user information.
var Elem = XMLData.createElement("RequestUserId");
Elem.text = SubmissionForm.UserIDStr.value;
Root.appendChild(Elem);
Elem = XMLData.createElement("RequestPassword");
Elem.text = SubmissionForm.PasswordStr.value;
Root.appendChild(Elem);

// Add the request data.
Elem = XMLData.createElement("DetailLevel");
Elem.text = "0";
Root.appendChild(Elem);
Elem = XMLData.createElement("ErrorLevel");
Elem.text = "1";
Root.appendChild(Elem);
Elem = XMLData.createElement("Query");
Elem.text = SubmissionForm.QueryStr.value;
Root.appendChild(Elem);
Elem = XMLData.createElement("SiteId");
Elem.text = "0";
```

```
Root.appendChild(Elem);
Elem = XMLData.createElement("Verb");
Elem.text = "GetSearchResults";
Root.appendChild(Elem);

// Add the request data to the XML request.
XMLData.appendChild(Root);
```

It's not essential that you understand every nuance of this code—Chapter 6 will provide detailed information on how it works. However, it's time to look at a few of the details. This request message performs an item search. Notice that it begins by creating the XML header processing instruction. This instruction includes the <xml> element and both the version and encoding attributes.

The code creates the root node next. Remember that there's only one root node in any XML document. In this case, the code creates a <request> node that includes the eBay namespace as an attribute. If you find that your request isn't working, you'll definitely want to check for the eBay namespace in your request. The namespace could change at some point, but that's very unlikely because the namespace doesn't actually affect the content of the message.

Within the <request> node are a series of elements that define the request. Every request contains user information. You must define the username and associated password using the <RequestUserId> and <RequestPassword> elements.

Once the user information is added, you also need to add some request-specific information. Most requests will include the <DetailLevel>, <ErrorLevel>, <SiteId>, and <Verb> elements. The value of the <Verb> element changes for every kind of request. This is another message component to check if eBay doesn't recognize your request. You won't get the proper response without the proper verb. Make sure you check the spelling of the verb— your verb must match the verb eBay Web Services is expecting precisely.

This example includes one piece of mandatory request information, the <Query> element. Because this is a GetSearchResults request, you must provide a query value or eBay won't know what to look for. Note that this call could also include a number of optional pieces of information. The "Using the eBay API Test Tool" section describes these optional elements in more detail. After the root node is completed, the code adds it to the XML message and sends it to eBay Web Services.

Determining Where XML Fits into eBay Web Services

All forms of communication with eBay Web Services ultimately rely on some form of XML. The XML that you've seen in this chapter is at the center of every message exchange between an application and eBay. However, you won't always see the XML when you use the SDK technique for communicating with eBay because the SDK hides some of the harder aspects of working with XML. Even so, there are always ways to access the XML when you need it.

The question, of course, is why you would want to access the XML or even worry about it if it's hard to work with at times. The problem is communication. To ensure the message you send is the one that eBay needs, you must monitor the outgoing request from your application. The eBay API Test Tool provides you with an example of what that kind of message should look like—all you need to do is compare it with the message your application actually sends. Likewise, you might need to monitor the incoming message. Again, you need to verify that the XML matches what your application expects based on the information provided by the eBay API Test Tool.

Don't get the idea that the need to work with XML will go away once your application is fully debugged. No, you don't need to monitor the XML your application generates and receives on a daily basis. However, at some point eBay will likely change the messages the Web service sends and receives. Consequently, you'll need to turn the monitoring features of your application back on and retune it to the improved eBay setup. In short, knowing XML isn't optional—you need to know how eBay is interacting with your application, which means being able to view the XML.

How big a part XML plays in your application depends on several factors. A developer who needs to use the API technique of accessing eBay will definitely spend a lot of time working with XML. A developer who uses the SDK technique with one of the supported languages will find less need to use XML. As the complexity of your application increases, so does the need to use XML. In some cases, you might even want to use the API technique with a language that could use the SDK technique to gain better control over the communication stream. In short, XML will play some role in your eBay application, but you determine the precise role it plays in your application code.

Understanding Privacy Issues

Unlike many Web services that you might use, eBay Web Services applications will generally collect a lot of personal information. At a minimum, you'll know the person's name and address because you need to know where to send items that you sell. However, it's quite likely that you'll know more information than that—a telephone number is likely and you might even need to work with a credit card number or other sensitive information. Because privacy is such an important issue, eBay places significant restrictions on what you can do with personal information and describes in some detail how you should protect it. The following sections describe some general privacy policies you should consider implementing and those required by eBay. (You might also want to review Appendix B, which provides privacy requirements in a checklist format.)

Privacy Required by the eBay License

One of the biggest issues that that eBay license covers is that you can't begin to collect any information until the user gives you permission. Make sure the user knows precisely how you'll use the information. Encrypt the information before the user sends it to you using a secure setup such as Secure Sockets Layer (SSL)—generally enabled using HyperText Transfer Protocol Secure (HTTPS). It's generally a good idea to have an actual agreement page as part of the user sign-up to ensure there's no doubt that the user agreed to provide you with personal information as part of a transaction. In short, make sure you have a strong agreement with the user and stand by that agreement.

The privacy requirements also affect the statistical use of eBay information. For example, you can't use statistical analysis to compute the gross merchandise sold for any eBay category. You also can't use statistical analysis to develop a user profile, such as the user's identifying information. Obviously, you can still check on a user if you're engaged in a transaction— eBay isn't trying to limit your ability to protect your business interests.

eBay limits the user tasks that your application can perform. A new user must use the eBay site to sign up. In addition, your application can't provide a means for a user to change privacy settings—the user must make privacy setting changes using the eBay interface. The only exception to this second rule is that your application can help a user make changes to listing preferences. These preference setting rules might seem a bit harsh, but they ensure that any changes the user makes are through eBay and that your application hasn't acted as an intermediary. This restriction reduces the number of failure points for transferring the information.

Many of the eBay privacy requirements are commonsense issues. For example, you can't go out of your way to collect user information unless you actually need it for your application. In addition, information collected while working in the sandbox is only for testing your application. There isn't any way to even know if this data is real, and it's most certainly outdated if it is. You also have to provide a means for letting the user tell you that you can't use their information any longer. Section 2, User Data, of the licensing agreement has some other restrictions that you'll want to verify before you complete your application.

Privacy issues extend to your use of eBay as well. The licensing agreement you agree to says that you won't tell others about your developer keys and that you won't expose the special information that eBay has provided you to anyone else. These requirements are the reason I've been very careful about providing any details about my personal information in this book and you should exercise the same care. Although it's very likely that you'll end up showing your new creation to other people, make sure you do so with privacy in mind. Obviously, you can't give other people a copy of the application until eBay certifies it and you have a commercial license (rather than an Individual Tier license).

One bit of privacy information that you need to consider is that eBay does reserve the right to give other developers your email address. When you agree to the license, you also agree to this disclosure requirement. Given that most developers will have public email addresses anyway, this shouldn't pose a problem. However, you might want to set up a separate email address for use with eBay if privacy is a concern.

General User Privacy

You can add a few commonsense principles to ensure your own privacy policy will reduce your liability for user information. For example, many businesses store user information in a database. When crackers breach that database, the information becomes public knowledge and you have a public relations nightmare on your hands. Even if you use stringent methods and encrypt every piece of information in your database, someone with enough time and a good enough reason will likely break through your protections. The best policy is not to store the information at all.

Unfortunately, it's not always possible to get rid of the user data as soon as a transaction is complete. When you need to store user data for a while, make sure the database is encrypted and that you store the information on a server that lacks access to the Internet. Employ automatic aging if possible to ensure the data is automatically removed from the database after a certain time. Keep only the data that you actually need. For example, although you might need to retain the user's name and address, you probably don't have to keep their credit card number on file.

Understanding Security Issues

If you think eBay is serious about privacy issues, they're even more serious about security. When you think about it, your Web site is tied into the eBay site in some rather important ways. For example, you can readily upload new items to the eBay site through your site. A breach in security could allow a third party to do the same and perhaps without your knowledge. This is just one of many security issues to consider when working with eBay Web Services. The following sections discuss security in more detail.

General Security Issues

Security can be subtle in some respects. For example, it's possible for someone to intercept your eBay requests and learn more about you personally or your company. When this information gathering leads to some type of valuable deduction, you have a security leak on your hand. For example, Company A might be interested in knowing whether Company B is bidding on a given product. When someone in Company A monitors the search queries users in

Company B make, it becomes obvious that Company B is interested in the product and Company A takes actions to make sure their bid is accepted. The queries don't represent a security breach, but the analysis of the queries does present a problem. Company B could have protected itself by making generic queries and performing local analysis as necessary.

You need to consider security for your site when it performs Web service tasks. One of the better white papers on how the standards groups are meeting security needs appears on the Microsoft site at `http://msdn.microsoft.com/library/en-us/dnwssecur/html/securitywhitepaper.asp`. This discussion also provides a road map of security services.

It's also important to consider other sources of security information. For example, the Worldwide Web Consortium (W3C) and Internet Engineering Task Form (IETF) released the XML Signature specification in 2002. An XML Signature can help a recipient validate the sender of XML data and the integrity of that data. You can read about this standard at `http://www.w3.org/TR/2002/REC-xmldsig-core-20020212/`. The W3C and IETF are still working on two other XML security standards: XML Encryption and XML Key Management.

Given the strong eBay security requirements, you should consider some form of physical security for your system. This could be something as simple as ensuring the system is locked in a room where no one but you can get to it. You could also keep the data held by your system safe by placing the information on a removable disk, removing the disk after each session, and locking it away. There are a number of ways that you can ensure the physical security of your system. For example, companies such as Interface (`http://www.crocodile.de/`) provide physical security add-ons for your computer.

Using SSL to Contact eBay

All of your communication with eBay must rely on SSL (using the HTTPS protocol). The reason for this requirement is to ensure your data is encrypted as you send it. A good application designer will probably use SSL for all user interaction as well. It's important to secure the data stream to reduce the chance of someone peeking at the data. You can learn more about the HTTPS protocol at `http://www.w3.org/Protocols/` and `http://www.faqs.org/rfcs/rfc2818.html`. Learn about the SSL specification at `http://wp.netscape.com/eng/ssl3/`.

Security Required by the eBay License

One of the most important security measures from a developer perspective is protecting the developer keys that eBay provides. Each of these keys contains identifying information that helps eBay ensure that you're the only one using the Web service. You need to make eBay aware of any compromise of these keys. eBay also verifies the security measures provided by your application as part of the certification process. If your application uses eBay in a nonsecure manner, eBay has the option of revoking your developer keys and disallowing access.

> ▶ **NOTE**
>
> Make sure you check Exhibit B of the developer license for a complete set of security guide-
> lines. Appendix B provides a checklist of these issues.

Your application has to provide every possible security measure. For example, you'll want to verify that you check data for accuracy before sending it to eBay. This means ensuring the data is the proper length and data type, and that it doesn't contain any character data that could cause problems (such as a hidden script). Whenever possible, check the data against a list of acceptable entries and verify that the user has provided complete entries. You can often use regular expressions, a type of check that validates the form of the data, to ensure the data meets a particular requirement, such as a telephone number.

eBay assumes there are going to be security breaches, as any good security-minded com-pany would. Consequently, you need to maintain a log of access events for your application for 60 days. The event log needs to include the user identifier and the time of access (includ-ing both log on and log off).

You'll also find that eBay specifies minimum encryption key lengths for the data you submit. The best rule of thumb to follow is to use 128-bit encryption for everything. Not only does this policy ensure that you'll meet the minimum eBay requirements, but it also simplifies coding and reduces the potential for error.

One requirement that would be easy to miss is that eBay wants you to secure all storage media. This means that you shouldn't expose a system with sensitive data to the Internet if possible and that you must take precautions to safeguard the system when you do. However, the requirement goes further than actual application requirements. You might decide to get rid of your current machine and get the latest model. To ensure that you meet the eBay guidelines, you must have your system disk securely wiped before you discard this system. Usually this means destroying the disk or at least exposing it to a strong enough magnetic force to ensure complete data erasure.

Your Call to Action

You now know how to work with XML. This may not seem like much, but considering how important XML is to Web services, knowing how to work with XML is essential. Without knowing XML, you can't successfully build many eBay Web Services applications. Viewing the XML you receive from eBay helps you understand how various requests affect the infor-mation flow, which increases the chance that you'll develop efficient applications without a lot of extra effort.

This chapter is a beginning. You need to spend more time working with XML to become truly proficient with it. Make sure you visit at least some of the Web sites listed in this chapter to learn more about XML and related technologies such as SOAP and XSLT. Finally, if you don't have privacy and security policies in place, make sure you create the required documentation now, before something happens. Written policies are the best way to reduce risk. If you do have written policies, make sure you revisit them annually to ensure they still meet requirements of your organization, no matter how big or small.

Chapter 5 is the start of a new section. Rather than spending time looking at various techniques for developing applications and theoretical knowledge you need to implement a eBay Web Services application, this section shows you how to perform the task. Chapter 5 presents concepts and techniques that everyone needs to work with eBay Web Services. The chapters that follow begin looking at individual language requirements. In sum, Chapter 5 is the first chapter where you begin writing application code.

Part II

▶ **Writing** eBay Web Services Programs

Chapter 5

Determining Which Communication Method to Use	Choosing a Platform

▶ Starting the Development Process

Choosing a Development Language	Creating Internationalized Applications

You might be one of the many people who think they can't write an application or have no interest in doing so. The applications demonstrated in Chapters 2 and 4 might not look like much, but they really are applications. Writing applications shouldn't fill you with fear or trepidation, because most people have the skills needed—all you really need is a desire to do something and to know how to write a procedure. Coding is often more a matter of discipline and technique, art rather than science.

Designing software includes a number of tasks this chapter doesn't consider, such as how to create the user interface. In addition, the chapter won't discuss defining schedules and other tasks that don't really relate to the topic at hand—connecting to eBay Web Services and using the information it provides effectively. Consequently, this chapter discusses issues you probably didn't hear about in a computer science class, read in a book, learn about in a magazine, or discuss with a friend across the street.

Web services are all about communication. Your application uses some type of communication medium to transmit a request to a remote server and receive a response. The kind of communication you use makes a great deal of difference in the way you design and optimize your application. The communication method can also change the way your application operates and can affect performance.

You also need to consider the target platform for your application and choose the best language to meet your particular needs. eBay Web Services works well with a number of platforms and programming languages (as you'll see in the chapters that follow). Some developers attempt to take a one size fits all approach to selecting a language, but that's clearly not the best approach. This chapter helps you decide which platforms to target and which language to use for your specific needs.

Finally, most Web sites don't get visitors from just one country anymore. eBay recognizes this fact and provides its Web site in multiple languages (see the list of global sites on the eBay main page at `http://pages.ebay.com/`). In addition, you'll find that eBay takes a proactive stance on international sales (check the site at `http://pages.ebay.com/international-trading/index.html` for details). This final section discusses when internationalization can make your site more appealing and some of the steps you need to perform to do it.

Getting Additional Information about Application Design

This chapter doesn't discuss general application design. Make sure you augment the information in this chapter with some general design information from books such as *Designing Highly Usable Software* by Jeff Cogswell (Sybex, 2004). Another good book to consider is *Database Design for Mere Mortals: A Hands-On Guide to Relational Database Design*, Second Edition, by Michael J. Hernandez (Addison-Wesley, 2003). Finally, you might consider *Patterns of Enterprise Application Architecture* by Martin Fowler, David Rice, Matthew Foemmel, Edward Hieatt, Robert Mee, and Randy Stafford (Addison-Wesley, 2002).

Don't think that you're limited to reading books about design. You can also find a wealth of online sources for specific topics. For example, Microsoft provides a number of white papers online, such as the article entitled "Modeling Your Application and Data" at `http://msdn.microsoft.com/library/en-us/vsent7/html/vxoriModelingYourApplicationData.asp`. You should also consider sources such as Rational's (now IBM) article entitled "Modeling Web Application Design with UML" at `http://www.rational.com/products/whitepapers/100462.jsp`. Sometimes online magazines provide great input. Check out the article entitled "Magic Quadrants: Business Modeling, Application Design" at `http://www4.gartner.com/pages/story.php.id.2648.s.8.jsp`—it provides some great resources you can use.

Make sure you also get any application design software you need. There are moderately priced solutions such as Microsoft Visio (`http://www.microsoft.com/office/visio/`). However, you should also consider shareware from sites such as Tucows (`http://www.tucows.com/`), ZDNet (`http://downloads-zdnet.com.com/2001-20-0.html`), CNET (`http://www.cnet.com/`), and Nonags (`http://nonags.com/`). If your application is small enough, you can also use simple drawing programs such as Paint Shop Pro (`http://www.jasc.com`) or create the design by hand on paper. The point is to get the design down in print so that you can refer to it.

No matter what source of information you use and how you get your design in writing, you want to avoid one of the most common mistakes that developers make—starting an application without designing it. You wouldn't consider building a house without a blueprint—developing a blueprint for your application is the same. Although this chapter doesn't provide general design information, you'll find it essential in adding the eBay Web Services twist to your application design.

Choosing a Communication Method

All of the examples, to this point in the book, have relied on some form of communication to achieve their goals. In fact, every eBay Web Services application you create will include some type of communication with the remote server unless that application relies on static data. Even then, you need to consider significant licensing issues for updates because the updated data will have to come from some source. For example, a PDA could obtain updates from a local desktop, which avoids having the PDA connect to eBay Web Services, but the desktop will still need some source of updated information (usually a direct connection).

The following sections discuss the design issues surrounding the various communication choices you have. You'll find that eBay Web Services is extremely flexible. In fact, as the book goes on, you'll find that there's normally more than one good way to accomplish any given task. Choosing a method to accomplish the task often comes down to the need at hand and the business practices you have in place.

Choosing between the API and SDK

As of this writing, there are two techniques you can use to access eBay Web Services. The first is the API technique, which relies on the eXtensible Markup Language (XML) over HyperText Transport Protocol Secure (HTTPS) standard or REpresentational State Transfer (REST). This is the method where you build an XML message and send it to eBay. The second is the SDK technique, where you create an object within a programming environment and use that object to send a request to eBay. The object still creates an XML message in the background, but your application won't see the XML unless it specifically needs to.

In some cases, you have a choice between these two methods. Generally, if your language of choice has a strong Component Object Model (COM) support, you can use either technique with equal ease. However, when you use a less capable language, such as JavaScript, your only choice is the API. Here is a list of languages that do provide support for either choice, and there are most definitely others.

- ASP.NET
- C#
- Java
- PERL
- PHP
- Visual Basic (Version 6 and .NET)
- Visual C++ (Version 6 and .NET)

Some people have tried other languages and gotten them to work. For example, you'll read on eBay developer newsgroups that some people are using ColdFusion with the SDK. The key ingredient in getting SDK support is learning to work with the various interfaces—a task that most scripting languages don't perform well. Personal experience has shown that VBScript doesn't provide the required level of support, even though you can create COM objects with it, but Visual Basic for Applications (VBA) does provide the required support.

The big question is why a choice is even necessary. The quick answer is that the API technique offers better flexibility and more control. The SDK technique offers faster code creation and fewer opportunities to make mistakes. Neither technique is perfect or the solution for every problem. Each technique does work better for a particular class of problem. In general, I'd use the SDK technique for most applications because most applications don't require the extra flexibility that the API technique offers. As previously mentioned, however, you don't always have a choice.

Unfortunately, making a choice is seldom as easy as the quick answer would lead you to believe. You can use XML with the SDK technique. The SDK provides XML classes you can use to perform the task with essentially the same XML you'd use when using the API technique. However, this SDK technique isn't as straightforward and it uses more memory. The fact that you can combine standard objects with XML requests does make the SDK technique a little more appealing though.

You also need to consider the issue of familiarity. Some developers will be more familiar with the coding practices employed by the API technique, which means the learning curve is going to be smaller. If time is a factor and you don't want to learn the SDK technique, then the API technique will be a better choice.

This section gives you a little bit of information to think about, but it's not the end of the discussion. Wherever possible, I'll provide examples of both techniques in a given language chapter so you can determine for yourself which technique works best for a given need. You might find that learning both techniques is actually better so that you have a choice of tools to use.

Using XML over HTTPS

Of the communication choices, XML over HTTPS is the most flexible because you can use it from so many different programming languages. The "Using a Browser Example" section of Chapter 2 demonstrates that you can even write an application using a simple browser page—nothing exotic is needed. If you want, you can work with eBay using just the Notepad and Internet Explorer applications provided with Windows; although, this is admittedly not very efficient because dedicated Web page applications usually provide better information on designing Web pages and working with XML messages. You might want to look at the CoffeeCup HTML Editor as a low cost alternative to Notepad (`http://www.tucows.com/preview/194456.html`).

Chapter 6 demonstrates that you can actually perform quite a few tasks with the right browser pages and a little JavaScript. Unlike some other Web services, however, you must write some code to perform any task with eBay Web Services. The input you provide must be in the form of an XML message with specific header information. Given the right input, you receive an XML message from eBay that contains the information you need.

As previously mentioned, this method does have certain problems. For example, you don't get formatted output. Of course, there are any number of ways around this issue—everything from using eXtensible Stylesheet Language Transformations (XSLT) to parsing the XML and providing it as part of a report. All of these issues have solutions of some sort, so you can work around them.

> ▶ **TIP**

eBay has already announced a SOAP interface for their Web service (`http://developer`
`.ebay.com/DevZone/KB_SearchDocs/OReilly_Conference_Release-Final.pdf`), which
brings another factor into your design process. From a design perspective, the most critical
problem your application will have is performance. You'll find that SOAP is far faster than
using the XML over HTTPS request method because SOAP is formatted input that doesn't
require as much interpretation on the part of the server or the client. The additional work
required to use SOAP does boost performance. Just how much of a performance boost
depends on a number of factors, including communication speed, line conditions, and how
busy eBay is at any given time.

All types of communication are subject to damage. One of the issues you need to consider as you work with eBay Web Services is how to trap errors that eBay Web Services has already noted (usually an error in the request) and those that eBay Web Services didn't find (such as an error in the response). Many of the examples in this book point out methods of avoiding, detecting, fixing, and reporting errors. However, the robustness of the language you choose makes a difference in the level of error trapping you can perform. A browser application is the easiest to put together, but also the most fragile, because error trapping is nearly impossible.

Using XSLT

Formatting the response you receive from eBay is a requirement. Generally, the API method gives you more options in this area. If you want to use XSLT to automatically translate the response, then you must use the API technique to communicate with eBay. The reason that I included XSLT as a separate communication method is that some people will use this technique to communicate with eBay with scripts on a Web page, rather than write an application. For example, the "Viewing the XSLT Example" section of Chapter 2 demonstrates this technique.

Generally, you'll find that using JavaScript to create XSLT communication scenarios is the least complex method of providing full output to the user. You do have access to a number of underlying request methods, so this technique is also flexible when compared to other options, such as interpreting the XML from an XML request. Most browsers can also use both JavaScript and XSLT, so this is one of the few "universal" solutions at your disposal. Some developers might think otherwise, but this is also the easiest solution to debug because you don't need any special equipment.

The design considerations include performance. This is the slowest method you can use to work with eBay. Every request requires interpretation using some type of script reader. Unlike an application, the script reader must interpret the script and convert it into something the user's machine can understand every time the user makes a request. Don't use this solution if speed is a concern.

Another potential problem is browser compatibility. Using JavaScript and a Web page might seem like the ideal solution, but you can run into numerous pitfalls when a user with a different browser than yours visits. Users can also decide to disable scripting, which prevents your page from working properly. In short, although using XSLT does cross boundaries that you'd normally have a hard time crossing, it isn't perfect.

Defining the Common Communication Elements

No matter what form of communication you eventually select, you'll find that you need to provide some common pieces of information for all of them. Every communication requires your developer information—the keys that eBay provides when you sign up for the developer program. These include the developer identifier, application identifier, and the certificate identifier. You also need to provide user information, which includes a user identifier and a user password. The user information you provide must match a user for the environment in which you want to work. A sandbox user only works in the sandbox environment.

> ▶ **NOTE**
>
> eBay is deprecating (getting rid of) the user identification and password entries. Instead, you'll have to use the `<RequestToken>` element to provide a user token to the other API calls. See the "Getting a User Token" section for one technique of obtaining a user token.

Besides these critical pieces of information, you also need to provide some supplementary information that helps eBay Web Services fulfill your request. One of the most important pieces of information is the compatibility level. This entry determines how eBay Web Services interprets your request. The current minimum compatibility level you can specify is 305, which is the level most of the examples in this book use. You can learn more about the compatibility levels at `http://developer.ebay.com/DevZone/docs/API_Doc/index.asp` (the SDK documentation doesn't appear to contain this information).

You also need to define a detail level. The detail level defines the amount of information that a particular call returns. This value varies by call. Unfortunately, the SDK documentation doesn't tell you what detail levels to use, or whether they're even applicable for a certain call. (You always have to provide this value, but a call such as `AddItem()` only has one detail level.) Look at the API documentation online to determine the applicable detail level values. For example, you can find the detail levels for the `GetSearchResults()` call at `http://developer.ebay.com/DevZone/docs/API_Doc/Functions/GetSearchResults/GetSearch-ResultsInputArguments.htm`.

Each of your calls also require an error level setting, which is a value of 0 (for minimal information) or 1 (for maximum information). For a production application, you'll always want to set this value to 0 to improve performance by reducing the size of the error message. Setting it to 1 as you debug your application lets you get more information about the error from eBay.

The site identifier is another required input. This is one of the settings you need to consider when working with an internationalized application. If you're working in the United States, this value is always set to 0. The "Using the *SiteId* to Your Advantage" section of this chapter describes this entry in more detail.

The final piece of required information is a verb—a term that describes the action you want to perform. When you use the SDK, the code automatically sets this value for you. However, users of the API technique will need to supply the name of the function.

Getting a User Token

At the time of this writing, eBay has a lot of kinks to iron out in the authentication and authorization process. The process is designed to work with Web applications. To be more precise, it's designed to work with Web applications where the server has a connection to the Internet and support for SSL. Needless to say, this assumption could leave a lot of developers scratching their heads looking for a solution.

The actual process isn't difficult. You begin by getting a unique name for your application using the `GetRuName()` call. Once you have a unique name for your application, you need to use the `SetReturnUrl()` call to tell eBay where to redirect a user after they log in. You receive the user's token as part of the return information. The `GetReturnUrl()` call lets you retrieve your application information from eBay whenever you need it.

Most developers who have the resources to set up a Web application of the type that eBay is expecting won't have a problem. This section is devoted to helping developers who don't have the required setup to create a workaround. It's not a pretty workaround, but it does work. All you need is a hosted site—the one you get with your email will do. For that matter, it's possible to set up this system to work with your local PC so long as you have a local Web server set up, have a connection to the Internet, and provide the connection information for your Internet Service Provider (ISP) as the return URL.

Registering Your Application

The workaround performs the required task in two steps. The first step is to register your application. It's possible to perform this step from your local machine, but using a Web site does improve the chances of success. You'll find two Web pages for this task in the \Chapter 05\ RegisterApplication folder of the source code found on the Sybex Web site. (This chapter won't discuss the actual code used—just the procedure. See the "Using JavaScript to Access eBay Web Services" section of Chapter 6 for implementation details.)

The main page is named StartReg.HTM. This page requests a unique identifier for your application. All you need to provide for input is the same five inputs you always provide: developer identifier, application identifier, certification identifier, username, and password. When you click Submit, code in the StartReg.HTM file requests a unique name for your application using the GetRuName() call. After making the call, the code obtains the RuName value and passes it along with all of your information to a second page stored in the EndReg.HTM file.

At this point, you need to provide a successful and unsuccessful login page value for your application. You can use a single page for both events, but I chose to use two pages so that it would be evident whether the login is successful. The EndReg.HTM file provides entries for both values. When you click Submit on this page, the code uses the SetReturnUrl() call to register your application with eBay. Figure 5.1 shows typical results from the call.

Notice the Results field. This field is filled in after the call. If you see success, your application is registered and ready to use. Any other value in the Results field signifies an error of some type. Normally, if the call to eBay fails, then you'll see a Failure message, rather the Success message show in Figure 5.1.

Understanding the Web Server Alternatives

Your application is registered, but you still don't have the required user token—that's the second part of the process. In this case, I didn't find any way to perform the task from the local hard drive. You must have a connection to the Internet. What most people don't realize is that your hosted account normally includes a Web page. Some people set up their Web page with pictures of their children or information about their hobbies. No matter what you use your hosted site for, it normally provides SSL capability—a requirement for the procedure in this section to work. To test the SSL functionality of your site, type the full URL for your home page using the HTTPS protocol rather than the normal HTTP protocol. For example, the full URL for my home page is `https://www.mwt.net/~jmueller/welcome.html`. Normally, I can simply type `http://www.mwt.net/~jmueller/` to get to my Web page, but the short version doesn't work when you use HTTPS. If your home page is accessible using this technique, then you can use the authentication pages described in this section. Note that your home page might not display some features that you're used to seeing, such as graphics.

Unfortunately, your hosted site might not support SSL or you might not even have a hosted site. You still have options for making this setup work. One of those options is to install a local Web server on your machine. This book doesn't have space to discuss all of the options, but most new versions of Windows such as Windows XP and Windows 2000 come with a Web server right out of the box. You'll find the option for installing a Web server in the Add/Remove Windows Components portion of the Add or Remove Programs applet shown in Figure 5.2. Notice that the Internet Information Services (IIS) option is highlighted in the screenshot—that's the option you need to install if it isn't installed already. Make sure you spend some time learning how to work with IIS as well. You can find a tutorial at `http://www.trainingcenter.com/series2/IIS_4.asp` (normally for Windows 2000 users) or `http://www.simongibson.com/intranet/iis5/` (normally for Windows XP users).

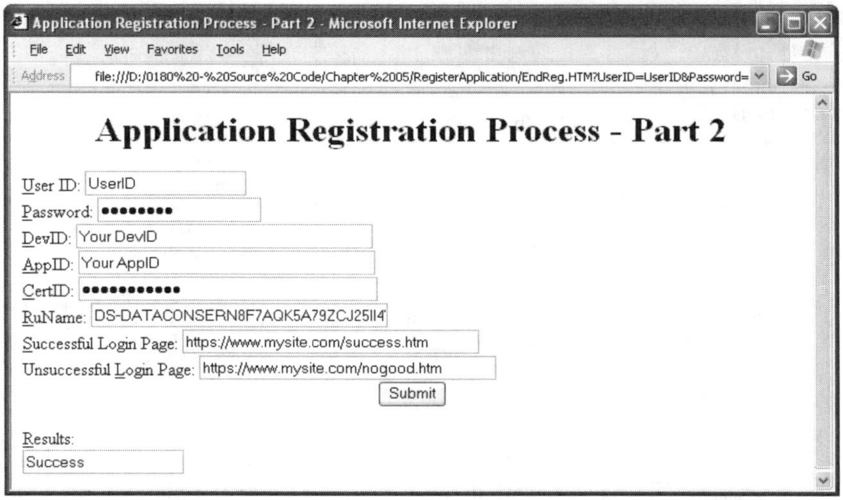

FIGURE 5.1:
Typical results of the initial registration process.

FIGURE 5.2:

Many versions of Windows come with a copy of IIS that you can use.

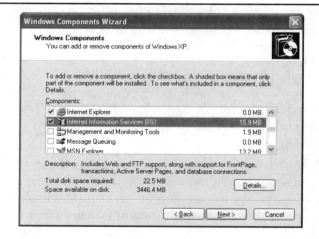

Once you have a local copy of IIS installed, you still have a problem connecting it to the outside. Or do you? Most people don't understand the reason that IIS isn't installed by default on many Windows operating systems. The fact is that if you have a connection to the Internet, then IIS also has a connection to the Internet. Even if you're using a dial-up connection, this connection exists. However, you don't have a domain, so you need to use the actual Internet Protocol (IP) address for your server when you communicate with eBay. To learn the IP address of your server, open a command prompt, type **IPCONFIG**, and press Enter. You'll see a display similar to the one shown in Figure 5.3.

FIGURE 5.3:

You can obtain your IP address using the IPCONFIG utility.

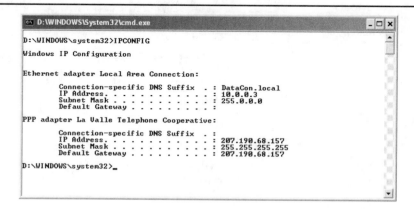

Notice that I have two connections. The first is to my network and doesn't affect this discussion. The second says it connects to La Valle Telephone Cooperative. That's the connection I would need. Your connection will use the name that you assigned to it. The number that you want is the IP Address, which is 207.190.68.157 in this case. This number will change every time you connect, so you need to maintain the connection during this entire process. In other words, you must register your application and get the authentication token in one session or the procedure won't work. Now you need to feed that number to eBay as part of the URL. Look again at Figure 5.1. If I were to change the success URL to point to my local machine, it would probably be `https://207.190.68.157/success.htm`. In fact, you'll want to verify the URL before you send it to eBay to ensure it works as anticipated. Simply use your browser and place the URL you think will work into the Address field.

> ▶ **NOTE**
>
> Always verify the information about your connection before you use this procedure. Check with your ISP about obtaining a fixed IP address for your connection if you use a connection such as DSL. These always-on connections make it possible to create easier interaction with eBay. In addition, you might find that you can't use this technique when working with a cable modem. In some cases, the ISP blocks the ports eBay needs to communicate with your system.

Authenticating the User

At this point, you've registered your application and you have a Web server that eBay can access. To authenticate the user and obtain the token you need, you must provide a connection to eBay and a means for eBay to redirect the response to your site. The three Web pages to perform this task appear in the `\Chapter 05\GetUserAuth` folder of the source code on the Sybex site.

The `Default.HTM` file begins the authentication process. It contains a simple script that combines the URL for the eBay sandbox site (`https://scgi.sandbox.ebay.com/aw-cgi/eBayISAPI.dll?signin`) with the `runame` argument you obtained when you registered your application with eBay. It's the combination of these two items that tell eBay to register this user with your application.

When the user clicks Submit, they'll see a standard eBay login page. After the user logs in, they'll see a special consent agreement page similar to the one shown in Figure 5.4. This page lists the actions that your application can take on the user's behalf.

After the user clicks Agree and Continue, eBay will redirect them to your Web site using the URLs that you provided when you registered your application. That's why it's important that the URLs are valid and current. Otherwise, the redirection won't work and you won't receive the required authentication token. A successful login will display a page similar to the one shown in Figure 5.5.

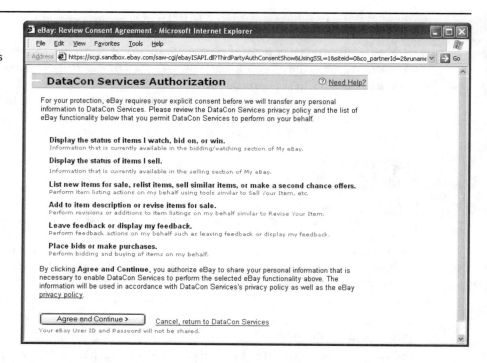

Make sure you save the authentication token somewhere safe. It consists of two elements. The first is the actual token, which is a long string of nonsense characters that you must supply with every request you perform on a user's behalf. The second is an expiration date. At some point, the user is going to have to go through the authentication process again. Even though you have to cut and paste the resulting authentication token, at least this process works. Other examples in Chapters 7, 8, and 10 demonstrate some language-specific techniques you can combine with the techniques discussed in this section to make the process more seamless for desktop applications.

> ▶ **WARNING**

> Don't use the authentication token that appears as part of the URL in the Address field of your browser as input to eBay. This form of the authentication token contains escape characters and will cause your application to fail. Use only the authentication token that appears in the Results field of the sample as input.

Selecting a Platform

You might think at the outset that only desktop users will need the eBay Web Services application you create. In some cases, you might be right. Other kinds of users might not have a need to access your application in any way. However, it's surprising how many applications are seeing use on alternative platforms that many people would have considered impossible even a year or two ago. The problem for developers is seeing past preconceived ideas of how users will employ an application and deciding which platforms the user could use. Once you make that determination, you have to go further and decide which platforms you want to support. The economic benefit of supporting a platform must outweigh the cost of implementing it.

The following sections discuss several platform design options. You'll find recommendations on ways to optimize your platform design decisions. These sections also contain a few surprises—things you might not have considered important. For example, the first section answers the question of whether you always need to implement a desktop application solution.

Writing Desktop Applications

Desktop applications can serve a variety of needs. You can use a desktop application for everything from a corporate reference that incorporates information from eBay Web Services to a site for selling surplus equipment that your company has either purchased or produces. A desktop application can help you bid on items with greater efficiency and provide direct connections with your database. This kind of application works well for family events such as setting up an online garage sale for all of those extras that have accumulated over the past year. A small store could make an application available as a kiosk to help customers locate hard to find items and provide an exchange for items that might not sell well in the local community. The application possibilities are endless.

> ► **TIP**
>
> One of the most important additions you can make to your Web site is a survey form. The survey should ask users questions about the usability and information content of your site. In addition, you need to know what type of device the responder used to access your site, as well as the devices the responder would like to use to access your site. In some cases, you might find that you could double sales if you support an additional platform such as a cellular telephone.

The following sections describe three kinds of desktop applications. Obviously, you can write myriad application types for a desktop machine, but these three types work well with eBay Web Services. Each application type has something special to offer in the way of flexibility, usability, performance, or compatibility. It's important to weigh your choices carefully, because even desktop machines aren't a one size fits all environment.

Using Standard Applications

Many users are unaware of the communication that goes on behind the scenes with many desktop applications today. The application could rely on standard desktop application controls—the same controls that developers have always used for this kind of application. In fact, you saw an example of this kind of application in the "Viewing the Desktop Example" section of Chapter 2. This application doesn't look like it has any type of connectivity to the outside world, but it does use an Internet connection to retrieve data from eBay Web Services.

Use standard desktop applications for corporate needs. In many cases, even though the user is aware that their main interaction is with eBay, they need not know every nuance of that interaction. This kind of application could pull data in from a number of sources in a way that helps the user perform a task quickly and with less frustration than using a number of independent applications to perform the same task. For example, the application could pull in the list price of a product that the user wants to bid on through eBay—the addition of this information would help the user to know when it's time to stop bidding because the auction price is too high. Data source hiding is an important development principle to keep in mind. Hiding the source of the data means you don't have to retrain users every time the source of the data changes.

Using Web-enabled Applications

Some developers use the term *Web-enabled* to mean any browser application that sits on the desktop. However, this description doesn't really fit today's application development products. You can easily create an application that looks like a standard desktop application, but uses a browser interface by adding one of many HTML controls to the application. It doesn't matter whether you use a high-end product such as Visual Studio or an Office product such as Word—the interface still looks like a standard application, but the presentation is all HTML. Microsoft actually uses this technique for most help setups in their applications today.

This kind of application can work well when you need to combine local and remote sources. For example, consider an office supply need. An employee search could begin with the local storeroom. If the company is out of that supply, a check of eBay could show that the company could obtain that product for a low cost. At this point, the application sends a request with the eBay information to the person who can make such purchases. Only when these two sources fail, does the application resort to putting an order in for the office supply at full price from a local store.

A side benefit of this approach is that you can combine sources into one page. The application could show local quantities of the office supply and help the user make a good decision about reordering when stocks are low. Perhaps there's an auction where the company could restock a little sooner than necessary at a significant savings. The idea is to maximize the efficiency of a search so that you can address a range of requirements using a simple interface.

Using Browser Applications

A browser application can reside on a desktop or anywhere else for that matter. The user clicks on a link that opens Internet Explorer and takes them to the location of the application. The application could reside on a local intranet or on the Internet. A desktop browser application is usually simple compared to other kinds of browser applications. At most, the application needs to determine what type of browser the user has so that it can account for any compatibility issues.

It's important to consider browser compatibility because you don't know which of the many browsers available a user will choose. However, getting the vendors to tell you the facts is nearly impossible. You can find various charts that show browser compatibility issues online. One of the better charts is the Webmonkey Browser Chart at `http://hotwired .lycos.com/webmonkey/reference/browser_chart/index.html`. The advantage of using this chart is that the owner updates it regularly to reflect new browsers. Figure 5.6 shows a typical example of this chart.

FIGURE 5.6:

Always check the assumptions you make about browser compatibility against a reliable chart.

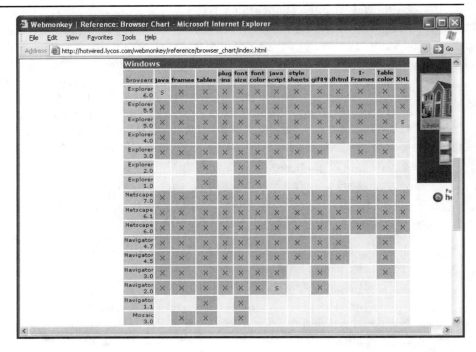

As you can see, the Webmonkey Browser Chart presents a wealth of information about the features that each browser supports. Note that this chart only supports Windows browsers—Webmonkey also provides charts for the Macintosh (http://hotwired.lycos.com/webmonkey/reference/browser_chart/index_mac.html), Unix/Linux (http://hotwired.lycos.com/webmonkey/reference/browser_chart/index_nix.html), and other platforms (http://hotwired.lycos.com/webmonkey/reference/browser_chart/index_other.html). Make sure you consider Webmonkey's other offerings, such as a chart that shows how to create special characters and a JavaScript reference library.

Use browser applications when you think you might need to connect to other platforms. For example, using a browser application makes it much easier to move the application to the Pocket PC or even a cellular telephone. Browser applications do tend to face a variety of compatibility problems, and they're not very fast when compared to other application types, but they're the flexibility option of choice.

Writing Small Form Factor Applications

Many users now carry some type of small form factor device such as a Personal Digital Assistant (PDA). The PDA is the most popular form, but you could consider some types of notebook computers in this category too. The small form factor device is very portable, generally sees use on the road, and has limits in processing power, memory, and local storage. Notebooks and PDAs don't suffer quite the limitations of a cellular telephone, but you may still find it difficult to write a program that fits on these devices and delivers everything needed.

The following sections discuss two kinds of small form factor application: desktop and browser. The Pocket PC is one of the easiest and most powerful PDAs to program, so the first section discusses how you can create desktop applications for this platform. Most people use a Web application of some type for less capable devices, such as the Palm, because local storage and the difficulty of writing an application for these platforms becomes a factor.

Using Pocket PC Applications

The Pocket PC provides a number of great programming options. For example, you can write directly to Windows CE or use the .NET Compact Framework. Developing a Pocket PC–specific application has many of the same advantages of creating standard desktop application. (See the "Using Standard Applications" section for details.) One of the biggest benefits of the Pocket PC application is that you don't need a Web server to host it in most cases.

Currently, many businesses favor the programmability the Pocket PC provides for applications such as warehouse inventory. The user has a need for a mobile device, a laptop or notebook won't work, and the user can carry a Pocket PC in a holster.

Like many other uses of eBay Web Services, this one is nontraditional. A company can use eBay as just another means for finding products, but, in this case, the products can cost considerably less. Given slow sales, your warehouse manager might decide to offload certain products through eBay as well. It's a lot easier to perform these two tasks when the manager is actually in the warehouse looking at the current product inventories. So, a mobile setup can make the manager a lot more efficient.

Obviously, you can also perform searches and buy products using a Pocket PC. The advantage of the Pocket PC application, however, is that you can also do the unexpected. Many users will see the advanced applications and say that they didn't know you could do that.

Using Generic PDA Applications

All PDAs can use a Web interface, including the Palm and Pocket PC. When you create a generic PDA application, you normally need to host it on a Web server because you can't assume anything about the processing power of the client. A host can detect the type of mobile device and provide output for that device in the form of a Web page.

From a design perspective, you need to consider the devices you want to support at the outset of the project. Everything from screen design to coding technique must consider the devices you expect to use the application. In fact, you normally need to provide settings within the application that instruct the server how to react to specific devices. A Palm might require three pages to display a Web site, while a Pocket PC can display the same information in two pages. The information is the same, but the form factor of the device is different.

One of the biggest advantages of using this approach is that you can support any device. Many users find the advanced features of the Pocket PC less than useful and the larger size of the device annoying. An office manager doesn't want to carry a Pocket PC around in a holster all day. A Palm that fits in a pocket is much better because it stays out of the way until needed.

> ▶ **NOTE**
>
> Although it might be possible to use a cellular telephone to work with eBay, the devices lack the resources to perform any significant work. Consequently, I haven't provided a special section for cellular telephones in this chapter.

Writing Mixed Environment Applications

It's important to consider the fact that you might not be able to support just one device and make your eBay Web Services application work. Sometimes you need to support two or even three platforms to ensure that everyone who wants to contact you can do so. You might think that this means writing separate applications for each device, but that's not necessary anymore as long as you consider the requirements of each device before you begin writing code.

Mixed environment applications commonly work on more than one device or environment (and sometimes both). In the past, you wrote mixed environment applications using Web programming techniques because the various platforms didn't offer much in the way of commonality. For example, you can write an ASP application that detects the device type (desktop browser version, PDA model, or cellular telephone model) and outputs a page specifically tailored for that device. The essential code doesn't change and you use a single code base for every device. Only the interface changes to meet the needs of a particular device.

Today, it isn't necessary to write your application as a Web application. For example, you can use Visual Studio .NET to write an application that works on a PDA or a desktop machine. Your code base remains the same, but you do need to compile the application for each kind of device. In addition, you must work within the confines of the .NET Compact Framework, rather than assume the full resources of the .NET Framework are available.

The ability to write applications that work on more than one platform or in more than one environment is so compelling that other vendors will follow suit. Eventually, you might be able to write an application that works equally well on any device without much thought.

Unfortunately, although the development environment is better today, it's still not perfect—the goal of writing mixed environment applications that truly work everywhere with little effort on the developer's part is a long way off.

Selecting a Development Language

Some developers have a mind-set that their particular language is the only perfect language in the world and they never plan to use anything else. I'd love to say these developers are really onto something because it would greatly reduce the efforts I go to in order to maintain proficiency with multiple languages. The sad truth is the world has yet to discover the perfect language and probably never will. Some development languages work best for one situation, and others work best in another situation. Good developers either realize the limitations of the one language they do know or have multiple languages available in their programming toolkit.

Of course, the question is how language choice affects your use of eBay Web Services. Look again at the examples in Chapters 2 and 4. You'll notice that all of the examples return a result from a simply constructed request. The problem is using the data you receive in some useful way. Displaying a search result with XSLT isn't a problem and you can add scripting to the resulting page to make it more flexible, but trying to build a high-end application using this technique is difficult. The sections that follow won't tell you specifically which language to use to meet your development needs, but they will help you match a language to a specific kind of project.

Choosing a Language that Meets Specific Needs

Some developers look at me rather strangely when I tell them that I develop applications in VBA about as often as I do in other languages such as C++ or C#. I find that using VBA provides me with a way to quickly prototype Office-specific applications and reduce the user's learning curve by using an environment they already know. In addition, VBA is enough like other languages I know that I don't have a big learning curve to contend with every time I start a new project. That's also the reason you'll find a VBA chapter in this book.

In fact, the language-specific chapters (Chapters 6 through 11) each demonstrate the functionality provided by a specific language. For example, the VBA examples deal with tasks you can perform more easily in Office than you can any other environment, such as creating reports or generating a list of items you want to sell. You'll also see how to perform statistical analysis and generate graphs. Perhaps you sell items on eBay and want to track the bidding process on your various offerings to see how each item performs. You might use this information to create a better presentation for the next auction.

However, VBA and Office don't provide the level of accessibility needed for some tasks and you definitely wouldn't want to set up a Web site that relies on VBA. The other chapters in the book cover other kinds of applications such as a Web site that offers items for sale, along with the information you have always provided. The idea is to select a language that meets the needs of the application so that you don't become frustrated trying to use a hammer where a screwdriver would work better.

Considering Your Skills and Abilities

It would be easy to assume that you want and can devote hours to your eBay project simply because you're reading this book. However, the fact is that many of you have time constraints and probably don't have much of an inclination to become a developer (unless you're already a professional developer). It may be that you won't want to create a Web site that instantly produces sales or tracks sales records—maybe you just want to do a little research. Along with considering the needs of the application, you also have to consider your skills and abilities. Trying to create a full-fledged warehouse auction application when all you need is the equivalent of a garage sale is a waste of time and effort.

The development language you choose has to match the project, but it also has to match your skills and abilities. Often, the choice of language determines just how much you should attempt to do with eBay Web Services. In other cases, you might know that you want to perform certain tasks, but that the programming language skills you possess don't quite fit in with your plans. The planning process can point out the need to call in a consultant to help with the programming part of the job. In addition, by knowing your skills and understanding the needs of the job, you can find a developer with the qualifications you need from a point of knowledge.

Honestly assessing your skills and abilities can have another effect. One person I know went back to school to learn the skills required to develop their Web application. The person didn't have nearly as many time constraints as he did cash flow problems (a consultant was out of the question). Although he didn't graduate with a degree in computer science, this person now knows how to maintain a Web site that has built his business. In short, this book might help you choose a programming language that you want to learn to use eBay Web Services to meet a specific need effectively.

Defining Language Limitations

Part of the design process is to understand the limitations of the language you choose. You must consider both the current application requirements and those that you need to address in the future. Moving an application from one language to another is definitely not a fun task. Consequently, you need to consider what you plan to do today and how you plan to expand the application in the future. In some cases, accomplishing this task means defining the limitations of the language.

If you choose JavaScript to create an application for your Web site, it's going to be quite flexible and most browsers won't have a problem accessing the information. In addition, you can perform most eBay Web Services tasks without buying an expensive server or incurring many startup costs. JavaScript is the low-price solution for many developers. However, JavaScript is hardly the most robust programming language, and you'll find your expansion opportunities limited. For example, this probably isn't the right choice for creating complex reports, but it's a good solution if you want to offer a means to make purchases on eBay or perform quick searches for products.

You might think that Java or Visual Basic .NET will solve all of your development problems. They're certainly robust enough to help you perform any task you might want to do. However, I probably wouldn't use either language if my main goal were tracking product statistics. In addition, both Java and Visual Basic .NET require the skills of a good programmer to create successful applications. Good programmers don't come cheap—plan to spend quite a bit to create the Web application of your dreams.

Understanding Internationalization Issues

Many developers don't consider internationalization issues when they develop a Web application today, but it's an important issue. Unless you know that no one who speaks another language will ever have any reason to access your site, you have to consider the possibility that internationalization could benefit your site. Not every site requires internationalization, but many do. You also have to consider how to handle the internationalization of your site. In many cases, you can simply ensure that the site handles more than one type of currency; but in others, you need to provide pages in more than one language. The following sections discuss these issues as they apply to eBay Web Services.

Learning the Limits of Translation

It's important to consider not only how to internationalize your site, but also when. Sometimes the question is even "if" you should internationalize your site. Adding a second language or a second country to your site isn't a small undertaking. Even if you choose to use the least expensive approach possible, supporting two languages still means providing two sets of identical Web pages in most cases. (Some developers solve the problem by placing the language-specific strings outside the application so that the content and functionality of the application are separate.) Experience shows that even with the best of intentions, one language is bound to remain behind the other in updates. Adding more languages only compounds the problem. The point is that you need to consider the monetary problems of maintaining more than one language. You need to be sure that the cost of supporting more than one language is going to result in a quantifiable gain.

When you internationalize a site, it often means using other languages. Unless you know the target language well enough to perform the translation, you need to find someone who can translate the pages. Sometimes you can get the translation free. For example, the Free-Translation.com site at `http://www.freetranslation.com/` will accept your input and output translation in a number of languages. Figure 5.7 shows an example of such a translation from English to Spanish. The free translations on this site focus on translating English to another language, although you can find some translations that go the other direction (from Spanish to English, for example). Unfortunately, the quality of the translation on these sites varies from acceptable to poor. In many cases, you'll want to use a professional translator to ensure the quality of a translation remains high. (It's interesting to note that many of the sites providing free translation services also offer paid human translations.)

FIGURE 5.7:

Sometimes you can translate a limited amount of text free.

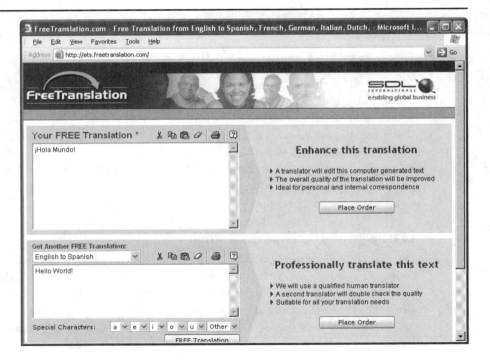

Considering the User's Location

The user's location affects the way you handle internationalization from more than one perspective. Of course, the first problem to avoid is confusing the user's language with the user's location—the two aren't always the same. Someone in the United States could prefer speaking Spanish, even though the language spoken by most Americans is English. Likewise, someone in the United Kingdom could prefer to speak Hindi. However, even when you offer your page in Hindi or Spanish, you still need to consider the user's location because the location affects presentation issues, such as the format of dates.

> ▶ **TIP**
>
> It's important to consider language issues when you develop a Web site. For example, many people have never even heard of Hindi, yet 180 million people use it as their first language and another 300 million use it as their second language (see `http://www.cs.colostate .edu/~malaiya/hindiint.html` for details).

Using the *SiteId* to Your Advantage

The book hasn't devoted very much time to the `<SiteId>` element of the XML request yet because it doesn't matter for most of the examples. However, the `<SiteId>` element can play an important role in making your site better from an internationalization perspective. For example, when performing a search, you might want to use the `<SiteId>` element to ensure your application looks in the current country for the item first, and then in other areas if the user can afford to pay higher shipping charges. You can find a list of the `<SiteId>` element value at `http://developer.ebay.com/DevZone/docs/API_Doc/Functions/Tables/SiteIdTable.htm`.

Your Call to Action

This is the first chapter that really discussed programming techniques to the extent that you're planning for a Web site or application that relies on eBay Web Services. Previous chapters have demonstrated the useful features of eBay Web Services and even shown how these features work by exposing the Web service process. Completing this chapter means that you're ready to look at language-specific issues and get your application running.

Now that you've spent some time discovering the Web service process and deciding what eBay Web Services can do for you, it's time to consider the design of your application. This chapter presented useful information that you need to develop a good design. However, it concentrated on eBay Web Services, rather than general development principles. Now is the time to learn about these other principles, if you haven't worked with them already. In addition, you need to consider the design of your application. A written specification is nice (and required for larger companies), but just the act of thinking about what you want to do is essential.

Chapter 6 is the first language-specific chapter in the book. This chapter concentrates on using JavaScript to create specialized Web pages. I found that using JavaScript at the outset gave me a better understanding of how eBay Web Services works. There's little (if any) cost associated in using this particular language, so you can experiment to see if eBay Web Services will meet your needs. I would consider this chapter one that everyone should try, even if they intend to use another language to develop their application.

Chapter 6

Interacting with eBay Web
Services Using JavaScript

Authenticating
Application Users

▶ Writing Browser-Based Applications

Performing a
Category Search

Using XSLT
Display Techniques

Many people may begin their eBay Web Services experience using simple Web pages that employ JavaScript to interact with eBay. The main reasons for this choice are that JavaScript is relatively straightforward, easy to learn, works on multiple platforms, and provides instant feedback. You can use JavaScript without making a large investment—or any investment at all. Most browsers come with JavaScript support built right into the product.

The examples in this chapter demonstrate techniques you can use to access eBay with JavaScript. The first section concentrates on essential tasks. It begins with a simple example that demonstrates the principles you'll use for all of the other examples in the book. Next, you'll see an example of one technique for registering your application and authenticating a user.

The next few sections discuss common tasks you can perform with JavaScript. For example, you'll discover some unique search techniques you can add to your application or use as a stand-alone addition to the support eBay provides. This single chapter can't discuss every potential use of eBay, but it does provide a good start. You might want to combine some of the ideas presented here with ideas that appear in other chapters.

Using JavaScript to Access eBay Web Services

Many people find that JavaScript is a great solution for Web-based application tasks. Accessing eBay Web Services is no different. You'll find that you can create a basic application in just minutes. The first example in this section discusses a simple access technique. The goal is to demonstrate the basic techniques you'll use for all eBay Web Services applications. For instance, you'll discover how to send your developer keys as a header using JavaScript—a task you need to perform for every application. After you create a basic access application, you'll probably want to extend it with eXtensible Style Language Transformation (XSLT). The second example extends the basic technique by providing support for XSLT.

> ▶ **NOTE**

JavaScript is a very flexible language, and it runs on a lot of platforms. In fact, you'll find that JavaScript provides moderately good support for various types of object technologies, including Microsoft Component Object Model (COM). It was a little surprising to learn that working with the SDK technique in JavaScript just isn't possible. The main problem is that JavaScript doesn't provide good interface access. Consequently, all of the examples this chapter use the API technique to access eBay Web Services.

JavaScript Resources

This chapter doesn't provide a nuts and bolts discussion of JavaScript. I'm assuming you have some experience using this language. Because this language is used in so many ways, you can find great JavaScript resources online. Many sites include tutorials, a reference, and sample code. If you want to be sure your code runs in as many environments as possible, make sure you download a copy of European Computer Manufacturer's Association (ECMA) standard 262 from `http://www.ecma-international .org/publications/standards/Ecma-262.htm`, which is the standard for JavaScript.

If you've never used JavaScript before, you'll need a good tutorial. The W3Schools.com site at `http://www.w3schools.com/js/default.asp` provides an excellent tutorial for first time users. Webmonkey provides several JavaScript tutorials including a basic tutorial at `http://hotwired.lycos.com/ webmonkey/98/03/index0a.html` and an advanced tutorial at `http://hotwired.lycos.com/webmonkey/ 98/29/index0a.html`. You might also want to view their crash course index at `http://hotwired .lycos.com/webmonkey/programming/javascript/tutorials/jstutorial_index.html`.

It's important to have a good JavaScript reference. One of the better standards-based JavaScript references is at `http://devedge.netscape.com/central/javascript/`. If you want to learn about the Microsoft perspective on JavaScript, the Microsoft Windows Script Technologies site at `http:// www.script-info.net/jsvbs/msscript/misc/vtorimicrosoftwindowsscripttechnologies.php` contains a wealth of helpful information.

eBay is deprecating (getting rid of) the user ID and password technique of identifying the user of your application. The problem is that eBay would prefer that third party developers not store eBay usernames and passwords locally. A new authentication scheme provides an authentication token that you can use for some period of time before the user has to authenticate again. This new technique requires Web access for a number of reasons discussed in the "Getting a User Token" section of Chapter 5. The third example shows how to register your application and then authenticate a user to obtain the authentication token for use in an application. All of the remaining applications in the chapter rely on the authentication technique.

> ▶ **NOTE**
>
> You might be tempted to think that you need an expensive product to work with the examples in this chapter. The fact of the matter is that Notepad provides all the text editing capability you need. However, if you want an editor that does a little more than Notepad and won't cost anything to try, check out NoteTab Light at `http://download.com.com/3000-2352-10008280.html`. This editor provides HTML functionality that makes the editing processing much easier. It also includes a good glossary of computer terms, templates to make designing Web pages easier, and a number of useful toolbars. What I really like is the drag-and-drop functionality it provides. You find a tag you want to use from the list of available tags, drag it to the required position, and drop it on the page. The editor also promotes good design strategies by performing tasks such as automatically creating opening and closing tags for you.

Understanding the Basic Access Technique

As previously mentioned, eBay relies on a request and response mechanism to communicate with your application. eBay Web Services requires you to provide an XML formatted request for the information you need. Unlike other Web services, you can't use the HyperText Transport Protocol (HTTP) GET method to perform this task—you'll generally use the POST method to do it. In addition to the request message, you must also provide special headers so eBay knows about you through your developer keys and how you want the Web service to interpret your request. Listing 6.1 shows how to create the headers and a simple request message. You'll find the complete source for this example in the `\Chapter 06\SimpleBrowser` folder of the source code located on the Sybex Web site.

Listing 6.1   Creating a Simple Access Page

```
function GetData()
{
   // Create the request.
   var Req = new ActiveXObject("Msxml2.ServerXMLHTTP.4.0");
   Req.open("POST", "https://api.sandbox.ebay.com/ws/api.dll", false);
```

```javascript
// Define the header information for the request. These headers
// appear in the same order recommended by the documentation at
// http://developer.ebay.com/DevZone/docs/API_Doc/index.asp.
Req.setRequestHeader("X-EBAY-API-SESSION-CERTIFICATE",
                        SubmissionForm.DevIDStr.value + ";" +
                        SubmissionForm.AppIDStr.value + ";" +
                        SubmissionForm.CertIDStr.value);
Req.setRequestHeader("X-EBAY-API-COMPATIBILITY-LEVEL", "305");
Req.setRequestHeader("X-EBAY-API-DEV-NAME",
                        SubmissionForm.DevIDStr.value);
Req.setRequestHeader("X-EBAY-API-APP-NAME",
                        SubmissionForm.AppIDStr.value);
Req.setRequestHeader("X-EBAY-API-CERT-NAME",
                        SubmissionForm.CertIDStr.value);
Req.setRequestHeader("X-EBAY-API-CALL-NAME", "GetSearchResults");
Req.setRequestHeader("X-EBAY-API-SITEID", "0");
Req.setRequestHeader("X-EBAY-API-DETAIL-LEVEL", "0");
Req.setRequestHeader("Content-Type", "text/xml");

// Create the XML request object.
var XMLData = new ActiveXObject("Msxml2.DOMDocument.4.0");

// Add the XML request header.
var ProcInst =
   XMLData.createProcessingInstruction(
      "xml", "version=\"1.0\"  encoding=\"iso-8859-1\"");
XMLData.appendChild(ProcInst);

// Construct the XML request message.
var Root = XMLData.createElement("request");
Root.setAttribute("xmlns", "urn:eBayAPIschema");

// Add the user information.
var Elem = XMLData.createElement("RequestUserId");
Elem.text = SubmissionForm.UserIDStr.value;
Root.appendChild(Elem);
Elem = XMLData.createElement("RequestPassword");
Elem.text = SubmissionForm.PasswordStr.value;
Root.appendChild(Elem);

// Add the request data.
Elem = XMLData.createElement("DetailLevel");
Elem.text = "0";
Root.appendChild(Elem);
Elem = XMLData.createElement("ErrorLevel");
Elem.text = "1";
Root.appendChild(Elem);
Elem = XMLData.createElement("Query");
Elem.text = SubmissionForm.QueryStr.value;
Root.appendChild(Elem);
Elem = XMLData.createElement("SiteId");
Elem.text = "0";
```

```
    Root.appendChild(Elem);
    Elem = XMLData.createElement("Verb");
    Elem.text = "GetSearchResults";
    Root.appendChild(Elem);

    // Add the request data to the XML request.
    XMLData.appendChild(Root);

    // Send the request.
    Req.send(XMLData);

    // Write the data to screen.
    if (Req.status == 200)
        SubmissionForm.ResultStr.value = Req.responseText;
    else
        alert("Request Failed!");
}
```

The code begins by creating an XML HTTP request object, Req. It uses Req to open a connection with the sandbox server that relies on the POST technique with the open() method. The only code you'd change when working with the production server is the URL for the open() method.

The next task is to build a series of headers using the setRequestHeader() method. There's no law that says you must submit the headers in the order shown. However, submitting them in this order ensures you don't miss a header. eBay Web Services requires that you provide all of the headers shown in the example. The X-EBAY-API-SESSION-CERTIFICATE header is actually a combination of the three keys that eBay provides. You'll also need to provide these keys as separate headers. You must provide the correct X-EBAY-API-CALL-NAME header, even though this value is provided as part of the XML message; otherwise, eBay sends a somewhat ambiguous message telling you there's something wrong with the header, but not the precise problem. You'll also want to adjust the headers for the compatibility level, detail level, and site identifier to meet your specific needs. The only header that will never change is Content-Type.

You can use a number of techniques to create the XML message. The example shows the least error-prone approach based on a lot of experimentation. The code begins by creating a document to hold all of the data. This document doesn't include the XML header (a processing instruction), so you need to add it. Notice that the processing instruction includes both the version number and encoding. The code adds the processing instruction to the XML document.

The next task is to create the root node, <request>. The code sets the namespace attribute so the XML parser knows how to interpret the remaining entries in the document. Notice the code doesn't add the root node to the document, at this point, because the root node contains child nodes that describe the actual request.

A request begins with the user information. This example shows the user identifier and password technique. Other examples in the chapter will show the authentication token technique. No matter which technique you use, you must provide the user information to make a request.

> ▶ **NOTE**

There are exceptions to every rule. You can make three eBay Web Services API calls without user identification. These calls include `GetRuName()`, `SetReturnUrl()`, and `GetReturnUrl()`. The reason you don't need user information for these calls is that the user isn't involved—these are application-specific calls.

The code builds the request next. Again, the actual order of the entries isn't essential, but placing them in order ensures you don't forget anything. The eBay API Test Tool (described in the "Using the eBay API Test Tool" section of Chapter 4) provides one of the better ways to discover what eBay Web Services requires as input. The example begins with all of the essential elements including the detail level, error level, site identifier, and verb (the action you want eBay to perform). Because this is a search request, the code also adds the <Query> element to the root node.

Now that the root node is complete, the code finally adds it to the XML document. The `Req.send()` method transmits the data to the server. Many programming languages would send the request and automatically generate an error should one occur. JavaScript doesn't appear to provide this functionality, so you must check the error status of the communication before you try to do anything with the response. When `Req.status` equals 200, the communication is successful, even if the actual request failed.

> ▶ **WARNING**

Don't confuse the communication status with the request status. The communication status information only refers to the ability of your application to send data to the server and the server's ability to receive the document. The request status tells about all other forms of error, including most header errors. Consequently, the code must make two checks to ensure it receives a valid response from the server.

At this point, you'd normally check the error status of the response and then process the data in some way or ask the user to try the request again. The example displays the raw XML contained in the `Req.responseText` property on screen.

Modifying the Basic Technique to Use XSLT

At some point, you're going to want to process the data you receive from eBay Web Services. The basic example is helpful while you experiment because you can see the raw XML that eBay Web Services returns. The application user won't be quite as thrilled to see the information in this form. Using XSLT to translate the data is extremely flexible and quick. The "Using XSLT for Presentation" section of Chapter 4 provides more details on working with XSLT. The code in this section describes one technique for calling on XSLT to perform the required work from JavaScript. Listing 6.2 shows the essential code for this example. You'll find the complete source for this example in the \Chapter 06\XSLTBrowser folder of the source code located on the Sybex Web site.

Listing 6.2   **Turning Control Over to XSLT**

```
// Write the data to screen.
if (Req.status == 200)
{
    // Place the resulting information in an XML document.
    var ProcDoc = new ActiveXObject("Msxml2.DOMDocument.4.0");
    ProcDoc.async = false;
    ProcDoc.loadXML(Req.responseXML.xml);

    // Determine the response status.
    var StatusCheck = ProcDoc.childNodes[1].childNodes[1];

    // If there is an error, display the information.
    if (StatusCheck.nodeName == "Errors")
    {
        // Get the first error.
        var ErrorData = StatusCheck.childNodes[0];

        // Create an error string.
        var Code = ErrorData.childNodes[0];
        var ErrorClass = ErrorData.childNodes[1];
        var SeverityCode = ErrorData.childNodes[2];
        var Severity = ErrorData.childNodes[3];
        var LongMessage = ErrorData.childNodes[7];

        // Display the error and exit.
        alert("Error!\r\nCode: " + Code.text +
            "\r\nError Class: " + ErrorClass.text +
            "\r\nSeverity Code: " + SeverityCode.text +
            "\r\nSeverity: " + Severity.text +
            "\r\n" + LongMessage.text);
        return;
    }

    // Create an XSLT document and load the transform into it.
    var XSLTData = new ActiveXObject("Msxml2.DOMDocument.4.0");
    XSLTData.async = false;
```

```
        XSLTData.load("Default.xsl");

        // Display the output on screen.
        document.write(ProcDoc.transformNode(XSLTData));
    }
    else
        alert("Request Failed!");
```

The code performs all of the same tasks as for the basic example. The point of interest is the check after the application receives a response from eBay Web Services. As usual, the code verifies the Web server status by checking the Req.status property. However, now that the application is going to do something other than just display the raw XML, it also needs to trap potential errors. The first step in this process is to load the response into an XML document. Normally, this document will contain data that the application can process, but sometimes it will contain an error message. Figure 6.1 shows a typical error message—this one for a bad username.

You can handle the error in a number of ways. For example, you could create a special XSLT file for displaying error messages. Because eBay could send more than one message, the XSLT solution is an elegant way to display them all. The example assumes that most errors are going to be simple and require just one error message. The code separates the node that would normally contain the <Errors> element from the rest of the document. If this element really is an error, the nodeName property will contain Errors. Otherwise, this is a good result and the code will process it as normal.

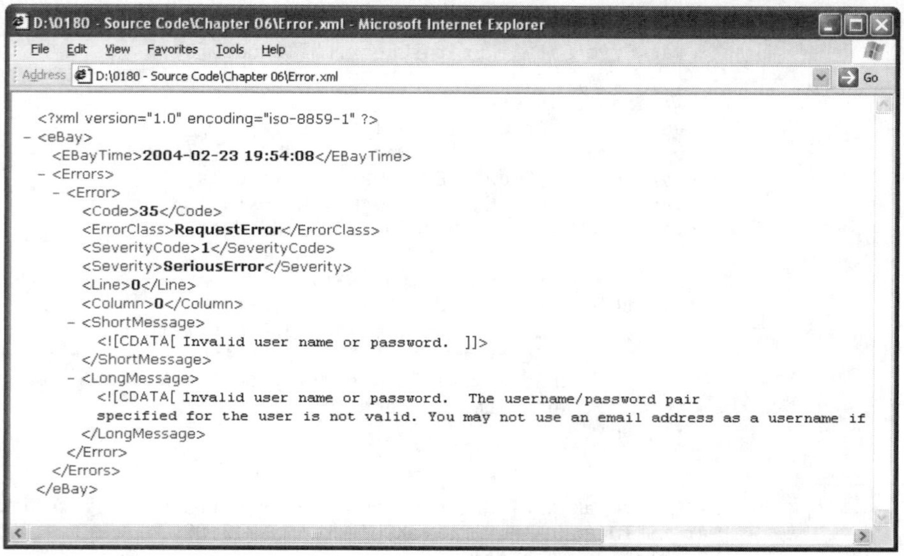

FIGURE 6.1:

An XML response containing an error message regarding the username.

Processing the error data means removing at least the first <Error> node and obtaining the content of various siblings. The code performs this task next—placing the text for each sibling into an error string. It then combines these strings to display an error message such as the one shown in Figure 6.2.

Once the code knows that the eBay Web Services response contains good data, it loads the XSLT file as another XML document. Remember that you can use any XSLT document capable of processing the data to provide different reports. The data is the same, just the XSLT file changes. The final step is to process the eBay Web Services response through the XSLT file using the `ProcDoc.transformNode()` method. The code writes the resulting Web page to the screen.

FIGURE 6.2:

An error message displayed as a message box, rather than a Web page.

Modifying the Basic Technique to Perform Authentication

At some point, everyone who works with eBay Web Services will need to obtain an authentication token for users, rather than ask for a username and password. As discussed in the "Getting a User Token" section of Chapter 5, this is actually a two step process. First, you must register your application using a unique name. Second, the user must log into eBay using this unique name and agree to allow your application to perform specific management tasks. The following sections show coding techniques you can use to perform these tasks with JavaScript. The use of JavaScript ensures that just about anyone can perform the required authentication, even if they don't own a high-end server—any connection to the Internet will do.

Registering the Application

The first step of the authentication process is to register your application with eBay. The important issue here is that you must provide a unique identifier. In addition, you can only register each identifier one time. A success message the first time is all you need—subsequent add requests, even those with good data, will fail because the application is already registered. (You can request an update from eBay, which will succeed so long as the application is already registered.) Listing 6.3 shows the first part of this process—creating a unique name to ensure your request will succeed. You'll find the complete source for this example in the \Chapter 06\ RegisterApplication folder of the source code located on the Sybex Web site.

Listing 6.3 **Creating a Unique Application Name**

```
function GetData()
{
    // Create the request.
    var Req = new ActiveXObject("Msxml2.ServerXMLHTTP.4.0");
    Req.open("POST", "https://api.sandbox.ebay.com/ws/api.dll", false);

    // Define the header information for the request. These headers
    // appear in the same order recommended by the documentation at
    // http://developer.ebay.com/DevZone/docs/API_Doc/index.asp.
    Req.setRequestHeader("X-EBAY-API-SESSION-CERTIFICATE",
                         SubmissionForm.DevIDStr.value + ";" +
                         SubmissionForm.AppIDStr.value + ";" +
                         SubmissionForm.CertIDStr.value);
    ... Other Headers ...
    Req.setRequestHeader("X-EBAY-API-CALL-NAME", "GetRuName");

    // Create the XML request object.
    var XMLData = new ActiveXObject("Msxml2.DOMDocument.4.0");

    // Add the XML request header.
    var ProcInst =
        XMLData.createProcessingInstruction(
            "xml", "version=\"1.0\"  encoding=\"iso-8859-1\"");
    XMLData.appendChild(ProcInst);

    // Construct the XML request message.
    ... All the Usual Entries ...

    // Add the request data.
    Elem = XMLData.createElement("DetailLevel");
    Elem.text = "0";
    Root.appendChild(Elem);
    Elem = XMLData.createElement("ErrorLevel");
    Elem.text = "1";
    Root.appendChild(Elem);
    Elem = XMLData.createElement("SiteId");
    Elem.text = "0";
    Root.appendChild(Elem);
    Elem = XMLData.createElement("Verb");
    Elem.text = "GetRuName";
    Root.appendChild(Elem);

    // Add the request data to the XML request.
    XMLData.appendChild(Root);

    // Send the request.
    Req.send(XMLData);
```

```
// Write the data to screen.
if (Req.status == 200)
{

    // Create a parse string.
    var ParseStr = Req.responseText;

    // Locate the RuName tag.
    var Posit1 = ParseStr.indexOf("<RuName>");
    Posit1 = Posit1 + 8;
    var Posit2 = ParseStr.indexOf("</RuName>", Posit1);
    ParseStr = ParseStr.substring(Posit1, Posit2);

    // Create a new URL string.
    var NewPath = location.href;
    Posit1 = NewPath.lastIndexOf("/");
    NewPath = NewPath.substring(0, Posit1) + "/EndReg.htm?"
            + "UserID=" + SubmissionForm.UserIDStr.value
            + "&Password=" + SubmissionForm.PasswordStr.value
            + "&DevID=" + SubmissionForm.DevIDStr.value
            + "&AppID=" + SubmissionForm.AppIDStr.value
            + "&CertID=" + SubmissionForm.CertIDStr.value
            + "&RuName=" + ParseStr;

    // Go to the new URL.
    window.navigate(NewPath);
}
else
    alert("Request Failed!");
}
```

The code begins by creating all of the usual headers and the XML document for the request. Notice that both the X-EBAY-API-CALL-NAME and the <Verb> element reference the GetRuName() call. In this case, you don't have to supply any special data, just the usual information that eBay always requires.

The response from eBay contains all of the usual information, plus an <RuName> element. This element contains a name that is partly based on your developer identification and partly random so the resulting name is almost guaranteed to be unique. Although I've never had a name repeated, there's a chance you could receive the same name type. However, the probability is so small that you can probably forget this issue. (If a name does repeat, eBay Web Services displays an error message—simply try the call again.)

The code separates the value from the <RuName> element. In previous examples, you saw that you could treat the XML as a document and parse through the nodes, or you could hand it off to an XSLT document for processing. This code shows a third technique—using string parsing methods to locate a specific value.

Once the code has the value separated (parsed), it builds a GET request for the next page to pass the information to it. The code uses the `window.navigate()` method to transfer control to the next page. You don't have to use anything this fancy to get the job done, but it does save you from having to type the same information on the next page.

The next page uses the `SetReturnUrl()` call to actually register the application with eBay. This call works much like the others in the chapter, so the code in Listing 6.4 concentrates on the unique areas of the call. You'll want to review the full source code to see all of the changes. The source code also shows how I accept the input arguments and place them into the text boxes on screen.

Listing 6.4   **Setting the URL Request Entries**

```
// Add the request data.
Elem = XMLData.createElement("DetailLevel");
Elem.text = "0";
Root.appendChild(Elem);
Elem = XMLData.createElement("ErrorLevel");
Elem.text = "1";
Root.appendChild(Elem);
Elem = XMLData.createElement("SiteId");
Elem.text = "0";
Root.appendChild(Elem);
Elem = XMLData.createElement("Verb");
Elem.text = "SetReturnUrl";
Root.appendChild(Elem);
Elem = XMLData.createElement("Action");
Elem.text = "Add";
Root.appendChild(Elem);
Elem = XMLData.createElement("RuName");
Elem.text = SubmissionForm.RuNameStr.value;
Root.appendChild(Elem);
Elem = XMLData.createElement("AcceptURL");
Elem.text = SubmissionForm.SuccessPgStr.value;
Root.appendChild(Elem);
Elem = XMLData.createElement("RejectURL");
Elem.text = SubmissionForm.UnsuccessPgStr.value;
Root.appendChild(Elem);

// Add the request data to the XML request.
XMLData.appendChild(Root);

// Send the request.
Req.send(XMLData);

// Write the data to screen.
if (Req.status == 200)
{

    // Create a parse string.
```

```
        var ParseStr = Req.responseText;

        // Locate the RuName tag.
        var Posit1 = ParseStr.indexOf("<Status>");
        Posit1 = Posit1 + 8;
        var Posit2 = ParseStr.indexOf("</Status>", Posit1);
        ParseStr = ParseStr.substring(Posit1, Posit2);

        // Output the response.
        SubmissionForm.ResultStr.value = ParseStr;
    }
    else
        alert("Request Failed!");
```

As you can see, the SetReturnUrl() call requires several important pieces of information. The <Action> element defines the kind of change that eBay makes. Notice that it uses the Add keyword in this case. You can also Update and Delete applications. The <Action> element is especially important because you must use the correct action to obtain a successful request. Trying to add an application more than once will always fail unless you delete the application between tries. You register an application only once, but you can update it as often as needed. Read more about the <Action> element at http://developer.ebay.com/ DevZone/docs/API_Doc/Functions/SetReturnURL/SetReturnURLLogic.htm#Actions.

The <RuName> element must be unique. eBay doesn't require you generate this name as shown in Listing 6.3—you can use any technique that provides a unique <RuName> element value. However, using the GetRuName() call does tend to reduce potential problems.

The <AcceptURL> and <RejectURL> elements contain the URLs for a login that succeeds and fails respectively. The example uses separate URLs for each login result, but you could just as easily use a single page for the task. All eBay needs to know is where to send the results.

Once the code receives all the required input, it sends the request to eBay as normal. The code checks the return status and uses the string parsing technique to learn the value of the <Status> element. This element contains a value of Success when the call succeeds. However, don't assume that a failure means that your code is wrong—check issues such as the value of the <Action> element first to ensure you've used the correct value for the situation.

Authenticating the User

After you register your application, you need a way to use that registration to authenticate the user. The "Authenticating the User" section of Chapter 5 describes what the user will see. Listing 6.5 shows the first part of this process—creating a special URL that you can use to direct the user's request. You'll find the complete source for this example in the \Chapter 06\ GetUserAuth folder of the source code located on the Sybex Web site.

Listing 6.5 **Defining the Sign-in URL**

```
function GetData()
{
   // Create the URL.
   var NewPath =
      "https://scgi.sandbox.ebay.com/aw-cgi/eBayISAPI.dll?signin" +
      "&runame=" + RuNameStr.value;

   // Go to the new URL.
   window.navigate(NewPath);
}
```

The code comes down to a matter of building a custom URL. The sign-in URL always remains the same. To the sign-in URL, you must add an runame argument and the unique name of your registered application. If you're creating a page for a single application, you don't even need to use a script—just create the URL as part of an anchor tag.

This example doesn't show an extra feature you can add, the ruparam argument. eBay passes this argument without change to your results page. You can use this argument for a number of purposes. For example, you might allow users to authenticate from a number of locations, so the ruparam argument could indicate the initial sign-in location. You can even add multiple arguments to ruparam by separating them with ampersands. Make sure you escape the ampersand as discussed in the "Sending Special Characters Using URL Encoding" section of Chapter 4. The API Technical Documentation explains this feature in more detail at http://developer.ebay.com/DevZone/docs/API_Doc/Developing/AuthAndAuth.htm.

After the user authenticates, eBay will redirect them back to your site. That means having at least one Web page that can process the results. Listing 6.6 shows a simple example of accessing the data that eBay returns. What you'll see are two parameters. The first contains the user's authentication token, while the second contains the expiration date of that token. Even if you use screen-scraping techniques to work with the information, you need some way to gain access to it and this script provides one of the better ways to accomplish the task.

Listing 6.6 **Parsing the Sign-in Results**

```
function window_onload()
{
   var IndParm = "";
   var Parm = "";
   var Value = "";

   // Get the variables passed to the page.
   var ParmArray =
      location.search.substr(1, location.search.length).split("&");
```

```
// Parse each of these variables in turn.
for (Counter = 0; Counter < ParmArray.length; Counter++)
{
    // Split the parameter from the value.
    IndParm = ParmArray[Counter].split("=");

    // Place the parameter and the value in separate variables.
    Parm = IndParm[0];
    Value = IndParm[1];

    // Replace any escaped characters in the value.
    Value = decodeURIComponent(Value);

    // Display the results on screen.
    ResultStr.value = ResultStr.value +
                      "Parm=" + Parm + " Value=" + Value + "\r\n";
}
}
```

The code begins by using the split() method to divide all of the arguments into separate array elements. What you end up with is an array of strings that contain information like ParameterNameA=ValueA.

Once the code has an array of arguments, it can split the parameter from the value using a loop. The for loop uses the split() method again to divide the resulting arguments into parameter and value pairs.

Notice the special code used to decode Value. The decodeURIComponent() function removes any escaped characters from the string. For example, eBay must replace the / (slash) with %2B to transfer the data to your system. You must use the unescaped form of the value or eBay won't accept the authentication token even if it's valid.

> **WARNING**

Don't use the authentication token that appears as part of the URL in the Address field of your browser as input to eBay. This form of the authentication token contains escape characters and will cause your application to fail. Use only the authentication token that appears in the Results field of the sample as input.

In this case, all of the data ends up in a single textbox. However, you could easily add a switch statement to detect the individual parameters and place them into hidden controls for screen scraping. (Screen scraping is a technique where an application retrieves the data on a Web page and leaves the tags that format the data behind.) The EndReg.HTM file contains code that demonstrates this technique.

Performing a Category Search

One of the more important considerations for buyers is finding what they need quickly. The search pages that eBay provides work well for many (if not most) needs, but the interface isn't necessarily optimal for certain user needs. A custom search page can help the user perform a detailed search without getting lost in options they don't need. For example, you can create a category search that concentrates on a specific class of item and also filters out items that you would never be interested in buying. The following sections present a few unique search ideas that you could use to create a specific presentation of eBay items.

Developing the Basic Category Search

You've seen the list of categories on the left side of some eBay site pages, most notably the home page. Click a link and you often drill down to the next level of categories. Click another link and you can go further. Adding search terms helps define the search as well, but often, all the clicking ends up with nothing worthwhile or too many results for the average human to process. The example in this section shows how you can overcome that problem by creating your own category search—one that specifically meets your search requirements. Listing 6.7 shows the essential code for this example. You'll find the complete source for this example in the \Chapter 06\CategorySearch folder of the source code located on the Sybex Web site.

Listing 6.7   **Performing a Category Search**

```
// Add the user information.
var Elem = XMLData.createElement("RequestToken");
Elem.text = SubmissionForm.AuthTokenStr.value;
Root.appendChild(Elem);

// Add the request data.
Elem = XMLData.createElement("DetailLevel");
Elem.text = "0";
Root.appendChild(Elem);
Elem = XMLData.createElement("ErrorLevel");
Elem.text = "1";
Root.appendChild(Elem);
Elem = XMLData.createElement("CategoryId");
Elem.text = SubmissionForm.CatStr.value;
Root.appendChild(Elem);
Elem = XMLData.createElement("SiteId");
Elem.text = "0";
Root.appendChild(Elem);
Elem = XMLData.createElement("Verb");
Elem.text = "GetCategoryListings";
Root.appendChild(Elem);
```

```
// Process the Optional Request Items.
if (SubmissionForm.ReturnStr.value.length > 0)
{
   Elem = XMLData.createElement("ItemsPerPage");
   Elem.text = SubmissionForm.ReturnStr.value;
   Root.appendChild(Elem);
}
if (SubmissionForm.PageStr.value.length > 0)
{
   Elem = XMLData.createElement("PageNumber");
   Elem.text = SubmissionForm.PageStr.value;
   Root.appendChild(Elem);
}
if (SubmissionForm.OrderStr.value.length > 0)
{
   Elem = XMLData.createElement("OrderBy");
   Elem.text = SubmissionForm.OrderStr.value;
   Root.appendChild(Elem);
}
if (SubmissionForm.RegionStr.value.length > 0)
{
   Elem = XMLData.createElement("RegionId");
   Elem.text = SubmissionForm.RegionStr.value;
   Root.appendChild(Elem);
}
```

Most of the required arguments for this call act as they do for every other call that you'll make. Of special importance for this example is the use of the <RequestToken> element, which replaces the <RequestUserId> and <RequestPassword> elements. Make sure you have a good token to use—one that isn't expired. In addition, check the token for escaped characters. The token that eBay passes to your application after a user login includes these characters, which can cause your application to fail.

This is one of the calls where the <DetailLevel> element is especially important. Instead of controlling the quantity of information, it controls the type of information you receive. A value of 0 returns all of the items, while a value of 1 will return just featured items. The range isn't continuous because the next value is 3, which returns the super featured items.

You must provide a valid category number, the <CategoryId> element, for this call. The category table at http://developer.ebay.com/DevZone/docs/API_Doc/Functions/Tables/ CategoryTable.htm provides a list of current category numbers. Figure 6.3 shows a typical list of categories for the United States. As you can see, the category numbers appear in parentheses to the right of the category name. All you need is the number. For example, if you wanted to use Cell Phones & Plans as the category, you should add 15032 to the <CategoryId> element.

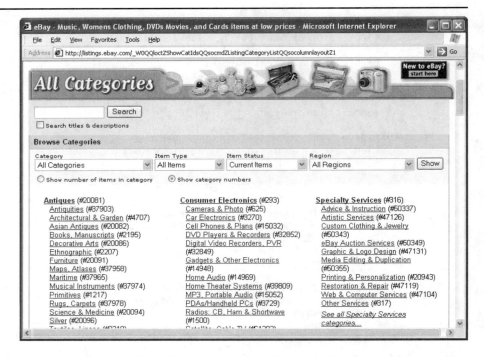

This application includes four optional entries. The code verifies that the user has actually entered a value for the optional entry, which is an important check because you don't want to send a blank entry to eBay. (Blank entries tend to result in errors.) The `<ItemsPerPage>` element controls the number of entries the user sees per page. The only legal values for this entry are 50, 100, 150, or 200. Any other value normally results in an ambiguous 8003 error.

> ▶ **WARNING**
>
> Some of the API calls have certification restrictions that you must follow to get your application certified. One of the restrictions for the `GetCategoryListings()` call is that you can't issue the call for a single category more than once every 30 minutes. Any application you submit for certification must include code that prevents more than one request. You can call other categories within that time frame. This and other call specific restrictions appear at `http://developer.ebay.com/DevZone/docs/API_Doc/Certification/CertificationRequirements.htm`.

The <PageNumber> element defines the number of the page you want to return. You can calculate the number of pages in a result set by dividing the total number of results by the items displayed per page. The only problem is that you have to call eBay Web Services at least once to obtain the total number of items from the <GrandTotal> element. You won't receive an error when the <PageNumber> element value is too high—eBay Web Services returns the first page of results, in most cases, instead.

Some developers will almost certainly confuse the <OrderBy> element with a method of sorting. This entry is actually a filter. When you set this value to 1, eBay Web Services returns only those items that were listed within the last 24 hours.

You might also want to provide a region identifier for your call. This filter ensures you get listings from a specific area. For example, you might want listings from Massachusetts, in which case you'd use the Boston filter. (You get listings from the entire region—not from a particular city.) A list of regions appears at http://developer.ebay.com/DevZone/docs/API_Doc/Functions/Tables/RegionTables.htm.

Augmenting the Category Search with XSLT

The category search example includes the idea of using XSLT to present different views of the data. In this case, the example presents two views. After the user makes the first call, it's easy to switch between views without making another call. The data looks different, but it all comes from the same source. The idea is to present the information that eBay Web Services provides in a number of ways, rather than force the user to use a particular view. Listing 6.8 presents a simple function you can use to make the transition. You'll find the complete source for this example in the \Chapter 06\CategorySearch folder of the source code located on the Sybex Web site.

Listing 6.8   **Transitioning between XSLT Views**

```
function ChangeData(XSLDoc)
{
    // Check for data in the data store.
    if (SubmissionForm.DataStore.value.length > 0)
    {
        // Load the XML document from the hidden variable.
        var ProcDoc = new ActiveXObject("Msxml2.DOMDocument.4.0");
        ProcDoc.async = false;
        ProcDoc.loadXML(SubmissionForm.DataStore.value);

        // Create an XSLT document and load the transform into it.
        var XSLTData = new ActiveXObject("Msxml2.DOMDocument.4.0");
        XSLTData.async = false;
        XSLTData.load(XSLDoc);
```

```
        // Display the output on screen.
        document.write(ProcDoc.transformNode(XSLTData));
    }
    else
        alert("Please Submit the Data First");
}
```

This function accepts the name of an XSLT file as input. You can provide any XSLT file that includes instructions for handling the output from the GetCategoryListings() call. The secret to this particular function is the use of a hidden field on the original form. The GetData() function discussed in Listing 6.7 saves the data from the initial call in this hidden field.

The process of transforming the document is relatively simple. In this case, the code creates an XML document containing the original results and loads the XSLT file from disk. The ProcDoc.transformNode() function performs the actual translation and the document.write() function displays the information on screen.

The XSLT files include a function to return the user to the main page. The user could also click the Back button on their browser if desired. In either case, a series of buttons at the bottom of the main page controls the display the user sees:

Submit button The application submits a new request to eBay Web Services.

Show Items button The application shows the items returned as the result of the GetCategoryListings() call.

Show Categories button The application shows a list of categories associated with the current category, along with the number of items in each subcategory.

Your Call to Action

The main goal of this chapter is to get you started with browser-based applications. When you reach this point of the chapter, you should know how to perform two essential tasks: make a request and authenticate a user. As long as you know how to perform these two essential tasks, you can extend what you know to other areas of eBay. Web services are technically specialized applications that communicate with remote servers using a request and response strategy.

The chapter does show more than the two basic tasks. What you need to do now is check the list of functions that eBay provides to perform specific tasks at http://developer.ebay .com/DevZone/docs/API_Doc/Functions/FunctionsOverview.htm. Every function in this list is a request and response pair. The documentation tells you what you have to provide as part of the request and what eBay will provide in response. Spend time looking at this list of functions as you develop ideas using the examples in this chapter and the other chapters of the book.

You can do a lot with JavaScript. In fact, it's possible to build fairly complex applications using this technique. However, JavaScript isn't the best approach to use when you want to analyze the data or create stunning reports on your eBay auctions. Those tasks are best performed by Microsoft Office (or another product like it). Chapter 7 shows how to perform these tasks using Visual Basic for Applications (VBA). Even though this chapter does use Microsoft Office for demonstration purposes, you'll be surprised at the number of applications that rely on VBA for macro capability. Chapter 7 shows that you can make eBay very friendly by using the correct desktop application effectively.

Chapter 7

Considering the Benefits of Using VBA

Getting Resources to Learn VBA

▶ Writing Applications Using VBA

Understanding How to Script Web Services

Writing Applications with Microsoft Excel

Writing Applications with Microsoft Access

Many people associate Visual Basic for Applications (VBA) with Microsoft Office. While it's true that Microsoft Office does rely on VBA as a development language, you'll find VBA used with other applications too (see the list at http://msdn.microsoft.com/vba/companies/company.asp). Therefore, even though the examples in this chapter do rely on Microsoft products, you can use the information with any product that supports VBA.

This chapter explores methods of coupling eBay Web Services to an application with VBA capability. You can use eBay Web Services to meet a number of needs. For example, you can write an application that draws current sales information for an item that you're auctioning using eBay Web Services and then uses Excel to chart the progress of that product. Likewise, you can obtain information from eBay Web Services to create a report in Word. You might use such a report to help management understand the current resources available on a particular subject—perhaps a new area the company plans to target for business.

Unfortunately, one chapter can't do everything that you normally find in a whole book. You won't learn how to use VBA in this chapter, and I'm assuming you also know how to use the application in question. The chapter doesn't leave you completely in the dark, however. The "Resources for Learning VBA" section contains information on where you can learn more about VBA. Knowing how to use VBA is a prerequisite for this chapter.

Understanding the Benefits of Using VBA

Most of the examples you'll see for eBay Web Services outside this book probably focus on Web technologies. Developers use eBay Web Services to create connections to their Web site (to make sales) or their Pocket PC (to perform quick searches or auction updates). However, VBA lets you view eBay Web Services from an entirely different perspective. Instead of looking for the next sale or generating some type of search result, using VBA with your application lets you concentrate on data—it helps you decide how to use the data that eBay provides for your own needs.

It's possible to create the kind of links described in the previous paragraph using full-fledged programming environments such as Visual Studio. You can also create a great Web environment that mimics some of these features using languages such as PHP Hypertext Processor (PHP). However, the point is that VBA works in concert with the host application. You don't have to write a lot of the code that you normally need to write because the host application provides the required functionality for you. In fact, if you choose the right host application, writing an eBay Web Services interface can become mind-numbingly simple. Just a few lines of code will help you perform tasks in seconds, rather than hours.

So, why not write every application in VBA? To say that VBA is a cure-all for every problem is incorrect. VBA answers a specific range of needs, but doesn't handle every need. In fact, the needs that VBA answers are somewhat specialized. This chapter helps you understand some of the applications where VBA can save you considerable time and expense. It also demonstrates that you can achieve truly amazing results with just a modicum of programming. The important point is to match VBA and the host application to a particular eBay Web Services application need.

Resources for Learning VBA

This chapter won't teach you how to use VBA. I'm assuming that you already know enough about VBA to create your own simple applications. If you don't already have this knowledge, you can get it from a number of sources. The first place to look is my book, *VBA for Dummies*, Fourth Edition (Wiley, 2003). This book introduces you to VBA and takes you through examples using all of the major Microsoft Office applications.

You'll also want to look at some of the resources that Microsoft provides. For example, you'll find the various Microsoft Office Resource Kits at: `http://www.microsoft.com/office/ork/home.htm`, `http://www.microsoft.com/office/ork/xp/default.htm`, or `http://www.microsoft.com/office/ork/2003/default.htm`. Make sure you check out the Office Developer's Center at `http://msdn.microsoft.com/office/`.

The Microsoft Office site includes some interesting tools at `http://www.microsoft.com/office/ork/2000/appndx/toolbox.htm`. Office 2003 users can find similar information on their product at `http://www.microsoft.com/office/ork/2003/tools/default.htm`.

It's amazing to see how many third party sources you can find online for VBA. Many sites have free code, specialized examples, chat forums, tutorials, or other offerings that make your VBA experience better. For example, you can download a VBA tutorial at `http://freedownloadswindows.com/windows/Visual-Basic/656996/L-Basic.html` (L-Basic isn't a new form of Basic—it's a tutorial about Visual Basic in general and very good for learning VBA—you download the program, install it, and run it on your desktop). Online Excel VBA tutorials appear at `http://lacher.com/toc/tutvba1.htm` and `http://lacher.com/toc/tutvba2.htm`.

Don't forget to visit newsgroups with your VBA questions. Microsoft sponsors VBA newsgroups at `microsoft.public.office.developer.vba`, `microsoft.public.excel.programming`, `microsoft.public.frontpage.programming.vba`, `microsoft.public.office.developer.outlook.vba`, `microsoft.public.outlook.program_vba`, `microsoft.public.project.vba`, `microsoft.public.visio.developer.vba`, and a series of Word newsgroups beginning with `microsoft.public.word.vba`.

Understanding Scripting of Web Services

In many respects, VBA is a scripting or macro language, rather than a full development language such as Visual Basic or C#. The host application interprets the VBA code when you run the macro based on an event such as selecting a menu entry, clicking a button, or opening a file. Consequently, the host application performs every task in real time—you can't decide much in advance. Although VBA is far more powerful than Web scripting languages such as JavaScript, it still has some of the benefits and problems of any scripting language. The following sections discuss how VBA scripting can affect your application and one technique for circumventing scripting issues.

An Alternative to VBA

One issue to consider before you invest a lot of time in VBA is whether you need VBA at all. Most Office 2003 applications and many third party applications can work with XML data directly. You can even format that data using XSLT. Consequently, you could download the information you need using any of the browser techniques discussed in Chapters 2, 4, and 6. Simply save the resulting XML file to disk and you have the raw information you need to perform an analysis, develop a report, or create a chart.

You still need to call the XSLT file in some way. When working with the browser examples, you indicated which XSLT file to use as part of a script. This technique works fine when you have a script to use, but the most basic technique for working with desktop applications doesn't allow this technique. However, you can add a special processing instruction to your downloaded raw file to ensure the desktop application knows how to format the information. Listing 7.1 shows a typical example of this addition. You'll find the complete source for this example in the `\Chapter 07\SimpleInput` folder of the source code located on the Sybex Web site.

Listing 7.1   XML Referral Example

```
<?xml version="1.0" encoding="iso-8859-1"?>
<?xml-stylesheet type="text/xsl" href="SimpleInput.XSL"?>
<eBay>
    <eBayTime>2004-02-23 11:37:27</eBayTime>
    <Search>
        <Items>
            <Item>
... Additional Input ...
```

The listing isn't very long, but the actual file contains all of the entries you'd normally find in a response from eBay Web Services to a GetSearchResults() call. However, it does contain two essential entries that work with the XSLT file. First, notice that this file contains the XSLT reference that the XML from eBay Web Services doesn't contain in the form of an XML stylesheet processing instruction. You must include this glue between the input file and the XSLT file. Second, notice that the root node is <eBay>. The XSLT file looks for this same element.

You have everything needed to get formatted data from eBay using a simple XML/XSLT file pair. You can open the SimpleInput.XML file directly using many of the desktop applications that support XML. However, this combination is more suited to use within Word or another presentation application, rather than Excel, which is an analysis application.

When you open the file, you may see a Convert File dialog box. Make sure you select the XML Document option (Word should highlight it automatically) and click OK. When the document opens, you'll see the SimpleInput.XML file, which might be a little disappointing. However, look at the XML Document pane shown on the right side of Figure 7.1 and you'll notice that you can select Default.XSL (select Browse to load the file). Once you select this option, you'll notice that the Word view changes to the same structured presentation used for XML and HTML documents. When you combine this display with the proper stylesheet, you can create reports directly from Word without relying on any VBA code.

As with many alternatives, this one has problems. First, you might have noticed that I hard coded the Web service query into the XSLT file, making each XSLT file good for only one request. Unfortunately, you probably won't find a way around this problem, which means that you have to use this technique carefully. Second, this solution means that the data often appears in your browser, rather than as part of the application display. Even when it does appear as part of the application display, the data is still HTML, not your document's native format. (You can correct this second problem using specially constructed XSLT files.) Consequently, while this technique does work well, it has limitations that make it unsuitable for some needs.

FIGURE 7.1:
Word 2003 can
also interpret XML
files for you.

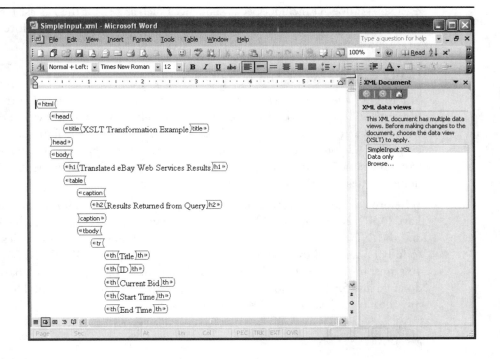

Using the eBay API Test Tool to Authenticate a User

The "Getting a User Token" section of Chapter 5 discusses a technique for authenticating a user with a series of Web pages. You can find the code for performing this task in the "Modifying the Basic Technique to Perform Authentication" section of Chapter 6. However, it's not always convenient for a developer to authenticate a test user with these techniques. Fortunately, you have an alternative available in the eBay API Test Tool. A special call named GetToken() lets you authenticate a user for testing purposes only. To use this call, you must rely on the special authentication keys discussed on the Getting Started with eBay Authentication and Authorization page at `http://developer.ebay.com/DevZone/get-started/authauth.asp`.

To use this technique, open the eBay API Test Tool at `http://developer.ebay.com/DevZone/build-test/test-tool.asp`. Select Sandbox mode. Input the authentication keys and provide your test user's name and password. Select GetToken as the request template and click Submit. You'll receive a message containing the token as a response. This is a short-term token that lasts either 10 minutes or 2 hours depending on which set of authentication keys you use. Unlike the real user token created in Chapters 5 and 6, this token isn't escaped—it doesn't include special sequences such as %2F for the / (slash) or %2B for the + (plus sign), so you don't need to worry about any special conversion before using the authentication token.

Using the Microsoft and eBay Examples

You might have noticed when you installed the eBay Web Services Kit that there isn't an example of how to work with VBA. Unfortunately, unless you know where to look, you won't find a good VBA example online. Microsoft and eBay collaborated to create such an example, and you can download it at http://developer.ebay.com/DevZone/KB_SearchDocs/ MicrosoftSample.zip. In fact, you'll find three example folders in the Zip file, each of which demonstrates a particular aspect of working with eBay.

Before you go any further, these examples require some extraordinary resources. You must have Office 2003 (Office 2003 Professional if you want to work with the Access example) and the .NET Framework 1.1 installed on your system to use the examples at all. If you want to fully understand the example, you must install Office 2003 with .NET integration and you must install Visual Studio .NET 2003 on your system. If you don't have these resources, don't go any further because the sample application won't work at all. The following sections provide a brief description of these examples.

> ▶ NOTE
>
> You should also take time to read The Globe and Mail article about Office 2003 integration with eBay at http://www.globetechnology.com/servlet/story/RTGAM.20031204 .gtfldec4/BNStory/Technology/. This article describes how the sample application can post information from Excel to eBay as one or more new items. It's a good write-up of the sample applications in this section.

Performing the Configuration

The example won't work unless you configure it for use. Actually, you need to perform this configuration for any Visual Studio .NET application written for Microsoft Office. The .NET Framework applications require this configuration as a security precaution—to ensure add-ins have your permission to run. The process is relatively simple, but you must have administrative privileges. The following steps show you how to perform this task.

1. Use the Start ➤ Programs ➤ Administrative Tools ➤ Microsoft .NET Framework 1.1 Configuration command to open the .NET Configuration 1.1 console shown in Figure 7.2. You can also open this console using the Microsoft .NET Framework 1.1 Configuration icon in the Administrative Tools folder of the Control Panel.

FIGURE 7.2:

Use the .NET Configuration 1.1 utility to set up the eBay Lister DLL.

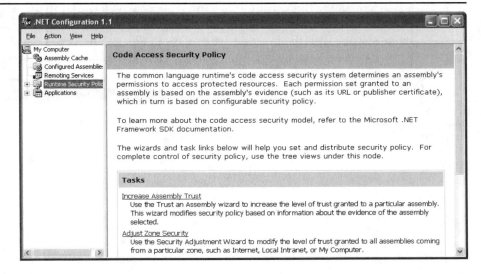

2. Select the Runtime Security Policy folder as shown in Figure 7.2. This folder contains the security settings for the assemblies, a Dynamic Link Library (DLL) in this case.

3. Click Increase Assembly Trust. You'll see a Trust an Assembly dialog box.

4. Select the Make Changes to This Computer option and click Next. The wizard will ask you which assembly you want to trust.

5. Locate the eBayLister.DLL file that is part of the example. You'll normally find this file in the \MicrosoftSample\eBayLister_bin\ folder of the example, but the location could vary. Click Next. The wizard will ask what level of security you want to assign to the assembly.

6. Set the slider for this assembly to Full Trust. Click Next. You'll see a Completing the Wizard dialog box similar to the one shown in Figure 7.3. Notice the settings in this dialog box.

7. Click Finish. The assembly is now ready for use at its current location. If you move the assembly, you must also reset the security.

Using the eBay Lister

This part of the program contains the actual Office document and is the one you should concentrate on if you're interested mainly in how a partnership between Office and eBay can exist. Open eBayLister.xls and you'll see an opening page named Settings with the same information requirements as every other example in the book. Depending on how you configure Office, you might also see a macro warning; you can dismiss it to use the application. You must provide your eBay keys, as well as a valid username and password. Once you enter information on the Settings page, you're ready to go. Simply click Verify to ensure the settings will work.

The remaining three items in this spreadsheet let you work with items on eBay without ever leaving the Excel environment. The pages are listed in the order that you'd normally use them, starting with the Inventory page show in Figure 7.4. As you can see, this page contains a list of items to sell on eBay. You can add, remove, or modify items as needed.

FIGURE 7.3:

Verify the security settings before you complete the wizard.

FIGURE 7.4:

The Inventory page contains the items that you want to sell on eBay.

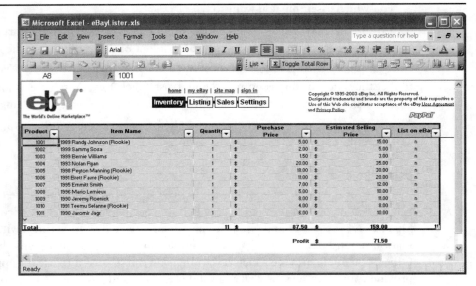

The most important column on the Inventory page is the List on eBay column. You must change this column to "y" (for yes) for every item you want to list.

The Listing page shown in Figure 7.5 comes next. You use this page to list new items and to check the status of current listings. This page doesn't tell you about sales, but it does keep track of your listings. The page even tells you the current high bid and the identity of the high bidder. You can also check on issues like the BuyItNow price and the number of days the auction has left to run.

FIGURE 7.5:

Keep track of your current listings using this page.

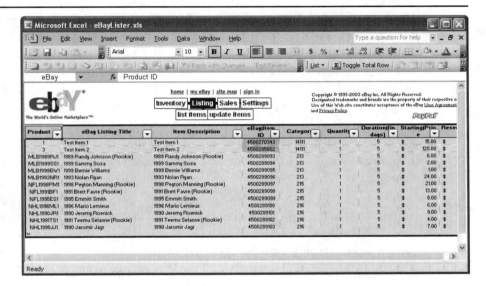

The final page is Sales. This page tells you which items have actually sold. In addition, it combines features of eBay Web Services with Excel to determine information such as the gross profit for the item and whether you have sent an invoice to the buyer.

Although this isn't the most complex example of working with eBay, the fact that it combines so many new technologies to produce this unique result makes it extremely interesting. This example shows how you can build an add-on for Excel using Visual Studio .NET that makes eBay access almost trivial. It's the type of example you'd want to study if you needed to build a simple application for a lot of users in a corporate setting.

Using the eBay Demo

This portion of the example is a Web service that you can access from within your Office application. In fact, it's not really limited to Office at all. Any language or development environment that supports Web services can also use this portion of the example. The wonderful part about using Web services is that they're not language dependent—you can use them with a number of languages. To use this application, you must set it up on a Web server that supports .NET. If you want to modify the application, you'll very likely need to change the project files to match your setup. The "Using the ASP.NET Applications in This Book" section of Chapter 11 tells you how to make this kind of modification.

After you place the files on your Web server, you need to make sure you've set it up as an application. To perform this task, right-click the folder in the Internet Information Services console (listed as Internet Services Manager in the Administrative Tools folder), and choose Properties from the context menu. You'll see an eBayDemo Properties dialog box. Select the Directory tab. Click Create (next to the Application Name field). Click OK and you'll notice that the folder icon has changed to an application icon.

To test the Web service, open a browser and select the eBayService.asmx file within the eBayDemo folder. After a few seconds, you'll see the eBayService window that contains the main Web service description page. This page contains two test links as shown in Figure 7.6.

Click the GetSellerList link and you'll see a test page. The page contains an actual test area if you use the Web service locally or a test entry if you use it remotely as shown in Figure 7.7. In both cases, this page also contains information about the SOAP request and response message formats.

When you click the Service Description link from the main Web service page shown in Figure 7.6, you'll see the Web Service Description Language (WSDL) file for the Web service. The application generates this page dynamically—it doesn't actually exist on disk. Figure 7.8 shows a typical example of the WSDL file for this Web service. Generally, you'll access this page when you want to add the Web service to an application.

In most cases, all you need is the link shown in Figure 7.6 to create the connection in your application. However, you might need to save the WSDL locally to ensure your application will create the connection. Try the link first because it's the best way to create a Web services connection.

FIGURE 7.6:
The main Web service description page contains two test links.

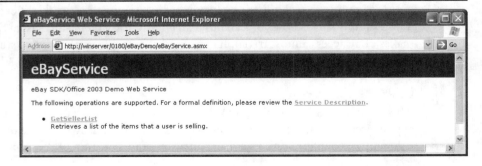

FIGURE 7.7:
The GetSellerList
test page contains
information about
the SOAP message
structures.

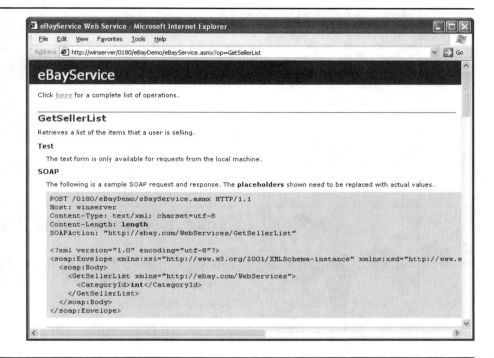

FIGURE 7.8:
Use the WSDL file to
add the Web service
to your application.

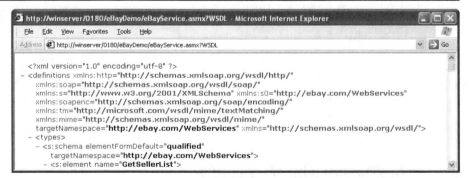

Using the Code Comment Report

This portion of the example consists of a number of Web pages. The name of the folder doesn't really tell you very much about the purpose of the Web pages. In fact, it's downright misleading. You can copy this portion of the example to a Web server. It's a help file that describes the various DLLs provided with the example. The help files are divided into two areas—one for the eBayLister application and a second for the eBayService Web service.

The main page for this portion of the example is Solution_eBayDemo.HTM. It contains two links, eBayLister and eBayService. Select one of the two entries and you'll see detailed description of the DLLs for that entry as shown in Figure 7.9. The left side of the display contains a selection of classes, while the right side of the display contains a detailed listing of the contents of the selected class.

Once you find an interesting method or property, you can click its link to see detailed information. Using this technique lets you drill down to the information you need to use the DLLs in the example. Unfortunately, the help files don't tell you much about the example itself. Consequently, if you run into questions about why a security message pops up or how to configure the application for use, you really don't have any resources except what you can figure out on your own.

FIGURE 7.9:
The help file uses a succession of links to let you drill down to the information you need.

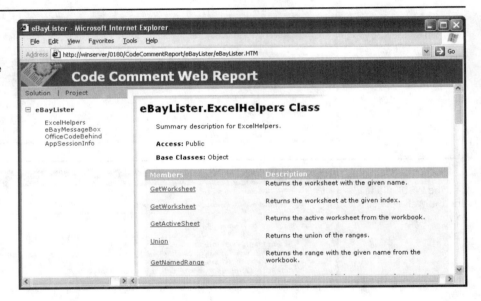

Developing with Microsoft Excel

Microsoft Excel provides a number of interesting features that can help you manipulate the data you receive from eBay Web Services. Sometimes you have to gather this data over time. For example, you might collect the current bid for an item every hour during the auction to chart the times of highest activity. After some time, you can chart the information for several auctions to see the general direction of sales for your product—at least on eBay.

> ▶ **TIP**
>
> Some types of statistical analysis for eBay Web Services are very time sensitive. Consequently, you'll want to use something like Task Scheduler to ensure the system gathers the data at the specified interval. You can perform this task in a number of ways, including relying on the automatic document execution feature of Excel. Simply opening the document ensures the macro runs.

The following sections demonstrate some ways to use Microsoft Excel with eBay Web Services. It's important to remember that these sections are just examples—you can use eBay Web Services in other ways. All you really need is an idea of how the data you can obtain from eBay works into your company's use of the Web site. For an in-depth treatment of the topic, see *Mastering Excel 2003 Programming with VBA* by Steven M. Hansen (Sybex, 2004).

Developing an Application with the SDK

By far, the easiest method to develop a VBA application for eBay is using the SDK technique. When using this technique, you simply create objects as you might for any other kind of development. These objects tend to hide the complexities of online communication and make the development process much faster. However, before you can use the SDK technique, you need to add some references to the VBA environment to allow access to the eBay Web Services SDK. Use the Tools ➢ References command to display the References dialog box shown in Figure 7.10. Notice that there are four eBay libraries to choose from, but that you only need three of them unless you're also adding database support to your application. The `eBay_SDK_Integration` library provides built-in database support for your Database Management System (DBMS).

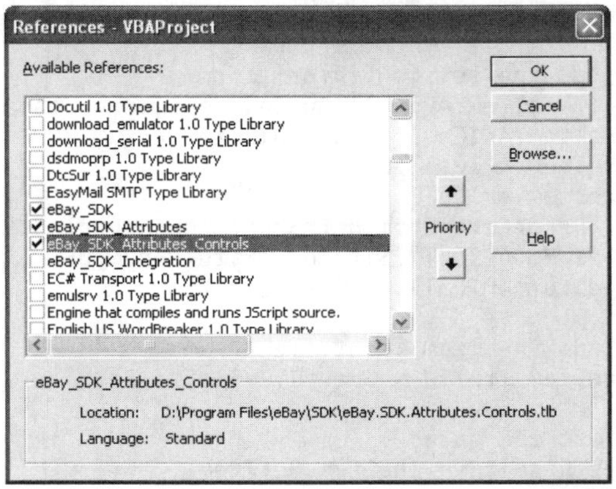

FIGURE 7.10:

Add eBay support using the References dialog box.

The example in this section gets item information based on its identifier. You can find the identifier in the upper right corner of the eBay item display or within the <Id> element of any call that returns item information, such as a GetSearchResults() call. Listing 7.2 demonstrates one technique for using the GetItem() call. You'll find the complete source for this example in the \Chapter 07\Excel\SDK folder of the source code located on the Sybex Web site.

Listing 7.2   **Getting a Specific Item Using the SDK Technique**

```
Public Sub Contact_eBay()
    ... Variable Declarations ...

    ' Handle errors inline.
    On Error Resume Next

    ' Create the session.
    Set Session = New ApiSession

    ' Add the user authentication token.
    Set AuthToken = New ApiToken
    AuthToken.Token = Sheet1.Cells(3, 2)
    AuthToken.ExpirationDate = Sheet1.Cells(4, 2)
    AuthToken.RuName = Sheet1.Cells(8, 2)
    Set Session.Token = AuthToken

    ' Add the developer keys.
    Session.Developer = Sheet1.Cells(5, 2)
    Session.Application = Sheet1.Cells(6, 2)
    Session.Certificate = Sheet1.Cells(7, 2)

    ' Add the sandbox URL.
    Session.URL = "https://api.sandbox.ebay.com/ws/api.dll"

    ' Create a new item call.
    Set TheItem = New GetItemCall

    ' Add the session information.
    Set TheItem.APICall.ApiCallSession = Session
    TheItem.APICall.CompatibilityLevel = 323
    TheItem.APICall.DetailLevel = 14
    TheItem.APICall.ErrorLevel = _
        ErrorLevelEnum_BothShortAndLongErrorStrings
    TheItem.APICall.SiteId = SiteIdEnum_US
    TheItem.APICall.Verb = "GetItem"

    ' Add the Item identifier.
    TheItem.ItemId = Sheet1.Cells(9, 2)

    ' Get the data.
    Set Results = TheItem.GetItem
```

```
' Check for errors.
If Results Is Nothing Then

    ' If there is an error, display it and exit the Sub.
    MsgBox "Description: " + Err.Description + vbCrLf + _
           "Source: " + Err.Source
    Err.Clear
    Exit Sub
Else

    ' Display the information on screen.
    Sheet1.Cells(13, 2) = Results.Title
    ... Other Information ...
End If

' Make a second call to get the item attributes.
TheItem.APICall.DetailLevel = 16
Set Results = TheItem.GetItem

' Display the attribute information on screen.
If Results Is Nothing Then

    ' If there is an error, display it and exit the Sub.
    Sheet1.Cells(21, 2) = Err.Description
    Err.Clear
    Exit Sub
Else

    ' Determine whether there are car attributes to process.
    If Not Results.Attributes.Car Is Nothing Then

        ' If so, get the attributes.
        Set ThisCar = Results.Attributes.Car

        ' Process attributes for a car.
        ' Some attributes you can use directly.
        Sheet1.Cells(21, 1) = "Doors"
        Sheet1.Cells(21, 2) = ThisCar.Doors

        ' A few will require processing against an enumeration.
        Sheet1.Cells(22, 1) = "Engine Type"
        Select Case ThisCar.EngineType
           Case CarEngineTypesEnum.CarEngineTypesEnum_Engine_2_Cyl
              Sheet1.Cells(22, 2) = "2 Cylinders"
           ... Other Engine Types ...
        End Select

        ' Some attributes are Boolean values.
        Sheet1.Cells(23, 1) = "Is Car Inspected?"
        If ThisCar.Inspected Then
            Sheet1.Cells(23, 2) = "Yes"
        Else
```

```
            Sheet1.Cells(23, 2) = "No"
        End If

        ' A few are combinations of data.
        Sheet1.Cells(24, 1) = "Options"
        OptCount = 0
        If ThisCar.Options.Cassette Then
            Sheet1.Cells(24 + OptCount, 2) = "Cassette"
            OptCount = OptCount + 1
        End If
        ... Other Options ...
      End If
    End If
End Sub
```

The code begins by creating an `ApiSession` object, `Session`. This object contains all of the information to create a connection with the server. Note that this example relies on a user token rather than the older username and password technique. The `Token` property contains the user authentication token the user receives from eBay after a login. The `ExpirationDate` is the date provided as part of the authentication token information. The `RuName` is the unique identifier for your application. You must provide a `Token` property value, but the `ExpirationDate` and `RuName` property values are optional.

> ▶ **WARNING**
>
> It's absolutely essential that you provide some form of error handling with your application when using calls such as `GetItem`, because not every item provides every value and some calls will generate errors. The example shows one technique you can use to handle the errors, but the technique you use depends on your application's requirements.

The developer information comes next. The code must provide values for the `Developer`, `Application`, and `Certificate` values. These are the keys that you receive from eBay after you sign up for the developer program.

Now that the code has created the session information, it creates a call to use that information. In this case, the call will create a `GetItemCall` object, `TheItem`. The first task is to assign `Session` to the `ApiCallSession` property. It's possible to perform this task as part of the `GetItemCall()` constructor in other languages, but VBA requires that you perform the task as a separate assignment. Notice that this application uses a higher compatibility level than the browser-based application in Chapter 6. The application requires the higher compatibility level to obtain attribute information about the item. The detail level also differs—you must

Listing 7.3   **Getting Seller Events Using the API Technique**

```vba
Public Sub GetSalesEvents()
    ... Variable Declarations ...

    ' Create the request.
    Set Req = New ServerXMLHTTP40
    Req.Open "POST", "https://api.sandbox.ebay.com/ws/api.dll", False

    ' Define the header information for the request. These headers
    ' appear in the same order recommended by the documentation at
    ' http://developer.ebay.com/DevZone/docs/API_Doc/index.asp.
    Req.setRequestHeader "X-EBAY-API-SESSION-CERTIFICATE", _
                         Sheet1.Cells(5, 2) + ";" + _
                         Sheet1.Cells(6, 2) + ";" + _
                         Sheet1.Cells(7, 2)
    ... Other Important Headers ...

    ' Create the XML request object.
    Set XMLData = New DOMDocument40

    ' Add the XML request header.
    Set ProcInst = XMLData.createProcessingInstruction( _
        "xml", "version='1.0'  encoding='iso-8859-1'")
    XMLData.appendChild ProcInst

    ' Construct the XML request message.
    Set Root = XMLData.createElement("request")
    Root.setAttribute "xmlns", "urn:eBayAPIschema"

    ' Add the user information.
    Set Elem = XMLData.createElement("RequestToken")
    Elem.Text = Sheet1.Cells(3, 2)
    Root.appendChild Elem

    ' Add the required request data.
    Set Elem = XMLData.createElement("DetailLevel")
    Elem.Text = "0"
    ... Other Required Request Data ...

    ' Add the call specific information.
    Set Elem = XMLData.createElement("NewItemFilter")
    Elem.Text = "0"
    Root.appendChild Elem
    If Sheet1.Cells(11, 2) = "Started" Then
        Set Elem = XMLData.createElement("StartTimeFrom")
        Elem.Text = Format(Sheet1.Cells(12, 2), "yyyy-mm-dd hh:mm:ss")
        Root.appendChild Elem
        Set Elem = XMLData.createElement("StartTimeTo")
        Elem.Text = Format(Sheet1.Cells(13, 2), "yyyy-mm-dd hh:mm:ss")
        Root.appendChild Elem
```

```
      End If
      ... Other Event Types ...

      ' Add the request data to the XML request.
      XMLData.appendChild Root

      ' Send the request.
      Req.send XMLData

      ' Write the data to screen.
      If Req.Status = 200 Then

          ' Create a new document for parsing.
          Set ParseData = New DOMDocument40

          ' Make sure the document loads correctly.
          If ParseData.loadXML(Req.responseText) Then

              ' Get the usable data from the document.
              Set Elem = ParseData.childNodes(1).childNodes(1)

              ' Display the number of return values.
              Sheet1.Cells(16, 2) = Elem.childNodes(1).Text

              ' Don't do any more processing if there weren't any events.
              If Elem.childNodes(1).Text = 0 Then
                 Exit Sub
              End If

              ' Display headings for each value.
              Set Item = Elem.childNodes(2)
              For NodeCount = 0 To Item.childNodes.Length - 1
                 Sheet1.Cells(18, NodeCount + 1) = _
                     Item.childNodes(NodeCount).nodeName
              Next

              ' Process the individual items.
              For Counter = 2 To Sheet1.Cells(16, 2) + 1

                  ' Select a single item and display each value it contains.
                  Set Item = Elem.childNodes(Counter)
                  For NodeCount = 0 To Item.childNodes.Length - 1
                     Sheet1.Cells(17 + Counter, NodeCount + 1) = _
                         Item.childNodes(NodeCount).Text
                  Next
              Next
          End If
      Else
         MsgBox "Request Failed!"
      End If
   End Sub
```

The code begins with the same techniques as used for the browser-based examples in Chapter 6. As usual, the API technique begins by creating the required headers, an XML document to hold the data, and a root node to act as a starting point for the data entries. One change from many of the browser-based examples is the use of the <RequestToken> element in place of the normal username and password. The example also requires the normal required nodes, including the <DetailLevel> node, which determines the number of return values, as well as the depth of content in this case. When you set the detail level to 0, eBay will return a maximum of 3,000 entries. Otherwise, eBay returns a maximum of 2,000 entries.

The GetSellerEvents() call lets you look for three kinds of events: auctions that have just started, auctions that have just ended, and auctions with modified information. The kind of information you want to retrieve determines which pair of time entry elements you use. Events for auctions that have just started use the StartTimeFrom and StartTimeTo elements, while an auction that has just ended uses the EndTimeFrom and EndTimeTo. If you just want to look for modifications, then use the ModTimeFrom and ModTimeTo pair. Each of these pairs must contain a time in the year, month, day, hour, minute, second format shown. In addition, the time must reflect Greenwich Mean Time (GMT), so you normally need to add or subtract a few hours to get the correct time. The easiest way to learn how much time to add or subtract when using Windows is to double-click the Clock in the Notification Area of the Taskbar. This action displays the Date and Time Properties dialog box shown in Figure 7.12. Notice that the drop-down list box shows the time compared to GMT. If you live in the Central Time Zone of the United States, you'd need to add 6 hours to the current time to get GMT (which is GMT –06:00 as shown in the dialog box).

After the code successfully returns the requested data, it creates a new XML document, ParseData, which contains a list of items. The first check you'll want to perform is to ensure the result set actually contains items by checking the <Count> element. The code places this value on screen as shown in Figure 7.13.

FIGURE 7.12:

Make sure you compensate for GMT in your time calculations.

FIGURE 7.13:

The input range you provide determines the number of events you get.

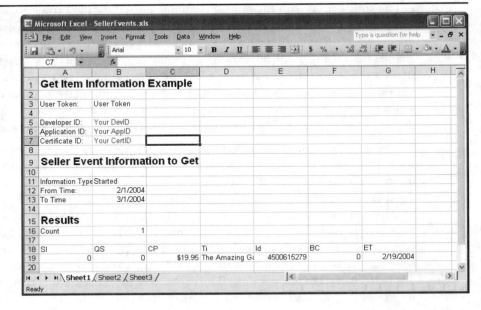

The next step is to look at individual items. The code uses a loop to process each item in turn. Notice the technique used to create a series of headings first. The heading entries reflect the names of the elements provided for each item. The nodeName property always contains this value. The final step is to display the actual item entries. The process is similar to displaying the header, but the code uses the Text property in this case.

Using Microsoft Access as a Database

Sometimes it's simply not efficient to query eBay Web Services repeatedly throughout the course of a single session for the same information. It's true that items listed on eBay change daily. In fact, one of the reasons for the GetSellerEvents() call described in the "Developing an Application with the API" section is that things do change rapidly, in some cases, and this call helps you keep up-to-date without a lot of effort. However, it's likely that some items will remain somewhat constant. You'll probably deal with the same buyers and sellers regularly. It's also possible that some items will appear with regularity and you won't always want to download every piece of information about them.

The eBay Web Services SDK also provides support for the Integration Library, which is a set of features that make it easy to work with eBay using your favorite database for local caching. In fact, the SDK provides special calls that load and save database information directly—you don't need to perform any special calls to accomplish the task. For this and many other reasons, it's often easier to simply cache the data locally. The sections that follow discuss caching techniques and methodology.

Caching as a Practical Performance Enhancing Technique

Cached searches work on the principle that people tend to look for the same things, so placing these common items in a cache can improve application performance and reduce resource usage. For example, if you have a small business that sells antiques, then it's quite possible that the employees in your organization will consistent look for the same types of information from eBay, even if the actual items differ slightly. If you can identify a request commonality in your company or for your personal use, a cached search can be quite productive. In fact, you'll receive the following benefits from cached searches.

Faster Searches　The one benefit that everyone can agree on is that you can search more quickly using a local data store—especially if that data store is optimized for a specific use. No matter how fast your Internet connection, it can't compete with the speed of your LAN and local database.

Improved Application Performance　A cached application can also improve application functionality in tasks such as uploading new items to eBay. The database stores the data and uploads it as soon as possible to eBay using a background routine. This technique makes the user faster by returning control to the application faster. The data isn't actually uploaded at the time the user enters the next item in most cases—it resides in the database until eBay can accept the input.

Offline Data Store　It's impossible to interact with eBay when you don't have a connection to the Internet. You can still perform a cached search, however, and might obtain everything you need from the offline database. In fact, this technique works especially well when the data doesn't change very often. For example, you could cache data on sellers and buyers that you work with regularly. As users become more mobile, the need to develop and enhance offline storage becomes more critical. Of course, given the dynamic nature of eBay, you also don't want to retain the data too long—it's a balance between application performance, user convenience, reliability (both data access and application), and age of the data.

Personalized Notes　Using a cached application can provide quantifiable benefits for the application user. One of the most important benefits is the ability to add notes and comments to the eBay data. You might keep track of which buyers and sellers you prefer to deal with from a personal level. A caching system could help you prioritize the items that you're bidding on so you ensure that you bid on the items with the greatest importance—stretching your money and making each purchase better tuned to your particular needs.

Reduced eBay License Usage   One of the big reasons to use a cache is so you don't eat away at the limited number of requests you can make on eBay every day. Remember that you only get 5,000 sandbox or 50 production requests per day (unless you upgrade to one of the higher license levels). Consequently, a cached search presents an opportunity to save one of the searches for that day.

Creating a Cached Application

This example is the next step in the GetItem() call example described in the "Developing an Application with the SDK" section of the chapter. The main difference is that this example uses caching to reduce the need to request information from eBay. In addition, it uses the eBay SDK Integration library to reduce the amount of coding required to keep the database in synch with eBay Web Services. To ensure you have full SDK access, add all of the libraries used in the previous example, plus the eBay_SDK_Integration library that the previous example didn't use.

> ▶ **NOTE**
>
> You'll need a copy of the eBaySdk.mdb database for this example. It's supplied in the \Program Files\eBay\SDK\Database folder. This database contains information about the application, the application users, and the application data itself. It's also important to set up test users for the example. The easiest way to perform this task is to have the sample application do it for you using the procedure found in the "Configuring the Sample Application" section of Chapter 8.

Listing 7.4 shows the essential code for this example—it doesn't repeat the code already explained in Listing 7.2. You'll find the complete source for this example in the \Chapter 07\ Access folder of the source code located on the Sybex Web site.

Listing 7.4   **Using Caching with the *GetItem()* Call**

```
Public Sub GetData()
    ... Variable Declarations ...

    ' Create a connection to the database.
    Set dbStore = New DataStore
    dbStore.Connect Sheet1.Cells(9, 2)
```

```
' Load the sandbox environment.
Set dbEnv = _
   dbStore.LoadEnvironment(EnvironmentEnum.EnvironmentEnum_SANDBOX)

' Load the user information.
Set dbUser = dbEnv.UserManager.LoadUser(1)

' Create the connection between eBay and the database.
Set dbSession = dbStore.GetEBaySession(dbUser)

' Get all of the saved items.
Set AllItems = dbSession.LoadItems(AppStatusEnum_Saved)

' Check for the saved item.
For Counter = 0 To AllItems.ItemCount - 1
   If AllItems.Item(Counter).ItemId = Sheet1.Cells(11, 2) Then

      ' Load the item when found.
      Set Results = AllItems.ItemAt(Counter)

      ' Check the last time the data was updated.
      Set ThisApp = Results.AppData
      If DateTime.DateDiff("d", ThisApp.AppModDate, DateTime.Now) > 2 Then

         ' Create the deleted item object.
         Set Item2Delete = New IntCollection
         Item2Delete.Add ThisApp.appItemId

         ' Remove the item from the database.
         dbSession.SetItemStatus Item2Delete, AppStatusEnum_Deleted

         ' Don't use these results.
         Set Results = Nothing
      End If

      ' Exit the loop.
      Exit For
   End If
Next

' Verify the database contains the required data. If not, get it
' from eBay.
If Results Is Nothing Then

   ' Get the data.
   Set Results = Call_eBay

   ' Check for errors.
   If Results Is Nothing Then

      ' If there is an error, display it and exit the Sub.
```

```
        MsgBox "Description: " + Err.Description + vbCrLf + _
                "Source: " + Err.Source
        Err.Clear
        Exit Sub
    End If


    ' Create application update information.
    Set ThisApp = New ItemAppData
    ThisApp.appEnvId = EnvironmentEnum.EnvironmentEnum_SANDBOX
    ThisApp.AppModDate = DateTime.Now
    ThisApp.AppStatus = AppStatusEnum_Saved
    ThisApp.AppUserId = 1


    ' Add application data to the results.
    Set Results.AppData = ThisApp


    ' Save the data to the database.
    AddResult = dbSession.SaveItem(Results)
    End If

' Display the information on screen.
... Display Code ...

End Sub
```

The code begins by creating a connection to the database. It requires a connection string to make the connection. The connection string contains a number of arguments separated by semicolons as shown here (the text normally appears on a single line, but appears on multiple lines in the book):

```
Provider=Microsoft.Jet.OLEDB.4.0;User ID=Admin;Data Source=D:\Chapter
07\Access\eBaySdk.mdb;Persist Security Info=False;Jet OLEDB:Database
Password=;Jet OLEDB:Encrypt Database=True
```

The information you provide is important. The Provider is a device driver that accesses the database. The Provider shown is the most common for Access users. The User ID argument must include the name of a valid database user—Admin is the default user for many single user setups. If your database is password protected, you must also provide a Database Password argument. The Source argument shows the physical location of the database on your hard drive. These are the mandatory arguments. The remaining arguments are those that eBay suggests for testing and requires for certifying the application. Notice especially the Jet OLEDB:Encrypt Database argument, which encrypts the content of the database when set to True.

Once the code has created a connection to the database, it uses the connection to load the application environment stored in the database. This environment includes information such as your developer keys and the URLs to use for calls to eBay. Notice that you must supply an environment type as part of the input to this call. The database stores information for several environment types, which means that you can use the same database for multiple applications if desired.

Now that the application knows about the environment in which it will work, the code loads a user. The example code shows a simple number. You obtain this number by looking in the AppUserId field of the AppUser table found in the database. The call is only successful if the user exists and is set up for the application environment. In other words, the call will fail if you try to load a user from the production environment into an application set up for sandbox use.

The code moves on to the next step of creating an eBay session. This session is set up to use the application environment and the user you've loaded. At this point, you can begin working with data.

The first date-oriented task is to load the appropriate items from the database—those that are saved from previous sessions—and check for the target item. The code uses the Load-Items(AppStatusEnum_Saved) method to load items with a specific status—saved. A loop checks each of the items in the AllItems collection for the target ItemId value. If the code locates the appropriate record, then it checks the date the record was last modified using the DateTime.DateDiff() method. At this point, the application has data to display in Results. However, if that data is too old, then the code sets the status of that item to deleted and removes the data from Results. Note that the Integration Library doesn't actually remove the record, so you'll need to perform database maintenance from time to time to remove all of the deleted records. Depending on how much you use eBay, performing maintenance weekly should provide good results.

The next step is to check the status of Results. If the code determines that Results is blank (either because the database didn't have the appropriate record or the data was too old), it obtains the data from eBay using the same technique described in Listing 7.2. The code also saves the data into the database. The data you receive from eBay lacks application data because eBay doesn't know anything about your application. Consequently, the code creates an ItemAppData that contains the application data, fills it with the appropriate information, and saves the record using the SaveItem() method.

Your Call to Action

This chapter has demonstrated how you can use VBA to write programs that use eBay Web Services. It's essential to remember that the techniques in this chapter work with any application that supports VBA, not just Microsoft Office. The capabilities of the application also affect how you interact with eBay Web Services. Yes, you can force a spreadsheet to act as a word processor, but the results usually aren't easy to use, flexible, or robust. Finally, this chapter demonstrates that you can do a lot more than just list items using eBay Web Services—this product definitely provides room for all kinds of application types.

It's your turn to begin creating macro add-ons that rely on eBay Web Services for your favorite application. VBA is a very flexible programming language. When you couple this language with the unique functionality provided by a specific application, you can create robust add-ons using a minimum of code and time. Of course, you can't confuse theses add-ons with full-fledged applications—the macro couples the add-on to the host application.

You might decide that you really do need a full-fledged application—that working with a specific host application just won't work for your needs. Chapter 8 discusses techniques you can use to write full-fledged applications using Visual Studio. Chapter 8 doesn't target a specific version of Visual Studio because many people don't have the latest product. Instead, it discusses several languages included with both Visual Studio 6 and Visual Studio .NET so that you can choose the language that works best for your specific needs.

Chapter 8

Using Web Services from Any Visual Studio Version

Resources for Learning Visual Studio

Developing with Visual Basic 6

▶ Writing Applications Using Visual Studio

Developing with Visual C++ 6

Developing with Visual Basic .NET

Developing with Visual C# .NET

One of the best ways to work with eBay Web Services when you want to create a free-form desktop application is to use Visual Studio. With Visual Studio, you have access to a full user interface, Web service, and database tools. Given time and resources, you can create seamless access to eBay Web Services for any need, including many forms of Web application access. If you use Visual Studio .NET, mobile applications become relatively easy to create as well. In sum, this is the approach to use when you require maximum flexibility, have the required development skills, and have the time and resources to create a complete application.

The two most popular versions of Visual Studio now are Visual Studio 6.0 and Visual Studio .NET. This chapter explores both versions of Visual Studio. Visual Studio 6.0 developers will find examples for Visual C++ and Visual Basic. Visual Studio .NET developers will find examples for Visual C# and Visual Basic .NET. Most developers will find a Visual Studio flavor they like in these sections.

This chapter also considers the use of a database for various kinds of data storage, both short and long term. You might find that you need to use local storage that provides automatic data entry updates to achieve a given level of performance for your application. In some cases, you might also need to store customer or company specific short-term information as part of your application. This chapter relies on SQL Server. You can use other database managers, such as Access (see the "Using Microsoft Access as a Database" section of Chapter 7) and MySQL (see the "Using MySQL as a Database" section of Chapter 9).

Using Web Services from Any Visual Studio Version

Chapter 5 demonstrates the two common techniques for working with eBay Web Services—SDK and API. Visual Studio developers also have these options, but implementing the solutions is a lot easier because Visual Studio provides a number of additional tools that Office developers can only dream about. For example, you can easily mix eBay Integration Library support with standard database calls.

Just because Visual Studio provides a robust development environment, doesn't mean that all versions of Visual Studio are equal. You have a number of choices when working with Visual Studio. The .NET version has a definite ease-of-use advantage not provided by previous editions. Many of the features that you have to program manually when using Visual Studio 6 are drag-and-drop easy in Visual Studio .NET. The functionality that Visual Studio .NET provides is especially important when working with a database.

I'd love to say that Visual Studio .NET is a positive advance in every way, but it isn't the right choice for some needs. This version of Visual Studio relies on the .NET Framework to perform tasks. The .NET Framework is a library of programming routines similar in purpose to the Windows API. The difference is that it also relies on a runtime engine in the form of the Common Language Runtime (CLR). Unless the person who needs your application has both CLR and the .NET Framework installed on their system, they can't run your application. In addition, the memory and hard drive requirements for the .NET Framework and CLR can be hefty for older systems to accommodate.

Visual Studio 6.0 has a distinct advantage in that it's familiar and you can produce native or Windows 32-bit Application Programming Interface (Win32 API) code using it. Every version of Windows can use applications created by this version of Visual Studio. Consequently, you have decisions to make when selecting which version of Visual Studio to use. Although all of the languages in this chapter can access eBay Web Services, each language has features that make it better suited to specific needs.

Resources for Learning Visual Studio

This book assumes that you already know how to use Visual Studio and at least one supported language. Except as needed, I won't discuss the IDE or basic programming techniques. Of course, the chapter will discuss how to use eBay Web Services in detail, but you still need to know the essentials of the IDE and language you want to use. The following sections provide some resources you can use to learn Visual Studio (although these lists are by no means complete).

Using Visual Studio 6

Visual Studio 6 is the last version of Microsoft's language product to provide full support for native applications—those that run directly from the Win32 API. Developers who don't want to adopt Microsoft's .NET strategy have continued to use this version of Visual Studio and it will probably remain viable for a long time. This book discusses the two most popular languages included with Visual Studio 6: Visual Basic 6 and Visual C++ 6. I'm assuming that you have installed the latest service pack from Microsoft (SP5 at the time of this writing, with SP6 on the way).

It helps if you have a good book when learning any computer language, but especially when working with the intricacies of Visual Studio. A good starting Visual C++ book is *Beginning Visual C++ 6* by Ivor Horton (Wrox, 2003). Visual C++ developers will probably want to look at my books, *Visual C++ 6 from the Ground Up*, Second Edition (Osborne, 1998) or *Windows 2000 Programming Bible* (IDG, 1999) as their second book. Make sure you check out *Mastering C++ 6* by Matthew J. Young (Sybex, 1998) as well.

For Visual Basic 6 developers, one of the best books on the market is *Visual Basic 6 for Dummies* by Wallace Wang (IDG, 1998). Another good book once you understand a few of the basics is *Mastering Visual Basic 6* by Evangelos Petroutsos (Sybex, 1998).

Make sure you also spend time looking at source code examples. For example, you can find great source code examples at Planet Source Code (`http://www.pscode.com/`). This site includes both Visual Basic and Visual C++ examples, along with helpful tutorials. Note that this site also caters to .NET users. Another good place to look for Visual Basic code is A1VBCode at `http://www.a1vbcode.com/`. The TutorGig site at `http://www.tutorgig.com/` provides tutorials for both Visual Basic and Visual C++. Other places to look for code include VB Forums (`http://vbforums.com/`), Tek-Tips Forums (`http://tek-tips.com/`), VBCode.com (`http://vbcode.com/`), and FreeVBCode.com (`http://freevbcode.com/`).

Normally, I recommend spending time on Microsoft's newsgroups such as `microsoft.public.vb.bugs` or `microsoft.public.vc.database`. However, if you're a Visual Basic developer, many online forums present great information without the usual Microsoft bias. For example, the Extreme Visual Basic Forum at `http://visualbasicforum.com/` provides a number of message lists you can use to discuss issues such as adding a Windows XP interface to your application.

Using Visual Studio .NET

Visual Studio .NET promises to deliver a lot in the way of language functionality, so it's almost a shame that I only cover C# and Visual Basic in this chapter. You still have an option to use Visual C++ for development purposes. See my book *Visual C++ .NET Developer's Guide* (Osborne, 2002) for details on using this language. In fact, the inclusion of new designer tools for Visual C++ developers in Visual Studio .NET 2003 makes this language a viable choice (the first version of Visual Studio .NET didn't provide Visual C++ developers with designer support). However, I'm currently working with PERL in .NET (see `http://www.activestate.com/Products/Visual_Perl/` for details) and there are other choices too. You can see a list of languages at `http://msdn.microsoft.com/netframework/technologyinfo/Overview/default.aspx`. It's also interesting to look at the language list at `http://www.gotdotnet.com/team/lang/`.

> ▶ **TIP**
>
> Many of the books that you'll see online say they're for the novice, but the author has targeted them to a specific need. For example, you might see a book for database programming or using Crystal Reports. These books are helpful, but first try to find a .NET book that focuses on the language, rather than tasks you can perform with the language.

One of the best places to learn about C# is *A Programmer's Introduction to C#*, Second Edition, by Eric Gunnerson (Apress, 2001). Once you get a basic start, check out my book *Visual C# .NET Developer's Handbook* (Sybex, 2002). If you want a great .NET book that includes both Visual Basic and C#, check out *.NET Programming 10-Minute Solutions* by Russell Jones and Mike Gunderloy (Sybex, 2003).

Visual Basic .NET developers also have a wealth of information sources at their disposal. One book to try is *Beginning VB.NET* by Richard Blair, Jonathan Crossland, Matthew Reynolds, and Thearon Willis (Wrox, 2003). Many people also find *Microsoft Visual Basic .NET Step by Step* by Michael Halvorson (Microsoft Press, 2002) quite helpful. Finally, you might want to read *The Ultimate VB.NET and ASP.NET Code Book* by Karl Moore (Apress, 2003).

As with any other language, seeing coding examples and trying them out on your machine is a good way to learn. One of the best places to obtain coding examples for Visual Basic .NET or Visual C++ .NET is GotDotNet (`http://www.gotdotnet.com/`). Some of the Microsoft developers frequent this site, as well as expert programmers who don't have any Microsoft affiliation. You can also learn a lot from my free .NET Tips, Trends & Technology eXTRA newsletter (sign up at `http://www.freeenewsletters.com/`). Send me your .NET questions and I'll answer them in the newsletter. I've also written a number of articles for InformIT (`http://www.informit.com/isapi/authorid~{67CBE1B0-99DC-4A19-8BFB-5D224A0F34A7}/authors/author.asp`). Finally, Matthew Reynolds' .NET 24/7 site at `http://www.dotnet247.com/` is packed with helpful examples and other information.

Getting the Latest Version of Microsoft XML

Visual Studio languages require use of Microsoft XML in many cases, especially if you want to use the API technique in place of the SDK technique. The main reason to use the API technique is to obtain better control of the programming environment. Using the API technique means that you work directly with the XML that eBay Web Services receives and sends. Of course, this technique does require a little more code than using the SDK technique.

Visual Studio .NET developers have access to the latest .NET wrapper for Microsoft XML through the .NET Framework. Generally, this support is all that you need to work with eBay. However, it's also possible to create a reference to the COM version of Microsoft XML for use with .NET applications. You might want to use this approach if the latest COM version provides features that the .NET Framework doesn't provide.

Make sure you use the newest version of Microsoft XML with your Visual Studio 6.0 applications. It's especially important that Visual Studio 6.0 developers update their product. You can learn about the latest version of Microsoft XML and associated products at `http://msdn.microsoft.com/library/default
.asp?url=/nhp/default.asp?contentid=28000438`.

Microsoft supports a number of .NET newsgroups. The important thing to remember is that most of these newsgroups have "dotnet" in the name. For example, if you want to learn about .NET Framework interoperability problems, you should visit the `microsoft.public
.dotnet.framework.interop` newsgroup. When you need help with Visual Basic .NET, check the `microsoft.public.dotnet.languages.vb` newsgroup. Likewise, you can visit the `microsoft.public.dotnet.languages.vc` newsgroup for help with Visual C++ .NET questions.

Using the eBay Visual C++ Example

One of the examples you get with the eBay Web Services Kit is a Visual C++ application that demonstrates basic usage. In this case, like many others, the example shows how to upload a listing to eBay. You'll find this example in the `\Program Files\eBay\SDK\Samples\C++\
SimpleList` folder of your eBay Web Services Kit installation. Make sure you read the `ReadMe.TXT` file in the source code folder—it contains setup instructions you need for the example. In general, you need to add the folder for the .NET Framework to the list of linking libraries, as shown in Figure 8.1, and you must ensure the `eBay.SDK.TLB` in the `Simple-
ListDlg.CPP` source code file is correct. To add the .NET Framework reference, use the Tools ➤ Options command to display the Options dialog box. Select the Directories tab and click New. Locate the .NET Framework folder on your system, which is `\WINDOWS\
Microsoft.NET\Framework\v1.1.4322` for the 1.1 version.

FIGURE 8.1:

The Visual C++ 6 example won't run without a copy of the .NET Framework installed on your system.

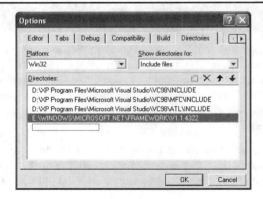

> **▶ NOTE**
>
> Depending on how you have your programming environment set up, you might see an error message when you compile the application: "warning C4146: unary minus operator applied to unsigned type, result still unsigned." Testing shows that you can probably ignore this warning message.

The application starts with a dialog that requests your developer keys, user information, and the URL for the development environment you want to use. The default environment is the sandbox. Enter the required information and click OK. You'll see the listing dialog box shown in Figure 8.2. Once you fill in the required listing information, click ListMe to send the information to eBay. After a few moments, you'll see a dialog box stating that AddItem succeeded. The dialog box also displays a new ItemId value that you can use for other calls to the API.

You won't find much code for the first dialog box—it consists of some variables associated with the dialog box and that's about it. The IDOK button performs the usual default action of closing the dialog box. The main code for this example resides in the SimpleListDlg.CPP file. The ListMe button shown in Figure 8.2 actually has an identity of IDOK, so you need to view the CSimpleListDlg::OnOK() method. (The process of adding and removing images is simply a matter of adding or removing a string from IDC_PICTURE_LIST, which is a CListBox control.)

The example uses the SDK method of communicating with eBay. Most of the interface definitions, such as IApiSessionPtr, appear in the eBay.SDK.TLI file that the Visual C++ IDE generates automatically for you because of the #import "..\\..\\..\\eBay.SDK.tlb" statement. It pays to spend some time looking through this file because the Visual C++ calling syntax isn't always the same as the information provided with the local SDK help file or the online API help. The code begins by creating a session and providing the developer keys, user information, and development environment URL as input.

After the code creates the session, it begins generating a log file of the session at C:\ SimpleList_C++.LOG. None of the example information tells you about this log, so you wouldn't learn about it without looking through the code. The log file is very helpful because it contains all of the XML messages generated during the session so you can learn how eBay Web Services communicates with the application. Using this technique as you build your own applications can save significant time because you can actually see the message content.

At this point, the code begins creating an item using the IItemPtr interface. The resulting item object contains a number of default values, such as the <Location> element value, that you'll want to request from the user in a production application. When the item information is complete, the code creates an IAddItemCallPtr interface object. This object defines the actual call and the code adds the item to it. The code performs the actual call next, returns the data to the user, and closes the application log. If an error occurs during any of the item manipulation procedures, a catch statement displays an error on screen.

You might wonder where the .NET Framework comes into play. Look into the eBay.SDK .TLH file and you'll notice that some of the interfaces, such as CatalogAttributeCollection, actually reference objects in the .NET Framework, such as IList. Even though you won't interact with the .NET Framework directly, the eBay Web Services SDK still requires the reference. The only way to avoid working with the .NET Framework with Visual C++ is to use the API technique to make calls.

FIGURE 8.2:

Use this dialog box to list a new item on eBay.

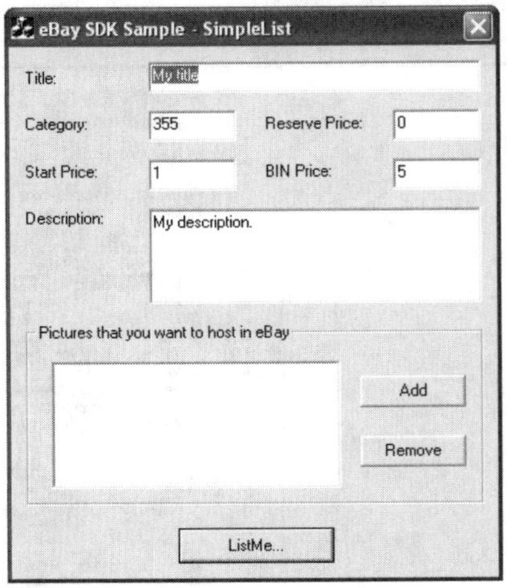

Developing with Visual Basic 6

Visual Basic 6 is still a favorite with developers today because it makes building applications easy, when they compare it to a language such as C, and still produces a native executable. Many organizations have documented the developer productivity benefits of using Visual Basic 6. You can produce both desktop and Web applications with equal ease. The design interface makes working with databases simple. In fact, if there's a problem with Visual Basic, it's that the product does too much and ends up hiding low-level functionality that developers need. Consequently, this is the language to use if you need a native code application to access eBay Web Services and developer productivity is high on your list of priorities. The following sections describe how you can use Visual Basic 6 to build an eBay Web Services application.

Using the eBay Visual Basic 6 Example

The Visual Basic 6 example looks and works much like the Visual C++ example shown in Figure 8.1. As with the Visual C++ example, you provide the developer, user, and environment information as input to the first dialog box. The second dialog box provides entries for adding a new item to eBay. If you run the application and get a "Can't find library or object." error, make sure you verify that all of the references are correct. To do this, open the Reference dialog box using the Project ➢ References command. Figure 8.3 shows a typical error—the eBay_SDK reference is missing. To correct this problem, deselect the entry, close the dialog box, and reselect it. If you find the reference isn't available, run the RegSDK.BAT file located in the \XP Program Files\eBay\SDK folder. Close Visual Basic, reopen the References dialog box, and try to select the reference again.

FIGURE 8.3:

Verify all of the eBay references are correct and that the eBay libraries are properly registered.

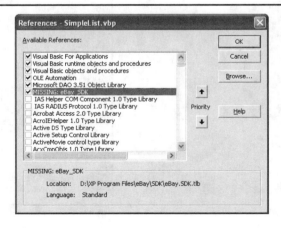

The `mBtnAddItem_Click()` Sub found in the `FormSimpleList.FRM` file contains the majority of the code for this example. The code begins by creating an `IApiSession` object, `callSession`. You can use `callSession` to perform a number of tasks, including creating an XML log so you can see the communication stream between eBay and the application (the example doesn't perform this task by default). To add logging support to the application, type **`callSession.Log.Open`** **`"C:\MyLog.txt"`** immediately before the call to `callSession.LogCallXml` = True. Make sure you close the log before the code exits, using `callSession.Log.Close`.

The code creates an `eBay.SDK.Model.Item.Item` object next. It uses this object to build a description of the item the user wants to sell. Once the item description is complete, the code creates an `IAddItemCall` object to send the data to eBay. The next step is to make the call. If the call is successful, the application displays the new `ItemId` value. Otherwise, the code displays an error message. As with the Visual C++ example, the Visual Basic example relies on the .NET Framework when using the SDK technique. If you want to create an eBay Web Services application that doesn't rely on the .NET Framework, then you need to use the API technique described in the "Using the API Technique with Visual Basic 6" section of the chapter.

Adding a Microsoft XML Reference to Visual Basic 6

Unlike many Web services that you'll use, eBay doesn't require you to install the Microsoft SOAP Toolkit—you can work with eBay Web Services using simple XML techniques. Chapter 4 discusses most of the XML techniques you'll use. However, before you use XML with Visual Basic 6, make sure you install Microsoft XML version 4.0, rather than use the older version that comes with the product. You can download Microsoft XML 4.0 Service Pack 2 at http://www.microsoft.com/downloads/details.aspx?familyid=3144B72B-B4F2-46DA-B4B6-C5D7485F2B42&displaylang=en#filelist.

To add the Microsoft XML reference to your project, use the Project ➤ References command to display the References dialog box shown in Figure 8.4. Check the Microsoft, XML v4.0 option, as shown in the figure, and click OK. If you have Office 2003 installed on your machine, you'll have a newer version of Microsoft XML that you should install in place of the 4.0 version shown.

This example will work with versions of Microsoft XML as old as 3.0 with reduced capability. The version of Microsoft XML you use must include the ServerXMLHTTP30, ServerXMLHTTP40, or newer object. This object helps you create a connection to the server.

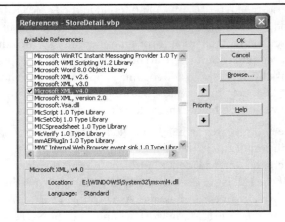

FIGURE 8.4:

Add the most current version of Microsoft XML to your project.

Using the API Technique with Visual Basic 6

The example in this section discusses the GetStoreDetails() call. Some sellers on eBay have an electronic storefront that offers specific benefits that improve sales and generally make using eBay easier. The GetStoreDetails() call helps you learn more about the stores. You can learn more about storefronts in the API help topic at http://developer.ebay.com/DevZone/docs/API_Doc/Developing/Stores/eBayStores.htm. A general discussion of this call appears at http://developer.ebay.com/DevZone/docs/API_Doc/Functions/GetStoreDetails/GetStoreDetailsLogic.htm. Most important of the features available to an eBay store is a special listing format called Store Inventory.

> **▶ TIP**
>
> You can find a list of real storefronts at http://www.stores.ebay.com/. However, these storefronts aren't accessible in the sandbox, so you'll want to create one for your test user. Make sure you go to the correct sandbox store setup at http://cgi6.sandbox.ebay.com/aw-cgi/ebayISAPI.dll?Storefrontlogin. Notice the word "sandbox" in the URL. Don't worry about any fees associated with a normal store—eBay doesn't charge these fees for stores created in the sandbox for testing. After you create the store, you can use the GetStoreDetails() call to test access to it.

Listing 8.1 shows the source code for this example. You'll find the complete source for this example in the \Chapter 08\VB6_StoreDetail folder of the source code located on the Sybex Web site.

Listing 8.1   **Using the *GetStoreDetails* Call**

```
Private Sub btnTest_Click()
    ... Variable Declarations ...

    ' Create the request.
    Set Req = New ServerXMLHTTP40
    Req.open "POST", "https://api.sandbox.ebay.com/ws/api.dll", False

    ' Define the header information for the request. These headers
    ' appear in the same order recommended by the documentation at
    ' http://developer.ebay.com/DevZone/docs/API_Doc/index.asp.
    Req.setRequestHeader "X-EBAY-API-COMPATIBILITY-LEVEL", "305"
    ... Fill Out Other Request Headers ...

    ' Create the XML request object.
    Set XMLData = New DOMDocument40

    ' Add the XML request header.
    Set ProcInst = XMLData.createProcessingInstruction( _
        "xml", "version='1.0'  encoding='iso-8859-1'")
    XMLData.appendChild ProcInst

    ' Construct the XML request message.
    Set Root = XMLData.createElement("request")
    Root.setAttribute "xmlns", "urn:eBayAPIschema"

    ' Add the user information.
    Set Elem = XMLData.createElement("RequestToken")
    Elem.Text = txtUserToken.Text
    Root.appendChild Elem

    ' Add the required request data.
    Set Elem = XMLData.createElement("DetailLevel")
    Elem.Text = "0"
    Root.appendChild Elem
    Set Elem = XMLData.createElement("ErrorLevel")
    Elem.Text = "1"
    Root.appendChild Elem
    Set Elem = XMLData.createElement("SiteId")
    Elem.Text = "0"
    Root.appendChild Elem
    Set Elem = XMLData.createElement("StorefrontOwner")
    Elem.Text = txtStoreOwner.Text
    Root.appendChild Elem
    Set Elem = XMLData.createElement("Verb")
    Elem.Text = "GetStoreDetails"
    Root.appendChild Elem

    ' Add the request data to the XML request.
    XMLData.appendChild Root
```

```
' Send the request.
Req.send XMLData

' Write the data to screen.
If Req.Status = 200 Then

    ' Create a new document for parsing.
    Set ParseData = New DOMDocument40

    ' Make sure the document loads correctly.
    If ParseData.loadXML(Req.responseText) Then

        ' Get the usable data from the document.
        Set Elem = ParseData.childNodes(1).childNodes(1)

        ' Display the store name.
        txtStoreName.Text = Elem.childNodes(1).Text

        ' Display the categories for this store.
        For Counter = 0 To Elem.childNodes(0).childNodes.length - 1

            ' Verify this is the correct node type.
            If Elem.childNodes(0).childNodes(Counter).nodeName = _
                "Category" Then

                ' Get the individual category.
                lstCategories.AddItem _
                    Elem.childNodes(0).childNodes(Counter).childNodes(1).Text
            End If
        Next
    End If
End If
End Sub
```

The application begins by creating a new request. You must set the request to use the POST method, rather than the GET method of communication. The URL shown in the example connects to the sandbox, rather than the production environment. To ensure the application works as anticipated, you want to use synchronous, rather than asynchronous, communication.

The next step is to set all of the headers for the request. Most of these headers are the same as all of the other examples in the book. Of special importance is the X-EBAY-API-CALL-NAME header, which is set to the GetStoreDetails() call.

After the code sets up the request, it begins building the XML message. The message relies on a DOMDocument40 object, XMLData. The first element added to the document is a processing instruction—the XML header. The code uses the XMLData.createProcessingInstruction()

method to create the header. The `XMLData.appendChild()` method adds the XML header to the document.

At this point, the code creates the `Root` node, but doesn't add it to `XMLData` immediately. As with most examples, the code adds all of the required child elements to the `Root` node first. The first child is the `<RequestToken>` element. The code then adds a number of required data elements. The `GetStoreDetails()` call doesn't provide any optional arguments. In addition, this is one case where the `<DetailLevel>` element doesn't provide any additional information, so always set it to 0, as shown in the code.

> ▶ **NOTE**
>
> Most of the examples in this chapter rely on the `<RequestToken>` element, rather than a username and password. The "Getting a User Token" section of Chapter 5 discusses one technique for getting a user authentication token; the "Using the eBay API Test Tool to Authenticate a User" section of Chapter 7 discusses a second technique. Use one of the two techniques to obtain a user authentication token for your test user.

The code adds the `Root` node to `XMLData` next, and sends the entire request to eBay Web Services. If the request succeeds, the `Req.Status` property is set to 200 on return from the call. All this property signifies is that the eBay Web Services server accepted the call, not that the Web service actually provided a response. If the Web service fails, you'll receive an error response. Listing 6.2 shows one technique you can use to handle an error response from eBay Web Services. Another technique is to handle it using error code, as shown in Listing 7.2. In general, you need to look for an error node and use the child nodes to obtain information about the error.

The return value from this call is a `<StoreDetails>` node that contains a series of nodes that list the store name, `<StoreName>` element, and the special categories, the `<CustomCategories>` element, that it uses. A new store will simply list default values for the special categories. Each `<Category>` element contains a `<CategoryNumber>` element and a `<Name>` element that define the category. The end of the `<CustomCategories>` element also contains a `<Count>` element that you can use to verify the category count.

Unfortunately, you can't access the various elements by name using Visual Basic 6—you must count out the node level, as shown in the code. However, you can use the `nodeName` property as shown to determine which node is present. The code uses this property to detect whether a `<CustomCategories>` element child is a `<Category>` element or a `<Count>` element. Figure 8.5 shows typical output from this example.

FIGURE 8.5:

Use the `GetStore-Details` call to learn about the special categories that a store uses.

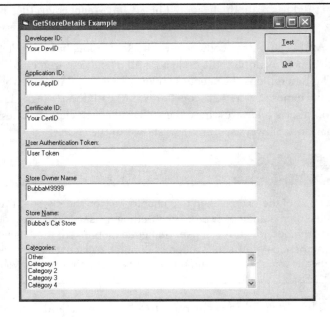

Developing with Visual Basic .NET

Visual Basic .NET isn't the same language as Visual Basic 6—the two are so different that many developers gave up trying to move code from one to the other. Many of the changes in Visual Basic .NET are actually advantageous, especially for eBay Web Services application designers. For example, you have better access to the low-level details of your application. In addition, Visual Basic .NET comes with many Web service support items built in. The following sections discuss how to use Visual Basic .NET to work with eBay Web Services.

> ▶ **TIP**
>
> If you don't own Visual Studio .NET, but would like to try it out, you can find a 60-day demonstration version at `http://msdn.microsoft.com/vstudio/productinfo/trial/default.aspx`. All you need to do is order the CD and install it. You can also find an online trial of Visual Studio .NET at `http://msdn.microsoft.com/vstudio/tryit/`. In general, the 60-day trial version is a better option than using the online version when working with eBay Web Services.

Using the eBay Visual Basic .NET Examples

eBay provides three Visual Basic .NET examples as part of the eBay Web Services Kit. Each example demonstrates a different technique for working with eBay. The following sections provide a brief overview of each example and some ideas on how to use them effectively. You'll find these examples in the `\Program Files\eBay\SDK\Samples\VB.NET` folder of your eBay Web Services Kit installation.

▶ TIP

It's also a good idea to look at the C# examples. They're different in some respects from the Visual Basic .NET examples, so you can get a better idea of how eBay Web Services works by looking at both.

API Library Example

The API example found in the `\Program Files\eBay\SDK\Samples\VB.NET\ApiLibraryDemo` folder uses a standard GUI interface. The first form requests your developer keys, a username and password, and the URL for the environment you want to use (sandbox or production). After you enter this information, you'll see a second form that contains a series of buttons, as shown in Figure 8.6.

To use any of the features, simply click the associated button and the application will display a form for that API call. Fill in the information and click the request button to obtain the information. You can use this example as a simple means to check results for the application you build. Given the same input, the example should provide the same output as your application.

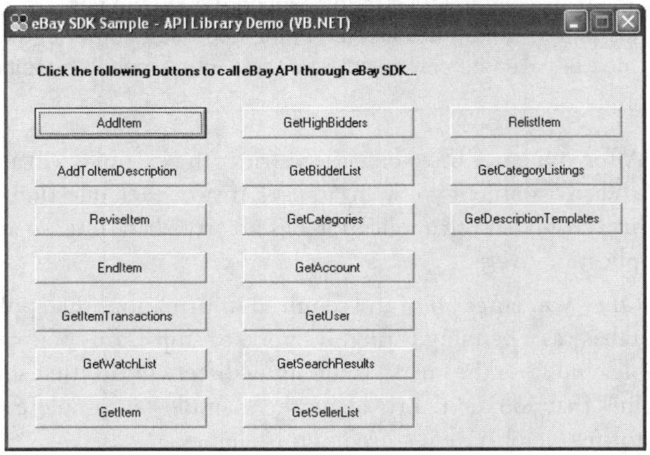

FIGURE 8.6:

This example shows how to use make calls to eBay using the API technique.

The only problem with the example code is that it doesn't show the whole picture. In general, you need to combine the code found in the `AccountForm.VB` file with the code located in the specific call file. For example, if you wanted to learn how to get an item, you'd need to combine the `AccountForm.VB` file code with the `FormGetItem.VB` file code. In addition, most of the examples show just the bare essentials to make the call and lack the optional arguments you can provide. Even so, the example code is a good way to get started if you want to use the API technique.

One feature that I especially appreciated about the examples is that they include basic error handling. The examples show which exceptions you can expect for a given call, at least from an eBay Web Services perspective. For this reason, it's important to at least view the various examples so you can see how eBay expects you to handle errors in your own code.

SDK Library Example

The SDK example uses a console interface, which removes some of the code you'd normally need to wade through to see the SDK at work. This particular example works with the Integration Library, so it probably isn't the best example to start with if you want to concentrate on using the SDK itself for the first time.

To use this example, you need to set up and use the eBay Sample Selling Application to ensure the database is ready for use. The sample application won't perform this setup for you. In fact, you'll need the connection string from the eBay Sample Selling Application to make this example work. You can learn more about the eBay Sample Selling Application in the "Using the eBay Sample Selling Application" section of the chapter.

> **▶ TIP**
>
> Remember that you don't have to type the connection string into the console window by hand. You can copy the string to the clipboard and then paste it into the console window by clicking on the control box located in the upper left corner of the console window and selecting the Edit ➢ Paste command from the context menu. Pressing Ctrl+V won't work in this case.

After you enter the connection string, the example will ask you a series of questions, such as the environment you want to use. Answer each question in turn, pressing Enter after each entry. Note that the application has no error handling, so an invalid entry means starting the application over.

Once you enter all of the required information, the application saves the entry to the database as a pending listing. It's good to stop at this point, open the database and the Items table, and view the entry. You'll immediately notice that some of the table entries contain values that you didn't provide in the example—a complete application would request this information or have it stored in the database.

At this point, the application offers to synchronize the database with eBay Web Services. Type **Y** and press Enter. The application displays a bunch of information (most of it scrolls by too quickly to see) and ends. You'll find that the item is now listed on eBay.

When viewing the application code, you'll notice that most of the required information appears in two functions within the `Module1.VB` file. Make sure you start with the `Main()` method. This method shows the main flow of the application. The `CreateItem()` method shows one technique for creating an item for listing.

Integration Library Example

The Integration Library example found in the `\Program Files\eBay\SDK\Samples\VB.NET\` `IntegrationLibraryDemo` folder relies on a connection string that you create for the Sample Selling Application to work.. You can learn more about the eBay Sample Selling Application in the "Using the eBay Sample Selling Application" section of the chapter. To begin using the example, open the `App.CONFIG` file and modify the following line of code to reflect the connection string for your database. (Even though the entry appears on multiple lines in the book, it should appear in a single line in the actual file.)

```
<add key="DbConnection" value="driver={SQLServer};provider=SQLOLEDB;server=
(LOCAL);trusted_connection=yes;database=eBaySales" />
```

Once you make this change, you can start the application. The first form you'll see contains a number of tabs, starting with the Setup, as shown in Figure 8.7. Make sure you click Edit and select the environment you configured for experimentation with the eBay Sample Selling Application or configure a new one using the options provided.

FIGURE 8.7:

Use the Integration Library example to experiment with eBay database support.

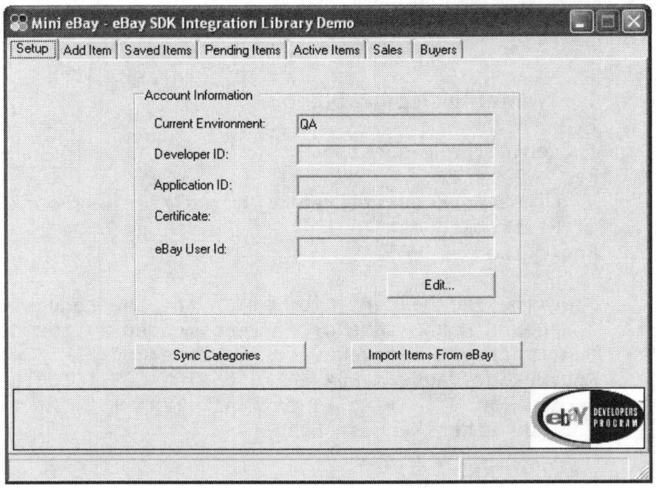

The example is a limited version of the eBay Sample Selling Application. It lets you see how such an application could be implemented without burying you in details. The best way to use this source code is to determine what activity you want to perform and look at the associated event handler code. However, it's important to realize that the application does rely on centralized setup, so the coding examples aren't self-contained. To implement a similar feature in your own application, you'd need to combine code from several areas.

Using the API Technique with Visual Basic .NET

Most developers will use the SDK technique to access eBay Web Services using Visual Basic .NET. However, the API technique comes in handy when you need to perform a little extra work with the request or response. In this case, you gain a little extra control over the response.

This example presents a special situation where a single auction could have multiple high bidders. Normally, you keep track of the high bidder by viewing the item statistics received from the GetItem() call. (See Listing 7.2 for an example of this call.) The high bidder appears as part of the <HighBidder> node on return from the call. The GetHighBidders() call only works with auctions where multiple copies of the same item are involved such as a Dutch auction. You can easily create a Dutch auction by sending an item with a quantity greater than 1 and no BuyItNow price. See the "Defining a Dutch Auction" section of the chapter for details. Listing 8.2 shows how to obtain a high bidders list using the GetHighBidders() call. You'll find the complete source for this example in the \Chapter 08\VBNET_HighBidders folder of the source code located on the Sybex Web site.

Listing 8.2   **Using the *GetHighBidders* Call**

```
Private Sub btnTest_Click(ByVal sender As System.Object, _
                    ByVal e As System.EventArgs) _
                    Handles btnTest.Click
   ... Variable Declarations ...

   ' Create the request.
   Req = _
      CType(WebRequest.Create("https://api.sandbox.ebay.com/ws/api.dll"), _
      HttpWebRequest)
   Req.Method = "POST"

   ' Define the header information for the request. These headers
   ' appear in the same order recommended by the documentation at
   ' http://developer.ebay.com/DevZone/docs/API_Doc/index.asp.
   Req.Headers.Add("X-EBAY-API-SESSION-CERTIFICATE", txtDevID.Text _
                  + ";" + txtAppID.Text + ";" + txtCertID.Text)
   ... Add Other Request Headers ...
```

```vb
' Create the XML request object.
XMLData = New XmlDocument

' Add the XML request header.
ProcInst = XMLData.CreateProcessingInstruction( _
    "xml", "version='1.0'  encoding='iso-8859-1'")
XMLData.AppendChild(ProcInst)

' Construct the XML request message.
Root = XMLData.CreateElement("request")
Root.SetAttribute("xmlns", "urn:eBayAPIschema")

' Add the user information.
Elem = XMLData.CreateElement("RequestToken")
Elem.InnerText = txtUserAuth.Text
Root.AppendChild(Elem)

' Add the required request data.
Elem = XMLData.CreateElement("DetailLevel")
Elem.InnerText = "0"
Root.AppendChild(Elem)
Elem = XMLData.CreateElement("ErrorLevel")
Elem.InnerText = "1"
Root.AppendChild(Elem)
Elem = XMLData.CreateElement("SiteId")
Elem.InnerText = "0"
Root.AppendChild(Elem)
Elem = XMLData.CreateElement("ItemId")
Elem.InnerText = txtItemID.Text
Root.AppendChild(Elem)
Elem = XMLData.CreateElement("Verb")
Elem.InnerText = "GetHighBidders"
Root.AppendChild(Elem)

' Add the request data to the XML request.
XMLData.AppendChild(Root)

' Place the string into a byte array.
Encode = New ASCIIEncoding
PostBytes = Encode.GetBytes(XMLData.OuterXml)

' Set the Request up to post information to the server.
Req.ContentLength = PostBytes.Length

' Reset DataOut to send data.
DataOut = Req.GetRequestStream()
```

```vb
        ' Transmit the data.
        DataOut.Write(PostBytes, 0, PostBytes.Length)
        DataOut.Close()

        Try

            ' Get the resulting page from the server.
            Resp = Req.GetResponse()

            ' Place the data in a data stream for processing.
            DataOut = Resp.GetResponseStream()

            ' Read the data.
            ReadMe = New StreamReader(DataOut)

            ' Parse the data.
            ParseData = New XmlDocument
            ParseData.LoadXml(ReadMe.ReadToEnd())

            ' Close the data stream after reading the data.
            DataOut.Close()

        Catch WE As WebException
            ' Display the server's error message if an error occurs.
            MessageBox.Show(WE.Message)

            ' Exit the routine.
            Return
        End Try

        ' Get the eBay node.
        eBayData = ParseData.ChildNodes(1)

        ' Get the bids.
        AllBids = eBayData("Bids")

        ' Process the bids.
        For Each SingleBid As XmlElement In AllBids

            ' Check for the bid count.
            If SingleBid.Name = "Count" Then
                txtBids.Text = SingleBid.InnerText
            End If

            ' Display an indidual bid.
            If SingleBid.Name = "Bid" Then
                lstBidders.Items.Add( _
                    SingleBid("TimeBid").InnerText + " " + _
                    SingleBid("User")("UserId").InnerText + " (" + _
                    SingleBid("User")("Email").InnerText + ") " + _
                    SingleBid("Quantity").InnerText + " @ " + _
```

```
                SingleBid("CurrencyId").InnerText + _
                SingleBid("ConvertedPrice").InnerText)
            End If
        Next
    End Sub
```

The code begins by creating the HttpWebRequest object, Req. Notice the technique used to convert the generic WebRequest type into a specific HttpWebRequest. Unlike calls to the Microsoft XML libraries, the .NET Framework routines require that you set the request Method property separately. The next step is to add all of the usual headers. Notice that you must use the ContentType property to define the data type.

Building the XML message uses the same steps as many of the other examples in the book. Notice this example uses the <RequestToken> element, in place of the soon to be deprecated (eliminated) username and password. Make sure the <ItemId> value you provide is for an item with a quantity greater than 1 or the call will fail. Fortunately, in this case, the error message is very clear as to the source of the error, so you won't have any problems figuring out when an item is incorrect because it's the wrong type. Always set the <DetailLevel> for this call to 0 because it supports only one level of detail.

You can't send the data directly to the server because of the way that the .NET Framework handles HTTP requests. The code converts the XML request into a Byte array and writes the information to the server using a data stream. This technique is actually more efficient when you have a large amount of data to write because you don't have to write the entire stream at one time. In addition, this technique is somewhat less error prone. Make absolutely certain that you close the data stream when you finish using it, as shown in the code. Otherwise, the application will display an error when the code attempts to receive the data.

The code receives the response at this point. Make sure you use error trapping because a server error will cause an application crash before you get the chance to check the server status information in most cases. The code receives the response as a data stream that it loads into an XML document, ParseData using the LoadXml() method. Again, make sure you close the data stream after receiving the XML response.

The XML document is a little hard to use compared to the features provided by an XmlElement, so the code loads the data into eBayData. Notice that using an XmlElement makes the code easy to read because all of the nodes are accessible using names, rather than numbers. The code processes all of the children of the <Bids> node. The first child is a <Count> element that contains the number of bidders. The remaining children are <Bid> elements that contain information about the various bidders. The code shows just a little of the information you can retrieve. Figure 8.8 shows typical output for this application.

The high bidder list contains a wealth of information about the buyer.

Developing with Visual C# .NET

Visual C# .NET is a new language that made its appearance as part of Visual Studio .NET. The language combines the flexibility of C++ with some of the programmer productivity benefits of using Visual Basic. In addition, it bears a striking resemblance to Java in many ways. In fact, many developers say that C# is Microsoft's attempt to create something as useful as Java.

No matter how you feel about C#, it's a capable language that lets you perform some tasks that Visual Basic .NET doesn't. For example, Visual Basic doesn't let you create unsafe code—that is, code that contains unmanaged pointers. C# lets you create such code so that you can perform some low-level tasks that Visual Basic isn't designed to perform. From an eBay Web Services perspective, the two languages are probably equivalent and the choice of language comes down to coding style. However, it's important to keep the differences between Visual Basic and C# in mind if you plan to create a complex application. The following sections show how to create a basic C# eBay Web Services application.

Using the eBay C# Examples

eBay provides two C# examples as part of the eBay Web Services Kit. These examples differ from the Visual Basic .NET examples, so you might want to look at both. Each example demonstrates a different technique for working with eBay. In the case of the SimpleXmlPost example, you might want to keep a copy around and augment it for personal use. The following sections provide a brief overview of each example and provide some ideas on how to use them effectively. You'll find these examples in the `\Program Files\eBay\SDK\Samples\C#` folder of your eBay Web Services Kit installation.

SimpleList Example

The C# version of the SimpleList example works much like the Visual Basic 6 version described in the "Using the eBay Visual Basic 6 Example" section of the chapter. However, this example does have an important difference: it shows how to handle SDK events. In this case, you'll find two check boxes for the `IAPICall.OnPostRequestXml` and `IAPICall.OnReceiveResponseXml` events. When you make a call with these two check boxes selected, you receive additional information from eBay Web Services. Handling the `IAPICall.OnPostRequestXml` lets you make last minute changes to the XML sent to eBay, as shown in Figure 8.9.

FIGURE 8.9:

The C# version of the SimpleList example shows how to handle events.

Likewise, handling the `IAPICall.OnReceiveResponseXml` lets you work with the response XML before the `IApiCall` class does any work with it. The event handler can work with the raw XML before it's processed. The C# example demonstrates that you can work with raw XML even if you choose to use the SDK. The task isn't any more convenient using an event handler, but the capability is there. The main reason to handle these events is for debugging or added processing needs.

SimpleXmlPost Example

The SimpleXmlPost example is one of my favorites because it mimics much of the functionality of the online API Tool without actually having to use a browser. As shown in Figure 8.10, you enter an XML request, click Post XML to eBay, and look at the response. This is another way that you can test your XML to ensure it works in your code.

FIGURE 8.10:

Send and receive XML that you want to test using this example.

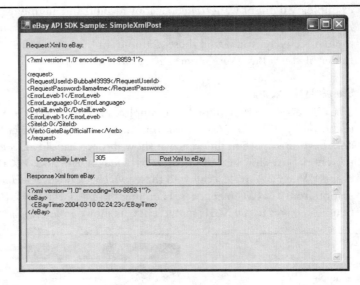

This example is interesting for another reason—it's the only one that eBay provides that uses the `IApiXmlPoster` interface. This interface is exceptionally useful because you can send data located in a file, a string, or in an XML document. The example program uses the `PostXmlText()` method to post information defined in a string that you create in the Request Xml to eBay field shown in Figure 8.10.

Using the SDK Technique with Visual C# .NET

The example in this section performs a standard search using the SDK technique. The unique feature of this example is the use of a `DataSet` to store the results. The use of `DataSet` means that you can perform a number of data manipulations at the speed of local memory, but with all of the benefits of a database. Listing 8.3 shows the essential source code for this example. You'll find the complete source for this example in the `\Chapter 08\CSharp_ItemSearch` folder of the source code located on the Sybex Web site.

Listing 8.3   Using the *GetSearchResults* Call

```
private void btnSearch_Click(object sender, System.EventArgs e)
{
    ... Variable Declarations ...

    // Create a session.
    Session = new ApiSession();
```

```
// Define the sandbox as the call location.
Session.Url = "https://api.sandbox.ebay.com/ws/api.dll";

// Add session security information.
Session.RequestUserId = txtUserID.Text;
Session.RequestPassword = txtPassword.Text;

// Add the developer information.
Session.Developer = txtDevID.Text;
Session.Application = txtAppID.Text;
Session.Certificate = txtCertID.Text;

// Create a search.
Search = new GetSearchResultsCall(Session);

// Add the search criteria.
Search.Query = txtQuery.Text;
Search.MaxResults = 20;

// Perform the search.
Results = Search.GetSearchResults();

// Clear the current results in the dataset.
dsOutput.Tables["ItemOut"].Clear();

// Interpret the results.
foreach (IItemFound Item in Results)
{
    // Add a row.
    DR = dsOutput.Tables["ItemOut"].NewRow();

    // Add the data to the row.
    DR["Title"] = Item.Title;
    DR["Current Price"] = Item.CurrentPrice;
    DR["Start Time"] = Item.StartTime;

    // Display the row on screen.
    dsOutput.Tables["ItemOut"].Rows.Add(DR);
}
}
```

The code begins by creating an API session using the ApiSession() constructor. As is normal, it adds the user and developer information to the session. You must always provide this information or the call will fail.

Once the code establishes a session, it creates the GetSearchResultsCall object, Search. Notice how the constructor for this call uses Session as an input. I've found that it's more reliable to always provide the session variable as an input to the constructor—one of the options is simply to create a new GetSearchResultsCall object.

The next step is to define a set of query parameters. eBay exposes a number of search arguments not shown in the code. These arguments help you refine your search. Chapter 3 discusses the search options at your disposal—using them carefully can make it easier to find the specific items you need. In this case, all the code defines is the required `Search.Query` property and the optional `Search.MaxResults` property. At this point, the code calls `Search.Get-SearchResults()` to return the results from eBay Web Services. The results appear as a series of `IItemFound` objects in a collection, `Results`.

The example uses a `DataGrid` to present the data on screen. The easiest way to fill the `DataGrid` is using a `DataSet`, `dsOutput`. This setup lets the user perform tasks such as sorting the information and reordering as needed. Your application can also work with the data in the same way that it does a database. To fill `dsOutput`, the code creates a row using the `NewRow()` method. It places data in each of the data fields, and then adds this row to `dsOutput` using the `Rows.Add(DR)` method. Figure 8.11 shows typical output from this application.

Using SQL Server as a Database

Using a cache to hold your eBay search data is a good idea for a number of reasons. For example, using a cache helps you improve application performance. For more information on how to use caching, see the "Caching as a Practical Performance Enhancing Technique" section of Chapter 7. The example in this section relies on SQL Server to provide caching functionality. However, you could easily adapt the example to use any Database Management System (DBMS). In fact, you don't have to use a DBMS at all—a simple XML file (or even a text file) works fine for personal needs.

FIGURE 8.11:

Desktop applications are platform specific, but offer great processing flexibility.

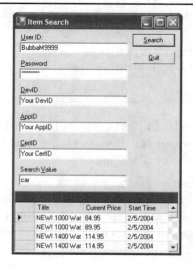

Using the eBay Sample Selling Application

The eBay Sample Selling Application provides you with a full-fledged example of a complete eBay management application. The example is heavily skewed toward the needs of a seller, but it contains a host of great ideas for the developer of any application. You can find this example in the \Program Files\eBay\SDK folder of the eBay Web Services Kit.

Unfortunately, the eBay Web Services Kit appears to lack the full source code for this example—making it of limited usefulness for learning coding techniques. However, I've found it makes a great developer tool. For example, you can use it to set up a quick auction for testing your latest creation. The following sections provide an overview of the application and some pointers on ways you can use it to develop ideas of your own.

Using the eBay SDK Configuration Wizard

In order to use eBay Sample Selling Application, you need to configure it by modifying the eBaySales.exe.config file located in the \Program Files\eBay\SDK folder. This configuration task is an important first step—you must perform it before you start the sample application. The following steps show you how to perform the task with an Access database. Working with other databases follows a similar sequence.

1. Start the eBay SDK Configuration Wizard using the Start ➢ Programs ➢ eBay SDK ➢ Database Configuration Wizard command. You'll see the eBay SDK Configuration Wizard dialog box.

2. Click Next. The configuration wizard will ask you to select one of the supported databases (Access, SQL Server 2000, or SQL Server 7.0) or provide a connection string.

3. Select your database and click Next. The configuration wizard will ask for a location for your database. The default for Access is \Program Files\eBay\SDK\Database\eBaySdk .mdb. The SQL Server option defaults to a local database connection. You can place the database anywhere you like. Make sure you select a location that's easy to back up so you can protect your data. The eBay supplied databases use a password of SecretKey as a default, make sure you change the password if you use the database to store data from the production system.

> ▶ **WARNING**
>
> The database you select must exist and it must contain all of the required tables. If you provide the name of a nonexistent database, the configuration wizard will display an error message. If the database is empty, the configuration wizard will run, but the sample application won't. You can still create the database without stopping the wizard—simply clear the message and continue after the database is ready for use.

4. Type a location and name for your database. Click Next. eBay will create a connection string for you. Make sure you copy this string by highlighting it and pressing Ctrl+C. Paste the string into a document or other safe location. Fortunately, you can also find this information in the eBaySales.exe.config file located in the \Program Files\eBay\SDK folder. At this point, the configuration wizard offers to create all of the required tables and other support the SDK needs for you.

> ▶ **NOTE**
>
> The connection string that the configuration wizard creates for you lacks a username. The lack of a username means the connection could fail. If you receive an error message from the configuration wizard stating the database is invalid, try again with a modified connection string. Add a User ID=Admin; entry to the list of configuration items. For example, a typical connection string might look like Provider=Microsoft.Jet.OLEDB.4.0;User ID=Admin; Data Source=D:\Chapter 07\Access\eBaySdk.mdb;Persist Security Info=False;Jet OLEDB:Database Password=;Jet OLEDB:Encrypt Database=True with the additional information.

5. Click Next. If configuration wizard is successful in accessing the database, you'll see a completion message and an offer to start the sample selling application. If the configuration wizard fails to connect to the database, you'll see an error message telling you about the error.

6. Click Finish. The database is now ready for use with the Integration Library.

Configuring the Sample Application

When you start the sample application for the first time, it asks you some simple questions. These questions add information to the database so it provides complete support for the Integration Library. For example, even though the database has a complete set of tables, it doesn't contain any users. You need to create a user in order to use the sample application—the configuration process accomplishes that task. The following steps take you through the initial configuration process.

1. Start the eBay Sample Selling Application, if it hasn't already started as part of the configuration process in the "Using the eBay SDK Configuration Wizard" section.

2. Click Next to get past the Welcome dialog box. The configuration wizard asks for a site, development environment (sandbox, production, or QA), and your developer keys.

3. Type the required information and click Next. The configuration wizard asks for a user identifier, password, and email address. This information must be for a user in the requested development environment—you can't use a sandbox user in the production environment, or vice versa.

4. Type the user information and click Next. The configuration wizard asks for an email template. If you're an individual user or a small company, use the incoming mail server for your account. Otherwise, provide a template for your company email system—one that has Internet access.

5. Provide the SMTP server information or the email template and click Next. The configuration wizard displays a message telling you about the application update it plans to perform.

6. Click Next. The configuration wizard performs the required updates. This process can take a long time, in excess of an hour, if you're using a dial-up connection (and it's not very fast with broadband either). The reason for the long download is that the sample application is loading categories, attributes, and other essential information.

7. Click Next. The configuration wizard will ask if you want to import items that have completed sale within the last 30 days. Generally, it's a good idea to import the items so click Next to begin the process.

8. Click Finish when the data import process completes. The eBay Sample Selling Application is ready for use.

Creating a New Item

One of the reasons to use this application from a developer perspective is to quickly create auction items for testing. The various listing test programs supplied by eBay do work, but they don't provide complete access to every listing feature. This program provides complete access to all listing features, including access to any store categories that you set up. Figure 8.12 shows the initial application window. As you can see, the application lets you track current sales, items that haven't sold (they won't sell to anyone but test users in the sandbox), items that you've saved (see Listing 7.4 for an example of how to save items), and items marked for deletion.

To add a new item, click New Item on the toolbar. Notice the list indicator next to this button. You can use this list to select special item listings such as a store listing or a fixed price listing. It's also possible to select from any templates you create using this list. The list doesn't include a few special sale types, such as the Dutch auction described in the "Defining a Dutch Auction" section. After you click New Item or select one of the new item types, the application displays a New Item window. Figure 8.13 shows a typical view of the New Item window—the actual contents can vary when you select one of the special options.

FIGURE 8.12:
Use the eBay Sample Selling Application to view the status of your test users.

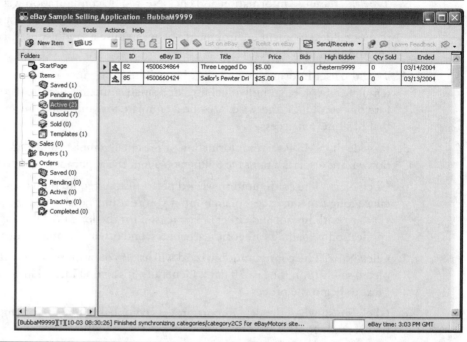

FIGURE 8.13:
The eBay Sample Selling Application helps you create new items quickly.

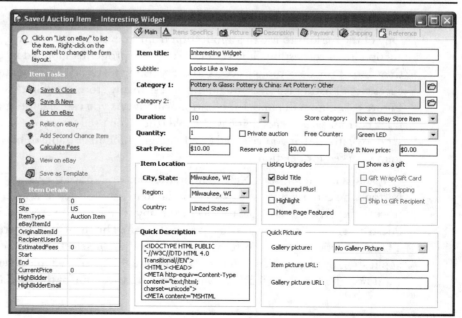

This form probably has too many blanks for the average user to fill out. That's why your custom application is needed. You can set some defaults for the particular business that is using the application. However, as a test application, this one is excellent because you can see the various options you do have available and how they interact. One of the first tasks you must perform is considering what type of auction to create. eBay supports the following auction types—only the Dutch auction requires special handling.

Ad-type   This auction doesn't actually sell anything—it's an advertisement. To create an ad-type auction, you must set one or both of the categories to a real estate value.

BuyItNow   This auction sells one item to the highest bidder. The first bidder has the option of buying the item at the BuyItNow price, which must be higher than the start price. If the buyer exercises this option, the auction ends immediately and the buyer pays the BuyItNow price. When the buyer chooses to ignore this option, the auction proceeds like a Chinese auction. To create an auction of this type, set the BuyItNow price field to a value other than 0 and higher than the start price.

Chinese   This auction sells one item to the highest bidder at the end of the specified duration. You can sell a store item using this method. To ensure your auction is accepted as a Chinese auction, you must set the Quantity field to 1 and the BuyItNow price field to 0.

Fixed price   This auction sells one or more items at a fixed price—there isn't any bidding. The buyer purchases one or more items at the price specified. The auction ends when the duration expires or the last item is sold. Use the Fixed Price Item form to create an auction of this type by selecting Fixed Price Format from the New Item drop down list. You can detect this form by the Fixed Price field it contains (rather than the usual Start Price field).

Store fixed price   This auction works much like the fixed price auction. However, you use the Store Fixed Price Item form in place of the Fixed Price Item form. The difference from an eBay perspective is that the item is listed in the seller's storefront on eBay, as well as the usual auction areas.

All of the auctions require that you provide some essential pieces of information. You must provide a location, at least one category, a price (starting or fixed), a title, and a description. Everything else is optional. Once you complete the form, click the List on eBay link and the application will upload it for you.

Defining a Dutch Auction

Some of the function calls, such as the `GetHighBidders()` call demonstrated in Listing 8.2, require the use of a Dutch action. A Dutch auction always offers multiple items for sale and never offers a BuyItNow price. The buyers can competitively bid on one or more items. The auction ends when the duration expires.

To create a Dutch auction, you must create a new item that has 2 or more in the Quantity field. After you create the item, verify that eBay views it as a Dutch auction item by clicking Calculate Fees. When the call returns, the Item Details area of the display should show Dutch Auction in the `ItemType` field, as shown in Figure 8.14.

Getting the Category List and Storing It

Almost every application you create is going to require some knowledge of the categories that eBay supports. In fact, most of the sample applications that eBay provides require a category entry or present category information. The reason for this concentration on categories is that effective selling relies on categorization of the item for sale. Consequently, one of the first database applications I built for myself was a tool to download, store, and display categories locally. The example in this section shows a category storage technique you can use when building your own applications.

> ▶ **NOTE**
>
> The eBay documentation warns that the category list is large—in the 1.5MB to 2MB range. Don't download the entire list every time you want to check the categories. To check the accuracy of your category list, make the `GetCategories()` call with the `<DetailLevel>` and `<ViewAll Nodes>` elements set to 0. eBay Web Services will return just the category list version number and the date of last update so that you can determine whether a complete update is warranted.

FIGURE 8.14:

Verify that you have actually created a Dutch auction before you save the item.

Listing 8.4 shows the essential source code for this example. You'll find the complete source for this example in the \Chapter 08\CSharp_CategoryList folder of the source code located on the Sybex Web site. The scripts and sample data for the example appear in the \Chapter 08\Data folder of the source code located on the Sybex Web site.

Listing 8.4   Getting a List of Categories

```csharp
private void CheckData()
{
    ... Variable Declarations ...

    // Create a session.
    Session = new ApiSession();

    ... Add the Usual Session Information ...

    // Create a category listing.
    Cats = new GetCategoriesCall(Session);

    // Use this criteria to get the version number.
    Cats.DetailLevel = 0;
    Cats.ErrorLevel = ErrorLevelEnum.BothShortAndLongErrorStrings;
    Cats.SiteId = 0;
    Cats.ViewAllNodes = false;

    // Check for a parent category number.
    if (Int32.Parse(txtCatParent.Text) > 0)
        Cats.CategoryParent = Int32.Parse(txtCatParent.Text);

    // Get the version number.
    Cats.GetCategories(out Version);
    txtVersion.Text = Version.ToString();

    // Open the database connection.
    CatConnect.Open();

    // Check the database to see if it contains any records.
    CSReader =
        daCategoryStats.SelectCommand.ExecuteReader(
            CommandBehavior.SingleRow);
    if (CSReader.HasRows)
    {
        // Read the data.
        CSReader.Read();

        // Verify the data is new enough.
        if ((Int32)CSReader.GetValue(0) >= Version)
        {
            // Display the last update date.
            txtLastUpdate.Text = CSReader.GetValue(1).ToString();
```

```
// Close the reader.
CSReader.Close();

// Use the same reader to read the Categories table. Determine
// whether the database has the requested top level category.
SrchCmd =
    new SqlCommand("SELECT * FROM Categories " +
                   "WHERE CategoryID=" +
                   txtCatParent.Text, CatConnect);
CSReader =
    SrchCmd.ExecuteReader(CommandBehavior.SingleRow);

// Verify the category is in the database.
if (CSReader.HasRows)
{

    // Add the parent node into Results. Note that this code
    // doesn't support the characteristic set (CS). This
    // feature doesn't seem to be used and requires special
    // handling.
    ThisCat = new Category();
    CSReader.Read();
    ThisCat.CategoryId =
        CSReader.GetInt32(CSReader.GetOrdinal("CategoryId"));
    ... Other Categories ...
    ThisCat.LeafCategory =
        Convert.ToBoolean(
            CSReader.GetInt32(
                CSReader.GetOrdinal("LeafCategory")));
    ThisCat.SiteId =
        (SiteIdEnum)CSReader.GetInt32(
            CSReader.GetOrdinal("AppSiteId"));
    Results = new CategoryCollection();
    Results.Add(ThisCat);

    // Close the existing reader.
    CSReader.Close();

    // Locate the second level of entries based on the
    // current parent.
    SrchCmd =
        new SqlCommand("SELECT * FROM Categories " +
                       "WHERE CategoryParentID<>CategoryID " +
                       "AND CategoryParentID=" +
                       txtCatParent.Text, CatConnect);
    CSReader =
        SrchCmd.ExecuteReader(CommandBehavior.Default);

    // Initialize the Parent array.
    CatIDs = new ArrayList();
```

```
        // Process this second level in the same way as the first.
        // Keep reading until all the records are process.
        while (CSReader.Read())
        {
            // Get the category information. Make sure you create a
            // new Category object for each entry.
            ThisCat = new Category();
            ... Add the Categories ...

            // Add the information to results. Make sure you
            // maintain the current object.
            Results.Add(ThisCat);

            // Add the current category ID to a list of IDs.
            CatIDs.Add(ThisCat.CategoryId);
        }

        // Close the existing reader.
        CSReader.Close();

        // The third level of processing the same, except now
        // you need to do it for each of the second level parents.
        foreach (Int32 CatID in CatIDs)
        {
            ... Process the third level entries ...
        }

        // Always close the database connection.
        CatConnect.Close();
    }
    else
    {
        // This routine assumes that the database contains current
        // information, but not the information needed.

        ... Essentially the same process deleting old data. ...

    }
}
else
{
    // Close the data reader and update the statistics database.
    daCategoryStats.DeleteCommand.Parameters[
        "@Original_CategoryVersion"].Value =
            (Int32)CSReader.GetValue(0);
    daCategoryStats.DeleteCommand.Parameters[
        "@Original_LastUpdate"].Value =
            (DateTime)CSReader.GetValue(1);
    CSReader.Close();
    daCategoryStats.DeleteCommand.ExecuteNonQuery();
```

```
                    // Add the new version information into the database.
                    daCategoryStats.InsertCommand.Parameters[
                        "@CategoryVersion"].Value = Version;
                    daCategoryStats.InsertCommand.Parameters[
                        "@LastUpdate"].Value = DateTime.Now;
                    daCategoryStats.InsertCommand.ExecuteNonQuery();

                    // Add the category download criteria.
                    Cats.DetailLevel = 1;
                    Cats.ViewAllNodes = true;

                    // Get the categories.
                    Results = (CategoryCollection)Cats.GetCategories();

                    // Delete all of the existing category records.
                    DelCmd = new SqlCommand("DELETE FROM Categories", CatConnect);
                    Int32 Rows = DelCmd.ExecuteNonQuery();

                    // Create the new database entries based on the results.
                    foreach (Category SingleEntry in Results)
                    {
                        // Add the record to the database.
                        daCategories.InsertCommand.Parameters[
                            "@CategoryId"].Value = SingleEntry.CategoryId;
                        ... Fill Out Other Parameters ...
                        daCategories.InsertCommand.ExecuteNonQuery();
                    }

                    // Always close the database connection.
                    CatConnect.Close();

                    // Set the last update day.
                    txtLastUpdate.Text = DateTime.Now.ToString();
                }
            }
            else
            {

                ... Call eBay, Get the Data, Store the Results ...

            }
        }
```

The code for this example is complex for a number of reasons. First, the code receives the categories as a listing. Your code must convert this listing into a hierarchy that correctly represents the category hierarchy on eBay. Second, the hierarchical structure of the data means you can't make any assumptions about it. Entries can appear out of sequence. Third, your code must handle inconsistencies in the data. For example, in most cases, the <CategoryParentId> element references the parent node of the current node. However, if the node is a top-level node, the <CategoryId> element and the <CategoryParentId> element are the same, which makes processing awkward.

The code begins as with any other SDK call. It creates an ApiSession object, adds user and developer identification information, and uses this information as a means for creating a connection. The code then creates a GetCategoriesCall object, adds required and optional data, and then makes the call. However, when you use the GetCategories() method, the eBay documentation suggests that you make two calls. The first call should just return the version number.

You might wonder why the code specifies a category for the version check when the documentation tells you not to provide a version number. If you make the call using the SDK technique without specifying a CategoryParent property value, the code appears to freeze for some length of time and eventually times out, forcing the application to crash. This same call works fine when used with the API technique, so the problem lies in the code that wraps the API for the SDK. When eBay fixes this problem, you'll be able to make the version part of the call without specifying the CategoryParent property value and the call will return very quickly.

At this point, the code must perform one of four tasks. First, the database could be empty, so the code might need to perform an initial fill of data. Second, the data in the database could be old, in which case the code will delete the existing data and fill the database with new information. Third, the database might not contain the required information since this application is designed to store only the categories you actually request. In this case, the code makes a request for the new information. Fourth, the database contains correct data, so the code can use the information without contacting eBay a second time.

> ► **TIP**
>
> This is a situation where the API technique provides a little more information than the SDK technique. With one call, the API technique provides the version number, the category count, the date eBay last updated the categories, and the GMT date eBay last updated the categories. Of these, you can obtain the category count with every call, if you know which properties to use. The version number requires a second call to obtain. You can't obtain the update dates using the SDK method.

To determine whether the database has any data, the code makes a daCategoryStats .SelectCommand.ExecuteReader(CommandBehavior.SingleRow) call. This call creates a SqlDataReader object, CSReader. If the CSReader.HasRows property is true, then the database contains information and the code doesn't have to start from scratch.

The database actually consists of two tables. The CategoryStats table contains two values: the version number of the categories stored in the database and the date those categories were last downloaded. The Categories table contains all of the category records. It's based on a similar table that eBay uses for the Integration Library. The code uses the version number stored in `CSReader.GetValue(0)` to check the current version number against the one obtained in the first `GetCategories()` call from eBay Web Services. If the version number in the database is equal to the one obtained from eBay, the data in the database is current. Otherwise, the code assumes the data is old, deletes it from the database, and calls eBay Web Services to fill the database with new information.

At this point, the code has to determine whether the database contains the information specified by the `txtCatParent.Text` property. This control lets the user determine the starting point of the eBay category listing. It's possible to select any point in the eBay category hierarchy. To perform this task, the code creates a special SQL Server command, `SqlCommand("SELECT * FROM Categories WHERE CategoryID=" + txtCatParent.Text, CatConnect)`. If after executing this command, the `CSReader.HasRows` property is true, then the database contains the required information. Otherwise, the code clears the current database information, and requests the new information from eBay Web Services. Note that you could retain the existing data since this data is current; the example takes this step for the sake of simplicity.

It's time to look at individual cases. The first case is one where the database contains the correct data. Remember that this data used to appear as a single object, but now it consists of individual records. Consequently, the code must rebuild a single object, `Results`, the same `Results` returned from a `GetCategories()` method call. The code already has access to the parent node because it had to look it up to determine whether the database has correct information.

The code begins by creating an individual `Category` object, `ThisCat`. It places the individual values from the current database record into `ThisCat` properties. It's important to note that you'll have to perform some data conversions to move the data. Notice the technique used. The code relies on specific methods of `CSReader` to obtain the data in the correct format. Since these methods all require an ordinal (a number) instead of a string, the code also uses the `CSReader.GetOrdinal()` method to define the number based on the column name. The Integration Library database format stores Boolean values as numbers. The example shows a technique for converting the numeric value back into a Boolean for use as a category. Finally, some values don't store in SQL Server at all because they're enumerations. Notice how the code uses coercion to convert the SQL Server numeric value into an enumerated value for `ThisCat.SiteId`. When `ThisCat` is complete, the code stores it in `Results` using the `Add()` method.

The first level search required that the code look at the `CategoryID` field of the SQL Server database. However, you don't know the category values for the second level. The only way to find the second level categories is to search for the first level category in the `CategoryParentID` field. However, there's a problem. When the parent category is also a top level node, the `CategoryParentID` field contains the same number as the `CategoryID` field. To handle this problem, the code constructs a complex `SqlCommand` and executes it. The result is one or more rows of second level category identifiers. The processing of the second level is about the same as the first level. The code stores the second level category identifiers in an array to use as a source of information for the third level of processing. The third level of processing is about the same as the second. The difference is that this level relies on the array of category identifiers created in the second level as search values for the `CategoryParentID` field.

The next two types of processing are essentially the same, so I'll only describe one in this section. Whether the data in the database is too old or the database simply didn't have the required information, the code still has to delete the old information and make a call to eBay Web Services to load the table with new information. The code begins by deleting the contents of the CategoryStats table and adding new values that show the new version number and download date. The code then changes the criteria for calling eBay Web Services so the call returns all of the requested category information. The `GetCategories()` method fills `Results` with data from eBay Web Services.

Now that `Results` has the latest information, the code uses a special `SqlCommand` object to delete all of the records from the table. The code then uses the standard `daCategories.InsertCommand.Parameters` properties to fill the `InsertCommand` with data and the `daCategories.InsertCommand.ExecuteNonQuery()` method to send that data to the database. When the code finishes, the table contains all of the records in `Results`.

The final type of processing follows the same process of calling eBay Web Services and storing the results in the table. The only difference is that there's nothing to delete, so the code skips the record deletion steps.

At this point, `Results` has the data needed to present the categories on screen. Listing 8.5 describes the process for taking what amounts to a list of node information and changing it into a hierarchical display.

Listing 8.5   **Presenting the Categories**

```
private void btnCheck_Click(object sender, System.EventArgs e)
{
    ... Variable Declarations ...

    // Get the data.
    CheckData();
```

```
// Display the number of categories.
txtNumCats.Text = Results.Count.ToString();

// Initiaize the category ID array.
CatIDs = new ArrayList();

// Assign images to the tree view.
tvCategories.ImageList = NodePics;

// Clear any existing results.
tvCategories.Nodes.Clear();

// Define the initial category level.
InitLevel = Results[0].CategoryLevel;

// Parse the child nodes.
foreach (ICategory ThisCat in Results)
{
   // Add each of the category IDs in order so we can find
   // specific categories.
   CatIDs.Add(ThisCat.CategoryId);

   switch (ThisCat.CategoryLevel - InitLevel)
   {
      case 0:
         // Create the root node.
         tvCategories.Nodes.Add(new
            TreeNode(Results[0].CategoryName, 0, 1));
         break;
      case 1:
         // Processing the first level is relatively easy because
         // you only need to look back one level to locate the
         // root node. The code adds the current node to the root
         // node.
         if (ThisCat.LeafCategory)
            tvCategories.Nodes[0].Nodes.Add(
               new TreeNode(ThisCat.CategoryName, 2, 3));
         else
            tvCategories.Nodes[0].Nodes.Add(
               new TreeNode(ThisCat.CategoryName, 0, 1));
         break;
      case 2:
         // Locate this child's parent.
         Level2 = 0;

         // Begin by checking the indext of category IDs.
         LevelChk = CatIDs.IndexOf(ThisCat.CategoryParentId);

         // Process only the nodes at the level above the current
         // level.
```

```
        foreach (TreeNode TN in tvCategories.Nodes[0].Nodes)
        {
            // LevelChk now contains the node number for the
            // parent in Results. Use this information to perform
            // a comparison and locate the correct node in
            // tvCategories.
            if (TN.Text == Results[LevelChk].CategoryName)
                Level2 = tvCategories.Nodes[0].Nodes.IndexOf(TN);
        }

        // Now the processing involves two levels of indirection.
        if (ThisCat.LeafCategory)
            tvCategories.Nodes[0].Nodes[Level2].Nodes.Add(
                new TreeNode(ThisCat.CategoryName, 2, 3));
        else
            tvCategories.Nodes[0].Nodes[Level2].Nodes.Add(
                new TreeNode(ThisCat.CategoryName, 0, 1));
        break;
    }
  }
}
```

The code begins with the call to CheckData(). This is the method shown in Listing 8.4 that fills Results with information. The code uses the Results.Count property to fill in the number of returned categories on screen. The code also takes care of a few initialization tasks. One of the most important initialization tasks is to create an ArrayList to hold the various category values.

The real processing begins when the code determines the current CategoryLevel value. The highest level nodes begin at a CategoryLevel of 1 and move down to leaf nodes with CategoryLevel values of up to 7 (although eBay could easily add more). The code uses a TreeView control to display the category levels, as shown in Figure 8.15. The code can process up to three levels of categories, depending on the starting level.

There are three cases to consider when working with three levels. The first case is easy—the code simply assigns the category to the root node of the tree. Because the root node is never a leaf, the code displays it using a folder icon, as shown in Figure 8.15. The TreeNode(Results[0].CategoryName, 0, 1) method defines the text that appears on screen, the number of an image in an ImageList for the nonselected mode, and a similar image for the selected mode.

The second case is a little more difficult. The code can still use the root node as a basis for adding new nodes to the tree view. However, the nodes could be leaf nodes, which means the code must check the ThisCat.LeafCategory value before assigning an image to the node.

FIGURE 8.15:

The category list can help you create other applications that require a category number.

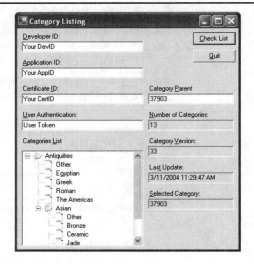

By the time the code gets to the third level, the root node is no longer in the picture. Notice the technique used to locate the parent of the target node. The CatIDs.IndexOf (ThisCat.CategoryParentId) method returns a number that tells where to locate the parent based on the content of the CatIDs ArrayList. Armed with this information, the code searches through the entire list in Results for the parent node and then uses that information to assign the current node to the correct position in the tree. You would need to extend this third level technique to the fourth and subsequent levels.

At this point, the nodes are displayed on screen and you can select them. The whole point of this application is to display the correct category number on screen so you can use it in an application. Listing 8.6 shows the final piece of the puzzle.

Listing 8.6   Selecting a Category

```
private void tvCategories_AfterSelect(
    object sender,
    System.Windows.Forms.TreeViewEventArgs e)
{
    // Get the name of the selected node.
    foreach (ICategory ThisCat in Results)

        // Compare the current node name to those in Results.
        if (ThisCat.CategoryName == e.Node.Text)
        {
            // If this is a top level node, we're done.
            if (e.Node.Parent == null)
                txtSelected.Text = ThisCat.CategoryId.ToString();
```

```
        // Lower level nodes require more processing.
    else
    {
        // Locate the parent node in Results.
        foreach (ICategory ParentCat in Results)
            if ((e.Node.Parent.Text == ParentCat.CategoryName) &&
                (ThisCat.CategoryParentId == ParentCat.CategoryId))
                    txtSelected.Text = ThisCat.CategoryId.ToString();

    }
  }
}
```

The code begins by creating a loop that checks every node in Results. Unfortunately, Results doesn't provide a means to search for a category by name, you must provide a number. The code performs the search by comparing each ThisCat.CategoryName against the node name passed into the event handler from the TreeView control. If this is a top level node, the result is immediate and the code displays the CategoryId property value on screen.

Other nodes require a little more processing because two nodes can have the same name— Other is one of the most common names that eBay uses. When this occurs, the code must also verify the parent node text against the parent in Results. If the two match, the search is done. Otherwise, the code continues looking for a node that has a parent with the correct name.

Your Call to Action

This chapter demonstrates various techniques you can use to access eBay Web Services using Visual Studio products such as Visual C++, Visual Basic, Visual Basic .NET, and Visual C#. Most developers will select one of these languages to create most applications, but all of them work well. The choice of language depends on personal taste and existing application infrastructure as much as the techniques for accessing eBay Web Services. You also learned how to mix Visual Studio applications with SQL Server. In most cases, you'll use SQL Server for short-term storage of intermediate results, item data, current sales information, buyer data, or seller data. However, you can use SQL Server with eBay as you would any other database application. The use of a database simply makes it easier to manipulate and analyze the data.

It's time to consider how you'll use Visual Studio to create applications to access eBay Web Services. The choice of language is important because each language does excel in specific areas. Visual C++ is a great choice when application performance and flexibility are prime considerations, but Visual Basic provides the best database access for many purposes. Visual C# and Visual Basic both provide superior database access and developer productivity. However, the cost of using these products is that every machine that uses the resulting application must have the .NET Framework loaded. Because .NET is a relatively new programming technology, you can't make assumptions about the user's machine unless you have control over the machine configuration.

Chapter 9 is the first Web-specific chapter in the book. It demonstrates techniques for accessing eBay Web Services using PHP. You'll find that working with PHP is relatively easy and that support for PHP is very good. Many developers create all of their Web applications in PHP because the language is so popular and short-term costs so low. Whether PHP is the right solution for your eBay Web Services application or not depends on how you plan to work with eBay Web Services in the long term. Chapter 9 can help you make a good decision about the viability of using PHP for your eBay Web Services project.

Chapter 9

Resources for Learning PHP

Downloading and Installing PHP

Working with the eBay Example

▶ Writing Applications Using PHP

Creating a PHP Application

Using MySQL as a Database

Creating a PHP Application with Database Support

Many developers have used PHP over the years because it's a good solution for creating Web pages and the price is right. The PHP acronym is like many other new acronyms for the Internet—the acronym is recursive (refers back to itself). PHP stands for *PHP Hypertext Processor*. This general-purpose HTML scripting language works much like Active Server Pages (ASP) or other page description languages you might have used. Essentially, you mix HTML with scripting information. When the PHP process sees HyperText Markup Language (HTML), it sends the text directly to the user. It processes any scripting information and passes the resulting HTML to the user as well.

This chapter helps you discover how PHP works with eBay Web Services. I'm assuming that you already know something about PHP, but the first two sections suggest how to learn more about PHP. Because PHP runs on so many platforms, you'll also find suggested resources for getting and installing PHP for your particular server. These instructions require a little technical knowledge on your part, so make sure you understand the instructions before you perform them.

The examples in this chapter show how to use PHP to create an eBay Web Services application. The first two examples provide simple instructions for accessing the Web service without any fancy application features. You'll also find an application that shows how to use PHP with MySQL, an open source database. In fact, you can download every piece of software in this chapter free and try out all of the examples without spending a penny—that's one of the benefits of using open source.

> **▶ NOTE**
>
> I'm using the Apache 2.0.47 Windows and PHP 4.3.4 versions for this chapter. You might notice some differences between these product versions and other versions available on the download sites. Because of the way PHP works, the example code should work fine on any newer version of Apache and PHP you choose to use. Older versions of both Apache and PHP could encounter problems when they don't support the features found in the current products.

Resources for Learning PHP

This chapter assumes that you already know how to use PHP and simply want to learn how to use it with eBay Web Services. Consequently, the chapter doesn't include essential language instruction that you might need if you're a PHP novice. If you think you might want to learn to use PHP for your next Web application, the resources in this section will help. One of the first places you should look for PHP information is the PHP site at `http://www.php.net/manual/en/introduction.php`. Once you spend some time with the PHP tutorial, you'll also want to look at the PHP manual at `http://www.php.net/manual/en/index.php`. The manual tells you how to use various PHP commands.

> **▶ NOTE**
>
> The PHP materials come in languages other than English. All you need to do is change the two-letter language abbreviation in the URL to your language. For example, to see the PHP manual in Spanish, you'd use a URL of `http://www.php.net/manual/es/index.php` instead of the English URL provided in this chapter. German readers can use the `http://www.php.net/manual/de/index.php`, while French readers can use `http://www.php.net/manual/fr/index.php`.

The Webmonkey Web site has an excellent PHP tutorial (`http://hotwired.lycos.com/webmonkey/01/48/index2a.html?tw=programming`). Another tutorial that will help you understand PHP and MySQL Usage is `http://hotwired.lycos.com/webmonkey/programming/php/tutorials/tutorial4.html`. However, you may also want to view other PHP topics on this Web site (`http://hotwired.lycos.com/webmonkey/programming/php/index.html`) to learn more about PHP and see how you can use it with other products such as Oracle.

A number of other sites also provide PHP tutorials. For example, the Free Webmaster Help.com site at `http://www.freewebmasterhelp.com/tutorials/php` provides a seven-part tutorial that includes information on using forms. You'll also find great articles and tutorials on the PHPBuilder site at `http://www.phpbuilder.com/`. The tutorials on Dev Shed (`http://www.devshed.com/Server_Side/PHP/`) are a little more advanced. The tutorials on this site help you discover how to work with the local hard drive and even create PDFs as output from your application. You'll also find a number of articles about error handling and other developer topics. However, you'll want to save this site as your last stop because many of the articles get quite detailed and you could find yourself lost quickly.

It's also helpful to have a good book on the topic. Take a look at *Creating Interactive Web Sites with PHP and Web Services* by Eric Rosebrock (Sybex, 2004). This book shows how to install and configure development and production platforms of Apache, PHP, and MySQL on both Windows and Linux systems, and teaches Web development with PHP from a problem-solving viewpoint. Also visit Eric's wildly popular Web site PHP Freaks (`http://www.phpfreaks.com`).

Downloading and Installing PHP

One of the first places you'll want to visit is the Webmonkey site at `http://hotwired.lycos.com/webmonkey/00/44/index4a.html?tw=programming`. Use this tutorial to get PHP set up on your system and learn a little about this product. This PHP tutorial will also introduce you to the language. Unfortunately, the tutorial is also a little outdated and many of the links no longer work. Here's a list of links you can use instead of the links provided with the Webmonkey article (the article information is still very good, so don't be concerned about the outdated links).

- Apache Server Download (`http://httpd.apache.org/download.cgi`)
- Apache Documentation (`http://httpd.apache.org/docs-2.0/`)
- PHP Download (`http://www.php.net/downloads.php`)
- PHP Manual (`http://www.php.net/manual/en/index.php`)

Because the Webmonkey article is a little outdated, you'll also want to spend time with the official PHP installation documentation found at `http://www.php.net/manual/en/installation.php`. Although this text isn't quite as readable as the Webmonkey version, it's definitely current. Make sure you base any installation decisions, such as whether to use Common Gateway Interface (CGI) or Internet Server Application Programming Interface (ISAPI), on the content of the official documentation.

> ▶ **TIP**
>
> Instead of installing Apache, PHP, and MySQL separately, you can use one of the package products on the market. For example, the Apache Friends site at `http://www.apachefriends` `.org/xampp-en.html` provides a product named XAMPP that includes all three products plus PERL. Best of all, this product is free and comes in versions for both Linux and Windows. Note that you might find the mirrors in the United States are slower than those in some European countries. Because this is a large download, you might want to try another site if you find the initial download is slow.

One thing you won't need to do to work with eBay Web Services is add any extensions. All of the examples in this chapter work fine with the default extensions. You might need to add extensions to process the data, but it's a good idea to work with eBay Web Services for a while using the default PHP configuration. Using the default configuration ensures you won't run into any extension-specific errors.

> ▶ **TIP**
>
> Like most programming languages, you'll find a variety of third party support sites for PHP. One of the better sites, ByKeyword.com (`http://www.bykeyword.com/pages/php.html`) includes a list of utilities to edit, manage, and even convert your PHP code. Make sure you also visit sites like Tucows (`http://tdconline.tucows.com/`). A simple search can net a list of useful shareware and freeware products you can use.

Don't get the idea that PHP only comes in versions for Apache users. It's true that many people use PHP with Apache, but you can also use it with Internet Information Server (IIS), Personal Web Server (PWS), and Xitami (among other servers). Many of the other servers require that you use the CGI version of PHP, but you can also get an ISAPI version for IIS. The ISAPI version will provide superior performance and a little more flexibility, as well as improved reliability and recoverability. If you want the ISAPI support, you must download the Zip version of the PHP file, not the installer version, which includes only the CGI files.

You can run into a number of issues with Apache that none of the documentation mentions. For example, you might run into a situation where Apache installs and even starts, but you can't access it. Make sure you don't have another Web server installed on the same system. The second Web server could make it difficult or impossible to access the Apache server. This problem is especially prominent on Windows systems because Microsoft simply assumes that every server should have IIS installed.

> **▶ WARNING**
>
> Make sure you take care of security when you set up Apache. Thawte is offering a free guide that shows how to secure your Apache server using a digital certificate. You can obtain the guide at `http://www.thawte.com/ucgi/gothawte.cgi?a=e39560143317026000`.

If you want to use the API technique for accessing eBay Web Services, you need to add XML functionality to your PHP installation. The examples in this chapter use the Microsoft supplied XML functionality as COM components with the `COM()` method. A similar technique can work on other platforms, but you need to configure your system differently.

> **▶ WARNING**
>
> Make sure you read the installation instructions for PHP XML support at `http://www.php.net/manual/en/ref.domxml.php`. Most Windows developers need to move a file from the PHP folder to the `System32` folder. The name of the file varies by XML version. In addition, the XML support in PHP is experimental—it could change in future versions.

In some cases, the first task is to download and install a copy of Gnome Libxml2. Newer versions of PHP already include the required XML support, so you don't need to perform this step. You can download this product from `http://www.xmlsoft.org/`. The second task is to add XML support to your PHP setup in such a way that Apache automatically loads it. Open the `PHP.INI` file (or equivalent on your system) and check the extension directory to make sure it's correct. You should see something like this:

```
; Directory in which the loadable extensions (modules) reside.
extension_dir = "D:\PHP4\extensions\"
```

Uncomment the correct PHP extension library for your system. For example, if you're using PHP version 4.3 or above, you need to uncomment the `extension=php_domxml.dll` and `extension=php_xmlrpc.dll` entries. Restart the Apache server to ensure the library loads as expected. You can verify the presence of the library using the `phpinfo()` function. Figure 9.1 shows the information you should see.

It helps to have a SOAP library installed when you work with PHP and Web services. Because PHP doesn't have native SOAP support, you'll need to download a SOAP library to use with PHP. There are currently two good options: NuSOAP and PEAR:SOAP. You can find the NuSOAP library at `http://cvs.sourceforge.net/cgi-bin/viewcvs.cgi/nusoap/lib/nusoap.php`. This file must appear in a central location or in the same folder as your other application files. Download the PEAR:SOAP library at http://pear.php.net/package/ SOAP/. There's a good article about using PHP with NuSOAP to create Web services at http://www.phpbuilder.com/columns/kramberger20031226.php3 that you'll want to read before you get too involved in working with Web services.

> ► NOTE
>
> If you intend to use PHP with the upcoming eBay SOAP toolkit (see http://developer .ebay.com/DevZone/KB_SearchDocs//OReilly_Conference_Release-Final.pdf for details), make sure you read about any requirements before you choose a SOAP product. As of this writing, the NuSOAP library appears to present problems for eBay Web Service developers. Hopefully, these issues will be resolved soon.

FIGURE 9.1:
Ensure that your PHP setup has the correct XML support installed.

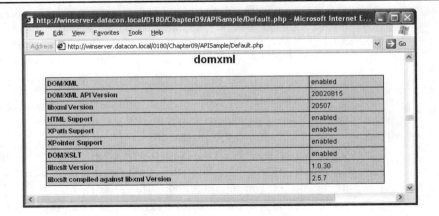

Using the eBay PHP Example

The eBay PHP example is a bare bones demonstration of what you can do with PHP using the SDK technique. The example runs from the command line and doesn't make use of any of the PHP Web features at all. (You can theoretically run it from a browser, but you'd need to modify the code a little first.) The example creates a new listing and sends it to eBay Web Services. Your server must have the eBay Web Services Kit installed to run this example, along with the proper PHP support. You don't need any special libraries to run this example and it even works without having Apache installed. You'll find the code for this example in the \Program Files\eBay\SDK\Samples\PHP\SimpleList folder of the eBay Web Services kit.

The code begins by requesting the developer keys that eBay issues to you as part of the developer program signup. After you enter this information, the program asks for the user information. The second phase of the application requests some basics about the item you want to list for testing purposes. The application only requests required information, not all of the optional information that you could provide. The final step is to send the data to eBay. If the listing is successful, you receive an item identifier. Figure 9.2 shows typical output from this application. Note that my personal information is blocked out in the example.

> ▶ **NOTE**
>
> The example has several problems. First, it doesn't include any error trapping, so any mistakes you make will cause the application to crash. Fortunately, not all errors are fatal as shown in Figure 9.2. In this case, I chose not to provide a BuyItNow price and the application wasn't prepared for that. Second, it's easy to surpass the default 300 second processing time built into the PHP processor if you don't have all of the information you need collected before you make the call.

PHP doesn't have any method for creating a Component Object Model (COM) reference directly, so it uses a special method for the task. The code begins by creating a reference with the COM("eBay.SDK.API.ApiSession") method. You have to watch carefully for any error messages because the example simply assumes the method worked. The instantiated object resides in $apiSession. The next several steps fill $apiSession with data, including your developer keys and the user information.

FIGURE 9.2:

The PHP example is a pure text display that provides bare bones coding help.

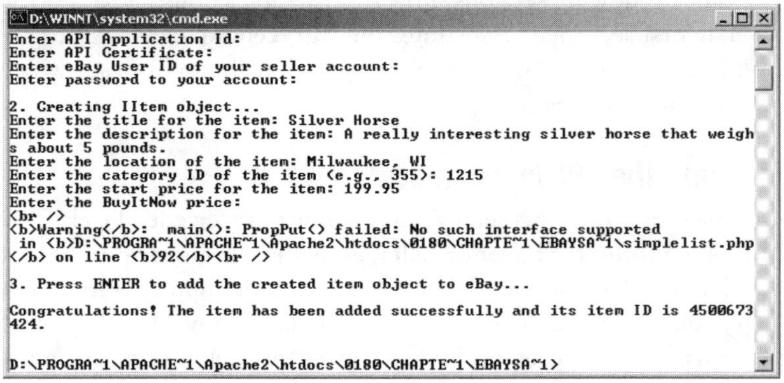

The next step in the process is to create an `Item` object using the `COM("eBay.SDK.Model`
`.Item.Item")` method. The application provides queries for some of the required values such
as the item title and description. Note that even though you can provide a long description,
the application automatically cuts the description to 256 characters. It automatically fills in
other values such as country property using statements such as `$item->Country = "us"`.

The third step is to make the actual API call by creating an `AddItem` object using the
`COM("eBay.SDK.API.AddItemCall")` method. The call executes much as you would expect
from other examples in the book. However, the error trapping is a little different in this
example. Instead of checking for an error code from the server or looking for information
using other techniques described in the book, this example checks the `$item->ItemId` property value. If this property value is empty, the application assumes the call has failed, but it
never determines an actual reason for the failure.

Developing a PHP Application

You can use two techniques for accessing eBay Web Services currently, with the SOAP technique on the way sometime later. The API technique has several advantages for PHP developers. For one thing, you don't have to worry about having the .NET Framework installed
to access the Web service. If you want to use the PHP-specific libraries, you can also get by
without using the `COM()` method, but I wouldn't recommend this approach on Windows systems because it's very code intensive. As with every other API example in the book, the downside to using the API technique is the additional code you need to write; although the actual
difference in coding is less than with other languages such as C#. The SDK technique does
simplify access. You don't have to worry about creating a perfectly formatted XML message.

The following sections show two examples of using PHP to access eBay Web Services.
The first section demonstrates the API technique, while the second section demonstrates the
SDK technique. Make sure you try both techniques to see which one works best for your
particular application.

Using the API Technique

The example in this section shows how to receive feedback. The send and receive process
doesn't differ for buyer or seller, except in the content of the feedback. When a buyer provides feedback about a seller, the seller has an opportunity to respond to that feedback. This
system ensures that everyone has a chance to say what they need to say about a particular
transaction. As previously mentioned, this example relies on the Microsoft XML support
that you can obtain for Windows. The code uses the `COM()` method to create the required
objects. The benefit of using the approach shown in Listing 9.1 is that you gain a great deal

of flexibility and reduce the code you have to write when using native PHP objects. You'll find the complete source for this example in the \Chapter 09\APISample folder of the source code located on the Sybex Web site.

Listing 9.1   **Using the *GetFeedback* Call**

```php
<html>
<head>
  <title>API Request Example</title>
</head>
<body>

<?php
    // Create the request.
    $Req = new COM("Msxml2.ServerXMLHTTP.4.0");
    $Req->open("POST",
                "https://api.sandbox.ebay.com/ws/api.dll",
                false);

    // Define the header information for the request. These headers
    // appear in the same order recommended by the documentation at
    // http://developer.ebay.com/DevZone/docs/API_Doc/index.asp.
    $Req->setRequestHeader("X-EBAY-API-SESSION-CERTIFICATE",
                            "Your DevID" . ";" .
                            "Your AppID" . ";" .
                            "Your CertID");
    ... Other Headers ...

    // Create the XML request object.
    $XMLData = new COM("Msxml2.DOMDocument.4.0");

    // Add the XML request header.
    $ProcInst =
        $XMLData->createProcessingInstruction(
            "xml", "version=\"1.0\"  encoding=\"iso-8859-1\"");
    $XMLData->appendChild($ProcInst);

    // Construct the XML request message.
    $Root = $XMLData->createElement("request");
    $Root->setAttribute("xmlns", "urn:eBayAPIschema");

    // Add the user information.
    $Elem = $XMLData->createElement("RequestToken");
    $Elem->text = "User Token";
    $Root->appendChild($Elem);

    // Add the request data.
    $Elem = $XMLData->createElement("Verb");
    $Elem->text = "GetFeedback";
    $Root->appendChild($Elem);
```

```php
        $Elem = $XMLData->createElement("UserId");
        $Elem->text = "BubbaM9999";
        $Root->appendChild($Elem);
        ... Other Request Data ...

        // Add the request data to the XML request.
        $XMLData->appendChild($Root);

        // Send the request.
        $Req->send($XMLData);

        // Determine whether the data is good.
        if ($Req->status == 200)
        {
                // Create a document to parse the data.
            $ParseData = new COM("Msxml2.DOMDocument.4.0");

            // Continue parsing the data if the code can load it.
            if ($ParseData->loadXML($Req->responseText))
            {
                    // Get the usable data from the document.
                $eBayLevel = $ParseData->childNodes(1);
                $FeedbackLevel = $eBayLevel->childNodes(1);

                // Get the list of feedback items.
                $Detail = $FeedbackLevel->childNodes(0);
                $Details = $Detail->childNodes();
                print_r("<h2>Feedback Items</h2>");

                // Display the feedback items on screen.
                for ($Counter = 0; $Counter < $Details->length; $Counter++)
                {
                        // Get an individual feedback item.
                    $Elem = $Details->item($Counter);

                    // Display the username.
                    $Value = $Elem->childNodes(3);
                    print_r("Name: " . $Value->text . "<br/>");

                    ... Other Feedback Items ...
                }

                // Get the feedback ranks.
                $Detail = $FeedbackLevel->childNodes(2);
                $Details = $Detail->childNodes();
                print_r("<h2>Feedback Level Summary</h2>");
?>

<table border="1" cellpadding="5" width="90%">
   <tr>
      <th width="200pt">Feedback Type</th>
```

```
    <th width="100pt">Number</th>
</tr>


<?php

        // Process each of the feedback levels in turn.
        for ($Counter = 0; $Counter < $Details->length; $Counter++)
        {
                // Get an individual level.
            $Elem = $Details->item($Counter);

            // Determine the feedback level type.
            $baseName = $Elem->baseName;
            switch ($baseName)
            {
                // The three levels of bid retraction are 7,
                // 30, 180 days.
                case 'BidRetractionCountINT1':
                    print_r("<tr><td>Bids Retracted ");
                    print_r("(7 Days)</td>");
                    print_r("<td>" . $Elem->text . "</td></tr>");
                    break;
                ... Other Intervals ...

                // eBay provides four levels of positive, neutral,
                // and negative comments. However, the first level
                // is just for compatibility purposes; it doesn't
                // serve a useful purpose now.
                case 'PositiveFeedbackCountINT1':
                    print_r("<tr><td>Positive Comments (7 Days) ");
                    print_r("Not actually used.</td>");
                    print_r("<td>" . $Elem->text . "</td></tr>");
                    break;
                ... Other Intervals ...
            }
        }
    }
?>

</table>
</body>
</html>
```

The code begins by creating a ServerXMLHTTP object, Req. This object creates the connection between the client and the server. In this case, even though PHP is running on your server, it's making a request of another server on behalf of the user, so the principle is the same. This example connects to the sandbox, but you could just as easily connect with the production environment with the correct keys. The code uses the `setRequestHeader()` method to add all the eBay required headers to `Req`. Make sure you check the headers carefully because it's relatively easy to create headers that PHP won't flag as errors, but eBay Web Services won't accept.

The next step is to create the XML request object. A processing instruction comes first, after which the code begins creating the `<request>` node. The example uses the newer `<RequestToken>` element, rather than the older username and password. Most of the request data is the same as any other call. You need to include elements such as the detail and error levels. The unique elements for this example are `<Verb>`, which contains `GetFeedback`, and `<UserId>`, which contains the name of the user you want to check.

At this point, the code calls eBay Web Services and receives the data. Make sure you check `$Req->status` to ensure the call succeeded. An error on the server returns a value other than 200. It's also important to check for an error message as part of the eBay Web Services return value. This example leaves out the error handling for the sake of clarity. Listing 6.2 shows one technique for checking for the `<Errors>` element in the return value.

The `<Feedback>` node actually contains four elements, but you can divide them into two categories. The first category contains the individual comments made by each person. The `<FeedbackDetailItem>` elements include information such as the user's name, the time they made the comment, the kind of comment, and the comment itself. It's also possible to track whether you made a response to the comment and whether there are any other details to consider. Along with this information, eBay Web Services also provides a `<FeedbackDetailItem-Total>` element that tells you how many `<FeedbackDetailItem>` elements it returned.

The second category of information is the feedback score. The `<FeedbackScoreSummary>` element contains all of the statistics. A `<Score>` element contains the overall score for this person. Figure 9.3 shows typical data you'll receive for each category of information.

The code for parsing this information is relatively simple. PHP won't let you access the XML data more than one level deep, so you need to access it one level at a time. The code shows how you can use a combination of `IXMLDOMNode` and `IXMLDOMNodeList` objects to work with the data. Use the `IXMLDOMNode` object to obtain individual data values and the `IXML-DOMNodeList` to loop through the data values.

All of the feedback items are straight text. However, when you get to the statistics, the return elements can look a little odd. eBay Web Services provides statistics based on intervals of so many days. For example, bid retraction statistics are in intervals of 7, 30, and 180 days. The positive, neutral, and negative comments have intervals of 7, 30, 180, and 365 days. According to the documentation, the 7-day interval isn't active—eBay provides it for compatibility purposes.

FIGURE 9.3:

Use the GetFeeback call to obtain pending feedback as well as feedback statistics.

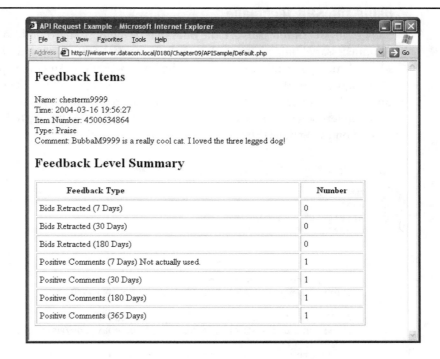

Creating Test Feedback

You can use the GetFeedback() call at any time. However, the normal response is to send you empty feedback. Before you can use the GetFeedback() call effectively, you need to create some for the buyer or seller. The easiest and fastest approach is to create feedback for the seller.

To begin this process, the seller must list an item for sale. The buyer must then bid on the item and win it. When the auction ends, the buyer must pay for the item by clicking its link in the Items I'm Bidding On section of My eBay. Obviously, no money changes hands in the sandbox, but you still have to go through the process. Normally, I set the listing up for Cash On Delivery (COD) transactions to make things simple. Note that selecting "other" as a payment technique is almost certain to cause the system to go into a continuous loop. After the buyer pays for the item, it will appear in the Items I've Won area of their My eBay page.

To create test feedback, click the Leave Feedback link in the right side of the page. Select the feedback rating, type a comment, and then click Leave Feedback. Follow the remaining steps to complete the feedback process. At this point, you can query the seller's feedback and receive the data left by the buyer.

Using the SDK Technique

Sometimes the simple calls are the ones that developers fail to find, so they end up creating an unnecessary kludge. One of these calls is the GetLogoUrlCall call. It's one of those necessary calls that you could easily miss in the documentation. Any time you want to display the eBay logo as part of your application, you should use this call to obtain the most current version and location. Listing 9.2 shows how to obtain the logo URL for a given size. You'll find the complete source for this example in the \Chapter 09\SDKSample folder of the source code located on the Sybex Web site.

Listing 9.2   **Using the *GetLogoUrlCall* Call**

```
<html>
<head>
  <title>SDK Example</title>
</head>
<body>

<?php
        // Create a session.
    $Session = new COM("eBay.SDK.API.ApiSession");

    // Define the sandbox as the call location.
    $Session->Url = "https://api.sandbox.ebay.com/ws/api.dll";

    // Add the session security information.
    $Session->Token = new COM("eBay.SDK.Model.ApiToken");
    $Session->Token->Token = "User Token";

    // Add the developer information.
    $Session->Developer = "Your DevID";
    $Session->Application = "Your AppID";
    $Session->Certificate = "Your CertID";

    // Create the GetLogoURL call.
    $GLU = new COM("eBay.SDK.API.GetLogoUrlCall");
    $GLU->ApiCall->ApiCallSession = $Session;

    // Set the logo size.
    $GLU->LogoSize = 1;

    // Make the call.
    $Results = $GLU->GetLogoURL();

    // Display the results on screen.
    print_r("<h2>Medium eBay Logo</h2>");
    print_r("<img height=" . $Results->Height .
        " width=" . $Results->Width .
```

```
            " src=" . $Results->Url .
            " alt='eBay Logo'>");
    ?>

</body>
</html>
```

The example begins by creating an `ApiSession` object, `$Session`. As with the eBay example, this example relies heavily on the `COM()` method to perform its work. However, the code still relies on the presence of the .NET Framework at a low level, so you must have it installed.

The next task is to fill out session information including the user and developer identification. This example relies on a request token. Notice that the `ApiToken` object isn't part of the `eBay.SDK.API` namespace—it's part of the `eBay.SDK.Model` namespace. You need to exercise care when creating objects in PHP to ensure you use the correct namespace. Other languages that support the SDK tend to hide some of these details from you. Make sure you initialize the `$Session->Token` object before you use it. PHP won't complain about the omission. If you fail to initialize this object, you'll receive an error from eBay Web Services that won't quite tell you where the problem lies and you'll spend hours troubleshooting it.

Creating the `GetLogoUrlCall` object, `$GLU`, is a two-step process. First, you create the object, and then you add the `$Session` object to `$GLU->ApiCall->ApiCallSession`.

According to the API Technical Documentation, you need to specify the logo size using a word such as small, medium, or large. The SDK approach is different. Normally, you'd use an enumeration, but the enumeration is essentially inaccessible to you from PHP. Consequently, you need to provide the numeric equivalent of the enumeration as input to the `$GLU->LogoSize` property. Because the eBay SDK Reference doesn't provide actual numbers for the enumerations, you'll find that you need to count them out. I haven't found any enumerations where the value didn't start at 0 at the top of the members list in the documentation. The enumerated values appear in order.

At this point, the code makes the call and places the return value in `$Results`. This object only contains three properties: `Height`, `Width`, and `Url`. The code shows a typical way to use the three values to create an `<img>` tag.

Using MySQL as a Database

You'll probably want to improve the efficiency of your PHP application, at some point, by storing some data locally. It's likely that you'll use a database to perform this task. One of the more popular databases on the market is MySQL. It provides robust capability and the price is right. In addition, MySQL seems to enjoy better than average support from a cadre of developers who use it.

Like everything else in this chapter, MySQL is open source. Normally, you don't have to buy this product—just download it. However, in some situations you do need to buy a license, such as when you create an application for commercial (shrink-wrap) distribution where you'll realize a profit from the sale of the application. Make sure you understand the distribution requirements for MySQL by reading them at `http://www.mysql.com/downloads/index.html`.

The example in this chapter relies on MySQL 4.0, the latest production version at the time of writing, which you can download at `http://www.mysql.com/downloads/mysql-4.0.html`. You'll notice that MySQL comes in quite a few versions for various platforms including Linux, Windows, Solaris, FreeBSD, Mac OS X, HP-UX, IBM AIX, Novell NetWare, SCO OpenUnix, SGI Irix, and DEC OSF. You can also download the source code and create your own flavor of MySQL if necessary. The test system for this chapter uses the compiled Windows version with default settings applied by the installer. If you use some other form of MySQL, your screen shots will vary from mine.

Once you download the version of the product you need, install it according to the vendor directions. In most cases, this means starting the installer or unpacking the product and performing a manual install. The Windows Installer version is very easy to use—just double-click the executable that you download and follow the prompts.

Learning to use MySQL is relatively straightforward. You can find the product documentation at `http://www.mysql.com/documentation/index.html`. The documentation comes in two formats: PDF, for a printed version, or HLP, for a desktop electronic version. Part of the documentation is a tutorial that you'll find at `http://www.mysql.com/doc/en/Tutorial.html`. The vendor provides training and certification courses that you can learn about at `http://www.mysql.com/training-and-certification.html`. The Webmonkey site at `http://hotwired.lycos.com/webmonkey/programming/php/tutorials/tutorial4.html` provides an excellent online MySQL tutorial. Another good tutorial appears on the TAASC site at `http://www.analysisandsolutions.com/code/mybasic.htm`. In addition, take a look at *Mastering MySQL 4* by Ian Gilfillan (Sybex, 2003).

Writing a PHP Application with Database Support

One of the most important techniques you have at your disposal for creating a truly efficient eBay Web Services environment is database caching. Using caching means your application won't have to make every request from eBay Web Services. Of course, you have to follow any storage guidelines eBay provides to ensure your data doesn't get too old. The big question about this technique is whether it actually provides a benefit. Using a cache implies that someone makes the same query more than once. The "Caching as a Practical Performance Enhancing Technique" section of Chapter 7 discusses many of the issues surrounding caching. However, there's a significant difference in usage between a desktop application and a Web application.

You have to know how people use the Web site to make any assumptions about the benefits of caching. In many cases, you might not know the habits of the people using your site. Public Web sites with ill-defined goals will experience the biggest problems because you can't narrow the focus of the caching in any way. For example, you'd need to consider whether it's efficient to store all item searches. Fortunately, some items such as a category search are consistently good choices for caching.

Setting Up the Database

Before you can begin using PHP with MySQL, you need a database. The `\Chapter 09\Data` folder of the source code located on the Sybex Web site contains a Structure Query Language (SQL) script called `eBayData.SQL`. Copy this file into the `\MySQL\bin` folder of your server (assuming you used a default setup). At the command line, type `MySQL MySQL < eBayData.SQL` and press Enter. Your system will pause for a moment and return to the command prompt. That's all you need to do to create the database for this example.

You can use the MySQL utility to verify the presence of the database, table, and data at the command line. Simply type `USE eBayData;` and press Enter. If the `eBayData` database is present, the utility will use that database. Type `SELECT * FROM DataStore` and press Enter. You'll see a lot of data stream by if the script successfully created the table and filled it with data. An easier way to achieve the same results on a Windows system is to use the `WinMySQLadmin` utility shown in Figure 9.4. Simply select the Databases tab and you'll see the database, table, and associated fields.

The database is similar to, but not precisely the same, as the eBay Integration Library tables. The database stores the search criteria and associates it with multiple responses. The example doesn't store all of the data found in the Integration Library database—it concentrates on information you'll need to locate items. The sample database also contains a few special fields, one of which is the search criteria. Another special field is a link to the location of the information on eBay. Although the `GetSearchResults()` call returns the link information, the integration database doesn't store the information. In short, this database is optimized for use with searches, not the general caching that the integration database provides.

FIGURE 9.4:

The `WinMySQLadmin` utility validates the success of the script on a Windows machine.

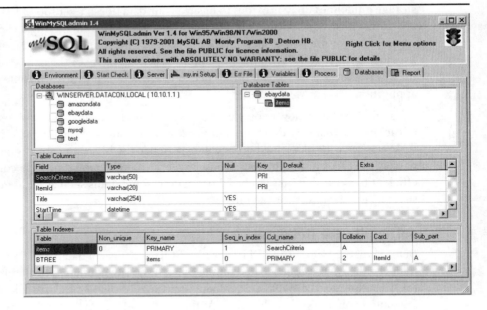

Writing the Sample Application

This example will perform a simple item search and store the results in the database. I've simplified the interface and the code to concentrate on the actual database functionality. With this in mind, the code contains three parts. The first part interacts with MySQL to determine whether the data is available locally. The second part obtains the data from eBay Web Services when necessary. The third part displays the data (whatever the source) on screen. Listing 9.3 shows the first part of the code. You'll find the complete source for this example in the \Chapter 09\MySQL folder of the source code located on the Sybex Web site.

Listing 9.3   Using the *GetSearchResults* Call

```php
<?php
   // Create a database connection.
   mysql_connect("localhost")
      or die ("Cannot connect to the database.");

   // Select the database.
   mysql_select_db("eBayData")
      or die ("The database doesn't exist or is inaccessible.");

   // Get the scan date.
   $Output = mysql_query("SELECT ScanDate FROM Items " .
```

```php
                              "WHERE SearchCriteria = 'Silver'");

   if (mysql_num_rows ($Output) > 0)
   {
      // Get the current date and convert it to a timestamp.
      $ScanDate = mysql_fetch_row($Output);
      $ConvDate = strtotime($ScanDate[0]);

      // Add 24 hours.
      $ConvDate = $ConvDate + 86400;

      // Verify the data isn't too old.
      if ($ConvDate < time())
         $Results = GetData();

      else
      {

         // Obtain the data.
         $Output = mysql_query("SELECT ItemId, Title, StartTime, " .
                               "EndTime, CurrentPrice, BuyItNowPrice" .
                               ", Link FROM Items " .
                               "WHERE SearchCriteria = 'Silver'");

         for ($Counter = 0; $Counter < mysql_num_rows($Output);
              $Counter++)
         {
            if (count($Results) == 0)
               // Get the display data.
               $Results = array($Counter, mysql_fetch_row($Output))
                  or die ("No Data in Query Row.");
            else
               // Add to the current data.
               array_push($Results, mysql_fetch_row($Output))
                  or die ("No Additional Data in Query Row.");
         }
      }
   }
   else
      // The database doesn't contain the information.
      $Results = GetData();

   // Display the results on screen.
   ... Some Display Code ...
?>
```

The code begins by creating a connection to the local database host and selecting the eBayData database. It makes a query to the Items table to whether the query is available (it's hard coded to Silver for the example, but you could use any query value). The mysql_num_rows

($Output) method returns 0 when the query fails, in which case the code calls GetData() to retrieve the information from eBay Web Services. The GetData() function contains standard code for making an eBay Web Services request, plus code to save the data to the Items table.

When the query is available, the code obtains the scan date from the table. This value is the date that the application downloaded the information from eBay, not the date that any of the auctions started. To determine whether the data is viable (not too old), the code converts the scan date to a time value. It adds 86,400 seconds to this value (24 hours). If the data is more than 24 hours old, the code calls GetData() to replace it.

When the data is viable, the code makes another query. In this case, it retrieves the fields that contain the data it needs to display on screen. The code uses mysql_fetch_row() to retrieve the data as a two-dimensional array. The first dimension is the record number, while the second dimension contains the individual field values for that record. Notice the use of the array_push() method to build the array after the code adds the first element.

The GetData() method works much like the SDK request method discussed in Listing 9.2. However, you need to add code to save the information to MySQL. Listing 9.4 shows the essential code for the GetData() method.

Listing 9.4   **Obtaining the Cached Data from eBay Web Services**

```php
function GetData()
{
    // Create a session.
    ... See Listing 9.2 for Details ...

    // Create the GetSearchResults call.
    $GSR = new COM("eBay.SDK.API.GetSearchResultsCall");
    $GSR->ApiCall->ApiCallSession = $Session;

    // Define the query.
    $GSR->Query = "Silver";

    // Make the call.
    $Results = $GSR->GetSearchResults();

    // Create an array to hold the data.
    for ($Counter = 0; $Counter < $Results->ItemCount; $Counter++)
    {
        // Get the item information.
        $ItemFound = $Results->ItemAt($Counter);
        $Item = $ItemFound->Item;

        // Create an array to display the individual item values.
        if (count($ResultArray) == 0)
```

```
        $ResultArray = array($Counter,
            array($Item->ItemId, $Item->Title, $Item->StartTime,
                $Item->EndTime, $Item->CurrentPrice,
                $Item->BuyItNowPrice, $ItemFound->ViewItemLink));
    else
        array_push($ResultArray,
            array($Item->ItemId, $Item->Title, $Item->StartTime,
                $Item->EndTime, $Item->CurrentPrice,
                $Item->BuyItNowPrice, $ItemFound->ViewItemLink));

    // Update the database. Create the query string.
    $UpdateQuery =
        'INSERT INTO Items (SearchCriteria, ItemId, Title, StartTime,
            EndTime, CurrentPrice, BuyItNowPrice, Link, ScanDate)
        VALUES ("Silver" , "' . $Item->ItemId . '" , "' .
            $Item->Title . '" , "' .
            strftime("%y/%m/%d %H:%M:%S", $Item->StartTime) . '" , "' .
            strftime("%y/%m/%d %H:%M:%S", $Item->EndTime) . '" , "' .
            $Item->CurrentPrice . '" , "' . $Item->BuyItNowPrice
            . '" , "' . $ItemFound->ViewItemLink . '", "' .
            strftime("%y/%m/%d %H:%M:%S") . '")';

    // Update the database.
    mysql_query($UpdateQuery)
        or die ("Error Updating Database");
    }

    // Return the data.
    return $ResultArray;
}
```

The code begins by creating a session using the same technique as shown in Listing 9.2. The differences, in this case, are the use of the GetSearchResultsCall object. To make the $GSR->GetSearchResults() call, the code provides a query value, which is hard coded to Silver for this example.

The code has to perform two tasks once it obtains the results from eBay Web Services. First, it has to create an output array that mimics the array the database provides as output. The code relies on a two-dimensional array for this task. Notice it uses the same technique as in Listing 9.3. The only difference is the source of the data.

Second, the code has to update the database so it contains the new data. To make the update process work correctly, the code creates an INSERT query. Notice how the code lists the values. It's important to convert some data values so MySQL will accept them. In this case, the most important conversions are the time values. The code uses the strftime() function to make the input format acceptable.

The display code for this example consists of tag output and simple array processing. Make sure you look at the full source code to see how the example handles this requirement. Figure 9.5 shows typical application output.

FIGURE 9.5:

Using a caching mechanism improves application performance.

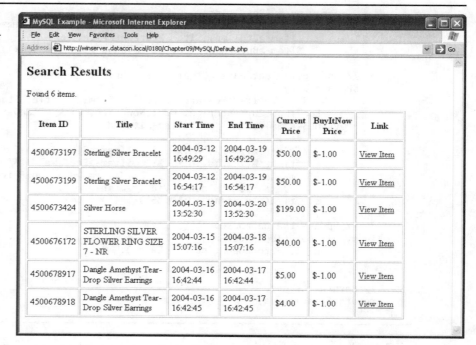

Your Call to Action

This chapter demonstrates the techniques you can use to access eBay with PHP. As with most applications, the idea is to reduce the amount of work the user must perform to accomplish any given task. When using a database, it also means keeping requests local, rather than obtaining the information from eBay Web Services. One of the best ways to improve user efficiency is by controlling the presentation and weighting of the data. However, PHP also opens the possibility of site-specific services such as performing topic-specific searches or improving the characteristics of a general application.

You have some decisions to make at this point. The first is whether you want to use caching to reduce the number of eBay Web service requests. Not only does caching provide better performance, but also it helps you keep within the confines of the eBay licensing agreement.

The downside is that you have to watch out for old data. It's also important to consider the kinds of input you want to allow and how to use that data to perform tasks such as creating a new listing or checking on auction results. Make sure you provide some type of user feedback form (discussed in the "Adding Feedback to Your Application" section of Chapter 14) so that you can improve the quality of the search for users who might have different ideas on what they'd like to look for.

Chapter 10 moves from PHP to Java. You'll find that Java is another extremely popular choice. Although Java isn't quite as easy as PHP to transfer from one platform to another, it's a more popular choice. In addition, you'll find that Java applications run faster because Java performs some of the interpretation required to run the application during a compile cycle. Java still doesn't run as fast as a native code application, but it's a very good choice.

Chapter 10

Understanding Java Benefits · Learning Java · Overcoming Java Browser Issues

▶ Writing Applications Using Java

Building Applications with the eBay-Supplied Code · Creating a Simple Java Application · Creating a Java Application with the eBay Request Library

Most people have heard about Java and many people have worked with it. Java appears on Web sites with some regularity because it lets Web designers create solutions that work with a number of browsers. Developers create Java applets for many Web-enabled applications as well as desktop applications. In short, Java appears in numerous places, so it's no wonder that you can use Java with eBay Web Services too.

This chapter discusses techniques for using Java with eBay Web Services. The examples show various strategies you can use to improve the user experience, while keeping the cost of development low. In general, you'll find many resources for using Java online. In addition, because Sun essentially owns Java, you'll find that it enjoys a level of support that most solutions can only dream about and openness not normally found with fully proprietary solutions.

However, using Java can become problematic in some cases. Java isn't fully proprietary, nor is it fully open. Consequently, some contention surrounds Java, and you need to consider the issues using Java can cause. (Read about these issues at http://www.infoworld.com/article/03/05/12/HNfowler_1.html.) This chapter doesn't examine these issues in detail, but it does provide enough information that you can learn more about the issues yourself and make a decision about the suitability of Java for your next application. As part of the Java overview, you'll also learn where you can find more information about the language. As with all other languages in the book, I assume you've already learned Java and performed the required software installation before you begin this chapter.

> ▶ **NOTE**
>
> The examples in this chapter rely on the Java 2 Platform, Standard Edition (J2SE) version 1.4.2 available at `http://java.sun.com/j2se/1.4.2/download.html`. Older versions of the product might work, but you may need to modify the example code to exclude new features or functionality. In addition, I used the Windows platform for writing many of the applications and associated explanations. While the source code will work on any platform that supports the latest version of Java, you might need to modify some of the usage instructions slightly for other platforms.

Understanding the Benefits of Using Java

Java is popular because it can do so many things well. You can use Java on either the client or the server, or even both at the same time. This feature makes Java different from other solutions such as PHP because it provides flexibility in determining where an application runs. Unlike many other solutions, Java enjoys wide platform support, so a solution you create for one platform has a good chance of working on other platforms, too. In fact, you'll find numerous Java applications available for download that run on multiple platforms. For example, a single byte-code file (compiled code) can run on Macintosh OS X, OS/2, Unix, VMS, and Windows.

Many developers use Java for both desktop and Web-based applications, although most people equate Java with Web development where it's a much stronger presence. The fact that you can use it for multiple application types makes Java a good solution for many multi-environment scenarios. Even though you'd need to make changes to an application (desktop) to run it as an applet (Web), the changes are minimal compared to other languages. However, make sure you understand the limits of Java compared to platform-specific solutions such as Visual Basic before you decide to use it in more than one place.

Using Java for Web applications has many significant benefits. The most important benefit is that so many platforms support Java natively. You can develop Web-based applications using products such as Shockwave or Flash, but this solution often forces the Web site visitor to download a browser plug-in. Given Microsoft's loss of a lawsuit allowing plug-ins, using Macromedia Shockwave or Macromedia Flash might not even be an option in the future (see the eWeek article at `http://www.eweek.com/article2/0,4149,1269693,00.asp` for details). Java applications generally work without any additional effort at all on the part of the user. In addition, Java is more capable than most other languages used for Web application presentation because it allows full interactivity between the client and server.

One feature that could be a benefit or a problem, depending on how you view it, is the fact that Java applications rely on a runtime engine that keeps them in a secure environment known as a sandbox. A Java application can only use the resources allotted to it by the runtime engine or Java Virtual Machine (JVM). This feature is beneficial because it improves security and makes it less likely that an errant Java application will cause other applications to fail (crash). The feature can cause problems by making it difficult to access resources the application needs to perform essential tasks such as writing data to the hard drive.

Another feature that you can view as a benefit or problem is the fact that Java tends to take a one size fits all approach to platform support. Yes, every platform requires a special JVM, but that JVM tends to have the same functionality as every other JVM. This means you face fewer problems porting Java applications from one platform to the next. In fact, except for text-based products such as PHP, Java is one of the easiest languages to port. However, the one size fits all approach also means that you'll experience problems using advanced features a specific platform has to offer. Microsoft tried to address the lack of platform-specific support in Java by (among other things) creating its own version of the JVM (see the "Understanding Java Browser Issues" section for details).

Resources for Learning Java

Learning any high-end language is difficult. However, some developers have complained that Java is one of the harder languages to learn because it lacks tools that other high-end languages provide. Sun is apparently aware of the complaints because it's promised to provide better tools (see the article at `http://www.infoworld.com/article/03/06/09/23NNjavaone_1.html` for details). Ease of use issues aside, Java is still a very powerful and flexible language, so you should honestly consider this solution for your next eBay Web Services application. A single chapter can't show you everything about Java, so this section provides resources where you can learn more.

> ▶ **TIP**
>
> The court of public opinion on whether .NET or Java is the best solution to use for Web services is split. According to a survey late in 2002 (see `http://www.infoworld.com/article/02/10/09/021009hndevsurvey_1.html?1010thap` for details), developers are spending equal time on both technologies. In short, both technologies are popular—you need to decide which one meets your needs best.

Choosing a Java Editor

The Sun tutorial suggests using Windows Notepad or a similar text editor, such as Notepad+ (http://www.mypeecee.org/rogsoft/), for creating your Java applet code. However, you should consider using a good Java editor to make the development experience a lot better. The Sun ONE Studio 4, Community Edition IDE mentioned in the tutorial isn't available for download any longer—Sun has replaced it with a 60-day demonstration version of Sun ONE Studio 5, Standard Edition. You can get the Sun ONE Studio 5, Standard Edition IDE at http://wwws.sun.com/software/sundev/. The advantage of using the official IDE is that Sun designed it for Java and the IDE provides Java-specific help.

In some cases, a third party product such as SlickEdit (http://www.slickedit.com/) is actually a better deal. The SlickEdit solution provides support for multiple languages, which means you only have to learn one editor. Although it is a shrink-wrapped application, you can obtain a limited use trial version from the company Web site.

You might also consider using a product such as jEdit (http://www.jedit.org/) because the same executable runs on Macintosh OS X, OS/2, Unix, VMS, and Windows. The author wrote this editor in Java and it points out the platform independence this language provides in a real world application. You'll find that jEdit has great community support, so you can download any of a number of add-on products for it. I used the jEdit editor to write the eBaySearch and SimpleApplication examples in this chapter and found the color coding it provides extremely helpful. You can download this open source product free.

Another great IDE is JCreator (http://www.jcreator.com/). You can get the freeware version of the product and use it as long as you like. The professional version of the product is shareware, so you can download and use it free for 30 days. I also tried this editor while working on the ERLSample and SimpleSearch examples for this chapter. It's a great choice for developers who have worked with VBA or Visual Studio and are familiar with the IDE for those products. It is also one of the better editors for large projects because it helps you organize your project better and includes features such as a debugger.

One of the best places to learn about Java is the Sun Web site at http://java.sun.com/docs/books/tutorial/. This site provides a good overview of Java and some great introductory material you can use to learn the language. For example, this tutorial explains the difference between a stand-alone application and an applet. Note that this Web site does provide separate instructions for Windows, Linux/Unix, and Macintosh developers. You might find it helpful to read the instructions for your platform of interest, and then quickly glance through the other two sections to pick up platform-specific issues.

If you need another basic tutorial, then look at Brewing Java: A Tutorial at http://www.ibiblio.org/javafaq/javatutorial.html. The author of this tutorial actually expanded it into a book that he also mentions on the site. If you find the whole concept of object-oriented programming with Java difficult to understand, you'll want to view the Don't Fear the OOP tutorial at `http://sepwww.stanford.edu/sep/josman/oop/oop1.htm`. You can get interactive Java coding lessons at the Coder School (`http://www.coderschool.com/`). Many of the offerings on this site are free, but you'll also find some excellent paid offerings as well.

An excellent beginner tutorial is Phil Heller's *Ground-Up Java* (Sybex, 2004). *Ground-Up Java* assumes no programming experience, but gets the reader up and running as a Java programmer quickly. The unique aspect of this book is the collection of powerful animated illustrations on the accompanying CD-ROM. They provide a crash-free environment to experiment with Java programming. The animated illustrations combined with the graded exercises that conclude every chapter and Phil's clear explanations of concepts and techniques make *Ground-Up Java* a programming course and computer lab rolled into one.

Once you learn a little about Java, try some of the more advanced developer tutorials offered by Sun at `http://developer.java.sun.com/developer/onlineTraining/`. The tutorials on this site are diverse and some are complex, so make sure you understand the requirements for using the tutorial before you get too involved (the requirements normally appear as part of the tutorial's introduction). The feature I like most about this site is that all of the tutorials have dates, so you know how old the information is before you get started.

A number of third parties also provide advanced tutorials and this section doesn't even begin to list them all. One of the more interesting offerings is the Advanced Java/J2EE Tutorial at `http://my.execpc.com/~gopalan/java/java_tutorial.html`. This tutorial begins with a comparison of the various communication technologies (including Java/RMI, DCOM, and CORBA). You might also want to look at Java Coffee Break at `http://www.javacoffeebreak.com/` because it includes a wide range of tutorials (some advanced) as well as other resources.

Newsgroups can also provide essential information to the Java developer. One of the best newsgroups to try is `comp.lang.java`. Note that this newsgroup has numerous subfolders you'll also want to visit. For example, you can keep track of Java bugs on the `comp.lang.java.bugs` newsgroup. The `comp.lang.java` newsgroup enjoys broad support and some people even support it on their Web sites. For example, check out the comp.lang.java FAQ List at `http://www.ibiblio.org/javafaq/javafaq.html`. You can also try newsgroups such as `alt.comp.lang.java`. Make sure you check any vendor-specific Java newsgroups groups such as `borland.public.jbuilder.java` when you use a particular product.

Understanding Java Browser Issues

As previously mentioned, you can use Java in a client, server, or mixed solution. The problem with developing either a client or mixed solution is that you have to consider the user's browser. The media has documented the combat between Sun and Microsoft over the JVM. (See the

story at `http://archive.infoworld.com/articles/hn/xml/02/12/05/021205hnmsblames`
`.xml?1205tham` as just one example.) Microsoft, as usual, decided to produce its own version of
the JVM, which is incompatible with Sun's version. Some users might have this incompatible
version installed, even though Sun won a lawsuit over the issue and Microsoft no longer
produces it.

The latest twist in the battle is that some versions of Windows no longer come with the JVM
installed, which means that the client can't run your Java application at all. In some cases,
Microsoft is withdrawing products from the market earlier than anticipated to ensure they meet
the court-ordered deadline for restricting distribution of their custom JVM solution (see the
eWeek article at `http://eletters.eweek.com/zd1/cts?d=79-353-2-3-67152-42164-1` for
details). Microsoft originally shipped Windows XP without a JVM, downloading the JVM on
demand, rather than supplying it as a default (see the InfoWorld story at `http://archive`
`.infoworld.com/articles/hn/xml/02/06/18/020618hnjavasupport.xml?0620thap` for details).

Sun is also active in the JVM battle. For example, the company is trying to get around the
Windows JVM problem by signing individual companies to distribute the Sun version of
the JVM (see the InfoWorld article at `http://www.infoworld.com/article/03/06/11/`
`HNjavadell_1.html` for details). The two companies are still in court over this issue (see the
story at `http://www.infoworld.com/article/03/04/03/HNmsorder_1.html`). Because of this
contention, you can't be sure which version of the JVM a client has or even if the client has
the JVM installed.

Even if the client has the JVM installed, crackers have made Java one of their tools of choice.
Consequently, many people turn off support for the JVM in their browsers. This task is
amazingly easy with products such as Internet Explorer. Because you don't know whether the
client has the JVM installed, telling them to turn the JVM on in an error message is unlikely
to produce the desired results in many cases.

Finally, it might seem like everyone would have a JVM installed and all the proper browser
support, but that's not true. Many browsers simply don't have the required support. You can
view the Webmonkey charts at the following locations for specific platform support of Java.

- Windows
  `http://hotwired.lycos.com/webmonkey/reference/browser_chart/index.html`

- Macintosh
  `http://hotwired.lycos.com/webmonkey/reference/browser_chart/index_mac.html`

- Linux
  `http://hotwired.lycos.com/webmonkey/reference/browser_chart/index_nix.html`

- Other
  `http://hotwired.lycos.com/webmonkey/reference/browser_chart/index_other.html`

The bottom line is that you have to know the client capabilities of the users of your application or develop a server-side solution. Java is a great solution because it's so flexible, but it also carries a number of problems that you might not run into with less flexible or less capable solutions. You need to decide whether the potential browser problems with Java are going to interfere with your eBay Web Services application.

Viewing the eBay-Supplied Code

eBay provides sample code that shows how to create an item listing. This example requires some special setup because it relies on a special library. In general, the example won't run until you perform the required setup. The following sections describe the setup, use, and functionality of the eBay-supplied example. You'll find this example in the \Program Files\ eBay\SDK\Samples\Java\SimpleListJava folder of the eBay Web Services Kit.

> ▶ **WARNING**
>
> After working with this example for a considerable time, it's apparent that this particular example isn't very stable, nor is the SDK access technique it uses. It is the only example in the eBay Web Services Kit that didn't run out of the box on any of my test systems. The number of messages on the eBay forums indicates that I'm not the only one with this problem. Unless you can find another COM bridge to replace the Jacob.DLL file described in the sections that follow, you'll probably get better results using the API technique. All of the other examples in this chapter use the API technique.

Performing the Required Setup

Java requires special support for accessing eBay Web Services. The example assumes you're using a Windows machine. You'll need to copy Jacob.DLL from the \Program Files\eBay\ SDK\Java folder to the Windows \System32 folder to ensure Java can find it when needed. As an alternative, you can add the \Program Files\eBay\SDK\Java folder to your system path.

JACOB is short for Java COM Bridge—the function that the DLL serves. Make sure that you don't have any other version of Jacob.DLL available on the test system. Older versions can cause the test application to fail. Fortunately, just installing the Java SDK won't install Jacob.DLL for you, so you shouldn't need to do anything special if you create a clean installation or haven't specifically installed Jacob.DLL for another purpose. You can obtain the current Jacob.DLL documentation, including the source code, at http://danadler.com/jacob/.

▶ **WARNING**

> The Jacob.DLL doesn't run well with some versions of Windows unless you have specific features installed. Make sure you install the .NET Framework version 1.0, not version 1.1 for the best results on both Windows 2000 and Windows XP. (You can download the .NET Framework 1.0 at http://www.microsoft.com/downloads/details.aspx?FamilyId= D7158DEE-A83F-4E21-B05A-009D06457787.) eBay provides this information as part of the ReadMe file in the example folder. Tests showed that a machine with the .NET Framework 1.1 installed did indeed experience problems. A second machine with a side-by-side installation didn't experience as many problems. Any test machine you set up should have all the current service packs and patches installed. eBay recommends that Windows XP developers have Service Pack 1 installed as a minimum (there's a SP1a available and Microsoft plans to release SP2 soon).

Running the Example

Most developers run example programs to see what's possible and then dissect the code to make their own development experience better than it could be learning from scratch. One of the most important benefits of using the eBay-supplied Java example is to ensure you have a viable setup before you begin developing an application. It doesn't pay to progress any further in the chapter unless you can get the sample application to work. If this example doesn't work, it means that Jacob.DLL is probably incompatible with your system and you need to use the API technique to write your code.

To use the example, open a command window in the \Program Files\eBay\SDK\Samples\ Java\SimpleListJava folder of the eBay Web Services Kit. Type **Make** at the command prompt and press Enter. Java will build the example. If Java doesn't build the example, make sure you have paths set up so the Java compiler can locate all of the files it needs. Run the example by typing **SimpleListJava** and pressing Enter.

▶ **NOTE**

> The example times out after a relatively short time. Consequently, you'll want to enter the information relatively quickly to ensure you get to see a result.

The example is a simple console application. It begins by requesting your developer keys and the user information. As with most of the eBay samples, this sample lacks any error trapping, so you need to enter the information carefully. Unlike most eBay examples, this one doesn't assume that you want to use the sandbox to make your request, so you have to supply the URL of the environment you want to use. The example does suggest the sandbox URL of `https://api.sandbox.ebay.com/ws/api.dll`.

> ▶ **TIP**
>
> As part of the Java example input, you can provide the name and location of a log file. It's tempting to simply press Enter as suggested, but the log file can provide some interesting information as you create your own application. Generally, it's a good idea to create the log file so you can follow the sequence of communication between the example application and eBay.

Once you enter the preliminary information, the example lets you make a series of calls to eBay, so this example isn't simply a matter of listing a new product online. If you're creating a communication log, it pays to make every call offered so you can see how they work with the example and Java. The first prompt asks whether you want to use the `GetCategoriesCall()`. Type **y** and press Enter. You should see a list of categories. This is the point where the application normally fails if it's going to fail. If you see an error that describes an access error at the current Java thread for `com.jacob.com`, you know the SDK setup won't work (at least, not well). Errors that don't mention `com.jacob.com` could have other causes such as an inaccurate entry.

After the example shows a list of categories, it asks you to enter information for listing a new item on eBay. This information includes the title, description, location, category, price, and BuyItNow price of the item. The example assumes certain pieces of information for you, such as setting the title bold and setting the region information. The application builds the new item, at this point, and sends it to eBay. You should see a success message that includes the item identifier.

Examining the Code

The example code is relatively straightforward. It begins by creating a new session by calling `IApiSession apiSession = new ApiSession()`. Notice that you must use the interface and not the actual object when creating the session variable. The code fills in the required `apiSession` variables using inputs from the command line. It also fills in one optional entry, the log file, when you provide a filename. Because the code creates an XML log, it must define a special object to hold the data. Here's the general procedure that you should follow when creating a log.

```
// Create log file object.
ILogFile log = new LogFile();
log.open(input);
```

```
// Assign the log to the session.
apiSession.setLogCallXml(true);
apiSession.setLog(log);
```

After the example completes creating the session, it creates the first session call object, `apiGetCats`, using the `IGetCategoriesCall` interface if you choose to get the category list. It appears that Java can't assign the session to the `GetCategoriesCall` object directly, so the code assigns this information indirectly. Normally, this would mean assigning the session to the `apiGetCats.APICall.ApiCallSession` property, but the example uses a two-step process to perform the task:

```
parentApi = apiGetCats.getAPICall();
parentApi.setApiCallSession(apiSession);
```

The first step retrieves the `APICall` property. The second step associates the session to the `APICall.ApiCallSession` property. The main reason for this convoluted approach is that `Jacob.DLL` doesn't appear to support multiple levels of indirection. Notice the use of get and set methods for the property values. The code completes the categories call by displaying the categories as a single list using a simple loop.

The code begins building an `IItem` object next. This object contains the item information for the new listing send to eBay by the `AddItemCall()` method. Creating the item is a matter of filling out the properties based on inputs provided by the user. After the code creates the `IItem` object, it creates the `IAddItemCall` object to make the call. This call uses the same convoluted approach to assigning the session to the object. When the call is successful, it displays the `item.getItemId()` value on screen.

At one point in the listing, you're going to run into a commented out call to `Build-Attributes()`. It isn't clear what this extra code is supposed to do in the example. However, the function does exist and you might want to work with it to build items, such as cars, that do rely on attributes.

Developing a Simple Java Application

This section shows how to create a simple Java application using the API technique to access eBay. As previously mentioned, the current SDK technique setup for Java is unstable. The API technique appears to work flawlessly. Despite the need to write more code when using the API technique, the stability is worth the additional effort.

Rather than use the command line approach of the eBay-supplied example, this example relies on a third party editor, JCreator. The code will work with any editor you choose to use, including a simple text editor. However, you'll find debugging and running the application goes a lot faster if you have a good editor.

Configuring the JCreator Editor

The professional version of the JCreator editor can make working with eBay Web Services a lot easier because it provides help with the various packages and libraries. You don't have to spend time working with batch files because the application compiles within the IDE. In addition, the debugger makes it easy to see how requests to and responses from eBay Web Services work.

Because there are a number of ways to work with eBay Web Services, I decided to create a setup that could work with them all. This section shows how to install support for the SDK technique, the eBay Request Library technique (depends on the API technique), and the future Simple Object Access Protocol (SOAP) technique. You only have to perform steps 1 through 3 if you want to use the API technique without any fancy add-ons.

When using the SOAP technique, you'll need the Axis 1.1 or above library you can download from `http://ws.apache.org/axis/` and a current copy of Xerces-J you can download from `http://xml.apache.org/dist/xerces-j/`. You'll likely need a copy of the eBay support for SOAP, but the production SOAP environment information isn't available as of this writing. When using the eBay Request Library, you actually need two libraries, the one supplied by eBay and the JDOM library. Download a copy of the eBay Request Library from `http://developer.ebay.com/DevZone/docs/Samplecode.asp` and the JDOM library from `http://www.jdom.org/downloads/index.html` (I used Beta 9 of this particular library for the examples).

> ▶ **NOTE**
>
> The JCreator Web site currently includes two versions of the product: 2.5 and 3.0. In addition, you can download a freeware or professional product of each of these major versions. The examples in this chapter assume you have JCreator 3.0 Professional. The steps will also work with the freeware product, but won't work with either 2.5 product.

1. Create a new workspace using the File ➢ New ➢ Project command. You'll see a Project Wizard dialog box shown in Figure 10.1.

2. Select the Basic Java Application option and click Next. The wizard will ask you to provide a project path.

3. Type a name for the project (the example uses SimpleSearch) in the Name field and click Next. (Click Finish if you intend to use the straight API technique.) You'll see the Project ClassPath dialog box shown in Figure 10.2. Notice that this dialog box has two tabs JDK Profiles and Required Libraries.

FIGURE 10.1:

Select a project type from the list of options.

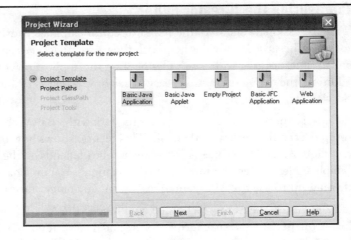

FIGURE 10.2:

Define one or more libraries as needed using the Project Wizard dialog box.

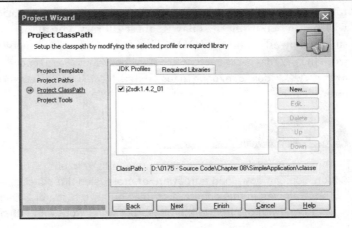

4. Select the Required Libraries tab so you can add the Axis, Xerces, JDOM, and custom eBay libraries.

5. Click New. You'll see the Set Library dialog box shown in Figure 10.3. This dialog box can add either archives, such as those used for Axis, Xerces, and JDOM, or library paths, such as the one used for the custom eBay Request Library.

6. Select Add ➤ Add Path or Add ➤ Add Archive as appropriate. In both cases, you'll see a dialog where you can select the required path or archive file. When selecting the custom eBay SDK library path, choose the \Program Files\eBay\SDK\Java folder because it's the top-level folder for the library. After you download the eBay Request Library, add its path

as a library. The default path is \eBayRequestLibrary\src. The default JDOM paths include \jdom-b9\build and \jdom-b9\lib. When working with Axis and Xerces, select all of the appropriate archive files in the \axis-1_1\lib or \xerces-2_5_0 folder.

> **NOTE**

You can also add source code and documentation files when available using the Sources and Documentation tabs of the Set Library dialog box. The Axis documentation files appear in the \axis-1_1\docs folder, while the Xerces documentation files appear in the \xerces-2_5_0\ docs folder. The eBay Request Library documentation appears in \eBayRequestLibrary\doc. The JDOM documentation appears at \jdom-b9\build\apidocs. You must use the external viewer when working with the SDK.

7. Type a name for the library in the Name field of the Set Library dialog box and click OK. JCreator will add the library to the list of available libraries for the project.

8. Repeat steps 5 through 7 for the custom eBay, JDOM, Axis, and Xerces libraries. When you complete the steps, check only the library entries in the Project ClassPath dialog box that you actually need. Figure 10.4 shows a typical library setup for eBay Web Services.

9. Click Finish. JCreator will create a new project and workspace for you.

> **TIP**

Once you configure the libraries you need for eBay Web Services, they're available for every other project you create. All you need to do is check the required libraries. Use the eBaySDK option for SDK technique projects, the Axis and Xerces options for SOAP projects. Select the eBayRequestLibrary and JDOM options for API technique projects that use this library.

FIGURE 10.3:

Add library paths or archives using the Set Library dialog box.

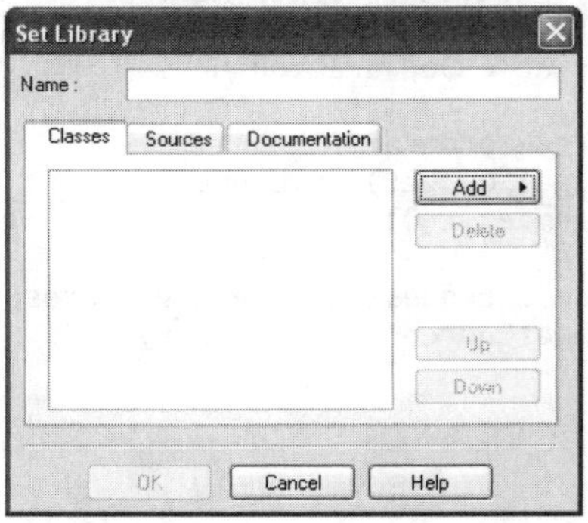

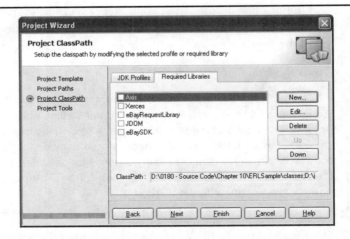

You've configured JCreator for use with eBay Web Services at this point. These steps probably seem like a lot more work than simply typing what you need into a batch file, but it's also less error prone and somewhat easier to configure. Generally, you'll find modification and updates are much easier to perform using this editor.

Writing the Application

This first example demonstrates the API technique without adding anything extra. You can call eBay Web Services and work with the data without anything more than the 1.4.2 (or above) version of the Java Development Kit (JDK). The example performs a simple GetSearchResults() call. Listing 10.1 shows the simple API technique for making the call. You'll find the complete source for this example in the \Chapter 10\SimpleSearch folder of the source code located on the Sybex Web site.

Listing 10.1   **Using the Simple API Technique**

```
public void actionPerformed(ActionEvent AE)
{
   ... Variable Declarations ...

   // End the program.
   if (AE.getSource() == btnQuit)
      System.exit(0);

   // Issue a request and receive a response.
   if (AE.getSource() == btnTest)
   {
      try
      {
```

```java
// Define the development environment URL.
eBayUrl = new URL("https://api.sandbox.ebay.com/ws/api.dll");

// Create a connection to eBay.
Conn = (HttpsURLConnection) eBayUrl.openConnection();

// Specify the connection is for input/output.
Conn.setDoInput(true);
Conn.setDoOutput(true);

// Set the data transmission method.
Conn.setRequestMethod("POST");

// Define the header information for the request. These
// headers appear in the same order recommended by the
// documentation at
// http://developer.ebay.com/DevZone/docs/API_Doc/index.asp.
Conn.addRequestProperty("X-EBAY-API-SESSION-CERTIFICATE",
                        txtDevID.getText() + ";" +
                        txtAppID.getText() + ";" +
                        txtCertID.getText());
... Other Request Headers ...

// Build a string that contains the request.
Req =
    "<?xml version='1.0' encoding='utf-8'?>\r\n"+
    "<request>\r\n" +
    "<RequestToken>" +
       txtAuthToken.getText() +
    "</RequestToken>" +
    "<DetailLevel>0</DetailLevel>" +
    "<ErrorLevel>1</ErrorLevel>" +
    "<Query>" + txtSearch.getText() + "</Query>" +
    "<SiteId>0</SiteId>" +
    "<Verb>GetSearchResults</Verb>" +
    "</request>";

// Create the output stream.
DataOut = Conn.getOutputStream();

// Send the data.
SendIt = new PrintStream(DataOut);
SendIt.print(Req);
SendIt.close();

// Recieve the response.
DataIn = Conn.getInputStream();
DataBuf = new BufferedInputStream(DataIn);

// Build a DOM document.
BuildIt = DocumentBuilderFactory.newInstance();
```

```java
RespDoc = BuildIt.newDocumentBuilder();
eBayDat = RespDoc.parse(DataBuf);

// Drill down to the Items node.
eBayLst =
 eBayDat.getElementsByTagName("eBay").item(0).getChildNodes();
Search = eBayLst.item(3).getChildNodes();
Items = Search.item(1).getChildNodes();

// Set the number of rows in the table.
RTM.setNumRows(
   Integer.parseInt
     (Search.item(3).getChildNodes().item(0).getNodeValue()));

// Set the table row count.
TblCnt = 0;

// Clear the response table.
for (int RCount = 0;
     RCount < 10;
     RCount++)
   for (int CCount = 0;
      CCount < 4;
      CCount++)
    tblResp.setValueAt("", RCount, CCount);

// Process all the items.
for (int Count = 0; Count < Items.getLength(); Count++)
   if (Items.item(Count).getNodeName() == "Item")
   {

      // Process an individual item.
      Item = Items.item(Count).getChildNodes();
      for (int ICount = 0;
           ICount < Item.getLength(); ICount++)
      {
         TheItem = Item.item(ICount);

         // Display the data.
         if (TheItem.getNodeName() == "Title")
            tblResp.setValueAt(
               TheItem.getChildNodes().item(0).getNodeValue(),
               TblCnt, 0);
         ... Other Display Statements ...
      }

      // Update the table row count.
      TblCnt++;
   }
}
catch(java.net.MalformedURLException e)
```

```
        {
            ... Lots of Error Trapping ...
        }
    }
}
```

The most important piece of API technique code appears in the `actionPerformed()` method of the `ButtonHandler` class. The code begins by building a new URL. It then uses the URL to create a secure connection to eBay. Notice that you must coerce the output of the `eBayUrl` `.openConnection()` method. The code then sets the connection up for both sending and receiving data. It also sets the request method to POST using the `setRequestMethod("POST")` call and begins setting the request headers using the `addRequestProperty()` method.

Unlike many of the other API examples in the book, creating the XML request for Java is relatively easy. You create a string containing the required elements, rather than an XML document.

After the code creates the request, it obtains the output stream using `Conn.getOutput-Stream()` and sends the data using `SendIt.print(Req)`. The process is actually viewed as printing from the Java perspective. Make sure you close the output stream or you'll experience errors in the application later.

The next task is to retrieve the response by creating an input stream using `Conn.getInput-Stream()`. The code creates a buffered input stream next using `DataIn` (the input stream) as the data source. The code hasn't read the data yet; it has only prepared to read the data. The data reading process occurs as part of building a DOM document. The code uses a three-step process in this case: it creates a document builder factory, uses the factory to create a document builder, and finally uses the document builder to read the data and use the information to create a document. The `RespDoc.parse(DataBuf)` call actually reads the data in a string and converts the string to an XML document.

Reading through the document can be a frustrating experience unless you know how Java interprets the eBay input. If you look at the raw data you'll notice that every other element is a `#text` node. After working with the data for a while, it appears that Java interprets the carriage returns between the other elements as text nodes. Consequently, you can't assume that the items appear as a list of `<Item>` elements. Every `<item>` element has an associated `#text` node. The ramifications of this little oddity become apparent when you look at the code required to drill down into the various node levels including `<eBay>`, `<Search>`, and `<Items>`.

The results window has a default of 10 rows. In many cases, you can store the result set in 10 rows, but, in other cases, you'll need more. Because you can't know how many rows to create in advance, the code sets the number of rows based on the `<Count>` element using the `RTM.setNumRows()` method (RTM is the template used to create the result rows).

The code now needs to track which row of the table it's using with the `TblCnt` variable. You can't use the item element counter, `Count`, because the `<Items>` node includes text elements.

At this point, the code processes the `<Items>` node using a `for` loop. The code begins by determining whether the child node is an `<Item>` node using the `Items.item(Count).get-NodeName()` method. If so, it begins processing the `<Item>` child nodes using another `for` loop. The code uses the `TheItem.getNodeName()` method to determine which data node it's processing (or whether it's another `#text` node). When the code does find a data node, it places the data in the table using the `tblResp.setValueAt()` method. Figure 10.5 shows typical output from this application.

Writing a Java Application Using the eBay Request Library

After working with the SDK technique and deciding I would rather commit hari-kari than use it with Java (it works great with many other languages) and wondering seriously if the API approach wasn't almost as bad, I stumbled on one of eBay's best kept developer secrets: the sample code at `http://developer.ebay.com/DevZone/docs/Samplecode.asp`. I would normally expect some fanfare or at least a well-placed pointer to the code in this area, but what you really need is a compass and a good map. You can't get there from anywhere—you must know it exists.

FIGURE 10.5:

The application creates typical output for the `GetSearch-Results()` call.

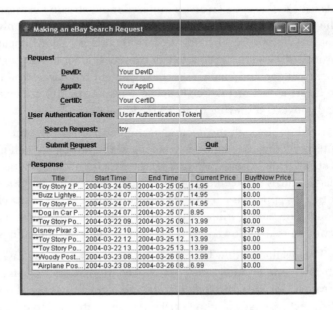

The example in this section uses the eBay Request Library, which is perhaps the best tool in the Java developer's toolkit. I chose to replicate the `GetSearchResults()` call shown in Listing 10.1 for this example so you could compare the differences for yourself. The code you see in Listing 10.2 performs the same task, produces the same result, and took about a quarter of the time to write. Not only did I write fewer lines of code, but it was easier to write as well. You'll find the complete source for this example in the `\Chapter 10\ERLSample` folder of the source code located on the Sybex Web site.

Listing 10.2   **Using the eBay Request Library**

```java
public void actionPerformed(ActionEvent AE)
{
    int                 TblCnt;     // Current table row.
    Properties          ReqData;    // Request properties.
    GetSearchResults    Req;        // The request.
    Result              Response;   // Request response.
    SearchResult        AllItems;   // All of the items.
    ItemResult          Item;       // One item.

    // End the program.
    if (AE.getSource() == btnQuit)
        System.exit(0);

    // Issue a request and receive a response.
    if (AE.getSource() == btnTest)
    {
        try
        {
            // Create the request properties.
            ReqData = new Properties();

            // Set the request properties.
            ReqData.put(EBayRequest.HostURL,
                        "https://api.sandbox.ebay.com/ws/api.dll");
            ReqData.put(EBayRequest.DeveloperId, txtDevID.getText());
            ReqData.put(EBayRequest.ApplicationId, txtAppID.getText());
            ReqData.put(EBayRequest.CertificateId, txtCertID.getText());
            ReqData.put(EBayRequest.CompatibilityLevel, "305");
            ReqData.put(EBayRequest.DetailLevel, "1");
            ReqData.put(EBayRequest.ErrorLevel, "1");
            ReqData.put(EBayRequest.SiteId, "0");
            ReqData.put(EBayRequest.UserId, txtUserName.getText());
            ReqData.put(EBayRequest.UserPassword,
                        txtUserPassword.getText());

            // Create the request object.
            Req = new GetSearchResults(ReqData);
```

```
            // Add the query.
            Req.setQuery(txtSearch.getText());

            // Get the response.
            Response = Req.execute();

            // Get all of the items.
            AllItems = Response.getSearch();

            // Set the number of rows in the table.
            RTM.setNumRows(AllItems.getCount());

            // Set the table row count.
            TblCnt = 0;

            // Parse the individual items.
            for (Iterator Count = AllItems.getItems().iterator();
                Count.hasNext(); )
            {
               // Obtain the single item.
               Item = (ItemResult)Count.next();

               // Place the values in the table.
               tblResp.setValueAt(Item.getTitle(), TblCnt, 0);
               ... Other Values ...

               // Update the row counter.
               TblCnt++;
            }

        }
        catch(java.net.MalformedURLException e)
        {
            ... Lots of Error Trapping ...
        }
     }
   }
}
```

The code begins by creating a series of properties to use to make the call. The ReqData object contains the same entries you'd normally need to add to the request header and parts of the request message. The difference is that you only need to supply the information once.

After the code creates the request data, it builds a request object using the GetSearch-Results() constructor. The constructor accepts ReqData as input to configure Req. It's important to note that the current incarnation of the eBay Request Library doesn't support the full set of API calls. It can easily be made to support the full set, but the developer of the library hasn't created support for all the API calls yet. The call also has to add the one special option that the GetSearchResults() call requires, a query, using the Req.setQuery() method.

> **▶ NOTE**
>
> The current version of the eBay Request Library only supports the username and password access method. However, the code for adding a user authentication token is trivial. Since eBay makes the full source code available, you should modify it to ensure you can use the user authentication token access technique.

The code makes the request and gets the response using a single line of code, `Response = Req.execute()`. It begins to process the information immediately by recovering the `<Search>` node data. Notice you don't have to go through a bunch of intermediate steps to go directly to the `<Search>` node.

At this point, the code sets the number of rows in the response table using the `AllItems.getCount()` method. It then uses a simple `Iterator` to process the list of items. The code places each iterated item into `Item` by coercing the `Count.next()` output. It sets the various table values using the `tblResp.setValueAt()` method. The output from this application is very similar to the output shown in Figure 10.5.

Your Call to Action

This chapter helps you understand how to use Java to build an eBay Web Services application. In fact, the chapter discusses how to build several application types so you get a better idea of just how flexible Java is. The chapter has also pointed out hurdles you might encounter when building the application. Java is an outstanding language with amazing flexibility, but it also has significant problems that you can't overcome with ease. The important issue is to determine whether the benefits of using Java outweigh potential problems when you decide whether to use this language.

Begin your preparation for using Java by using the Web site URLs in the "Resources for Learning Java" section of the chapter. Once you know Java well enough, you're ready to look at the requirements for your application. Make sure you spend enough time considering the issue of whether the intelligence for your application will reside on the client or the server (or something in between). You also need to consider the server setup you want to use and decide what kind of functionality to build into your application. You might decide to start with something as simple as a search site so you can see how eBay Web Services performs, as well as how you need to configure your setup for a more advanced application.

Chapter 11 moves development from desktop, laptop, notebook, and other large devices to the small, mobile devices that many people use today. These devices are lightweight, easy to carry, and generally allow the user to communicate everywhere. As great as these devices are for the general user, they're a problematic platform at best for the developer because they need to consider the limitations of such devices. Most mobile devices have small displays, lack full keyboard functionality, have limited memory, have reduced processing power, and have significant operating system limits. However, even with these problems, mobile devices can serve as an important platform for an eBay Web Services application and eBay certainly makes it easy to use these devices.

Chapter 11

▶ Writing Applications for Mobile Devices

Working with eBay using a mobile device is a natural extension of the services that eBay already provides. In fact, road warriors may well find themselves using a mobile device more often than their desktop machine. The only problem is that eBay doesn't offer much in the way of wireless service. You can find a basic service to raise your bid at `http://www.rebid.com/`. There's also a basic service for Palm users that's described at `http://www.workspot.com/ebay/techsupp.html`. eBay doesn't currently offer anything for Pocket PC users.

Mobile devices present special problems for the developer. The biggest problem is what to do with all the data eBay returns with every request. Trying to fit all that information on a small screen isn't going to work, so you need to create prioritized displays. The first section of the chapter discusses the limitations you need to consider in light of the physical and operational characteristics of a mobile device.

It isn't always possible to test your eBay Web Services application on the actual device. Although you should test the application on an actual machine before you give it to anyone, using an emulator can greatly decrease development time and make the development process easier.

Data management is also an issue. Many of the previous chapters discussed scenarios where you can store data locally to improve performance. However, a mobile device doesn't stay in the same place, so using this technique can prove problematic.

The remaining sections of the chapter discuss application development techniques for various devices. The mobile device you choose greatly affects the kind of development you perform. For example, a Pocket PC is perfectly capable of running an application locally. On the other hand, smaller devices might require some form of Web access through a custom server setup.

> **▶ NOTE**
>
> This chapter uses very specific terms for the various devices. A mobile device refers to any type of device the user can move from one place to another (including PDAs and cellular telephones). A cellular telephone refers to a standard version of this device without built-in intelligence. A Smartphone is a special kind of cellular telephone that includes built-in intelligence that a developer can program using a product such as Visual Studio .NET. A PDA is any kind of non-cellular telephone handheld device. For this book, the term *PDA* includes both Palm and Pocket PC devices. A Palm device specifically uses the Palm OS. A Pocket PC specifically uses some form of Windows. I won't discuss other PDA OSs in this book.

Understanding Mobile Device Limitations

Every device has limitations that you must consider. Whether these limits become a burden depends on what you plan to do with the device. The technique you use to perform a task is also a factor. The following sections discuss mobile device limitations of all types as they relate to eBay Web Services.

Special Add-ons

Most vendors design PDAs as electronic versions of the calendar, address book, and personal note taker. Early versions of these products didn't include the mini–word processors and spreadsheets you'll find in modern versions. In fact, you can extend many PDAs to double as cameras, scanners, and other devices now with special add-ons. Other mobile devices, such as cellular telephones, have followed suit, but to a lesser degree.

The PDA isn't exactly a standard device to begin with. There are many hardware implementations, more than a few operating systems, and even different capabilities to consider. When users start adding features to their PDA, you may find that it's nearly impossible to determine what features you can rely on finding. In short, try to standardize the device configuration whenever possible.

Networking

Distributed application development relies on a connection between the client and the server. Because most mobile devices have limited processing capability, distributed applications are especially important in this situation. The networking problems you'll encounter fall into three categories. The first problem is the limited networking potential of devices such as cellular telephones. These devices have good connectivity, but you'll find it difficult to run custom Web applications using them because it's tough to add any form of security.

You can't reliably determine the identity of the caller, secure the application, or ensure the integrity of the connection. Consequently, cellular telephones are good for downloading noncritical information or performing nonsecure queries.

The second problem is that even though newer PDAs have much better processing capability than any cellular telephone and include good connectivity through a wireless connection, you still can't secure the communication path between server and Pocket PC easily, so critical data could become compromised. At least it's possible to provide a reliable identity check with higher end systems such as the Pocket PC. In addition, you can provide some level of application security.

> **WARNING**

Lest you think that cracking of the sort mentioned in this section falls into the urban legend category, cracking does happen regularly at the various Internet cafés such as Starbucks and McDonald's. In fact, crackers have standard tools to perform the task. Find out more in the Computerworld article at `http://www.computerworld.com/mobiletopics/mobile/story/0,10801,87523,00.html?f=x68`.

A third problem is that older PDAs are far less capable than the newer products on the market. In some cases, you might not even have good networking capability. Some of these older models rely on an internal modem for communication. A few models I've seen use an add-in card to provide a wired connection to the network. In general, you won't want to use one of these older devices with eBay Web Services.

Operating System

The operating system you use for a mobile device affects the device functionality and your ability to interact with eBay Web Services. Generally, you don't have a choice of operating system when it comes to your cellular telephone. Even the Smartphone comes with a single operating system choice and that operating system really isn't capable of providing more than Web application access.

> **TIP**

Make sure you keep up-to-date with mobile device technologies by checking vendor sites often. For example, you can learn about updated capabilities for the Pocket PC and Smartphone devices by visiting Microsoft's site at `http://www.microsoft.com/windowsmobile/default.mspx`. Visit the Web site for your particular cellular telephone vendor to obtain cellular telephone updates. Finally, make sure you visit the Palm site at `http://www.palm.com/home.html` or `http://www.palm.com/us/`.

PDA users do have some choices to make, especially if they have a Pocket PC device at their disposal. Early versions of the Pocket PC used Windows CE. However, devices now come loaded with compact versions of Windows 2000 or Windows XP. No, you can't create a full desktop application for these devices, but the newer the operating system and the greater the device functionality, the better your chances are of creating an application that can perform most (perhaps all) tasks locally.

Early versions of the Palm are extremely limited and any hopes you have of creating a local application are dim (unless you want to do the equivalent of assembly language programming). These early versions require that you use a Web application to communicate with eBay Web Services. Newer versions of the Palm offer greater functionality, and you'll probably find a strong third party market for development tools as these versions gain support. In the meantime, you can use the developer resources provided directly by Palm at `http://www.palmone .com/us/developers/`.

Screen Size

Many users have 17-inch or 19-inch monitors capable of a minimum of 1,280 × 1,024 resolution today. Developers have taken advantage of the screen real estate to create better applications that display more data at one time. Even Microsoft uses higher resolutions as a baseline for applications—many of their application screens won't fit on an 800 × 600 display anymore.

Everything you want to do with your PDA has to fit within a small screen space (320 × 200 pixels if you're using a Pocket PC model like the Casio Cassiopeia). Developers working on cellular telephone applications have even less screen real estate—some models display just a few lines of information. In addition, some PDAs and most cellular telephones use black and white displays in place of color, so you can't even use the modern tricks to make the display look nicer.

Make sure you consider eXtensible Hypertext Markup Language (XHTML) for complex applications with many elements (`http://www.w3.org/TR/xhtml1/`). It helps you to display your application in segments with relative ease.

Other display options include using the Handheld Device Markup Language (HDML) (`http://www.w3.org/TR/NOTE-Submission-HDML-spec.html`) or Wireless Markup Language (WML) (`http://www.oasis-open.org/cover/wap-wml.html`). Both of these technologies use the concept of cards and decks to break up information into easily managed pieces.

Color

Developers have gotten used to seeing colors on their applications. Color dresses up a drab display and makes the application more fun to use. In addition, using color presents cues to the user. Depending on the mobile device you use, you may not have any color at all. For example, older Palm models present the world in shades of gray. Many cellular telephones also represent all data using either black or white and don't even provide for shades of gray.

The problem for mobile device users is that the screen is already small. If a user gets into an area with bright sunlight, seeing the screen might become impossible, especially if the screen contains colors that don't work well in such an environment, so don't rely on color for your main display.

Using color to display icons or to convey a message is still a good idea, even in the world of the mobile device. For example, a red icon could signal danger or tell the user to wait without using up screen real estate for words. Of course, you need to explain the meaning of the color changes within a manual or help file (preferably both).

User Interface

Cellular telephone users commonly have just a keypad as an interface device. In some cases, the vendor will also supply some control keys, including an arrow keypad, but that's about it. If you want to create an eBay Web Services application for a cellular telephone, you need to consider these limitations.

Most PDA users rely on a pointer to do all of their work. Sure, a few PDAs do offer a keyboard and mouse as separate items, but most of these offerings are bulky and difficult to use. Pointer use is one of the reasons that you want to keep your application on one screen, or use multiple screens when necessary. Scrolling on a PDA screen is less than intuitive and requires some level of skill to master.

Pointer friendly programs also make tasks yes or no propositions. Again, this allows the user to accomplish the task with a single click, rather than writing something down. The point is to make the PDA as efficient as possible so the user doesn't get frustrated trying to do something easy.

Working with Emulators

An important consideration for this chapter is that eBay offers data in response to a request. One of the problems that developers must solve when working with mobile devices is testing for multiple models. Because of this requirement, most developers turn to emulation software to help test their applications. An emulator provides the equivalent environment of the mobile device that it's supposed to model. I stress the word *equivalent*, because most of these emulators don't provide a complete picture of the mobile device environment. You can rely on an emulator to tell you whether the application fits within the screen area that the mobile device provides, but you can't rely on it to tell you about memory issues or whether a particular device has a piece of support software you need. These other issues require testing on an actual device—something you should do for at least a subset of the mobile devices you want to support.

> ▶ **TIP**
>
> Keep apprised of the latest Microsoft mobility and embedded system developments at `http://msdn.microsoft.com/mobility/`. This Web site includes many of the links you'll need to download the latest Microsoft products to make your eBay Web Services mobile application development easier.

I chose the emulators used to test the application in the sections that follow because they provide a broad range of support, and you can download evaluation units. Here are the download locations so that you can get your copies of the products before you begin this section. The following sections assume that you've downloaded the software required for the installation.

- Microsoft eMbedded Visual Tools 3.0 (2002 edition): `http://www.microsoft.com/downloads/details.aspx?FamilyId=F663BF48-31EE-4CBE-AAC5-0AFFD5FB27DD` (full development package) or `http://www.microsoft.com/downloads/details.aspx?FamilyId=25F4DE97-AE80-477A-9DF1-496B85B3D3E3` (emulators only) or `http://www.microsoft.com/downloads/details.aspx?FamilyID=2dbee84a-bd94-4167-b817-2b2e548b2e92` (older full development version)

> ▶ **TIP**
>
> Because it's such a large download (205MB), Microsoft provides eMbedded Visual Tools 3.0 (2002 edition) on a CD. You can order the CD to avoid the download time. In addition, even though Windows XP isn't listed as one of the supported platforms, developers find the product installed just fine on Windows XP. Make sure you copy the CD key at the bottom of the download page when you do download your copy of eMbedded Visual Tools 3.0 from the Internet.

- Openwave SDK: `http://developer.Openwave.com/download/`
- Microsoft Smartphone 2003: `http://www.microsoft.com/downloads/details.aspx?familyid=8fe677fa-3a6a-4265-b8eb-61a628ecd462` (requires eMbedded Visual C++ 4.0) or Microsoft Pocket PC 2003 emulator for eMbedded Visual C++ 4.0 at `http://www.microsoft.com/downloads/details.aspx?FamilyId=9996B314-0364-4623-9EDE-0B5FBB133652`

Visual Studio .NET Built-in Emulator

Visual Studio .NET 2003 comes with a built-in emulator you can use for various kinds of development. When you create a mobile project, the IDE automatically sets up the required emulator support as well. After you develop the application, use the Debug ➤ Start command to display the Deploy Pocket PC dialog box.

To use the emulator, simply select the Pocket PC 2002 Emulator (Default) option and click Deploy. The IDE will copy the application to the emulator folder, start the emulator, and load your application. At this point, you can begin testing the application as you would any another .NET application.

The emulator is configurable. Use the Tools ➤ Options command to display the Options dialog box. Select the Device Tools ➤ Devices option to display the list of devices available for this project. Select the device you want to configure and click Configure. You'll see a Configure Emulator Settings dialog box similar to the one shown in Figure 11.1.

You can change features such as the display size and color depth. More importantly, you can set memory restrictions on the System tab so that the application can model the memory restrictions of the target device to an extent. Note that the default Visual Studio .NET setup has a number of emulators including the Pocket PC and Windows CE devices.

> ▶ **TIP**
>
> Microsoft recently released the Visual Basic .NET Resource Kit, a must-have addition for mobile development. The kit offers additional samples and makes it much easier to create robust mobile applications. Learn more about this kit at `http://www.microsoft.com/downloads/details.aspx?FamilyId=EF4289B4-FFCB-40BD-9BFE-95256ABD0E13`.

FIGURE 11.1:

Configure the emulator to better model the mobile device you want to use.

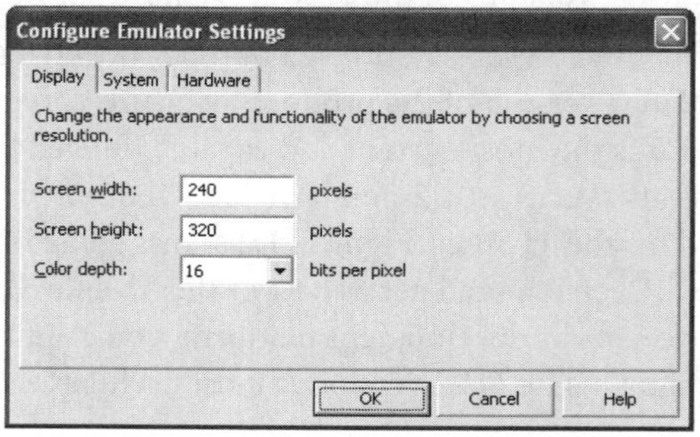

Microsoft eMbedded Visual Tools

The Microsoft eMbedded Visual Tools option is free. All you need to do is download the product and unpack it into an installation directory. You have a choice of two versions on the Internet right now, but the URL at the beginning of this section points to the latest version of the product. Developers have reported fewer problems with the newer version of the emulators and it does model the device more accurately. I'm assuming you have the latest version of the product.

The latest version of Microsoft eMbedded Visual Tools uses a self-extracting executable. When you start the application, it unpacks the contents of the executable into a temporary folder. It then displays a series of dialog boxes that help you install eMbedded Visual Tools 3.0, Microsoft Windows SDK for Pocket PC 2002, and Microsoft Windows SDK for Smartphone 2002. The newer version only includes the Pocket PC and Smartphone emulators—you can separately download SDKs for the handheld and palm-size emulators found in the older version of Microsoft eMbedded Visual Tools at `http://msdn.microsoft.com/downloads/list/handheldpc.asp`. The Smartphone SDK is only available for eMbedded Visual C++, so make sure you install this language if you want to create a Smartphone application.

When you finish installing everything, it's important to test each of the emulators to ensure you received a good installation. Open one of the sample projects to test the emulator when using the newest version of Microsoft eMbedded Visual Tools. If one of these emulators fails, rerun the setup program and select just that emulator for a reinstall.

Openwave SDK

Like the Microsoft emulators, the Openwave SDK is also a free download, but the Openwave Web site offers plenty of opportunity to purchase products as well. (You must complete a registration form to get the free download.) The Openwave file you download is an executable, so double-clicking it starts the installation process. Simply follow the prompts to install the product. Most versions of the product require yes or no answers to each question.

The Openwave Web site offers a number of versions of the product. I suggest you download the latest version of the product to ensure you get the latest features. The Mobile SDK Version 1.5 is the most current and capable full version product available. However, the 5.1 version is also very capable and it includes a number of features not found in the 6.2.2 version used for this chapter. Figure 11.2 shows some of the optional features you can install with the 5.1 version (and get as part of the Mobile SDK Version 1.5). If you want to use Openwave as your development platform, you might want to download the 5.1 version (or both versions). The 6.2.2 version is most useful as an emulator only.

FIGURE 11.2:

Select custom options as needed for your emulator setup.

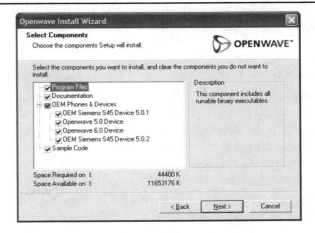

Once you get Openwave installed and have restarted your machine, you'll want to test this product. If you installed the 6.2.2 version, all you get is the emulator. To start the emulator, select the Start ➤ Programs ➤ Openwave SDK 6.2.2 ➤ Openwave SDK 6.2.2 HTTP option. You'll see the emulator start. The emulator automatically goes to the Openwave test site on first use, but you can change that location by opening the SDK Configuration dialog box using the Tools ➤ Options menu. Select the Browse tab and change the Homepage field.

As previously mentioned, Openwave SDK 5.1 has more to offer than other versions of the product. Unlike some of the other emulators you'll use, this one is actually part of a development IDE. Select the Start ➤ Programs ➤ Openwave SDK 5.1 ➤ Openwave SDK 5.1 option to open an IDE similar to other IDEs you may have used in the past. However, for this book, the important feature is the emulator that appears in the right side pane. To use this feature, you'll need to use the Simulator ➤ Go to Address command, enter an URL in the Go To Address dialog box, and then click OK.

Designing for Local or Remote Data Management

Most programming chapters of this book have mentioned the need to store commonly used eBay data locally to improve performance and provide a backup should the main connection to eBay fail. A desktop application can rely on any of a number of Database Management Systems (DBMSs) to perform the task of storing this data for future use. Given the static connection a desktop system enjoys, you can assume the user will always have access to the data. Unfortunately, it's not possible to say the same thing about mobile devices. Mobile devices have dynamic connections that might not be available when a user needs them.

The lack of connectivity means you have to make hard choices about how to make your eBay Web Services application perform well. You could rely on a server-based DBMS to perform this task for you. It's remote because you can't count on a connection, and the mobile device might actually need to rely on a nonstandard connection to obtain the data (as when the user is on the road).

An alternative for some devices is to use a product such as Microsoft SQL CE or Sybase iAnywhere. These DBMSs let you build a local connectivity solution that stores data short term on the local device. However, this solution also has problems. For one thing, you might not see as great a performance gain as you might anticipate—the limited memory and processing capacity device is now running your application and a DBMS. In addition, you'll find that many older devices aren't able to run either Microsoft SQL CE or Sybase iAnywhere.

The best solution is to use local storage when the processing power and storage capability of the mobile device is up to the task. When you can't rely on the resources provided by the mobile device, use a Web application with server-based storage instead.

Developing for a Pocket PC

The Pocket PC is the most capable of the mobile devices you can use for an eBay Web Services application. You can use local storage with this device and perform a multitude of tasks that some mobile devices can't, such as limited data analysis using the copy of Pocket Excel provided with the operating system. This platform even helps you create reports using Pocket Word. In sum, you can use a Pocket PC for most eBay Web Services tasks—at least in a limited way.

> ▶ **TIP**
>
> You may have to search the Internet for some Pocket PC resources. However, you can find many Microsoft-supplied developer tools at http://www.microsoft.com/windowsmobile/ resources/downloads/developer/default.mspx.

Using the .NET Compact Framework

The .NET Compact Framework offers a lot of XML functionality, so the techniques you use to build a desktop application for eBay Web Services generally work with small modifications for a Pocket PC application as well. The biggest changes are that you need additional error trapping to ensure the application doesn't fail in unexpected places and that you need to divide the content between several pages, rather than show a single page.

You also need to exercise some care in choosing methods and properties. For example, when you look through the list of supported properties for the `HttpWebRequest` class, you'll notice that the .NET Compact Framework doesn't provide support for the `ClientCertificates` property. Most of these omissions won't affect your use of eBay Web Services.

> ▶ **WARNING**
>
> The example in this section contains more error trapping than other .NET Framework examples and some of these routines are more generic than previous examples. The reason for the additional error trapping is that the Pocket PC emulator appears to have problems working with eBay at times. For example, you'll find it reports network blocking errors when the same code runs perfectly on the actual device or as part of a desktop application. To learn more about these blocking errors, see the Microsoft Winsock Reference at `http://msdn` `.microsoft.com/library/en-us/wcewinsk/html/cerefWinsockErrorCodes.asp`.

To work with eBay Web Services on the Pocket PC, you need to use the API technique. Several attempts to use the SDK technique on this platform failed—the SDK really isn't designed for mobile use. Listing 11.1 shows a typical search application for the Pocket PC. You'll find the complete source for this example in the `\Chapter 11\PocketPC_Search` folder of the source code located on the Sybex Web site.

Listing 11.1   Using the .NET Compact Framework to Call eBay

```
private void mnuFileSearch_Click(object sender, System.EventArgs e)
{
    ... Variable Declarations ...

    // Create the request.
    Req = (HttpWebRequest)WebRequest.Create(
        "https://api.sandbox.ebay.com/ws/api.dll");
    Req.Method = "POST";

    // Define the header information for the request. These headers
    // appear in the same order recommended by the documentation at
    // http://developer.ebay.com/DevZone/docs/API_Doc/index.asp.
    Req.Headers.Add("X-EBAY-API-SESSION-CERTIFICATE",
                    txtDevID.Text + ";" +
                    txtAppID.Text + ";" +
                    txtCertID.Text);
    ... Other Headers ...

    // Create the XMLData object.
    XMLData = new XmlDocument();
```

```csharp
// Add the header.
Header =
   XMLData.CreateProcessingInstruction(
      "xml", "version='1.0'  encoding='iso-8859-1'");
XMLData.AppendChild(Header);

// Create the root node.
Root = XMLData.CreateElement("request");
Root.SetAttribute("xmlns", "urn:eBayAPIschema");

// Add the user information.
Elem = XMLData.CreateElement("RequestToken");
Elem.InnerText = txtUserAuth.Text;
Root.AppendChild(Elem);

// Add the request data.
Elem = XMLData.CreateElement("DetailLevel");
Elem.InnerText = "0";
Root.AppendChild(Elem);
... Other Request Data ...

// Add the request data to the XML request.
XMLData.AppendChild(Root);

// Convert the data to a byte array.
Encode = new ASCIIEncoding();
Conv = Encode.GetBytes(XMLData.OuterXml);

// Create the request.
Req.ContentLength = Conv.Length;
DatSend = Req.GetRequestStream();

try
{
   // Send the request.
   DatSend.Write(Conv, 0, Conv.Length);
}
catch(System.Net.Sockets.SocketException excp)
{
   // Display an error message, close the stream, and exit.
   MessageBox.Show(excp.Message +
                   "\r\nStopping the Request Routine");
   DatSend.Close();
   return;
}

try
{
   // Get the resulting page from the server.
   WebResp = (HttpWebResponse)Req.GetResponse();
```

```csharp
            // Place the data in a data stream for processing.
            DatResp = WebResp.GetResponseStream();

            // Read the data.
            RespStr = new StreamReader(DatResp);
        }
        catch(System.Exception excp)
        {
            // Display an error message, close the stream, and exit.
            MessageBox.Show(excp.Message +
                            "\r\nStopping the Request Routine");
            DatSend.Close();
            return;
        }

        // Create the output form.
        OutFrm = new FrmResults();

        // Create a data set to store the data and associate
        // it with the grid.
        OutFrm.DS = new DataSet("ds_eBay");
        OutFrm.DS.Tables.Add("Results");
        OutFrm.DS.Tables["Results"].Columns.Add("Title");
        OutFrm.DS.Tables["Results"].Columns.Add("ID");
        OutFrm.DS.Tables["Results"].Columns.Add("CurrentPrice");
        OutFrm.dgOutput.DataSource = OutFrm.DS.Tables["Results"];

        // Process the data.
        Resp = new XmlDocument();
        Resp.LoadXml(RespStr.ReadToEnd());
        Items = Resp.ChildNodes[1].ChildNodes[1].ChildNodes[0].ChildNodes;
        foreach (XmlNode Item in Items)
        {
            // Add a row.
            DR = OutFrm.DS.Tables["Results"].NewRow();

            // Add a string to the output.
            DR["Title"] = Item["Title"].InnerText;
            DR["ID"] = Item["Id"].InnerText;
            DR["CurrentPrice"] = Item["CurrentPrice"].InnerText;

            // Display the row on screen.
            OutFrm.DS.Tables["Results"].Rows.Add(DR);
        }

        // Switch to the new form.
        OutFrm.Show();
    }
```

This example begins like many other API technique examples. The code creates a request that includes a posting method, headers, and an XML document. All of the developer-required information appears on the first page of the application and includes the developer keys, user authentication token, and the search query. The code builds the XML document containing the request. It converts the request to a `Byte` array using ASCII encoding. The sending process begins when the code creates `DatSend` using the `Req.GetRequestStream()`. At this point, the code begins to differ from any other search you have seen.

Notice that the `DatSend.Write()` method appears within a `try...catch` block. Theoretically, you should always include it in a `try...catch` block, but the call seldom, if ever, fails on a desktop machine. The call does fail regularly when using the emulator. Unless you want the application to constantly crash during testing, you'll want to include the `try...catch` block. Note that this problem doesn't seem to occur very often when using the real device.

Once the code sends the request, it retrieves the response using `(HttpWebResponse)Req` `.GetResponse()`. You must coerce the data type to ensure you can work with the resulting data. The code obtains a pointer to the data stream and uses a `StreamReader` to get the data.

The first form (page of the application) contains all of the inputs—there isn't any room for output, so the application creates an instance of a new form specially designed to hold the output, `FrmResults`. This form consists of a `DataGrid` that has a reference to a `DataSet` that contains the actual output. Normally, the IDE makes these members private. You must make them public in order to access them from the main form code. Once the code initializes the data output, it begins processing the data.

Before the code can access the data, it must gain access to the `<Items>` node. The `Items` `XmlNodeList` contains the reference. A simple `foreach` loop processes the individual items in the list. The code adds a new row to the `DataSet`, `OutFrm.DS.Tables["Results"]` using the `NewRow()` method. The resulting `DataRow`, `DR`, is updated with the current item information and added back into the `DataSet`.

Using Older Microsoft Products

You can use embedded Visual Basic (eVB) to create an eBay Web Services application. However, you need to bend the rules slightly to accomplish the task. The default eVB IDE doesn't include any form of XML on the Available References list in the References dialog box. Use the Project ➤ References command to see this dialog box.

Even though the reference doesn't exist, the Pocket PC does have at least one version of the Microsoft XML library available. Click Browser in the References dialog box and you'll see an Add Reference dialog box. Highlight the `MSXML.DLL` file in the `\System32` folder of your machine and click OK. The eVB IDE will complain that the library isn't marked for use with this platform. Click OK to ignore the warning and the IDE will add the reference.

The example in this section relies on the `GetSearchResults()` call again. The main reason for using this example again is so you can compare techniques using the same call. Nothing stops you from using eVB in place of the newer .NET Compact Framework on a Pocket PC, so the comparison is important. Note that this is also the first use of Microsoft XML 2.0 in the book—other examples have used newer versions because they're available on the desktop. Using this older library brings some interesting changes to the code, so the example concentrates on the calling process. Listing 11.2 shows the code you need for this example. You'll find the complete source for this example in the \Chapter 11\eVB_Search folder of the source code located on the Sybex Web site.

Listing 11.2   **Using eVB to Call eBay**

```
Private Sub btnTest_Click()
    ... Variable Declarations ...

    ' Create the request.
    Set Req = CreateObject("Microsoft.XMLHTTP")
    Req.open "POST", "https://api.sandbox.ebay.com/ws/api.dll", False

    ' Define the header information for the request. These headers
    ' appear in the same order recommended by the documentation at
    ' http://developer.ebay.com/DevZone/docs/API_Doc/index.asp.
    Req.setRequestHeader "X-EBAY-API-SESSION-CERTIFICATE", _
                         txtDevID.Text + ";" + _
                         txtAppID.Text + ";" + txtCertID.Text
    ... Other Headers ...

    ' Create the XML request object.
    Set XMLData = CreateObject("Microsoft.XMLDOM")

    ' Add the XML request header.
    Set ProcInst = XMLData.createProcessingInstruction( _
        "xml", "version='1.0'  encoding='iso-8859-1'")
    XMLData.appendChild ProcInst

    ' Construct the XML request message.
    Set Root = XMLData.createElement("request")
    Root.setAttribute "xmlns", "urn:eBayAPIschema"

    ' Add the user information.
    Set Elem = XMLData.createElement("RequestToken")
    Elem.Text = txtUserToken.Text
    Root.appendChild Elem

    ' Add the required request data.
    Set Elem = XMLData.createElement("DetailLevel")
    Elem.Text = "0"
    Root.appendChild Elem
```

```
    ... Other Request Data ...

    ' Add the request data to the XML request.
    XMLData.appendChild Root

    ' Send the request.
    Req.send XMLData.xml

    ' Create the output form.
    Set OutForm = frmResults

    ' Create a new document for parsing.
    Set ParseData = CreateObject("Microsoft.XMLDOM")

    ' Make sure the document loads correctly.
    If ParseData.loadXML(Req.responseText) Then

        ' Fill the form with data.
        OutForm.txtOutput.Text = ParseData.xml

    End If

    ' Display the form on screen.
    OutForm.Show

End Sub
```

The code for this example begins by creating a request. Notice that you must use the `CreateObject("Microsoft.XMLHTTP")` method when working with eVB because this language doesn't use the `New` keyword. The code defines the request information as with the other API technique examples.

Use the `CreateObject("Microsoft.XMLDOM")` method to create the XML document. The process of filling this document is similar to other API technique examples. Once the code creates the XML document, it can send it to eBay Web Services using the `Req.send` method. For some strange reason (totally unexplained by the Microsoft documentation), this particular version of Microsoft XML works better if you send the `XMLData.xml` property, rather than the object as in other API technique calls.

After the call returns, the code creates an output form to display the data and another XML document to hold the response information. The code loads this data using the `ParseData.loadXML()` method. You might have noticed that the test for the `Req.status` property is missing. Because of the way eVB handles errors, it displays any problems with server communications before you can catch them with the check. The code ends by placing the response XML into `OutForm.txtOutput.Text` and displaying the output form on screen.

Developing for a Cellular Telephone or Palm-type Device

Older versions of the Palm and most cellular telephones are so limited in processing capacity and memory that you really won't want to try to create a local eBay Web Services application for them. The best alternative is to create a Web application that retrieves and formats the data for the device before passing it along. The example in the section that follows relies on a special ASP.NET application specifically designed for mobile devices. The server detects the device type and pages forms as needed to ensure each form appears correctly on the device.

> ▶ **TIP**
>
> Many developers wrongly assume that cellular telephones will remain limited devices. Many companies are working on advanced versions that will let users perform some advanced tasks. For example, Cisco recently released an IP cellular telephone with XML support. This device could allow a user full access to eBay from any location. Read more about this new cellular telephone at http://www.eweek.com/article2/0,1759,1517502,00.asp. In addition, at least one company is working with Microsoft to include the Windows Mobile 2003 operating system in a cellular telephone (see the Computerworld story at http://www.computerworld.com/mobiletopics/mobile/story/0,10801,84923,00.html).

Creating the ASP.NET Application

The example in this section is a typical search application. Listing 11.3 shows the essential code you need for this example. Make sure you look at the form setup for this example in the source code. You'll find this example in the \Chapter 11\WebApp folder of the source code located on the Sybex Web site. It's also important to review the installation procedures found in the "Using the ASP.NET Applications in this Book" section when placing this code on your development machine.

Listing 11.3   **Using ASP.NET to Call eBay**

```
private void btnSearch_Click(object sender, System.EventArgs e)
{
    ApiSession            Session; // The eBay session.
    GetSearchResultsCall  Search;  // Search object.
    IItemFoundCollection  Results; // Returned items.

    // Create a session.
    Session = new ApiSession();

    // Define the sandbox as the call location.
```

```
Session.Url = "https://api.sandbox.ebay.com/ws/api.dll";

// Add session security information.
Session.Token = new ApiToken();
Session.Token.Token = "User Token";

// Add the developer information.
Session.Developer = "Your DevID";
Session.Application = "Your AppID";
Session.Certificate = "Your CertID";

// Create a search.
Search = new GetSearchResultsCall(Session);

// Add the search criteria.
Search.Query = txtQuery.Text;

// Perform the search.
Results = Search.GetSearchResults();

// Clear the current list of items.
lstResults.Items.Clear();

// Interpret the results.
foreach (IItemFound Item in Results)

    // Add a row.
    lstResults.Items.Add(Item.Title + " " + Item.CurrentPrice);

// Display the results.
this.ActiveForm = frmResponse;
}
```

It turns out that the ASP.NET example is the shortest and simplest in this chapter because you can use the SDK technique. The code begins by creating a new session and assigning the required values to it, including user identification, the developer keys, and the development environment. This is one situation where you want to keep the number of items on the display to a minimum, so make sure you program as many session inputs as you can in the background. In fact, you might consider giving each user a separate Web page with their settings stored in it.

The code creates a GetSearchResultsCall object, Search, and fills it with the query next. This is the one piece of information the user must supply. Now that the code has everything it needs, it calls eBay Web Services. The results you get back are the same as any other call, so you can pick and choose which data the user sees.

The example uses a list box to display the results. A grid won't work with devices such as cellular telephones. In fact, you might want to keep each item as small as possible while meeting user needs. In this case, the code displays just the item title and current price. After the code fills the list box with data, it displays the response form.

Using the ASP.NET Applications in this Book

All of the ASP.NET applications in this book follow the same pattern as the example in the "Creating the ASP.NET Application" section of the chapter. You'll find two folders associated with every example on the Sybex Web site. The first folder, such as `\Chapter 06\ASP_NET_Example`, contains the files that you should place on your development machine. The second folder, such as `\Chapter 06\ASP_NET_Example (Server)`, contains the files that you should place on your Web server in the appropriate `\Inetpub\wwwroot` folder.

Once you place the files on your system, open the SLN (Solution) file for the project using a plain text editor such as Notepad. The top of this file will contain several lines of information similar to the ones shown here:

```
Microsoft Visual Studio Solution File, Format Version 8.00
Project("{FAE04EC0-301F-11D3-BF4B-00C04F79EFBC}") = "ASP_NET_Example",
"http://winserver/0180/Chapter8/ASP_NET_Example/ASP_NET_Example.csproj"
```

Change the URL on the third line to match the location of the files on your Web server. Once you make this change, save and close the file. When you open the SLN file, the Visual Studio .NET will automatically open the correct project files on your Web server.

You also need to change one of the entries in the `ASP_NET_Example.csproj.webinfo` file on the server. This file contains a pointer for the information file for a particular project, as shown here:

```
<VisualStudioUNCWeb>
<Web URLPath =
"http://winserver/0180/Chapter8/ASP_NET_Example/ASP_NET_Example.csproj" />
</VisualStudioUNCWeb>
```

Again, you need to change the URL so that it matches you server setup. This technique lets you use a single machine by changing the Web server to localhost if desired. Make sure you recompile the application using the Rebuild Solution option to ensure that all of the compiled references also match your server setup.

Your Call to Action

This chapter has helped you understand some of the mobile device options at your disposal. You shouldn't consider this chapter complete or comprehensive—mobile device development kits abound. This chapter only discussed some of the more popular options. However, the concepts in this chapter apply equally well to other kinds of mobile development and you can apply the lessons learned to other language products discussed in the book. For example, it's perfectly acceptable to create a mobile device solution using PHP or Java—all you need is a little inspiration.

Now that you have a little more perspective of what's possible, it's time to consider what types of mobile device you want to provide for your eBay Web Services application. One mistake that developers make is to assume they must include support for every available device and that's simply not possible—at least not without a major investment in time and resources. A better path is to choose one or two devices to begin development and add additional devices as needed.

Chapters 5 through 10 introduced you to various language options. In each of these chapters, you learned how to access eBay Web Services using various techniques. Now it's time to refine those examples and explore other ways to use eBay Web Services. Chapter 12 takes you beyond simple applications into refined application development. Chapter 12 considers issues such as application performance and reliability. It also delves into additional caching issues.

Part III

▶ **Refining** Your eBay Web Services Program

Chapter 12

Creating Applications
with Performance in Mind

Creating Applications
with Reliability in Mind

▶ Crafting Your Application

Understanding the Data
Refresh Requirements

Adding Offline
Storage

All of the chapters so far have considered various ways to obtain data from eBay. However, great applications do more than just get data—a developer crafts them to get the data efficiently, reliably, and quickly. For example, you might use an application to track the trends in the auctions you start. You might find that your buyers respond better to certain eBay features, such as displaying the listing in bold type, than others. The storefront sales you create might actually become more profitable than other approaches you try. Crafting an application means knowing what kind of interaction to perform with eBay based on your specific needs.

This chapter assumes that you've read one or more of the preceding language-specific chapters (Chapters 6 through 10) and understand the concepts discussed in Chapters 1 through 5. This chapter answers the question of what comes next. You'll discover some of the concerns you need to address to move your application from *functional* to *usable*. In most cases, this means making your application efficient, reliable, and fast.

One of the major performance and reliability concerns you have to address is the use of databases in your application. Many of the examples in previous chapters showed how to create a database interface for your application so you can store information offline and therefore improve performance. However, the previous chapters left some questions unanswered, such as when to use database storage techniques to improve overall application performance. Sometimes, offline storage is more of a hindrance than a help.

Considering Performance Issues

Some developers confuse the concept of performance with the idea of speed. An application that performs well (has good performance) isn't necessarily fast. Performance is a measure of how well an application accomplishes the task that you set before it. Speed is only one aspect of performance. You also have to consider factors such as resource usage and user access speed (efficiency). In addition, you often have to consider the effect of task repeatability and network bandwidth availability (reliability). The following sections discuss performance concerns for eBay applications.

Addressing Speed Concerns

Speed measures how fast an application can perform a task. Many developers concentrate on this factor when developing an application because it's relatively easy to quantify. You can easily demonstrate that a particular coding change or technique improvement provides a corresponding increase in speed. Making changes that result in a speed increase is important when using a Web service such as eBay Web Services because your application incurs a performance penalty when it requests the data.

Quantifying speed is relatively easy for most applications because the developer has control over the environment. On the other hand, getting, proving, and quantifying a speed increase with eBay Web Services can prove elusive. For example, your application will always slow during peak activity periods on eBay—you can't control this factor and it always affects the overall performance of your application. Consequently, long-term speed measurement is essential when working with eBay Web Services. You need to consider whether a change actually provides a performance boost or eBay Web Services just happened to provide faster results during the initial test. In addition, make one change at a time because you can't accurately measure the effects of multiple changes.

> **▶ NOTE**
>
> This book doesn't even begin to address local application speed issues because the language you choose, application environment, and platform affect the speed of your application. Look in the language-specific chapters of the book for suggestions on third party resources you can use for that language. Writing code that executes quickly takes time, effort, and planning—make sure you begin with a good application specification.

It's also important to consider the state of eBay Web Services at the time of your test. Monitor the state of changes by visiting the developer forums at http://developer.ebay.com/DevZone/community/forums.asp. These newsgroups help you keep up-to-date on changes that eBay is making that could affect your application. eBay also sends you a newsletter with probable changes to eBay Web Services. You can also find the newsletters at http://developer.ebay.com/DevZone/community/newsletter/index.asp. Finally, make sure you keep track of the latest news at http://developer.ebay.com/DevZone/community/events.asp.

Initially, you might get the idea that you have to perform all kinds of weird programming to gain much of a speed increase. However, you can reduce all eBay Web Services application speed improvements into five main areas.

Use the Fewest Possible Calls   A combination of optimized searches, explicit input, and data ordering usually serves to reduce the number of calls your application has to make to eBay. Every call costs time, so even reducing the number of calls by one round-trip helps. When performing searches, requesting more items can be more efficient when you don't know precisely what you're looking for (you're browsing for an item). Conversely, getting fewer items when you know what you want is more efficient.

Handle Only the Required Data   Some developers parse and store every piece of data that a Web service has to offer with the idea that they might need the information later. In general, you only need to save the information your application uses. The important element to consider is that every data manipulation costs time and resources, so you want to work with just the data you need to make your application work well.

> **▶ NOTE**
>
> The exception to the optimized data storage rule is when you use the Integration Library to store data. In this case, the SDK takes care of many of the details for you. However, you might also consider this a performance cost of using the Integration Library since it does store everything. You're essentially trading programming ease and speed for application performance.

Use Offline Storage Effectively   Don't assume that every application has to use offline storage or that you need to store everything offline. An application used to perform research might not benefit from offline storage as most requests are unique and data input is unlikely to repeat. In addition, an application that requires a source of constant updates might not benefit much from complete offline storage—you might want to store just the essentials for locating the data such as the title and URL. (See the "Using Offline Storage Effectively" section for details.)

Improve the Local Application Speed   It's easy to become fixated on the speed of eBay Web Services communication and forget local application requirements. The local application has a large effect on application speed. Consider items such as how fast the application makes a request. Because eBay provides multiple communication techniques (with more on the way with SOAP) you should try various approaches to the application development problem to see which works best. Consider special programming needs as well. For example, don't rely on eBay to sort the data if none of the default sort criteria completely meet your needs—sort the data locally instead.

Define the Best Possible User Experience   Many developers assume that fast code always results in a fast application. When a user spends considerable time trying to figure out your application, code execution speed becomes a nonissue. Always check user performance when you consider the speed of your application because the user is going to be the main choke point. Whenever you make the user fast, you gain a significant improvement in application speed (not to mention reducing support costs). Chapter 13 discusses this concept in detail.

> ▶ **TIP**
>
> Always use the current version of eBay Web Services to get speed, efficiency, reliability, and request features. As eBay improves its Web service, you'll see options for additional task performance methods that will make your application faster.

Addressing Efficiency Concerns

Efficiency affects performance by modifying the resource requirements for the application. An efficient application uses resources to their fullest and therefore reduces the cost of using the application. Making an application efficient can improve application speed as well. For example, an application that uses memory efficiently won't have to rely on swap files or other memory enhancements as much, which usually results in a speed boost. However, an efficient application can just as easily slow performance. An application that uses disk storage rather than memory to improve overall system efficiency by freeing memory for other applications is almost certain to work slower than an application that relies exclusively on memory.

> ▶ **NOTE**
>
> It's important to understand that most performance tuning relies on assumptions that might not be true on the production system. The more control you exercise over the host machine, the better you can control the assumptions you make about performance tuning. Real systems run multiple applications, including background applications such as virus checkers. In addition, applications can experience problems such as memory leaks. (You can fix memory leak problems using applications such as RAM Medic that you can download at `http://www.iomatic.com/products/product.asp?ProductID=rammedic`.) Consequently, you need to make the best assumptions you can about the application environment and use those assumptions when tuning your application.

You'll also find that efficiency affects reliability. An application that uses resources conservatively is less likely to run out of resources to process the incoming eBay data. Resource deprivation is a major cause of application crashes, so using resources carefully means your application is likely to crash less often.

An eBay Web Services application developer only considers the client side of the data exchange because eBay takes care of the server side. When a user makes a request, you must consider the efficiency of that request. Inefficient requests can cause eBay to return more results than needed and reduces overall system performance. As a side effect, consider how inefficient requests will add to the load the eBay Web Services servers must handle. When multiple developers create applications that perform requests inefficiently, server load increases, and could increase the time the user waits for responses.

One of the most important efficiency considerations is the effect of false starts on application efficiency. A developer striving for efficiency might not provide enough information for the user to make a good decision, which means the user spends more time looking at items that obviously won't fulfill a need online. However, the system must also have some intelligence because not all item choices are obvious. Sometimes it's better to have the user assign a weight to each item entry so that ordering becomes easier and more appropriate to that particular user's requirements.

> ▶ **NOTE**

> It often pays to extend application customization to weight all data factors to the user's needs. For example, a user might have better experiences with a particular seller, so storing a weighting factor for that seller locally is helpful. Items sold by that seller will appear in the list of search results first. Sometimes a weighting factor is a matter of preference. The user might prefer sellers who accept personal checks to those who require credit cards, even though both payment options are acceptable.

Considering Reliability Issues

Reliable application performance is essential if you plan to use eBay Web Services for any type of business purpose. Most people associate reliability with availability, but that's only part of the picture. When working with eBay Web Services, you need to consider five reliability factors.

Availability of Data   Unless a user can access the eBay data, using the application you create is useless. Fortunately, eBay Web Services has a high availability rate, so most desktop applications will run fine even if you don't include backup data through a database.

However, you need some form of local and/or remote database support for mobile applications where high availability is a requirement and a connection isn't always available. Make sure you balance the need for data availability with the eBay Web Services licensing requirements, however. You can't store some information locally, even if doing so would increase the reliability of your application.

Consistency of Results   Providing consistent results to application users is important. Consistency means including all data (or a standard response to all data outputs). Sometimes, eBay won't provide an output that you need. For example, you might not receive a description of an item as part of the eBay information. In many cases, you can add this information by searching for it elsewhere, such as through Google. Make sure you let the user know you've relied on an alternative information source (this difference should be noticeable because the description will vary from the usual eBay description). The idea is to provide consistent information so the user can make good decisions. Consistency also means providing similar response times (when possible) and standard error notifications.

Accessibility of eBay Site   You have to decide, at some point, whether you can tolerate any availability problems with eBay Web Services because they'll eventually occur. For example, a line disconnection could result in loss of eBay contact, even if you can still contact your ISP. To provide maximum reliability, you must provide a cache of some sort. However, this requirement doesn't always mean creating a database to hold the data, although, that is one option. You can also use memory caches or disk-based browser caches. For that matter, your application can rely on the cache provided by a proxy server. The point is to provide some alternative, if you need it, for the few times that eBay Web Services doesn't respond.

> **NOTE**
>
> It's impossible to provide access to every eBay service when disconnection occurs. For example, you can't bid when no connection exists. However, a buyer could look through a list of cached items to purchase and a seller can prepare more items for upload when the connection is restored. The idea is to make as much functionality as possible available.

Availability of the Local Application   Strange things can happen to an application between the time it leaves your development machine and appears on the user's machine. In general, you need to perform complete application testing on several (more is better) user machines that don't include all the features of your development machine. Make sure you test obscure as well as common features. For example, test every search type that your application supports. It's also important to test features such as the use of cached pages. Make sure you verify that the cached page feature works as needed so that the user doesn't have to wrestle with your application to get the desired results.

Security of the Data It may seem peculiar to see an item on security in a reliability discussion, but given the sensitivity of the data you obtain from eBay, data security really is part of the reliability of your application. Any damage to your data can have a significant impact on the reliability of your application. In some cases, the damage is obvious—a customer relationship is ruined when personal information is released without permission. In other cases, the damage is subtle. For example, a cracker could get into that cache of downloaded items on your server. Changing the prices (making them higher) puts you at a disadvantage when looking for items to bid on.

Considering the Data Refresh Requirements

The eBay Web Services data refresh requirements are more complex than many Web services because you aren't just working with a single data source. Some data comes from eBay, some is generated as a result of your activities on eBay and in-house analysis, and some is generated by buyers. When you build an application it's impossible to separate the three data sources—your application needs them all. Consequently, you must consider the three data sources and incorporate refresh requirements for all of them. Even so, it helps to view all three data sources separately to make the problem of refreshing the data easier. The following sections provide general guidelines that ensure your data always remains fresh.

Working with eBay's Data

eBay doesn't require you to refresh your data for every call. However, the licensing agreement says that you can't display item data that is more than 6 hours old or other data that is more than 24 hours old. When you use cached data, you must also tell the user how old that data is compared to the data that is on eBay.

These requirements seemingly contradict certification requirements for certain calls such as `GetCategories()`. When you look at the certification requirements in the online API documentation (`http://developer.ebay.com/DevZone/docs/API_Doc/Certification/CertificationRequirements.htm`), it states that you merely need to check the version number and download a new category list when your version differs. The idea is that the data is versioned and you checked whether it was current, without actually downloading the data again. You still gain the benefits of caching, without the data aging that can occur when using a database.

You should also check the certification requirements to verify maximum refresh requirements. For example, you can't call `GetCategoryListings()` more than once in 30 minutes. To use this call more often than that, you must cache the data locally, so a local database store is essential. When using the `GetFeedback()` call, you should cache all of the old feedback and retrieve only the feedback records that you haven't retrieved previously. Essentially, you never have to refresh feedback data, even though this data does appear on eBay. In short, when you consider data refresh requirements, begin with the licensing agreement, and then augment that knowledge with what you find as certification requirements for the API calls you use.

Working with Your Data

Generally, you or your organization will generate two kinds of data. The first type is generated in-house as part of your analysis of eBay data. You might make notes about specific items you're bidding on or keep track of certain kinds of products you need. There aren't any refresh requirements for this kind of data—no one will ever see it but you.

The second kind of data is based on eBay information but is generated as the result of your activities on eBay. You need to consider the value of historical data to your organization. Depending on the licensing agreement you signed, you might find that you can't share many kinds of data with third party, but you can keep that data for your internal use. The historical data has beneficial use for your organization—collecting it isn't against the rules as it is with some Web services. These third party exclusions include:

- Sharing eBay site-wide statistics
- Sharing specific site statistics
- Providing information (take-up rates) for enhanced listings
- Discussing merchandise sales for any eBay site
- Providing performance statistics, sales or otherwise, for any eBay site
- Disclosing the average selling price for any eBay category
- Disclosing the gross merchandise sold for any eBay category

In many cases, you would have a hard time collecting the data mentioned without creating one of several application types that eBay prohibits. Generally, you can keep track of your own data, which is what most companies and individuals want.

The examples in this book help simplify the data refresh equation for you. All of the examples in this book take a dynamic approach. The application checks the date that it last retrieved any data in the database from eBay Web Services in response to a user request. If the data is too old, the application requests the information from eBay Web Services.

Unfortunately, this approach has some problems. For example, some users will observe an inconsistent delay in responses. You can partially solve the problem by building a database of non-item data and refresh that data every night at a convenient time—when no one is likely to need the information. It's possible to create an application where item data is refreshed immediately before anyone comes to work and again during lunch to ensure you meet the 6-hour requirement. The idea is to refresh the data at a convenient interval using the technique that best suits your organization.

▶ **NOTE**

Make sure you keep up with current eBay policy regarding offline data storage. As more people use eBay, the requirements could change to ensure the data is updated on your system with greater frequency (to accommodate the faster listing rate) or with less frequency (the ease the burden on the servers). The reason that I mention this particular potential change is that most Web services do require you to update your data at regular intervals to ensure your application accurately represents that Web service.

Working with Buyer Data

Using eBay means that you also retrieve buyer data. Given today's privacy climate, it's probably best to store the buyer information in encrypted format for just as long as you need it to receive payment and then get rid of it. For that matter, you can easily make an API call and get the data directly from eBay when you need it without storing it locally at all. Otherwise, you have responsibility for that data and anyone breaking into your network will most certainly go for the sensitive buyer information first.

Aside from the privacy issues of collecting buyer data, there's the issue of keeping that information fresh, which is the focal point of this section. Another good reason to get buyer information from eBay whenever you need it is to ensure you have the most current information. It annoys buyers to no end to have someone provide the wrong information to them as part of a transaction. You want to avoid old addresses and telephone numbers. Old buyer data causes far more problems than you might imagine in lost sales due to the negative image it provides.

It's interesting to note that the eBay licensing agreement doesn't have a prescribed refresh cycle for buyer data. There are many other restrictions to consider. For example, you must provide an opt-out system so the buyer can tell you when they no longer want you to use their data. Even so, you should consider getting rid of buyer data that's over a year old whether you use that information for other purposes or not. At the very least, contact the buyer, ensure the data is still correct, and ensure you still have their permission to use the data. Old data is simply too much of a liability.

Using Offline Storage Effectively

Many of the performance enhancements you can add to your eBay Web Services application revolve around some type of offline storage. How your application uses offline storage makes a big difference in performance enhancement. In most cases the vendor and product you choose will determine factors such as reliability and availability. The following sections describe a few of the issues you need to consider as part of your offline storage strategy.

Choosing the Correct Offline Storage Strategy

All of the examples so far in the book have considered offline storage from the perspective of storing the eBay data that an application needs to handle multiple requests for the same information. This technique is the most important strategy to learn from a speed and reliability perspective. However, it's not the only strategy to consider because some applications simply don't benefit from this approach.

Another offline storage technique to consider is storing just the categories you visit often in local storage. You could also consider creating a keyword storage setup to automate item searches. For example, a business that only deals with glassware will probably want to create a list of keywords for that topic. Given the right application, you could set up a search first thing in the morning that would execute automatically as you perform other setup tasks.

Task-based storage is also important. A database can store a list of tasks the application can perform automatically at a specific time of the day. You can create the list of tasks as you work with eBay. This strategy ensures that you work efficiently and offload as much of the mundane work as possible onto the application.

Don't become fixated on output data when working with eBay Web Services. All of the requests you make have value too. For example, you might create a database of recent request data to provide hints to the user. As the user fills in request data, your application can make suggestions for the next input value and reduce the chance the user will make an invalid request. Likewise, you can store requests that didn't work. Making a quick check for these requests before you send the data to eBay will save a round-trip over the Internet and improve application speed. The application can also alert the user to the fact that the request won't work and make suggestions on how to change the request.

The idea when working with eBay is to attack the problem of offline storage from a number of angles. Don't get trapped into thinking that data is the only potential storage issue. Make sure you remain efficient by keeping the number of things you have to do manually to a minimum. You paid good money for that computer; now make it sweat!

Selecting a Database that Suits Your Needs

The database-related examples in the book rely on one of three database managers: SQL Server, Microsoft Access, or MySQL. You can find many other alternatives—these are just a sampling of what's available. I chose these three database managers because they represent several steps in functionality, performance, ease of use, and cost. It's important to get a database manager that you can afford, that will perform the tasks you need it to do, and is easy enough to manage, so you might choose any of the myriad alternatives on the market.

SQL Server is the most expensive of the three, but it also provides the best functionality. Microsoft constantly touts the speed of SQL Server, but it's a memory hog and can consume copious amounts of hard drive space. Given the complex tasks that SQL Server can perform, you might not find it as easy to use as Access, but the GUI-based tools do make it easier to use than the command line interface of MySQL. (Newer versions of MySQL are supposed to come out with a GUI, but this version isn't released as of the time of writing.)

> **▶ NOTE**
>
> You can use the Microsoft Data Engine (MSDE) as a substitute for SQL Server in some cases. It always works as a good alternative to SQL Server for local development. In some cases, you can also use MSDE as an alternative to SQL Server for groups of up to five people. Make sure that MSDE actually meets your needs before you spend time installing it—this product doesn't include all the features of SQL Server. Because MSDE relies on the same DLLs as SQL Server in many cases, you'll also want to apply any required patches to ensure the integrity of your system. Learn more about MSDE at `http://www.microsoft.com/sql/msde/default.asp`. If you go the MSDE route, you might want to also look at MSDE Query (`http://www.msde.biz/`) a tool that provides a GUI for MSDE.

Microsoft Access is probably the easiest of the database managers to use because it provides a single GUI interface where you manage everything. Some developers feel that Access is only useful for local databases, but many small businesses rely on Access as their only multi-user database manager. From a speed perspective, Access is probably the slowest of the three database managers. However, it's very easy on hard drive use and relatively light on memory use as well.

MySQL is the least expensive of the three database managers—you simply download your copy from a Web site. You'll find that this database manager is the hardest of the three to use because almost everything happens at the command line. (You can get a GUI editor from Electronic Microsystems at `http://www.ems-hitech.com/mymanager/`.) Some midsized companies use MySQL because it has the speed required to handle larger applications. It's also relatively easy on memory use, but about equal with SQL Server when it comes to hard drive space requirements.

Considering Database Storage Alternatives

Don't assume that you need a database to provide the benefits of local storage. It's true that you need a database when the usage requirements are high or you need long-term storage of information. However, storing the eBay data isn't exactly rocket science—you can use any of a number of alternatives. For example, the "Using a Script to Call an XSLT Page" section of Chapter 4 discusses a technique where you rely on the capabilities of a browser to process the eBay data. In this case, the simple fact that the browser caches pages it downloads from the

Internet is enough to improve performance for multiple calls for the same data—at least for the local user. Obviously, the browser caching solution won't work for multiple sessions if the user sets the browser to clear the cache after each session.

Sometimes you need something a little more substantial than the cache provided by a browser, but still don't need permanent storage. In these situations, you can use an in-memory solution. The simplest solution is an array or other memory structure. However, many languages also provide actual caches you can use and some vendors provide caches as part of their third party product. For example, the DataSet object provided with Visual Studio .NET is actually a form of in-memory cache, but it definitely has database functionality and you can link it to a physical database.

> **▶ TIP**
>
> You can find a great article on caching techniques for PHP and Web services ("Caching With PHP Cache_Lite") at `http://www.devshed.com/c/b/PHP` or `http://www.devshed.com/c/a/PHP/Caching-With-PHP-Cache_Lite/`. This article considers important issues, such as using the browser cache and implementing server-based caching.

It's possible to get by without using a database even when you need some form of permanent storage. For example, you could store a list of categories in an XML file. In fact, you can easily extend XML storage to search request, search results, or other types of permanent data. At some point, the performance of such a system is going to become problematic, but it works for small amounts of data for one user and could even work for a few users if you use a central storage location for the XML files.

Your Call to Action

This chapter considers some of the fit and finish items for your eBay Web Services application. Making your application reliable, efficient, and fast is important if you want to get the most out of the features eBay Web Services provides. However, it's also important to remember that some choices are mutually exclusive—you might have to give up a little performance to obtain better application reliability.

While reading this chapter you considered options, not absolutes. The only absolute is your application needs. You need to use the information presented in this chapter to address your specific application needs. Consider elements such as the application platform and user environment as part of the option selection process. For example, a mobile device will probably give up a little reliability to ensure the application operates fast enough, but this isn't always a hard and fast rule. You might find that your particular mobile application helps locate sensitive information on eBay (such as links for an item you want to buy) and therefore requires superior reliability.

Chapter 13 continues the process of honing your application. However, instead of considering the application requirements, Chapter 13 considers user requirements. Making an application faster may net you an overall gain in performance, but making the user faster always nets an overall gain in performance because user task speed is usually the critical performance factor for an application.

Chapter 13

Working with
Specific User Types

Creating Flexible
Interfaces

▶ Considering User Needs

Writing Applications for
Users with Special Needs

Developing with the
GetMyEBay Call

No matter what kind of application you write, you must consider the user's needs to ensure someone will actually use the application. Targeting the application to meet that user's need is a big part of the application development equation. Because many developers don't have direct contact with individual users, or must create an application to meet the needs of a lot of users, targeting a user type (a group description) is essential.

Accessibility is an important issue for applications today. Most developers realize that a Graphical User Interface (GUI) is better than a character mode interface and a few even realize that help is a requirement—not a nicety. A few developers understand that tooltips are also important and speed keys (shortcut keys) help users keep their hands on the keyboard so they can remain efficient. All of these elements, along with layout and design, are common to any application you might create. The market already has a number of good User Interface (UI) design books, so I won't replicate their information here (you'll find some of them listed in the "Selecting User Interface Design Resources" sidebar in the "Targeting a Specific User Type" section). This chapter helps you decide how to create a great interface for your eBay Web Services application using a combination of general and specific coding techniques.

Most of the applications in the book either help a buyer find something to purchase or help the seller manage items. However, eBay also provides a user element in the form of My eBay. The example in this section shows how to access My eBay from an application. It won't discuss every potential use of this method, but it will concentrate on the techniques you should use.

Targeting a Specific User Type

You'll invest a lot of time honing your eBay Web Services application if you plan to present it to other people. For that matter, it doesn't hurt to hone your application even if you only plan to use it to meet your own needs. No matter who uses your application, you have to consider their needs or the user will quickly tire of the application and not use it. Targeting specific user types helps you design an interface that works well, meets the user's needs, and requires less maintenance time.

Many books and Web sites on application design target generic applications—the type that anyone could use. However, this book considers a more specific application type—the one that relies on eBay Web Services. Even so, the number of uses for applications in this group is quite large, so you need to consider your specific application. It's essential to consider how the user will interact with the application and the user's skill level. In fact, you should consider the following elements when targeting your application to meet a specific user's needs.

- The nature of the user's exposure to eBay—sellers often have greater needs than buyers do because sellers have to perform management tasks.
- The environment in which the application executes—Web applications often have different requirements than desktop applications.
- The device the user will use to access your application—mobile devices have strict limitations that will affect your user interface design.
- The user's skill level—advanced users require less help and will quickly tire of repetitive help offers.
- The input and output requirements for the application—complex applications (those with more input or output) could require multiple screens.
- The request parameters of the application—simple eBay searches are the easiest to accommodate, but eBay users seldom stop with searches.
- The user's expectations for the application—a user who simply wants to browse will have fewer expectations than one making a purchase or listing an item.
- The kind of eBay searches performed—item searches are more complex and require more explanation than a category search. Automobile item searches are inherently more complex than other kinds of item searches.
- The availability of localized help—users of Web applications typically receive less help than users of desktop applications.

It's relatively easy to use these criteria to build a profile of an individual user, but assessing the needs of multiple user types can become more difficult. In this case, you need to build a profile of each user type and then organize the users by priority. This exercise lets you determine how much weight to give each requirement. An advanced user who only uses the application once a month can easily turn off the extra help you provide to novice users (assuming that you provide a switch for turning the help off).

Sometimes several user types will conflict, making prioritization essential. For example, if most of your users will employ a cellular telephone to access the site, you might need to provide alternatives for the few desktop users who visit. In many cases, careful development will allow both groups to access the site—the desktop users might notice that the site is a little plain, but that's about it. The goal is to accommodate the needs of each group based on their level of access to your site—don't accommodate the needs of a small group to the detriment of the users who normally support your site.

Designing Flexible Interfaces

No matter how well you design your application, someone will complain that some feature doesn't work as expected. During my years of programming, I've personally seen arguments between users about the order of fields on a form. One discussion about a screen degenerated into an intense argument about the order of name elements on the form (one user wanted last name first—the other wanted the first name to appear first). Users will grumble about every aspect of your application given a chance and you'll never satisfy all the users. Some developers solve the problem by giving up and creating the application they want. However, this solution probably works least often because the user's immediate reaction is that the developer isn't listening and lacks any form of human interaction skills.

Flexible user interfaces resolve the user problem by letting each user design the interface that meets their specific needs. Just how flexible you can make the interface depends on a number of factors including the application environment and the programming language you use. Making Web applications flexible is somewhat harder than for most desktop applications because many browsers lack the support required to move visual elements around and perform other manipulations the user would like. Depending on your programming skill, schedule, programming language, and patience, you can make some desktop applications so flexible that the user has control over every display element and the application will remember its configuration between sessions.

Let's start with something a little more reasonable than complete application configuration. Even the most mundane Web page allows configuration. For example, you can use Cascading Style Sheets (CSS) to format the Web page. Some browsers let the user substitute their CSS file for the default that you provide on your Web site—making it possible for the user to have complete control over the presentation of information even if you don't provide any other form of programming with the Web page. Some sites extend this principle by providing multiple CSS files. A simple cookie entry controls which CSS file the Web site uses when presenting information to the user. Desktop applications are even easier to control in this area. All you need is an Options dialog box containing the display element settings so the user can change them to meet specific needs. Most desktop applications already provide this feature. Make sure you save the user options in a file or other central location (such as the Windows Registry) if you offer this feature.

Selecting User Interface Design Resources

Getting great user interface design references helps you get started faster and ensures you won't make as many mistakes during the design process. Typically, you'll find that books are better than Web sites for this kind of information because books have more space to cover contingencies that articles or other online resources can't discuss. However, don't discount Web sites—you might find something that meets a specific need. Newsgroups can help, but you need to state the design issues you want to overcome very clearly and take any advice with a grain of salt because the developer helping you might not have a clear picture of the issues.

You can find a number of good books online. The trick is to find a book that is either completely generic or meets the need of a specific environment. For example, if you want to design a Web application, then you might consider reading *Designing Web Usability: The Practice of Simplicity* by Jakob Nielsen (New Riders, 1999). Although Web developers could rely on this book, desktop developers can benefit most from *The Humane Interface: New Directions for Designing Interactive Systems* by Jef Raskin (Addison-Wesley, 2000) and *About Face 2.0: The Essentials of Interaction Design* by Alan Cooper and Robert Reimann (John Wiley & Sons, 2003). A good generic book that addresses interface design as a component of total application design is *Designing Highly Usable Software* by Jeff Cogswell (Sybex, 2004).

It's possible to find good help online. For example, the Microsoft User Interface site at `http://msdn.microsoft.com/nhp/default.asp?contentid=28000443` provides a wealth of information on topics as diverse as accessibility and Microsoft Agent. Dr. Jakob Nielsen presents a number of usability articles at `http://www.useit.com/alertbox/`. This monthly column provides continuing help with your application as user needs and expectations change. In some cases, you can even find online books such as *Task-Centered User Interface Design* by Clayton Lewis and John Rieman at `http://www.hcibib.org/tcuid/`. The authors offer this book as shareware, so make sure you support them if you use it.

Locating a newsgroup that offers advice on user interfaces isn't hard—it's hard to find good advice. Generally, you'll need to find a newsgroup that caters to your language and choice of device (such as the .NET Compact Framework for mobile devices at `microsoft.public.dotnet.framework.compactframework`). Some newsgroups, such as `comp.human-factors` provide limited generic help should you need it. After many hours of searching, I couldn't find a suitable newsgroup devoted to the topic of user interfaces. Contact me at `JMueller@mwt.net` if you know of such a newsgroup and I'll post it on my Web site with the updates for this book.

The next level of application configuration is component selection. For example, not every eBay Web Services user will want to sort the output results. It might seem that simply ignoring the sort field would work, but unnecessary fields are annoying to some users. Again, Web pages can use a cookie to store a list of fields or controls the user doesn't want to see. You'll likely have to provide a configuration page to support this form of configuration—adding a simple link to the page to allow configuration usually works fine. Desktop applications can use an Options dialog box. Most desktop applications don't offer this feature—likely because the developer didn't think to offer the feature or assumed that everyone would want access to every field.

> ▶ **NOTE**
>
> Don't make every field on a form optional. A user will have to make some entries to perform even basic tasks. For example, a user can't perform an item number search without entering an item number, so the item number field isn't optional. However, hiding optional fields can make the application faster and easier to use. You might even find that you want to include some developer-only fields in the list that you control with special entries in the configuration file.

Web applications don't commonly use toolbars or special menus in the same way that desktop applications use them. However, both environments can benefit from some level of customization for both items. Quite a few desktop applications offer this feature. Generally, the user selects a special menu command that allows them to move menu or toolbar elements around, add new menu or toolbar options, or delete options the user feels aren't important. Trying to implement this feature on a Web site would be very hard, but doable if you use some technologies such as ASP.NET. Make sure you offer a feature that returns everything to its default state in case the user makes a few too many changes.

The ultimate level of interface flexibility lets the user move controls around on screen. This feature lets one user place names in last name order and another user place them in first name order. Complete interface control is difficult to implement on a desktop application and likely impossible for a Web application. Applications that allow complete interface configuration are extremely rare. However, an eBay Web Services application doesn't have to suffer from the level of complexity that some applications do, so this might be a viable solution in some cases. (Applications that meet a broad range of seller needs are going to be too complex to offer this level of customization unless you have an unlimited budget.) At least you can provide the user with enough flexibility to define precisely how the display appears so that your application works as efficiently for that user as possible.

> ▶ **NOTE**
>
> If you plan to provide complete interface flexibility for your application, you should go all the way by allowing the user to change even mundane features such a font size and typeface. To an extent, you could even let the user change the button captions and control the color of the tiniest text element. It's even possible to let the user add graphics and perform other odd configuration changes given the right programming language, a platform that supports the changes, and enough time.

Addressing Users with Special Needs

This section of the chapter considers some of the features that make an application easier to use for those with special needs. Don't automatically equate special needs with physical challenges faced by some people. As users age, they need better screens because their eyesight begins to fail. Older hands often suffer from arthritis and require more options for executing commands. Even someone who is very young can require help at the end of the day when a day full of eye fatiguing buying and selling means using a display with larger type. With this in mind, the following sections describe some things you can do to make your eBay Web Services application more usable without a large investment in time or effort.

> ▶ **NOTE**
>
> A section of a chapter can't possibly address every accessibility requirement. In addition, if you work for an organization that provides services to the government, you have certain legal requirements you must meet to address accessibility concerns. See my book, *Accessibility for Everybody: Understanding the Section 508 Accessibility Requirements* (Apress, 2003) for a complete treatment of this topic.

Adding Hints for Desktop Applications

Desktop applications commonly rely on hints to help a user understand its operation. For example, when you see a letter of a field underlined, you realize that pressing Alt+Letter selects that field. If the developer has wisely selected a different letter for each field, every field is a single key combination away. The use of speed keys helps touch typists work faster by allowing them to keep their hands on the keyboard, rather than using a mouse. However, speed keys also help those who can't use a mouse at all. In this case, the user has a choice of pressing Tab multiple times to locate the field or using a speed key to access it—the speed key is preferable because it's faster and requires fewer key presses. Adding speed keys to your application takes moments—all you need to do is type an ampersand in front of the letter you want to use for the speed key for most Windows languages.

Another common hint that also serves an accessibility need is the tooltip. Adding a tooltip for each control lets you explain the purpose of that control using a single sentence. If the user needs additional information, they can refer to the online help, but this feature usually provides enough information so that a trip to the help file isn't necessary. From an accessibility perspective, a screen reader or other piece of accessibility software normally reads the information in the tooltip to the user. Consequently, the tooltip helps users with vision needs build an image of the application and its functionality in their mind. The technique used to add a tooltip to an application depends on the language product used. For example, Visual Studio .NET developers can rely on the simple addition of a `ToolTip` control to make the tooltip addition. The `ToolTip` control adds a new `ToolTip` property to each of the other controls—just type the text you want to appear in the tooltip. The desktop applications in this book contain both speed keys and tooltips to ensure anyone can use them.

> ▶ **NOTE**
>
> Always try to support the accessibility features provided by the operating system. For example, Windows supports a number of accessibility features, including the use of high contrast displays for users with special visual needs. Some of these features, such as support for a screen reader, are so easy to implement that there's never a good reason not to implement them. Other features, such as the use of the Windows ShowSounds, can incur a higher cost in programming time because most programming languages don't support the feature.

Platforms such as Windows include a number of operating system–specific accessibility features as well. Windows includes a high contrast setting that displays images in just a few colors using large fonts. The display makes it a lot easier for people with less than perfect vision to see the display. However, many people with normal vision also use the setting at the end of a hard day when a standard display is apt to give them a headache. The problem for developers is that the high contrast setting tends to make labels and other text elements on a form difficult or impossible to see because the element consumes too much space. Figure 13.1 shows a typical example of this problem.

I chose this particular dialog box because it demonstrates two common problems. First, the information in the middle of the display is garbled—unreadable for the most part. Second, the application-specific text didn't size with the change in high contrast setting, so the application user receives minimum benefit. Generally, you can avoid problems with the high contrast display by testing this setting with your application. All you need to do is open the

Accessibility Options applet in the Control Panel, select the Display tab, and click Use High Contrast. Click OK and you'll see your display change to a high contrast representation. Note that Windows supports a number of high contrast configurations, so you might want to try several out with your application.

eBay Web Services returns some data that you might need to modify to make it accessible. For example, most products have an associated image. The problem with the images is that they assume you can see well. You might need to download a large version of an image for some users or create a dynamic description of the image for other users using the tooltip features provided by the language. Fortunately, many eBay sellers include descriptions with their items that you can use in place of the image description. When this approach fails, you might have to provide a description obtained through research on Google or simply tell the user there's no additional information available to describe the image. You need to ask users whether they prefer the image or description. It's also possible to automatically detect the presence of software such as JAWS (`http://www.freedomscientific.com/fs_downloads/jaws.asp`) or the high contrast setting and use the description automatically in those situations.

Another problem with eBay Web Services is that it provides a wealth of data—too much in some cases. It's easy to overwhelm someone with special needs with data they'll never use. The problem isn't quite as noticeable with many Web applications because the Web presentation format can reduce the problem. However, desktop applications can suffer significant information overload problems. In some cases, you'll need to present details one at a time or on separate displays to keep the display focused on the essentials.

FIGURE 13.1:
High contrast displays can make some information unreadable.

Adding Hints for Web Applications

Web applications use many of the same hints used by desktop applications, but the techniques for creating the hint differ. As with desktop applications, one of the more important hints is the use of speed keys. You implement a speed key using a combination of special text formatting and HTML tag attributes, as shown in the following code for a label.

```
<label id="Input">
    <span style="TEXT-DECORATION: underline">I</span>nput:
</label>
<input id="InputVal"
       type=text
       value="Hello World"
       name="InputVal"
       accesskey="I"
       title="Type the input string."
       autocomplete=on/>
```

The user needs to know which Alt+<key> combination to use to access the field, so the `style` attribute for the label is important—it underlines the target key. The `accesskey` attribute defines the speed key for the field associated with the label. The `title` attribute defines the tooltip text. When the user hovers the mouse over the input, the browser displays a tooltip, just like a desktop application. Use the `autocomplete` attribute to control the use of automatic completion for the field. Some fields benefit from this setting because the user is likely to type the same text more than one time, but for other fields automatic completion is a nuisance because the user will never type the same text twice.

Images require a little special handling because you can't easily determine whether the user can see the image or not. In this case, you don't use the `title` attribute because that would display a tooltip. In most cases, you'll use the `alt` attribute, as shown here, to provide a description of the image.

```
<img align="middle"
     src="OddImage.gif"
     alt="This image contains the words, 'An Odd Image'."
     height=130
     width=130/>
```

It's easy to use the item description information provided by the seller in most cases or provide one of your own when the seller doesn't (make sure you use an authoritative resource to provide a generic description to avoid problems). You'll find an example of an accessible Web page in the \Chapter 13\AccessibleWeb folder of the source code found on the Sybex Web site. Try this page out in a browser to see how your browser reacts to it. In most cases, browsers do provide support for accessibility features—at least the basic features described in this section.

The example is a little plain. Generally, you should avoid adding too much formatting to your Web page if you can help it, but most of us like a little color and some formatting to make the page interesting. You can follow some basic guidelines to avoid causing accessibility problems while you dress up the page. For example, use CSS to avoid formatting problems. Someone with special needs can substitute a CSS file of their choosing that makes the page easier to read and you still get the formatting you want. Make sure your page is compliant by testing it with any of a number of online testers such as Bobby (`http://bobby.watchfire.com/bobby/html/en/index.jsp`).

Considering Color-Blind Users

Before you read any further, it's important to understand that *color blind* doesn't mean the viewer can't see color. What a color-blind viewer sees is the wrong color. A red or green dot might appear brown or some other color. Generally, the viewer can still see the object as long as you don't surround it with the color their eyes substitute for the real color of the object. In addition, not everyone has the same kind of color blindness. Most doctors agree there are three main forms of color blindness to consider (read the explanation of the types of color blindness at `http://webexhibits.org/causesofcolor/2.html` for details).

Because eBay returns raw data and not color (at least until you display images), you have a choice about the color content of your desktop application or Web site. Even so, you might want to add a little pizzazz to your presentation and that usually means adding color. You can find information about working around color-blindness issues on a number of Web sites, but here are three exceptional sources.

- Can Color-Blind Users See Your Site?
  (`http://msdn.microsoft.com/voices/hess10092000.asp`)

- Color Vision Color Deficiency
  (`http://www.firelily.com/opinions/color.html`)

- Visicheck
  (`http://www.vischeck.com/vischeck/vischeckImage.php`)

The first two sites tell you about color blindness and provide example images that show how things appear to someone with a particular kind of color blindness. The third site lets you check your image for color blindness—all you need is a Web site URL. You can use this site to check an entire Web page by grabbing a screenshot of the Web site and uploading it to your site. The same technique works for desktop applications.

Using the *GetMyEBay* Call

A user's My eBay page reflects a lot of personal information about their buying and selling habits on eBay. Consequently, offering a customized version of this page as part of your application is one way to ensure you handle user needs. Personalization is one of the features that most users look for in applications now, so adding a My eBay connection is a great idea. The following sections describe this call in more detail.

> ▶ **NOTE**
>
> The current version of eBay Web Services only returns the information on the Bidding/ Watching tab of My eBay. Future versions will include support for other My eBay tabs.

Sorting the Data

This is one of the few calls where you should provide some type of sort value. You use the enumeration to select one of the values. The only problem is that the enumeration doesn't tell you which value to use for a specific item. Table 13.1 shows which values to use for a specific Bidding/Watching tab item.

TABLE 13.1: Sort Types by Bidding/Watching Tab Item

Sort Type	Watch List	Active List	Won List	Lost List
01—Item ID	X	X	X	X
02—Start time		X		
03—End time		X	X	
04—Price	X	X	X	X
07—Item ID (descending)	X	X	X	X
08—Start time (descending)		X		
09—End time (descending)		X	X	
10—Price (descending)	X	X	X	X
11—Start price		X		
12—Start price (descending)		X		
15—Number of bids	X	X		X
16—Number of bids (descending)	X	X		X
17—Quantity		X		
18—Quantity (descending)		X		
21—Seller user ID	X		X	
22—Time left for item's listing	X			
23—Time left for item's listing (descending)	X			
25—Seller user ID (descending)	X		X	

Writing the Code

The example in this section uses the `GetMyEBayCall()` method to retrieve the items that a user is watching, bidding on, has lost, or has won. Listing 13.1 shows how to work with this call to retrieve the required information. You'll find the complete source for this example in the `\Chapter 13\MyEBayDemo` folder of the source code located on the Sybex Web site.

Listing 13.1   **Using the *GetMyEBayCall()***

```
private void btnTest_Click(object sender, System.EventArgs e)
{
    ApiSession      Session; // The eBay session.
    GetMyEBayCall   MyEBay;  // My eBay Page Contents.
    FrmResults      Results; // Data output form.
    DataRow         DR;      // A single result.

    // Create a session.
    Session = new ApiSession();

    // Define the sandbox as the call location.
    Session.Url = "https://api.sandbox.ebay.com/ws/api.dll";

    // Add session security information.
    Session.Token = new ApiToken();
    Session.Token.Token = txtUserAuth.Text;

    // Add the developer information.
    Session.Developer = txtDevID.Text;
    Session.Application = txtAppID.Text;
    Session.Certificate = txtCertID.Text;

    // Create the My eBay call.
    MyEBay = new GetMyEBayCall(Session);

    // Set the standard criteria.
    MyEBay.DetailLevel = 0;
    MyEBay.ErrorLevel = ErrorLevelEnum.BothShortAndLongErrorStrings;
    MyEBay.SiteId = 0;

    // Define the watch interval, maximum results, and sorts.
    MyEBay.Days = Int32.Parse(txtDays.Text);
    MyEBay.MaxResults = Int32.Parse(txtReturn.Text);
    MyEBay.WatchListOption = new MyEBayGroupOption();
    MyEBay.WatchListOption.Sort =
        (MyEBaySorts)Int32.Parse(
            cbWatchSort.SelectedItem.ToString().Substring(0, 2));

    ... Other Sort Entries ...

    // Perform the call.
```

```
    if (MyEBay.GetMyEBay() == 0)
    {
        MessageBox.Show("No Items to Retrieve!",
                        "My eBay Status",
                        MessageBoxButtons.OK,
                        MessageBoxIcon.Exclamation);
        return;
    }

    // Create the results form.
    Results = new FrmResults();

    // Determine the number of Watched items.
    if (MyEBay.WatchItems.Count == 0)
        Results.dgWatch.CaptionText = "You're Watching 0 Items";
    else
    {
        // Display the number of results.
        Results.dgWatch.CaptionText =
            "You're Watching " +
                MyEBay.WatchItems.Count.ToString() + " Items";

        // Process the results.
        foreach (MyEBayItem ThisItem in MyEBay.WatchItems)
        {
            // Create a new row.
            DR = Results.dsItems.Tables["WatchItems"].NewRow();

            // Add the data.
            DR["Item ID"] = ThisItem.ItemId;
            DR["Title"] = ThisItem.Title;
            DR["Start Price"] = ThisItem.StartPrice;
            DR["Current Price"] = ThisItem.CurrentPrice;
            DR["Start Time"] = ThisItem.StartTime;
            DR["End Time"] = ThisItem.EndTime;

            // Add the row to the table.
            Results.dsItems.Tables["WatchItems"].Rows.Add(DR);
        }
    }

    ... Other Item Types ...

    // Display the results form.
    Results.ShowDialog();
}
```

The code begins by creating a session as normal. This example uses the authentication token, so it initializes Session.Token before adding the user authentication token to the Token property. After the code creates a session, it uses it to instantiate the GetMyEBayCall object, MyEBay.

The call doesn't provide multiple detail levels, so the code sets the `DetailLevel` property to 0. Because this is a test application, it's important to use the `ErrorLevelEnum.BothShortAnd-LongErrorStrings` setting for errors. Finally, the code sets the `SideId` property.

The interesting part of this code is the other settings you can, but don't necessarily have to, make. The `Days` and `MaxResults` properties both have default values. However, to get the maximum benefit from the sandbox environment, you should probably set the number of days to 30 and the maximum results to at least 10 to ensure you get enough data.

The code also sets sorting options for all four kinds of data the application retrieves: watches, active bids, won item, and lost items. The process is the same in each case. The code instantiates the target property using the `MyEBayGroupOption()` class. It then sets the `Sort` property. The problem is that the `Sort` property accepts an enumerated value the user is unlikely to understand. In addition, not every item can use every sort value. The example shows one way out of this problem using combo boxes as shown in Figure 13.2. The first two characters in the combo box entry contain the enumerated value as a number. All you need to do is convert that number into an enumerated value, as shown in the code.

At this point, the code makes the `MyEBay.GetMyEBay()` call. It's possible that the user has no activity within the specified time frame. The `MyEBay.GetMyEBay()` call returns the number of items for the entire call. If this value is 0, then you can assume there's nothing to process. The code displays a message in this case and returns immediately to save processing time.

This example displays the results in `DataGrid` objects using a `DataSet` for each item on a separate form. The code creates a form object, `Results`, to hold the data that eBay Web services returns.

FIGURE 13.2:

Use a combo box to present the sorting options in human readable form.

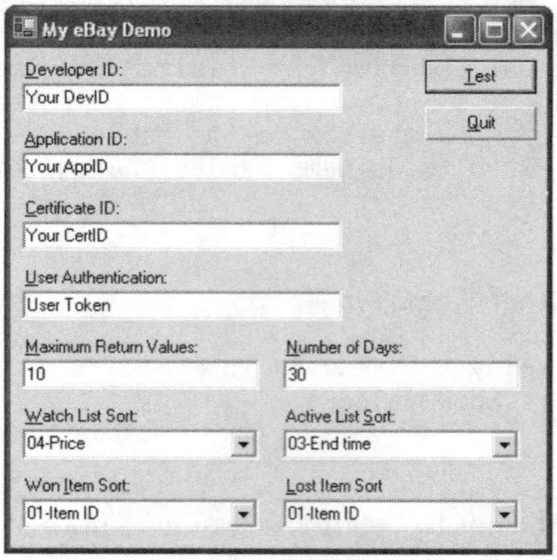

When the code does have data to process, there's nothing to guarantee that the results appear in a particular area, so you must again check for data using the `Count` property as shown. The code places the number of items that it finds in the `CaptionText` property of each `DataGrid`.

The processing of each item follows the same steps as many other examples in the book. The code creates a row, fills the row with data, and adds the row to the `DataSet`. A single `DataSet` with four tables serves all four `DataGrid` objects. Figure 13.3 shows typical results for this application.

This particular example demonstrates the need to perform proper setups before you make a call by ensuring you look for multiple return values. The `GetMyEBayCall()` method can return all four entries on the Bidding/Watching tab of the My eBay Web page. Future versions of the call will likely retrieve additional information, which makes proper setup even more important.

FIGURE 13.3:

The application output shows how a single call can return multiple item types.

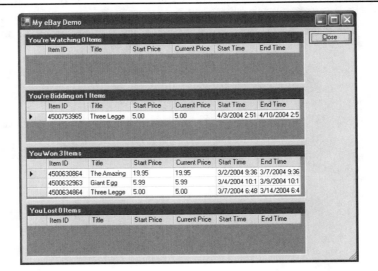

Your Call to Action

Chapter 12 discusses enhancement issues for your application and this chapter discusses enhancement issues for the user. Depending on your development goals, it's easy to miss opportunities to address one or both issues, but you must address both to create the best possible eBay Web Services application. The main point of this chapter is that you can address user needs without incurring an undo burden in terms of development time or effort. In fact, addressing user needs at the outset always reduces long-term application costs, so the little extra effort you apply today will pay dividends tomorrow. This chapter also addresses a special eBay user features in the form of My eBay access.

Now it's time for you to decide how to address user issues. You need to consider the kind of user that will use your application—advanced users require less help than novice users. It's also important to address special needs your users might have to ensure they can derive maximum benefit from the application. For example, the addition of a simple tooltip for every control is essential for users with vision needs. The same tooltip can help all users by providing a little more information about the control so they don't have to access help constantly.

Chapter 14 discusses some final enhancements—the optional types of application additions that you might consider. No, these additions won't make your application faster or more efficient. However, they do help you interact more easily with the users of your application. The chapter considers the essential issue of learning more about the user through feedback forms. You'll also discover uses for a few new eBay Web Services calls, including `GetShippingRates()`.

Chapter 14

Considering
Privacy Issues

Letting the User Tell You
about Your Application

▶ Other Refinements You Should Consider

Developing with the
GetShippingRates Call

Developing with the *Get-
SuggestedCategories* Call

Building an application that works with eBay Web Services means doing more than simply writing code that interacts with the Web service and making it perform well. You must consider refinements that don't improve application performance or affect the user directly. For example, a user is unlikely to notice that you've added extra features to protect privacy, but will definitely notice when you don't. Likewise, a feedback form might not seem like much, but providing one avoids public criticism and helps you resolve issues easier by communicating directly with the user.

Along with specific interface requirements for your application, this chapter also considers helpful design decisions. For example, although no one requires you to address privacy issues using the techniques in this chapter (they go beyond the eBay requirements in some areas), many users are beginning to request this functionality and might not visit your site more than once if you don't provide a privacy policy. In addition, it's important to personalize the user's experience with your site so you don't have to ask the same questions every time the user visits. A user might like to use a specific stylesheet with your Web site or request a specific setup for your application. Personalization helps users have a better experience and improves user efficiency.

Feedback is the most common feature that you'll use in this chapter because even a Web site that performs simple searches should include some type of user feedback form. Web sites that do more, such as help the user upload items for sale, should definitely include feedback in multiple places. Desktop applications also benefit from feedback, although far too few applications include this feature. The idea is to provide a means for a user to make a comment about your application immediately during use—when an idea, concern, or other comment is fresh and they're most likely to send it to you.

This chapter also addresses two special examples. The first shows how to get shipping rates from eBay for items you sell by providing a starting and ending location. This particular call is extremely helpful even during the planning stages of a sale because it helps you calculate your costs before you even list the item. The second call helps you obtain a list of suggested categories for your item. Sometimes, it's hard to know where to list an item on eBay. This call can help by providing insights into how the categories work.

Designing for Privacy Issues

Privacy has become a major concern for most people because the news contains numerous stories of personal information misuse. One of the major misuses of personal information is identity theft, but that's by no means the largest misuse. Many users also feel that gathering personal information for marketing purposes without permission and full disclosure of how the requestor will use the information is also a major misuse of personal information. People don't want to suffer through a barrage of unwanted sales calls as witnessed by the proliferation of "No Call" lists both locally and nationally. In fact, many people are taking positive steps to take back their personal information or at least block further attempts to acquire new information.

> ▶ **WARNING**
>
> eBay uses extreme measures, in most cases, to ensure the privacy of people using their service. It's small wonder that they do. According to an eWeek story, identity theft heads the list of complaints received by the Federal Trade Commission (FTC). Of these complaints, a full 15 percent are directly traced to online auction activities. See the story at http://www.eweek.com/article2/0,4149,1455941,00.asp for details. It's essential that you provide complete security for all user information when using eBay Web Services because the threat of identity theft is so high.

Personal information covers a range of topics today. Most developers recognize that name, address, telephone number, and other personally identifying information is private. However, users don't want developers to know a lot of other information that some developers see as belonging to the public domain. For example, some developers will try to get the Referrer (the previous Web page), User-Agent (the browser type, version, and host operating system), and From (the user's email address) headers of the user's browser. Brisk sales of products such as Norton Internet Security demonstrate that users don't want developers to collect this information. An interesting side effect of this battle between user and developer is that even though the user is using a new version of products such as Internet Explorer and Netscape, the Web site often reports that the user has an outdated version of the product.

Unfortunately, eBay provides a venue where buyer and seller can meet and doesn't take care of the actual sales details for you. When you sell products to someone, you must take care of setting up a payment option and sending them product to the buyer. Because of this requirement, your application will likely cache some user data until the sale is completed. However, it's still possible to keep the exchange of information under control through careful application design. For example, you don't always need to know every detail about the buyer (just as you wouldn't know these details if someone came to your store). Obtain only the information you actually need to complete the transaction and then dispose of the information if possible. You can also avoid collecting browser information through careful design and by following standards. The Webmonkey chart at `http://hotwired.lycos.com/webmonkey/reference/browser_chart/index.html` helps you understand which design features to avoid based on browser compatibility.

Even with the best design, however, you'll eventually encounter a situation where you want to use cookies (assuming the user has their browser set to accept cookies). Many users realize that cookies aren't inherently evil, but they also realize that a Web site could use cookies for nefarious purposes. All the pop-up ads that you see floating around on your favorite Web site are one reason that people are suspicious. Some of these vendors follow people around to the various sites they visit and keep track of their movements. However, you can overcome the fears of most users by maintaining a privacy policy and including special tags for that policy on your Web site. The most common way to publish and use a privacy policy is Platform for Privacy Preferences (P3P). The World Wide Web Consortium (W3C) sponsors this technique and you can read about the six easy steps for implementing P3P on your Web site at `http://www.w3.org/P3P/details.html`. The P3P standard (`http://www.w3.org/TR/P3P/`) also contains a wealth of information you should review.

> ▶ **NOTE**
>
> The example in this section uses the IBM P3P generator (`http://www.alphaworks.ibm.com/tech/p3peditor`). The W3C site lists several other generators—I chose this particular generator because it comes with a 90-day free trial. Your code might turn out different from mine if you use another generator for your code. For some reason, the IBM P3P generator doesn't work with the current version of the Java Runtime Environment (JRE)—version 1.4.2. IBM recommends using the 1.3.1 version of the JRE that you can download at `http://java.sun.com/j2se/1.3/`.

Your privacy statement will consist of several files, including at least one P3P file that you create using the P3P generator and an XML reference file. A good generator will also help you create a generic privacy summary that you can use for queries from the user and a compact policy statement you can use in the response headers of pages that contain cookies. If you own the server you use for the Web page, you can place the privacy information in the \w3c folder of the Web site. It's also possible to create linkage between the privacy information and your Web page using a <link> tag similar to the one shown here.

```
<link rel="P3Pv1" href="http://www.mwt.net/~jmueller/p3p.xml">
```

The problem comes in when you don't own the server that hosts your Web page—the situation for many people, including small business owners. Internet Explorer 6 has several levels of cookie protection built in. The highest level will likely reject your privacy information because Internet Explorer relies exclusively on the compact policy statement supplied as part of the response headers. Adding the compact policy statement is relatively easy if you own the server. Listing 14.1 shows an alternative you can try when you don't own the server, plus some test code you can use to verify the results. You'll find the complete source code for this example in the \Chapter 14\Privacy folder of the source code located on the Sybex Web site.

Listing 14.1   Adding a Compact Policy to a Web Page

```
<html>
<head>
<meta http-equiv='P3P'
      content='policyref="http://www.mwt.net/~jmueller/p3p.xml",
      CP="NOI DSP COR NID CURa OUR NOR NAV INT TST"'>
<title>Privacy Demonstration</title>
<script>
function SetCookie()
{
    var  UserCookie; // Stores the username.

    // Create the username cookie.
    UserCookie = "UserName=" + escape(InputVal.value);

    // Add the cookie to the document.
    document.cookie = UserCookie;

    // Tell the user the cookie was saved.
    alert("The cookies were saved.");
}

function ReadCookie()
{
    var  ACookie; // Holds the document cookie.
    var  Parsed;  // Holds the split cookies.
    var  Name;    // The username.
```

```
    // Get the cookie.
    ACookie = unescape(document.cookie);

    // Split the cookie elements.
    Parsed = ACookie.split("=");

    // Get the username.
    Name = Parsed[1];

    // Display the name.
    alert("Your name is: " + Name);
}
```

The `<meta>` tag at the beginning of the code is the essential addition to your application. The `http-equiv` attribute tells the server what kind of response header to add. Some servers don't honor this attribute, so this solution might not work completely in all cases. The `content` attribute tells the client where to locate the privacy policy for your Web site—it works much the same as the `<link>` tag discussed earlier in this section. Finally, the `CP` attribute defines the compact policy for your server. Most tools, such as the IBM P3P Policy Editor shown in Figure 14.1, tell you what these codes mean and generate a text file containing them for you.

FIGURE 14.1:

Make sure you generate a compact policy for Web pages that have cookies.

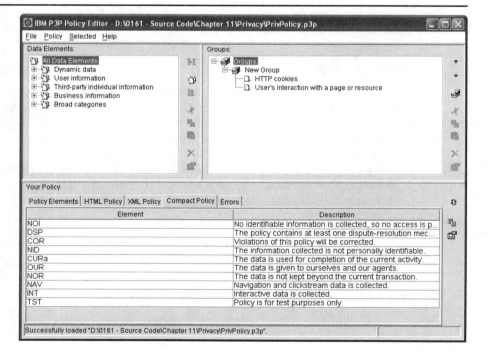

The test code consists of two functions attached to buttons on the example form. The first creates a cookie and attaches it to the document. The second retrieves the cookie stored in the document and displays the results on screen. Neither function is that exciting, but this is enough code to create an error with Internet Explorer 6 if the compact policy isn't accepted. You must have a compact policy in place and Internet Explorer 6 must accept it if you want users to use the high privacy setting. However, even if Internet Explorer 6 decides that it won't accept the compact policy, having a privacy policy in place and set up using the information provided in this section lets the user rely on the medium high privacy setting. Although the medium high setting isn't quite as comfortable as the high setting, it's much better than the low setting your Web site would require if it didn't have a privacy policy.

Adding Feedback to Your Application

Most people have an opinion. The opinion doesn't have a right or wrong value—it's simply how they feel about a particular topic. Getting an honest opinion from people can be difficult, but you can do it. When the topic concerns your application or Web site, the need to get an honest opinion is essential. Otherwise, changes you make to an application or Web site as the result of user feedback is going to be off target—you want to target the users of your site to ensure they have a great experience.

> ▶ **TIP**
>
> Don't assume that every positive feedback message you receive means that you're doing everything right with your application. Some people will tell you positive things to obtain benefits they might not normally receive or simply because they don't want to hurt your feelings. Likewise, not every negative message is an indictment against your programming practices. Sometimes a user will have a bad day and decide to take it out on you because you're the nearest target that can't attack back. Deciphering feedback often means reading the message several times and deciding just how it affects your application (or whether it affects your application at all).

When you mix interaction with another application (eBay Web Services in this case), the problems of getting honest feedback intensify. You need to consider whether the feedback relates to your application, a connectivity issue caused by an ISP, the user's environment, or eBay Web Services (among other things). It's not always easy to sort even a good opinion into the right area.

The following sections discuss user feedback. This information reflects issues you need to consider when working with eBay Web Services. For example, it discusses some of the problems of sorting information into the right area for consideration.

Designing User Feedback

One of the problems in getting good user feedback is designing the form so that it elicits a response, especially from users who don't normally express themselves well. A nebulous question such as "How do you feel about this input form?" won't net you a very good response. You need to direct the user to the kind of input you want, without contaminating the user's response. For example, "Does the item search form help you find the information you need to make a purchase, or do you find yourself using alternative search techniques?" offers the user a choice and makes them think about alternatives. The question is still specific enough that even a shy user can provide an answer. Offering yes, no, and other (with a comment field) lets the shy user off the hook, but also lets vocal users state their answers in precise terms.

The simplest method for obtaining user feedback on a Web page is to create a form and send it to your email (or other location). Although this method does require a little interpretation, it has the advantage of allowing you to get feedback almost free. If you use a programmable email reader such as Microsoft Outlook, you can write a macro to interpret and save the results for you. Otherwise, the careful use of form values will let you read the report with a little effort. Listing 14.2 contains an example of a simple form that works with almost all browsers even if the user has turned off scripting support and cookies. You'll find the complete source code for this example in the \Chapter 14\SimpleRespForm folder of the source code located on the Sybex Web site.

Listing 14.2   **A Simple, Low-cost Feedback Form**

```
<!DOCTYPE HTML PUBLIC "-//W3C//DTD HTML 4.0 Transitional//EN">
<html>
<head>
<title>Simple Response Form</title>
<meta name="vs_targetSchema"
      content="http://schemas.microsoft.com/intellisense/ie5">
</head>
<body>

<!-- Display a heading. -->
<h1 align=center>Simple Response Form</h1>

<!-- Define the form and anticipated action. -->
<form action="mailto:JMueller@mwt.net?subject=Test Message"
      method=post
```

```
        name=SimpleRespForm
        enctype="text/plain">

<!-- Ask about search engine performance. -->
<label>Did the search engine work as you expected?</label>
<input type=hidden
        name="Q1"
        value="Search Engine"/><br/>
<label>Yes</label>
<input type=radio name="1A" value="Y"/><br/>
<label>No</label>
<input type=radio name="1A" value="N"/><br/>
<label>Other</label>
<input type=radio name="1A" value="O"/><br/>
<label>Additional comment (40 characters max):</label><br/>
<input type=text name="1E" maxlength=40/><p/>

<!-- Ask about link descriptions. -->
<label>Were the link descriptions easy to understand?</label>
<input type=hidden
        name="Q2"
        value="Link Description"/><br/>
<label>Yes</label>
<input type=radio name="2A" value="Y"/><br/>
<label>No</label>
<input type=radio name="2A" value="N"/><br/>
<label>Other</label>
<input type=radio name="2A" value="O"/><br/>
<label>Additional comment (40 characters max):</label><br/>
<input type=text name="2E" maxlength=40/><p/>

<!-- Submit the form to email. -->
<input type=submit value="Send" accesskey="S"/>
</form>
</body>
</html>
```

For anyone who has spent considerable time working with Web pages, this might look like old technology crying for a makeover. However, this technique works quite well. I didn't include the accessibility information in this example for the sake of clarity. You could also dress it up a bit using Cascading Style Sheets (CSS). The underlying example, however, is easy to understand.

The focus of this example is the <form> tag. Notice that the action="mailto:JMueller@ mwt.net?subject=Test Message" attribute defines my email address as the destination for the data in the form. In addition, the email subject is Test Message. By giving each survey a different name, you know precisely where the user took the survey and what to expect as input. Most developers would stop here and complain about the results received in their email (a rather unattractive attachment). By adding the enctype="text/plain" attribute, you can change the output to something that's easy to parse using any script and not all that hard to read using the email application's preview pane, as shown in Figure 14.2.

▶ TIP

Many developers don't understand the mailto: URL very well. The problem is that the protocol doesn't appear very often on Web pages and most Web pages don't use the full potential of the mailto: URL. You can use most of the same fields with a mailto: that you use with an email program including such features a cc and bcc. You can find several good resources about the mailto: URL on the Internet. One of the better places to look is the Web Design Guides site at http://www.ssi-developer.net/design/mailto.shtml. Another good place to look for tips of this sort is the Ezine-Tips.com site at http://ezine-tips.com/articles/format/20001020.shtml.

Each of the entries in the email has a corresponding tag in the form that has the name attribute shown. Notice how the example separates the questions using a hidden <input> tag like this:

```
<input type=hidden
       name="Q1"
       value="Search Engine"/><br/>
```

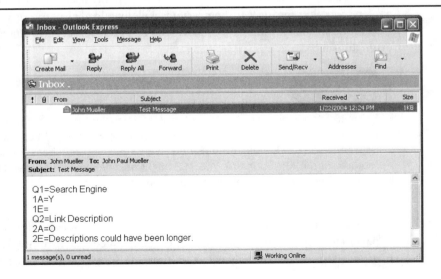

FIGURE 14.2:

Encoding your survey form correctly lets you read it directly in email.

The value you provide should include a reminder about the question content. In this case, I provided a reminder that the question asks whether the user found every product needed.

The main problem with using this technique is content size. Forms can have a 255-character limit on the amount of data they can send, although this limit is apparently uncommon. Generally, there isn't any character limit for forms. (Make sure you also check for potential limits with the Web server that you use.) This means you have to provide limits on the size of comment fields using the `maxlength` attribute, as shown in Listing 14.2. You also need to design your form carefully and make answers terse whenever possible.

Developing Automated Feedback

This chapter doesn't delve into automated feedback systems because there are a number of resources you can use for this type of programming. Here are a couple of resources you should consider.

User Feedback HTML Form   `http://www.bytesworth.com/learn/html00009.asp`

Creating Feedback Forms for Wireless Application Protocol (WAP) Sites   `http://www.aspfree.com/articles/1137,1/articles.aspx`

However, given that many eBay Web Services developers want to provide an application that does everything the user could possibly need to do on eBay, making the feedback page friendly is critical. In general, the more you automate the feedback to make things easier for your organization, the fewer users will be able to use the feedback system. This issue is especially true of form-based Web feedback because many users now turn off scripting, cookies, applets, and plug-ins for fear their systems will download viruses or experience other problems. Automation usually requires some level of client and server scripting, along with cookies and even plug-ins.

> ▶ **TIP**
>
> Some ISPs consider user feedback forms so important they make it part of the documentation for their service. For example, check out the AT&T site at `http://www.att.com/style/wc_feedback.html`. This site tells how to create a user feedback form using the special features of the AT&T servers. Your ISP might provide similar services that you can use to make development of automated pages easier.

The problem even occurs with desktop applications. Some vendors make feedback available as part of a Help menu option. In most cases, the feedback form works and sends the information to the vendor (usually over the Internet). However, problems arise when the vendor assumes the user has a permanent connection to the Internet—many users use dial-up connections. Fortunately, eBay Web Services developers can assume that the user has some kind of Internet connection (even if it's through a proxy server) because otherwise their application won't work at all.

Using the *GetShippingRates* Call

This example shows how to obtain an estimate of the cost for shipping an item based on a number of factors including the starting and ending point, the weight, packaging type, the method of shipment, and the value of the item. You can use this call to estimate the shipping costs before you put the item up for sale and also when you complete a sale. The call helps you determine what to charge for a product when the seller pays for shipping. Listing 14.3 shows the code for this example. You'll find the complete source code for this example in the \Chapter 14\ShippingRates folder of the source code located on the Sybex Web site.

Listing 14.3   **Obtaining Shipping Charges**

```
private void btnTest_Click(object sender, System.EventArgs e)
{
    ... Variable Declarations...

    // Create a session.
    ... Usual Session Code ...

    // Create a new shipping rate object.
    ShipRate = new GetShippingRatesCall(Session);

    // Create the shipping details object.
    Details = new ShippingDetails();

    // Define the shipping details.
    Details.PackagingHandlingCosts =
        Convert.ToDecimal(txtPackaging.Text);
    Details.ShippingService =
        (ShippingServices)(cbService.SelectedIndex + 3);
    Details.ShippingPackage = (ShippingPackages)cbPackage.SelectedIndex;
    Details.ShippingIrregular = cbIrregular.Checked;
    Details.ShipFromZipCode = txtFromZIP.Text;

    // Provide a new weight object and fill it with weight information.
    Details.Weight = new Weight();
    if (cbWeightUnit.SelectedIndex == 0)
    {
        Details.Weight.Quantity =
            Double.Parse(txtWeightMajor.Text) +
            (Double.Parse(txtWeightMinor.Text) / 16);
```

```
         Details.Weight.Unit = WeightUnits.Pounds;
      }
      else
      {
         Details.Weight.Quantity =
            Double.Parse(txtWeightMajor.Text) +
            (Double.Parse(txtWeightMinor.Text.PadRight(
               3, Convert.ToChar("0"))) / 1000);
         Details.Weight.Unit = WeightUnits.Kilograms;
      }

      // Add the details to the call.
      ShipRate.ShippingDetails = Details;

      // Add the items that aren't part of the details.
      ShipRate.ShipToZipcode = txtToZIP.Text;
      ShipRate.PriceSold = Convert.ToDecimal(txtPrice.Text);
      ShipRate.QuantitySold = Int32.Parse(txtQuantity.Text);

      try
      {
         // Make the call.
         Results = (ShippingRateCollection)ShipRate.GetShippingRates();
      }
      catch (eBay.SDK.Model.APIException ex)
      {
         // Display a message.
         MessageBox.Show(ex.Message,
                         "Request Error",
                         MessageBoxButtons.OK,
                         MessageBoxIcon.Error);

         // Exit the routine.
         return;
      }

      // Display the results.
      Output = new StringBuilder();
      foreach (ShippingRate Data in Results)
      {
         Output.Append("Shipping Service: " +
            Data.ShippingDetails.ShippingService.ToString() + "\r\n");
         Output.Append("Shipping Fee: " +
            Data.ShippingFee.ToString() + "\r\n");
         Output.Append("Insurance Fee: " +
            Data.InsuranceFee.ToString() + "\r\n");
         Output.Append("Package Handling Costs: " +
            Data.PackagingHandlingCosts.ToString() + "\r\n");
         Output.Append("Your Handling Costs: " +
            txtPackaging.Text + "\r\n");
         Output.Append("Total Costs: " +
            Convert.ToString(Data.ShippingFee + Data.InsuranceFee +
                             Data.PackagingHandlingCosts +
```

```
                    Convert.ToDecimal(txtPackaging.Text)));
    }
    MessageBox.Show(Output.ToString(),
                "Shipping Request Results",
                MessageBoxButtons.OK,
                MessageBoxIcon.Information);
}
```

The code begins as usual by creating a session. It then creates a new GetShippingRatesCall object, ShipRate. Within ShipRate is a ShippingDetails object that the code creates as Details. You can simply instantiate the existing entry in ShipRate when desired.

The Details object contains information about the item sender and the item itself including the type of packaging, the service used to send the item, the sender's ZIP code, and whether the item is irregularly shaped. A special Details.Weight property contains the weight of the item.

One of the more interesting problems with the SDK, in this case, is that you need to use the correct enumerated values. Unfortunately, you don't know what those values are based on the SDK documentation. Look at the eBay API Technical Documentation, however, and you'll see the values run from 3 (UPS Ground) through 11 (USPS Express Mail). Stranger still, the SDK ShippingServices enumeration doesn't include a value for USPS Express Mail. Consequently, since the cbService.SelectedIndex property starts at 0, adding 3 to the value obtains the correct value. Figure 14.3 shows that the input form uses combo boxes for some inputs to reduce user error. Make sure you use the order of items shown in the API Technical Documentation for the combo box because many IDEs sort enumerated values.

FIGURE 14.3:

Use combo boxes as needed to reduce user input errors.

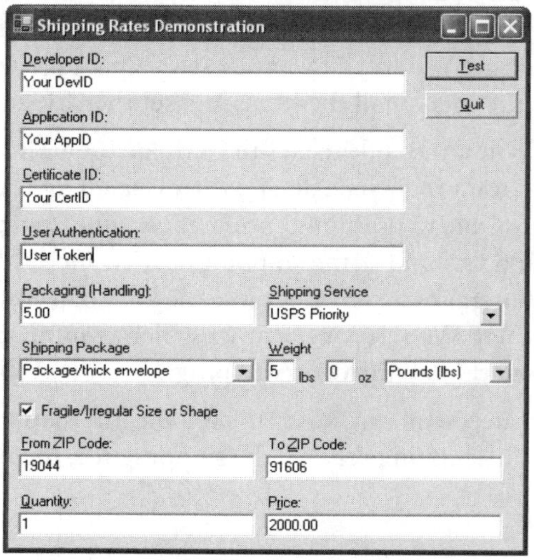

> ▶ **NOTE**
>
> The API examples shown at `http://developer.ebay.com/DevZone/docs/API_Doc/Functions/GetShippingRates/GetShippingRatesSample.htm` discuss two methods of using this call. The SDK only supports the first method where you obtain a single rate for a single service. If you want to use the second method, where you obtain the rates for all supported services, you must use the API technique.

The `Details.ShippingPackage` property also presents an interesting problem. In this case, the enumeration does begin from 0, so you don't have to do anything odd with it. However, if the user selects a value of None (see the `ShippingPackages` enumeration), the SDK returns an error message of "Invalid username or password. The username/password pair specified for the user is not valid. You may not use an email address as a username if the member has a User ID" of type `eBay.SDK.Model.APIException`.

Another issue to consider when working with this call is that the API uses two tags for the weight: `<WeightMajor>` and `<WeightMinor>`. The SDK uses a `Double` to store the value in a single property, `Weight.Quantity`. Consequently, you use two techniques to store the information depending on which technique you use to make the call. Given that most users won't know how to use a `Double`, create entries on screen for major and minor entries, and then convert the values as needed. The example source code shows one way to perform the conversion.

Once the code creates all the required entries in `Details`, it places this information in the `ShipRate.ShippingDetails` property. The client information appears as separate entries in `ShipRate`. You must include the destination ZIP code, the number of items, and the price for each time. The code assumes that you're sending multiple items of the same type in the same package. When you want to send a package with multiple items of different prices, calculate the total of all the items and set the `ShipRate.QuantitySold` property value to 1.

At this point, the code makes the `ShipRate.GetShippingRates()` call. This is one case when you might want to include detailed error handling because there are a number of situations that cause errors due to user input preferences. For example, you'll receive an error when the user selects UPS Ground as the shipping service and UPS Letter as the Shipping Package. (The combination raises an error because the kind of packaging is incorrect for the shipping service.) Because eBay Web Services knows which combinations work, it's easier to catch errors on return from the call than to try to program around all of the combinations the user could try.

After a successful call, `Results` contains the shipping cost information. This information includes the shipping service, the shipping fee, the insurance fee, and any handling fees. The information doesn't include any shipping fees that you require the user to pay, even though you provide this information as input to the call. You'll also find the `Data.ShippingDetails` property devoid of other information you provided, such as the shipping weight of the data. Because you already have this information, it's not a problem. Figure 14.4 shows typical output from this application.

Using the *GetSuggestedCategories* Call

Every time a user creates a new item listing, they have to research a category for it. The problem is that it's easy to miss categories that would work well if you list items in a number of categories. Consequently, it's helpful to get category suggestions. No one says you have to use a particular category, but these suggestions give you a good start on figuring out which ones you want to use.

> ▶ **NOTE**
>
> This is an interesting call because it provides a seller with some ideas on how to market an item effectively. You might want to combine this call with other calls, such as `GetCategory-Listings()`, to obtain a complete picture of a particular category. The eBay API Technical Documentation discussion at `http://developer.ebay.com/DevZone/docs/API_Doc/Functions/GetSuggestedCategories/GetSuggestedCategoriesLogic.htm` provides some additional insights into using this call.

The `GetSuggestedCategories()` call works much like a search. However, instead of using keywords to find an item, you use them to locate a list of categories. The keywords often reflect parts of a product name, although nothing prevents you from using other kinds of keywords as well. Listing 14.4 shows the code for this example. You'll find the complete source code for this example in the `\Chapter 14\SuggestedCategories` folder of the source code located on the Sybex Web site.

FIGURE 14.4:

Typical shipping price output from eBay Web Services

Listing 14.4   **Obtaining Category Suggestions**

```csharp
private void btnTest_Click(object sender, System.EventArgs e)
{
    ... Variable Declarations...

    // Create a session.
    ... Usual Session Code ...

    // Create the call.
    Cats = new GetSuggestedCategoriesCall(Session);

    // Add the query.
    Cats.Query = txtQuery.Text;

    try
    {
        // Make the call.
        Results =
            (SuggestedCategoryCollection)Cats.GetSuggestedCategories();
    }
    catch (eBay.SDK.Model.APIException ex)
    {
        // Display a message.
        MessageBox.Show(ex.Message);

        // Exit the routine.
        return;
    }

    // Process the results.
    foreach (SuggestedCategory SG in Results)
    {
        // Create a new data row.
        DR = dsCategories.Tables["Categories"].NewRow();

        // Add the data.
        DR["Category"] = SG.Category;
        DR["Full ID"] = SG.CategoryFullId;
        DR["Full Name"] = SG.CategoryFullName;
        DR["Percent Found"] = SG.PercentItemFound;

        // Add the data to the table.
        dsCategories.Tables["Categories"].Rows.Add(DR);
    }
}
```

The code for this example begins as usual by creating a session. Once the code creates a session, it creates the new `GetSuggestedCategoriesCall` object, `Cats`. The only property the code must define for `Cats` is `Query`, which contains the keywords you want to use for the category search.

> ▶ NOTE
>
> This call fails fairly often when used in the sandbox environment with an "Internal error to the application" error message. Consequently, you need to check for an `eBay.SDK.Model.APIException` exception with every call.

After the code makes the `Cats.GetSuggestedCategories()` call, `Results` contains a collection of `SuggestedCategory` entries. The example relies on a combination of a `DataSet`, `dsCategories`, and a `DataGrid` to display the information. In this case, the code relies on a `foreach` loop to process the collection.

The processing look creates a new `DataRow`, `DR`, to hold the individual data values for each result. Each `SuggestedCategory` object contains a `Category` (the actual category number), `CategoryFullId` (the list of category numbers that lead to this category), `CategoryFullName` (the hierarchical list of category names in human readable form), and `PercentItemFound` (the number of items in that category that match the keywords you provide) properties that describe the category entries. Interestingly enough, the API technique provides another value, `CategoryName`, that doesn't appear in the list of values returned by the SDK technique. This value contains the category name in human readable form. Using this information, the user can decide on which category to use for an item listing.

Your Call to Action

This chapter helps you discover some of the little noticed but decidedly important features that every application should have. Protecting a user's privacy is extremely important in a world where users feel companies violate their rights. No one is likely to compliment you about the addition of privacy to your application, but you can be sure that someone will complain if a lack of privacy makes personal information available to the public. Likewise, additions such as feedback forms, freight charge estimates, and category suggestions don't result directly in sales. However, by adding these features, you demonstrate to users that have you have considered their needs and want to provide the best computing experience possible.

The essential nugget of knowledge you can take from this chapter is that the user is important. Whether you have good communication skills or not, the user depends on you to create an application that not only works well, but also meets specific needs. It's up to you to decide to put the user first and make your application both useful and friendly. Empowering the user is one way to gain an order of magnitude in application performance and efficiency.

Congratulations! You've reached the last chapter of the book. However, your journey should also include the appendices for this book. Appendix A helps you locate useful third party utilities. Use Appendix B to ensure your application meets all of the eBay licensing requirements. Finally, use Appendix C to learn about late breaking eBay Web Services news—new technologies made available as this book went to press. If you've read from the beginning to the end of the book, you know that it covers a lot of ground. I encourage you to continue to use the book as a reference. eBay Web Services is a truly remarkable undertaking and I'd love to hear about your experiences with it. Make sure you contact me at `JMueller@mwt.net` if you have any questions about this book. Also, look on my Web site at `http://www.mwt.net/~jmueller/` for updates and additional information.

Appendix A

Finding Additional eBay
Web Services Resources

Seeing Demonstrations
Created by Others

▶ Helpful Third Party Resource Sites

Locating Other Interesting
Web Sites

Using the Office
2003 Add-on

Throughout the book you discovered a number of resources that would help you perform some tasks with less effort or faster. In some cases, a product added the special functionality required to make eBay Web Services access possible. I usually placed the special products in a separate section or used them to demonstrate a particular type of eBay Web Services access. The book also references a number of Web sites that feature special information—these helpful Web sites normally appear as part of notes or tips. This appendix is an extension of all those special sections, notes, and tips—it contains a number of helpful third party resources that will make your eBay Web Services experience better.

Of course, this appendix begs the question of why these third party products and sites don't appear somewhere in the main part of the book. In many cases, these products fulfill a special need that I didn't demonstrate or they duplicate a functionality that you'll already find. This appendix contains additional information that I thought you would find helpful, but didn't find a place in the main part of the book for whatever reason.

I'm always on the lookout for great third party products, and I like to know about Web sites with helpful information. These sites often appear in my newsletter (sign up at http://www .freeenewsletters.com/). I also provide them as updates to the book on my Web site at http:// www.mwt.net/~jmueller/. If you know of a special third party product or Web site that has special information that would help users of this book, please let me know by writing to me at JMueller@mwt.net.

eBay Web Services–Specific Web Sites

eBay Web Services has been so successful that many language vendors are beginning to take notice, as well as a number of third parties. The following list presents a few of the most interesting places to find eBay Web Services information. However, you should also check with the vendor that creates your programming language product and look around at other third party solutions too. For example, the "Microsoft Office 2003 Add-on" section describes how Microsoft is adding Web services support to their Office product.

Accessing the eBay API with PHP (uses a different technique than shown in the book)
`http://blog.php-tools.de/archives/12_Accessing_the_eBay_API_with_PHP.html`

Creating a Product Search Application Using the eBay SDK and Visual Basic .NET
`http://msdn.microsoft.com/library/en-us/dv_vstechart/html/ebaysearchbar.asp`

ePower and Profits `http://www.epowerandprofits.com/`

Ritz Auctions on eBay `http://www.ritzcamera.com/webapp/wcs/stores/servlet/CategoryDisplay?storeId=10001&catalogId=10001&langId=-1&categoryId=10000151`

Tannock.net CFHTTP Issues—Cold Fusion HyperText Transfer Protocol Programming Example `http://www.tannock.net/archives/001963.php`

> ► **NOTE**
>
> Although the Perl Server Side CGI Scripting site at `http://www.webmasterworld.com/forum13/` doesn't have a wealth of working examples, you can find some interesting PERL code and discussion about working with eBay Web Services. For example, the discussion at `http://www.webmasterworld.com/forum13/3261.htm` contains an example that appears to work fine (the author of the article couldn't get it to work at first and found that it worked fine later). Note that you need to join the Web site to see some of the resources provided, including the second URL.

Demonstration Web Sites

Sometimes a demonstration is better than any amount of descriptive text. Most of the demonstrations I've seen on the Internet are simple, at this point, but the potential for creating some very interesting Web applications is definitely there. Some of these applications are full-fledged setups designed for someone who makes their living buying and selling items on eBay. The following Web sites provide demonstrations you can try online. This list is by no means complete—at best, it's a representative sample of what you'll find online. The use of eBay Web Services is truly amazing.

Antique and Collectible Mall `http://tias.com/`

AuctionHelper `http://www.auctionhelper.com/ah/main/main.asp`

eBay Listings (RSS feed of search items) `http://www.ebaylistings.net/`

Kurant StoreSense `http://www.storesense.com/merchant/features/index.shtml`

Vivísimo Document Clustering `http://vivisimo.com/ebay`

> **▶ TIP**
>
> I've seen a few queries for developers who know how to work with eBay Web Services online. For example, the RentACoder site at `http://www.rentacoder.com/` recently had several requests for such a developer. You can also find somewhere to use your eBay Web Services programming expertise at places such as Elance (`http://www.elance.com/`) and Guru.com (`http://www.guru.com`). These online job sites provide opportunities for you to further increase your eBay Web Services expertise, as well as make a little money from the knowledge you've gained.

Web Sites That Provide Other Facts You Should Know About

You'll find helpful Web sites in every chapter of the book. However, some Web sites didn't quite fit in any of the chapters, yet they supply useful information for your eBay Web Services experience. For example, the "Sending Special Characters Using URL Encoding" section of Chapter 4 discusses the need to URL encode special characters before you send a request to eBay Web Services. Equally important is the need to *escape* special characters in some types of HTML and XML output by converting them to numeric sequences. The quote (') and double quote (") often cause problems, as do the angle brackets (<>). You can escape these characters as &#39, &#34, &#60, and &#62. The HTML Character Codes site at `http://home .online.no/~pethesse/charcodes.html` contains a good list of these codes.

Web accessibility is an extremely important topic and I hope that you take it as seriously as I do. You can find multitudes of statistics on Web sites that specialize in accessibility such as `http://www.w3.org/1999/05/WCAG-REC-fact`. An ExtremeTech article entitled "The State of Web Accessibility" (`http://www.extremetech.com/article2/0,3973,11774,00.asp`) says it all by stating that accessibility is for everyone—the 180 posts for this article provide some interesting insights as well. These additional Web sites provide some pointers you can use to make your site accessible and yet keep development costs to a minimum.

Confusing Words `http://www.confusingwords.com/`

Policies Relating to Web Accessibility `http://www.w3.org/WAI/Policy/`

Safe Web Colors for Color-Deficient Vision `http://more.btexact.com/people/rigdence/colours/`

Usability and Accessibility—Everyone Learning `http://www.cdlr.tamu.edu/dec_2002/Proceedings/david_peter.pdf`

Once you learn about Web services and understand how valuable they can be, you'll want to try out other Web services to learn whether they can help you with your application. One of the most interesting places to learn about new Web services is the Macromedia Flash site at `http://www.flash-db.com/services/`.

Sometimes you can find individual sites that include some eBay Web Services material. I like browsing through these because many of them include insights and perspectives you won't find on mainstream sites. Of course, some of them just repeat material you find elsewhere. Here are a few of the more interesting selections.

A Klog Apart `http://www.dijest.com/aka/2003/07/21.html`

Cover Pages `http://xml.coverpages.org/ni2001-03-15-d.html`

Java News Headlines `http://today.java.net/today/news/`

NY-PA Collector `http://www.mpnewspapers.com/nypacollector/features/351308489256274.php`

Windley's Enterprise Computing Weblog `http://www.windley.com/docs/EnablingWebServices.pdf` and `http://www.windley.com/2003/07/`

Microsoft Office 2003 Add-on

Most Microsoft Office users will need to use the VBA programming techniques found in Chapter 7 to access eBay Web Services. However, Office 2003 users have an alternative solution that works in some cases. Microsoft is creating a new add-on for the Research Task Pane that should be available when you read this. This add-on lets you perform research on eBay without ever leaving the Office environment. You can find the add-on at `http://www.office.microsoft.com/marketplace`.

This add-on provides a customizable interface. Generally, you'll interact with this add-on much as you interact with the eBay Web site, but you can also create a custom application to define the interface you want. You can find additional details at:

Creating Your Own Research Service for the Microsoft Office 2003 Research Library `http://www.devx.com/codemag/Article/18214?trk=DXRSS_XML`

Customizing the Microsoft Office 2003 Research Task Pane `http://msdn` `.microsoft.com/library/en-us/dno2k3ta/html/odc_customizingtheresearchpane.asp`

Gadgetopia `http://www.gadgetopia.com/2004/01/16/MicrosoftOffice2003Research-` `Library.html`

Appendix B

► eBay License Checklist

This appendix discusses some of the requirements you must fulfill to use eBay Web Services. The purpose of this appendix is to help you create a checklist to ensure you meet the legal requirements—the appendix doesn't tell you about your legal rights, act as a legal guide, or provide anything that would normally require a lawyer. The best policy is to ask eBay and to contact your personal legal department whenever you have a question about your licensing requirements.

> **► WARNING**
>
> eBay sets some requirements individually, so you need to consider any personal requirements for your use of eBay Web Services. These individual requirements consider issues such as how you plan to work with eBay (a question you answered when you signed up for the developer program) and your licensing level. This appendix only addresses general issues—you need to consider specific issues as well and add them to your personal checklist.

I often create checklists of this sort for my own use and find that many other people find them useful too. The main reason I create these checklists for myself is that they make it easier for me to determine whether an application I create fulfills the basic requirements of the license. If you do have questions about the legal requirements, make sure you contact eBay (`developer-support@ ebay.com`) to ensure you understand your role completely. In addition, although this appendix is current as of the date of writing, eBay could change the licensing agreement at any time—you must make sure that you keep current on all of the requirements. For example, whenever you see a change in one of the newsletters, make sure you update your checklist as well.

Addressing Certification Requirements

Before eBay accepts any application you create, it must go through a certification test and meet all of the certification requirements. These requirements apply to everyone equally. There's no ambiguity here; you must meet these requirements to get your application certified. Therefore, the first place you need to look for issues to address is the Certification Requirements page at `http://developer.ebay.com/DevZone/docs/API_Doc/Certification/CertificationRequirements.htm`.

You'll find that the information on the Certification Requirements is geared toward a developer, and not a lawyer. The information presents application scenarios and tells you how to address them. In fact, you'll find requirements in these areas:

- Handling System Errors
- Handling Request Errors
- Making Requests Using Multiple Threads
- Handling Multiple Items from a Single API Call
- Restricting Polling Frequencies
- Using the Correct Compatibility Level
- Understanding Requirements for Specific API Calls

The book already shows you how to address many of these issues. You already know how to handle both system and request errors. The code also demonstrated techniques for working with multiple items from a single call without relying on a specific number of returned items. You discovered how to work with compatibility levels. Finally, the book addressed any certification requirements for the calls actually discussed.

> ▶ **TIP**
>
> Make sure you verify any requirements for individual calls that you make using both the Certification Requirements page and the Certification Requirements Change History page at `http://developer.ebay.com/DevZone/docs/API_Doc/Certification/CertificationRequirementsChangeHistory`. Otherwise, you could find that your application fails certification due to a change in the requirements.

Besides these basic programming issues, you also need to consider thread usage when you write an application that relies on multiple threads for performance reasons. eBay restricts most users to using three threads. However, depending on your licensing level, you might have access to as many as 18 threads. The question to consider is how many threads you can actually use. When all is said and done, most desktop applications get by just fine with a single thread. You could possibly make a case for using two threads: one to send data and another to receive it. A third thread could retrieve essential information such as a category list, but this task would be something you'd do once a day at most. In general, the user isn't going to notice if you stick to one or two threads.

The reason an enterprise application might need more threads is that an application of this kind would make calls for multiple users. Each thread could represent the requests of one or more users accessing the application. When building an enterprise application, you need to consider how many users will make calls and find ways to throttle the requests so that you don't create too many threads. Most enterprise application server technologies now provide the required throttling as part of the system configuration, but you need to verify thread usage and ensure you keep things under control.

The other issue not discussed within the book is restricted polling frequencies. In general, if you begin requesting some data too often, eBay is going to restrict your ability to make that call. For example, you can't make the `GetCategoryListings()` call more than once every 30 minutes according to the certification requirements. To overcome this problem, you need to make the call at a specific interval and cache the information locally. When a user makes a category request, use the local data store rather than calling eBay Web Services.

Considering eBay User Requirements

Developers aren't immune to the eBay user requirements. If anything, eBay is going to hold you to a higher level of compliance than the typical user because your application affects the actions of more than one person. The basics appear in the User Requirements document at `http://pages.ebay.com/help/policies/user-agreement.html`. It's also a good idea to look through the list of essential information provided by the two user Frequently Asked Questions (FAQs) documents at `http://pages.ebay.com/help/policies/user-agreement-faqs.html` and `http://pages.ebay.com/help/policies/user-agreement-revisions-faqs.html`.

Understanding the User Agreement Essentials

Some of the requirements in the user agreement are definitely user related. For example, the first section states that the user can't participate on eBay if they can't form an agreement. In other words, someone under the age of 18 in the United States can't use eBay because they can't make a legal agreement to buy merchandise from someone else. In addition, users have to pay any required fees. Your application can control access to eBay to an extent, but it definitely doesn't need to include features for fees unless that's something you really want to do.

The third section contains a lot of information developers need to consider when creating the application. The important issue is that eBay is a venue and not an auctioneer. Some of the examples in the book demonstrate that eBay provides a number of sales models, some of which are auction based and others that aren't. This section also contains information that you really should consider when creating your application. For example, even though eBay does its best to verify user identity, absolute identification on the Internet is difficult. eBay encourages you to use whatever tools are necessary to ensure you know the buyer or seller with whom you're dealing. A well-designed application would do some of this work for the user and then tell the user what additional steps are necessary to avoid potential problems.

The fourth and fifth sections of the agreement discuss essential buyer and seller information. You can use this information to create a better application. For example, your application could provide reminders to a buyer who has won an auction to make prompt payment. Obviously, your application will end at the reminder stage in most cases, but any help is better than nothing. Likewise, your application can include seller aids to ensure that all listed items fairly reflect the seller's intent.

Interestingly enough, the seventh section of the agreement makes reference to the use of spyders (eBay's spelling) or screen scraping technology. Obviously, eBay frowns on their use. The same notice appears in many other places and you'll find it in your developer's license as well. The point is that eBay wants to ensure any application interaction occurs under strict control and follows required guidelines.

The eighth section discusses the matter of feedback. Given the popularity and necessity of this feature, a well-designed application can help a user create good feedback. For example, the inclusion of both spelling and grammar checkers can make the feedback easier to read. An application could suggest terms and even help the user create well-formatted and easily understood feedback.

Many of the remaining sections of the agreement are legal requirements such as what will happen when a breach of contract occurs and how eBay plans to protect the user's privacy. All of these issues are important and you should read them, but most of them won't provide you with new ideas for your application. In most cases, you won't have to act on these requirements because they're either user responsibilities or they don't take effect unless other events occur (events that you hope don't happen).

Getting All the Facts

eBay has a substantial number of procedures and policies in place. As a developer, you need to know about them all. This appendix can't discuss every policy in detail, but it's important to realize these policies exist. Make sure you create a strategy and add features to your application to ensure you meet the policy requirements listed here.

Privacy Policy http://pages.ebay.com/help/policies/privacy-policy.html

Outage Policy http://pages.ebay.com/help/policies/everyone-outage.html

Board Usage Policy `http://pages.ebay.com/help/policies/everyone-boards.html`

Non-Binding Bid Policy `http://pages.ebay.com/help/policies/non-binding-bid.html`

Listing Policy `http://pages.ebay.com/help/policies/listing-ov.html`

Half.com Policy `http://www.half.com/help/index.cfm?helpsection=halfpolicy`

Investigations Policy `http://pages.ebay.com/help/community/investigates.html`

Prohibited and Restricted Items Policy `http://pages.ebay.com/help/policies/items-ov.html`

Real Estate Policy `http://pages.ebay.com/help/community/re_agreement.html`

Non-Paying Bidder Policy `http://pages.ebay.com/help/sell/bidders_overview.html`

This document list could change at any time. You'll find a list of the current documents at `http://pages.ebay.com/help/policies/`. Click the link of the requirement that you want to see.

Reading Your *Individual.PDF*

The `Individual.PDF` document you receive from eBay discusses the requirements for using the API and your responsibilities as a developer. This document works with the API License–Appendix D HTML page you received. The two documents aren't the same—they're both parts of a single agreement that controls what you can do with eBay Web Services. Of the documents, you'll find Appendix D easiest to read. In fact, it's already in the form of a checklist and I recommend highly that you print it out and use it to check your application for potential problems.

> ▶ **WARNING**
>
> Appendix D spells out the ways you can personally use the API and might not reflect the uses of the API for other people. That's why you shouldn't answer licensing questions that someone asks on the developer forum—you don't know what their licensing agreement says. You can probably make certain assumptions because they appear in so many places in the licensing agreement and have even received some level of public exposure. For example, you can safely assume that eBay doesn't want anyone to use screen scraping techniques because this requirement appears in so many places in the licensing agreement. It normally appears as part of Appendix D and at least two places in the `Individual.PDF` file (Sections 1.2 and 6.2).

Understanding the Main Section

The `Individual.PDF` document begins with a list of things you can do. You combine this portion of the document with Appendix D to determine what kinds of actions you can perform (and consequently the kind of application you can create). It's essential to rely on this portion of the document as you design your application. Trying to work with the document after the application is designed simply wastes time. Some requirements also affect actual coding practices, such as the manner in which you display eBay content. The actual restrictions on your use of eBay content depends on your licensing level and the way you answered questions during the developer signup process. However, you can probably assume that some general issues such as reselling eBay content without permission are forbidden to everyone.

You'll want to pay particularly close attention to the display requirements usually found in Section 1.4, because this section spells out time intervals for displaying items (no more than 6 hours) and other content (no more than 24 hours). One of the more interesting requirements is that you can't display eBay content in a browser frame because other frames in a Web application could display other kinds of content. The idea is that your application should focus on eBay content.

The second section of the `Individual.PDF` document describes your interaction with the user. This section describes the minimum requirements for working with the user. For example, you can't collect any user information without express permission and you must provide an opt-out method for the user to withdraw permission. Given the nature of privacy today, you need to consider all of the requirements in this section during application design, testing, quality control, and maintenance. The best way to approach this section is that less is better—treat the user data as a hot potato that you don't want to keep around.

The third section considers licenses, such as your ability to nonexclusively use eBay content. Most of the items in this section are common sense. For example, you don't own the content, eBay does. In addition, eBay has to approve your use of their content. These items simply consider content as personal property. Even so, you need to ensure everyone creating or working with the application understands this point. An employee isn't allowed to take eBay data home because it doesn't belong to them.

In the fourth section, you learn the reason that cached applications are so great. eBay doesn't guarantee any level of uptime. This means you can be without access to eBay Web Services at any time and there isn't anything you can do or say about it. The best policy is to work around the issue. Either you can wait until eBay is back online (in which case, a cached application is optional) or you can't (in which case, you'd better use caching).

The fifth section describes payment issues. This section is completely individual and you need to set up some type of payment plan before you begin development. You also agree to pay any taxes for sales made by your application in this section. In general, you're going to pay something for using eBay Web Services, but make sure you understand the specifics before you get started.

The remaining sections of the agreement contain a number of interesting issues, but most of them are things that lawyers and accountants love, not developers. For example, the sixth section describes the termination of the contract and what events cause termination. The exception is the seventh section, which contains a few requirements for the stability and security of your application. This information is discussed in detail in Appendix B, which is where you should go for the particulars. Make sure you do read the tenth section because it describes eBay's intellectual property rights. Generally, it looks like the lawyers copied the same statement from every other lawyer out there—you have no rights. Saber rattling aside, don't tell anyone about eBay's intellectual property—keep it locked away and don't share it.

Understanding Appendix B

One of the main events for developers is Appendix B. This appendix spells out the security requirements for your eBay application. The requirements are stiff and you should consider making them even more extreme. The appendix even uses a term that I haven't heard since I left the military: "Need to know." If someone doesn't need to know about your interaction with eBay, don't tell them—they have no need to know. The best policy to follow is to ask whether a person needs to know every time you have to tell someone about anything. Yes, it's a bit extreme, but it's what Appendix B calls for.

The second section of Appendix B describes logging requirements for users who work with your application. According to this section, you must keep track of both logon and logoff information, the time, and the associated user identification. The appendix specifies that you must hold on to this information for a minimum of 60 days. You can bet that eBay is going to request this information if they detect an unauthorized access that's in any way connected to you.

The third section spells out the data storage and user identification encryption requirements. Some of this information is becoming outdated. For example, soon you won't be able to store the eBay user identification or password. However, you'll likely need to store the user authentication token. Just what eBay will require depends on the importance of the data. Until eBay updates the appendix, you should probably use 128-bit encryption. User email addresses require 56-bit encryption and credit card numbers require 128-bit encryption. To make things simpler, use 128-bit encryption for all data.

Make sure you look at the requirement that appears on the second page of Appendix B. It's in bold type to show eBay is really serious about this one. You're responsible for protecting any physical media, which means making it unreadable when you want to get rid of it. Because your data is important to you as well, this seems like a commonsense issue. However, I still read every day about someone who sent their system to the dump with a fully readable hard drive still installed. The effects can be devastating. While you protect eBay's data, make sure you protect your own too.

Understanding Appendix C

Appendix C, the final section of the `Individual.PDF` document, contains your license to use the SDK. Essentially, this agreement tells you that you can use the SDK within the limits assigned by eBay and then goes on to describe those limits. Generally, you need to treat the SDK with the same respect you would give to anyone's property, which means protecting it from abuse and not stealing it. eBay also states that you have access to the SDK source code and can use it to help develop your applications.

Interestingly enough, you can make small changes to the SDK and distribute the modified form in object format. In short, you can change a few items in the SDK to make them work better with your application, but you can't give the changed source code to anyone else and eBay is assuming that you'll only use the modified SDK to make your application work better.

Appendix C

| Understanding SOAP and eBay | Working with SOAP | Using the Improved Java API |

▶ Late Breaking eBay Web Services News

| Getting and Using Authentication Tools | Updating Your API Vocabulary | Discovering the PayPal Web Service |

This appendix brings you late breaking news about eBay Web Services as of the time of this writing. With many products, there are definite breaks in the development cycle so you can say one version is complete and another is beginning. The Web makes it easy to create products that have a continuous development cycle—there aren't any real versions to consider. eBay Web Services falls into this category.

The following sections describe some of the latest eBay Web Services features. eBay is trying a number of new strategies to make your programming experience better. For example, in addition to the API and the SDK techniques of working with eBay, you now also have access to the Simple Object Access Protocol (SOAP). In some cases, eBay is introducing features that make the environment more secure. For example, the new authentication and authorization feature creates a few problems (even though it does make the user feel more secure), so eBay is introducing some new tools to make the developer experience a little easier too. These new features make eBay more useful by helping you do more with less effort. You'll also find that these new features make it easier for you to create robust applications that fulfill more user needs.

A Few Words about SOAP

eBay is experimenting with SOAP as a means of reducing some of the problems developers have getting their applications to communicate well with eBay Web Services. You can download the support required to use SOAP with eBay Web Services at `http://developer.ebay.com/ devprogram/preview.asp`. An appendix can't provide everything you need to know about SOAP. However, the following sections describe SOAP basics, tell you about some important SOAP issues, and provide a few pointers on where you can learn more about SOAP. The idea is to understand SOAP well enough to use it with eBay Web Services for now and then build on that knowledge later.

> ▶ **NOTE**
>
> SOAP services for eBay Web Services are relatively new and still in the test phase as this book goes to print. You can read about the SOAP features in a number of places including the Communication System Design article at `http://www.commsdesign.com/csdmag/ sections/new_products/showArticle.jhtml?articleID=18700501` and the Information-Week article at `http://www.informationweek.com/story/showArticle.jhtml?articleID= 17602919`. It's also interesting to note that Microsoft is pursuing a number of integration strategies with Office as discussed in the InfoWorld article at `http://www.infoworld .com/article/04/03/01/HNebaymicrosoft_1.html`. The end of the article indicates that Microsoft is also pursuing this strategy with eBay Web Services and they already have an add-on for eBay Web Services, so Office users may soon have a wealth of Web service data from which to choose.

Determining Which SOAP Standard to Use

SOAP has gone through three major revisions. Each revision makes SOAP a better product to use for communication purposes. Almost no one uses the SOAP 1.0 standard anymore. Few vendors used this standard because it had some significant problems that the SOAP 1.1 standard quickly solved. The SOAP 1.1 standard is popular because it works well for most communication that doesn't require security. For example, you can safely use SOAP 1.1 products for most eBay Web Services tasks because you aren't passing along anything that's secret.

> ▶ **NOTE**
>
> Many developers who work with Visual Studio 6 and older versions of VBA rely on the Microsoft SOAP Toolkit. The features of this toolkit can also come in handy when you need to create a JavaScript application for your favorite browser. You can download this toolkit at `http://msdn.microsoft.com/webservices/downloads/default.aspx`. The examples all rely on the 3.0 version of the toolkit—the latest version available at the time of writing.

The SOAP 1.2 standard originally appeared on the scene on July 9, 2001 (`http://www.w3 .org/TR/2001/WD-soap12-20010709/`). However, the World Wide Web Consortium (W3C) didn't make it a recommendation until June 24, 2003 (`http://www.w3.org/TR/soap12-part1/`). Consequently, many of the products you see on the Internet today still rely on SOAP 1.1 and will probably continue to rely on this standard for some time. Even Microsoft's latest release of Visual Studio .NET still relies on SOAP 1.1.

> ▶ **TIP**
>
> You can find many SOAP 1.1 resources now. The ZVON Web site at `http://www.zvon` `.org/xxl/soapReference/Output/index.html` provides a great reference you can use to learn more about SOAP. You'll find a SOAP tutorial at `http://www.w3schools.com/soap/`. The SOAP 1.1 specification appears at `http://static.userland.com/xmlRpcCom/soap/` `SOAPv11.htm`. Microsoft provides a SOAP testing tool that you can download at `http://` `msdn.microsoft.com/library/en-us/dnsoap/html/soapvalidator.asp`. Learn more about SOAP messages with attachments at `http://www.w3.org/TR/SOAP-attachments`. Finally, if you want to learn all the ins and outs of SOAP 1.1 with both Microsoft and third party products, get my book *Special Edition Using SOAP* (Que, 2001).

Although SOAP 1.2 resources are still a little rare, you should look at the primer at `http://` `www.w3.org/TR/soap12-part0/`, the framework specification at `http://www.w3.org/TR/` `soap12-part1/`, and the adjuncts at `http://www.w3.org/TR/soap12-part2/`. You may also want to read about test collection methods at `http://www.w3.org/TR/soap12-testcollection/`. The W3C is also working on a number of additional specifications that aren't at the recommendation stage. These specifications include SOAP 1.2 attachments (`http://www.w3.org/` `TR/soap12-af/`), SOAP 1.2 email bindings (`http://www.w3.org/TR/soap12-email`), and SOAP 1.2 normalization (`http://www.w3.org/TR/soap12-n11n/`).

Given the current state of SOAP, you need to consider three things when you decide which standard to use. First, you need to know whether your product of choice even supports SOAP 1.2—most don't. Second, you need to consider whether the features SOAP 1.2 offers are essential to your organization. In many cases, using SOAP 1.1 still works fine. Third, you need to consider whether the remote sites you want to work with use SOAP 1.2. Using SOAP 1.1 until your partners catch up probably makes sense. You do want to use SOAP 1.2 sometime in the future, so planning for it today is a good idea.

Understanding the Parts of a SOAP Message

To understand SOAP, you need to consider the features that make up a SOAP message. A SOAP message includes the SOAP package, the XML envelope, and the HyperText Transfer Protocol (HTTP) or Simple Mail Transfer Protocol (SMTP) transport. Think about this system in the same way that you do a letter, with SOAP acting as the letter, XML as the envelope to hold the letter, and HTTP or SMTP as the mail carrier to deliver the letter. The most common transport protocol in use today is HTTP, so that's what we'll look at in this section. Keep in mind, however, that SOAP can theoretically use any of a number of transport protocols and probably will in the future. Figure C.1 shows a common SOAP message configuration. Notice the SOAP message formatting. This isn't the only way to wrap a SOAP message in other protocols, but it's the most common method in use today.

The HTTP portion of a SOAP message looks much the same as any other HTTP header you may have seen in the past. In fact, if you don't look carefully, you might pass it by without paying any attention. As with any HTTP transmission, there are two types of headers—one for requests and another for responses. Figure C.1 shows examples of both types.

FIGURE C.1:

An illustration of a typical SOAP message

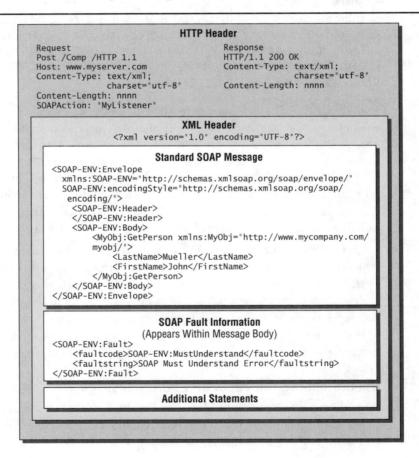

As with any request header, the HTTP portion of a SOAP message will contain an action (Post, in most cases), the HTTP version, a Host name, and some Content-Length information. The Post action portion of the header will contain the path for the SOAP listener. Also located within a request header are a Content-Type entry of text/xml and a charset entry of utf-8. The utf-8 entry is important right now because many SOAP toolkits don't support utf-16 or other character sets.

You'll also find the unique SOAPAction entry in the HTTP request header. It contains the Uniform Resource Identifier (URI) of the component used to parse the SOAP request. If the SOAPAction entry is " ", then the server will use the HTTP Request-URI entry to locate a listener instead. This is the only SOAP-specific entry in the HTTP header—everything else we've discussed could appear in any HTTP formatted message.

The response header portion of the HTTP wrapper for a SOAP message contains all of the essentials as well. You'll find the HTTP version, status, and content length as usual. There are two common status indicators for a response header: 200 OK or 500 Internal Server Error. The SOAP specification allows use of any value in the 200 series for a positive response, but a server must return a status value of 500 for SOAP errors to indicate a server error. Whenever a SOAP response header contains an error status, the SOAP message must include a SOAP fault section.

All SOAP messages use XML encoding. SOAP follows the XML specification, and you can consider it a true superset of XML. In other words, it adds to the functionality already in place within XML. Anyone familiar with XML will feel comfortable with SOAP at the outset—all you really need to know is the SOAP nuances. Although the examples in the SOAP specification don't show an XML connection (other than the formatting of the SOAP message), SOAP messages always contain an XML header similar to the one shown in Figure C.1.

A simple SOAP message consists of an envelope that contains both a header and a body (sort of the same arrangement used by an HTML page). The header can contain information that isn't associated with the data itself. For example, the header commonly contains a transaction ID when the application needs one to identify a particular SOAP message. The body contains the data in XML format. If an error occurs, the body will contain fault information, rather than data.

SOAP is essentially a one-way data transfer protocol. While SOAP messages often follow a request/response pattern, the messages themselves are individual entities. This means that a SOAP message is stand-alone—it doesn't rely on the immediate presence of a server, nor is a response expected when a request message contains all of the required information. For example, some types of data entry may not require a response since the user is inputting information and may not care about a response.

The envelope in which a SOAP message travels, however, may provide more than just a one-way transfer path. For example, when a developer encases a SOAP message within an HTTP envelope, the request and response both use the same connection. HTTP creates and maintains the connection, not SOAP. Consequently, the connection follows the HTTP way of performing data transfer—using the same techniques as a browser uses to request Web pages for display.

Understanding How WSDL Fits In

It's possible to build a SOAP message that eBay will understand from scratch, but that's typically the most difficult way to communicate. In fact, even though it might be tempting to give message building a try, you should probably avoid it. WSDL provides a means for describing a Web service so that the Integrated Development Environment (IDE) you use can create the definitions needed. When you use a product such as Visual Studio .NET, the IDE downloads the WSDL from the eBay Web site and you'll find that you don't actually have to worry about the construction of the SOAP message.

> ▶ **TIP**
>
> You can find a wealth of resources about WSDL on the Internet. One of the more interesting offerings includes the ZVON reference at http://www.zvon.org/xxl/WSDL1.1/Output/index.html. The W3C has a tutorial at `http://www.w3schools.com/wsdl/default.asp`. Originally, Microsoft and IBM promoted WSDL on their Web sites, but you can now find the specification on the W3C site at `http://www.w3.org/TR/wsdl`. You can find the IBM view of Web services at `http://www-106.ibm.com/developerworks/webservices/` and `http://www.alphaworks.ibm.com/tech/webservicetoolkit`. A WSDL search engine (where you can find services that rely on both SOAP and WSDL) appears at `http://www.salcentral.com/salnet/webserviceswsdl.asp`.

Like many other topics discussed, WSDL relies on XML as a basis for communication. Note that the Visual Studio .NET IDE automatically downloads this file as part of the process of creating a reference to the Web site. Use the following steps to create a reference to eBay Web Services.

1. Right-click the project entry in Solution Explorer and choose Add Web Reference from the context menu. You'll see an Add Web Reference dialog box.

2. Type `http://developer.ebay.com/webservices/latest/eBaySvc.wsdl` in the URL field. Click Go. After a few minutes, the Add Web Reference dialog box will display a list of methods available on eBay Web Services as shown in Figure C.2.

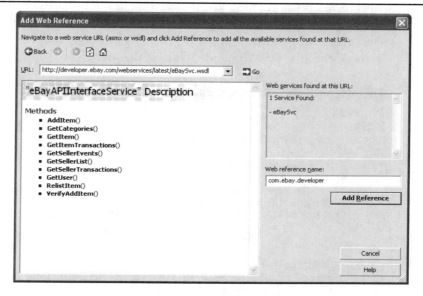

3. Type a new name for the reference in the Web Reference Name field if desired. The only time you need to perform this task is when you think your application could experience a naming conflict or you want to change the name to match your application better. The examples in this chapter will use the default name of com.ebay.developer.

4. Click Add Reference. After a few moments, you'll see a new reference added to Solution Explorer.

Adding the Web reference also adds a new file to the project. You'll find this file in the \Appendix C\SOAPExample\Web References\com.ebay.developer folder for the example in this section. The Reference.CS file contains all the information your application needs to interact with eBay Web Services. Other languages will create similar folders and reference files. It's interesting to look through this file to see how the Web service reference works. However, make sure you don't change any of the code in the file if you do open it. Changes can cause the Web service interface to stop working.

Creating an Application Using SOAP

Writing an eBay Web Services application that relies on SOAP is a little different than using either the API or SDK method. Many advanced language products simplify the process for you by encapsulating the SOAP functionality in standard objects. This is what happens when you create a reference for a Visual Studio application. The example in this section shows a simple SOAP call that you can use as a basis for building other applications. Listing C.1 contains the essential source code for this example. You'll find the complete source for this example in the \Appendix C\SOAPExample folder of the source code located on the Sybex Web site.

Listing C.1   SOAP Request Method

```
private void btnGetUser_Click(object sender, System.EventArgs e)
{
   ... Variable Declarations ...

   // Create the Web services.
   Service = new eBayAPIInterfaceService();

   // Define the call string.
   Service.Url = "https://api.sandbox.ebay.com/wsapi" +
                 "?callname=GetUser&siteid=0&appid=" +
                 txtAppID.Text + "&version=349";

   // Add the security information.
   Service.RequesterCredentials = new CustomSecurityHeaderType();
   Service.RequesterCredentials.Credentials = new UserIdPasswordType();
   Service.RequesterCredentials.Credentials.DevId = txtDevID.Text;
   Service.RequesterCredentials.Credentials.AppId = txtAppID.Text;
   Service.RequesterCredentials.Credentials.AuthCert = txtCertID.Text;

   // Add the user authentication token or the username and password.
   Service.RequesterCredentials.eBayAuthToken = txtUserAuth.Text;
   Service.RequesterCredentials.Credentials.Username = "User Name";
   Service.RequesterCredentials.Credentials.Password = "Password";

   // Define a detail level.
   DetLevel = new DetailLevelCodeType[1];
   DetLevel.SetValue(DetailLevelCodeType.ReturnAll, 0);

   // Create the request.
   UserDat = new GetUserRequestType();
   UserDat.UserID = txtUserID.Text;
   UserDat.DetailLevel = DetLevel;
   UserDat.Version = "349";

   //Response = new GetUserResponseType();
   try
   {
      // Make the call.
      Response = Service.GetUser(UserDat);
   }
   catch (System.Web.Services.Protocols.SoapException ex)
   {
         ... Error Handling ...
   }
```

```
    // Process the user response information.
    MessageBox.Show("User Name: " + Response.User.UserID + "\r\n" +
                    "Email: " + Response.User.Email,
                    "User Response Information");
}
```

The code begins by creating a new eBayAPIInterfaceService() object, Service, which is the connection between the client and the server. The first step is to create a value for the Service.Url property. Unlike either the API or SDK method, you must create a complex URL for a SOAP connection that includes the eBay Web Services environment (sandbox or production), the name of the method you want to call, a site identifier, the developer's application identifier, and the version number.

After the code creates the connection to the server, it begins building a series of credentials as part of the Service.RequesterCredentials property. As usual, you supply two kinds of credentials: developer and user. The only problem I ran into with the beta of the SOAP product is that it doesn't appear to accept a user authentication token as part of the Service.RequesterCredentials.eBayAuthToken property. The example shows how to add both kinds of user security. eBay will likely fix this problem shortly, so you should always try the user authentication token technique first.

Creating a request comes next. Part of this process is to define a detail level. When using the API and SDK methods, you provide a simple number. The SOAP technique requires that you create an array of the DetailLevelCodeType type and fill it with the kinds of data you want returned. In this case, the code returns all information by selecting the DetailLevelCodeType.ReturnAll enumerated value and adding it to the array.

This example requests user data from eBay Web Services by supplying a user identifier. The code creates a new GetUserRequestType object, UserDat, to hold the information. The request object must include the detail level and the compatibility level you want eBay to use. The actual call, Service.GetUser(UserDat), must appear in a try...catch block. It uses the connection to send the request data to eBay Web Services.

The returned data appears in Response. The example displays a simple dialog box containing the username and email address. However, eBay Web Services does supply other data that you can use in many cases.

Creating a Java SDK Application

The Java SDK currently distributed with the eBay Web Services Kit is admittedly difficult to use and error prone for some developers. Because eBay wants to make the development experience as easy as possible, you now have access to a new Java SDK. You can download the new eBay SDK for Java at http://developer.ebay.com/devprogram/preview.asp.

If you're using JCreator Pro, the product that I'm using for the example, you'll need to create a new library reference. The library files for this new SDK appear in the \eBaySDKforJava\ lib folder. You may also want to add a reference to the helper utilities located in the \eBaySDKforJava\samples\lib folder. This second reference isn't used in the example and you don't need it to create most applications, but it can come in handy.

The example application gets user information based on a user identifier. Listing C.2 shows the essential source code for this example. You'll find the complete source for this example in the \Appendix C\NewSDKDemo folder of the source code located on the Sybex Web site.

Listing C.2   **Making a Search Using the New Java Web API**

```java
public void actionPerformed(ActionEvent AE)
{
    ... Variable Declarations ...

    // End the program.
    if (AE.getSource() == btnQuit)
        System.exit(0);

    // Issue a request and receive a response.
    if (AE.getSource() == btnTest)
    {
        // Create a context.
        Context = new ApiContext();
        Context.setApiServerUrl("https://api.sandbox.ebay.com/wsapi");

        // Define the credentials.
        Cred = Context.getApiCredential();

        // Get the developer credentials.
        DevCred = Cred.getApiAccount();
        DevCred.setDeveloper(txtDevID.getText());
        DevCred.setApplication(txtAppID.getText());
        DevCred.setCertificate(txtCertID.getText());

        // Get the user credentials.
        Cred.seteBayToken(txtAuthToken.getText());

        // Use as an alternative with user name and password.
        //UserCred = Cred.geteBayAccount();
        //UserCred.setUsername("User ID");
        //UserCred.setPassword("Password");

        // Create the request.
        Req = new GetUserCall(Context);

        // Define the request arguments.
        Detail = new DetailLevelCodeType[]
        {
```

```
            DetailLevelCodeType.ReturnAll,
            DetailLevelCodeType.ItemReturnAttributes,
            DetailLevelCodeType.ItemReturnDescription
        };
        Req.setDetailLevel(Detail);
        Req.setUserID(txtSearch.getText());

        try
        {
            // Make the request.
            Response = Req.getUser();
        }
        catch (com.ebay.sdk.ApiException e)
        {
            ... Lots of Error Handling ...
        }

        // Display the response.
        txtUserName.setText(Response.getUserID().toString());
        txtEmail.setText(Response.getEmail());

    }
}
```

The code begins by creating a connection to eBay Web Services. Notice that this URL varies somewhat from the URL used by the API and SDK methods.

After the code creates the connection it adds credentials to it. The first step is to get the complete set of credentials using the getApiCredential() method. As normal, you provide two sets of credentials: user and developer. The developer credentials require that the code create an ApiAccount object, DevCred, and instantiate it using the getApiAccount() method. The preferred method of setting the user credentials is to provide an authentication token using the seteBayToken() method. However, the code shows how you would set the user credentials using a username and password. Be aware that this method is going to become unavailable.

As this point, the code creates a request. Notice that you instantiate the request object using the same technique as used for the API and SDK techniques. Always add the context as part of the constructor call. Creating the detail level is different from either the API or SDK techniques—you create an array with one or more of the DetailLevelCodeType enumeration members and add it to the request. To complete the request, the code adds the user identifier using the setUserID() method. The code finally makes the call using the same technique as the API and SDK techniques use now.

The code outputs the response. The Response object doesn't require much manipulation to get the data values. In this case, you see just the username and email address, but the Response object contains a wealth of other data.

Working with Single User Authentication

Part of the problem with the current authentication and authorization solution for eBay Web Services is that it relies on a Web application. Developers who create a desktop application are simply out of luck unless they create a Web component to that application. Fortunately, at least for now, there's a solution for developers who have limited authorization and authentication needs. You can find this single user tool at `https://developer.ebay.com/tokentool/Credentials.aspx`. The documentation for this tool appears at `http://developer.ebay.com/DevZone/docs/API_Doc/Developing/AuthAndAuthTool.htm`.

Before you get too overjoyed, this tool is less than automatic. You'll manually sign in and copy the resulting token. In other words, users will still know there's a Web component to the shiny new desktop application you've created. However, the tool is a step in the right direction. It helps you obtain the required user authentication token without a lot of extra work creating a custom setup.

This section of the appendix takes you through the process of using the single user tool in lieu of creating a special component for your application. Begin by going to the tool site at `https://developer.ebay.com/tokentool/Credentials.aspx`. The Web page includes entries to select the environment (production or sandbox) and your developer keys. Provide the required information and click Continue to Generate Token. This process takes a while, especially since you're using SSL, so be patient.

The next page you see is the login page for your organization. This is the same Web page the user sees when you set up the login for a Web application. Type the user ID and password you want to use. Make sure you use a user ID and password for the environment you're working in. Click Sign In. You see the same authorization page the user normally sees.

Read the agreement (if you haven't already) and click Agree and Continue. At this point, you'd normally see the token as part of a Web page you set up. However, the Auth & Auth Token Generator page contains the token you need as part of the Your Token field. Select the token, copy it, and paste it into your application. It's not a miracle cure for the authentication blues, but it does the job for small organizations or single developers.

Reading and Using the eBay Developer News

Everything in this book was accurate as of the day I wrote it. Yet, a week doesn't go by when a newsletter comes from eBay telling about new features, API fixes, and other useful information. Most developers have a hard time reading every newsletter or magazine that comes their way—information overload is a significant problem. However, you should take time to at least scan the eBay Developer News for breaking news that you're required to know to keep your applications current. You can always find the latest eBay Developer News at `http://developer` `.ebay.com/DevZone/community/newsletter/index.asp`. Word of updates to this site will arrive in your email, but a check before you begin something new is always a good idea.

As I write this, eBay Developer News contains information about a number of features that already appear in this book such as authentication and authorization. A few of the story items appear in this appendix including using SOAP and the new Java SDK. Unfortunately, not every item in the news is ready for prime time as I write this, so you'll need to discover them on your own. For example, eBay is working on an update to the API (version 353) that contains an interesting new call, `GetRecommendations()`, which provides recommendations for the attributes for the items you sell. eBay is also modifying the `ValidateTestUserRegistration()` call so you can modify test user values such as the registration date and feedback score. Sellers will also be able to offer multiple shipping services now, such as UPS and USPS.

Working with PayPal

Strictly speaking, PayPal Web Services are completely separate from eBay Web Services, even though both Web services are developed by eBay. PayPal is a system for taking care of all the financial details for purchases. For example, you can use PayPal on eBay to buy new products. However, eBay isn't the only place you can use PayPal. It's also possible to use PayPal to buy products on Amazon. In short, PayPal is another form of payment service akin to a credit card, but without the potential security problems of credit cards because your information is kept on a single secure site (at least you know where to go if your information is compromised).

You'd use PayPal Web Services if you wanted to add a simple payment mechanism to your own Web site. The purchases need not be for eBay or Amazon or any other particular online site—they can be for your own merchandise. Because this Web service is completely separate from eBay, you need to obtain new credentials from PayPal Developer Central at `https://` `developer.paypal.com/`. Your eBay credentials won't work.

Once you get past the new credentials though, you'll notice that many PayPal Web Service features look just like those used by eBay Web Services. For example, you work in a sandbox mode until your application is certified. eBay was able to use experience gained in the past to make PayPal Web Services better. For example, it relies on the same SOAP mechanisms described in the "Creating an Application Using SOAP" section of the chapter. Consequently, the information you learned in this book directly translates to your PayPal experience too.

PayPal Web Services is completely new at the time of writing, so I wasn't able to put an example together for you. The developer site is functional, but I found that some downloads aren't available yet. These downloads should be available by the time the book is in print, so you'll want to try out the PayPal Web Services when you need to add payment options to your own Web site.

▶ Glossary

This book includes a glossary so that you can find terms and acronyms easily. It has several important features you need to know about. First, every acronym in the entire book appears here—even if there's a better than even chance you already know what the acronym stands for. (The book does exclude common acronyms such as units of measure and most file extensions because these terms are easy to find in other sources and most people know what they mean.) This way, there isn't any doubt that you'll always find everything you need to use the book properly.

Second, these definitions are specific to the book. In other words, when you look through this glossary, you're seeing the words defined in the context in which they're used in this book. This might or might not always coincide with current industry usage since the computer industry changes the meaning of words so often.

Finally, I've used a conversational tone for the definitions in most cases. This means that the definitions might sacrifice a bit of puritanical accuracy for the sake of better understanding. The purpose of this glossary is to define the terms in such a way that there's less room for misunderstanding the intent of the book as a whole.

What to Do If You Don't Find It Here

While this glossary is a complete view of the words and acronyms in the book, you'll run into situations when you need to know more. No matter how closely I look at terms throughout the book, there's always a chance I'll miss the one acronym or term that you really need to know. In addition to the technical information found in the book, I've directed your attention to numerous online sources of information throughout the book and few of the terms the Web site owners use will appear here unless I also chose to use them in the book. Fortunately, many sites on the Internet provide partial or complete glossaries to fill in the gaps:

Acronym Finder   `http://www.acronymfinder.com/`

Free Online Dictionary Of Computing (FOLDOC)   `http://nightflight.com/foldoc/`

Microsoft Encarta   `http://encarta.msn.com/`

TechDis Accessibility Database   `http://www.niad.sussex.ac.uk/glossary.cfm`

Webopedia   `http://webopedia.internet.com/`

yourDictionary.com   `http://www.yourdictionary.com/`

A

Accessibility A measure of a user's ability to interact with an application. For example, applications should provide both mouse and keyboard access to every control to ensure the user can reach the control for use. In addition to direct user support, an application should support all devices without providing specialized support for a particular device unless necessary. A Braille input device should receive no special treatment beyond that required for a keyboard.

Active Server Pages (ASP) A special type of scripting language environment used by Windows servers equipped with Internet Information Server (IIS). This specialized scripting language environment helps the developer create flexible Web applications that include server scripts written in a number of languages such as VBScript, JavaScript, JScript, and PerlScript. The use of variables and other features, such as access to server variables, helps the developer create scripts that can compensate for user and environmental needs, as well as security concerns. ASP uses HTML to display content to the user. Recent extensions to ASP in the form of Active Server Pages eXtended (ASPX) provide a broader range of application support functionality, improved debugging, new features such as "code behind," and improved performance.

API See Application Programming Interface

Applet A helper or utility application that normally performs a task within a specialized environment such as a browser or as part of an operating system. Java is one of the most commonly used languages for creating applets for browser applications. Another example is the Control Panel applications used to configure Windows. In both cases, the applications perform a limited task within a specialized environment.

Application Programming Interface (API) A method of defining a standard set of function calls and other interface elements. It usually defines the interface between a high-level language and the lower-level elements used by a device driver or operating system. The ultimate goal is to provide some type of service to an application that requires access to the operating system or device feature set.

Array A structure that acts like an in-memory database. An array provides random or sequential access each element by number (also called a subscript). Arrays normally contain a single dimension. In some cases, arrays provide multidimensional access to data. A multidimensional array has the same number of elements in each sub-array in a given dimension. Jagged arrays treat each dimension as a separate sub-array, which means that each sub-array can contain a different number of elements.

ASP See Active Server Pages

Attribute An attribute expresses some feature peculiar to an object. When referring to a database, each field has an attribute that expresses what type of information it contains, the length of the field, the field name, and the number of decimals. When referring to a display, the attribute expresses pixel color, intensity, and position. In programming, an attribute can also specify some type of object functionality, such as the method used to implement security.

B

Bandwidth A measure of the amount of data a device can transfer in a given time. For example, the amount of data a processor can send to memory every second. In many cases, bandwidth also considers software limitations, such as the estimated bandwidth of an Internet connection.

Binary 1. A numbering system that only uses two digits: 0 and 1. 2. A method used to store worksheets, graphic files, and other nontext information. The data store can appear in memory, but most often appears in a file on disk. While you can use the DOS TYPE command to send these files to the display, the contents of the file remain unreadable. Other binary files include programs with extensions of EXE, DLL, or COM.

Boolean A method of determining whether a statement is true or false using rules of logic. Boolean values are often used to help a computer determine whether it needs to take a certain course of action based on current system or application conditions.

Browser A special application, such as Internet Explorer, Opera, or Netscape, normally used to display data downloaded from the Internet. The most common form of Internet data is the HTML (HyperText Markup Language) page. However, modern browsers can also display various types of graphics and even standard desktop application files such as Word for Windows documents directly. The actual capabilities provided by a browser vary widely depending on the software vendor and platform.

Buffer   The area in memory where program variables, data, or executable code is stored. Buffers often act as a means of caching data or code. For example, word processing applications will normally read more than one page from a document to improve performance. The applications store pages in addition to the one currently viewed by the user in the buffer until needed. Buffering is also used in applications where long request delays are anticipated, such as applications based on Web services.

C

Cache   A storage area for data, code, or other resources normally associated with memory or a special file on a hard drive. Both hardware and applications rely on the cache to improve performance.

CAD   See Computer-Aided Drafting

Cascading Style Sheets (CSS)   A method for defining a standard Web page template. This may include headings, standard icons, backgrounds, and other features that would tend to give each page at a particular Web site the same appearance. The reason for using CSS includes speed of creating a Web site (it takes less time if the developer doesn't have to create an overall design for each page) and consistency. Changing the overall appearance of a Web site also becomes as easy as changing the style sheet instead of each page alone. CSS is also a standards supported technology, so it represents an easy method for developers to create Web pages that will work in standards-compliant browsers. Note that there is a CSS Level 2, CSS2, that builds on the features of CSS Level 1. You can read about CSS2 at http://www.w3.org/TR/REC-CSS2/.

CFHTTP   Cold Fusion HyperText Transfer Protocol

CGI   See Common Gateway Interface

CIP   See Computer Investment Program

Client   The requestor and recipient of data, services, or other resources from a file or other server type. This term can refer to a workstation or an application. Often used in conjunction with the term *server*, this is usually another PC or an application.

CLR   See Common Language Runtime

COM   See Component Object Model

Common Gateway Interface (CGI)   One of the more common methods of transferring data from a client machine to a Web server on the Internet. CGI is a specification that defines how a Web server can launch EXEs and communicate with them. A developer normally writes a CGI application using a low-level language such as C. CGI receives input through the standard input device and output data through the standard output device. There are two basic data transfer types. The user can send new information to the server or can query data already existing on the server. A data entry form asking for the user's name and address is an example of the first type of transaction. A search engine page on the Internet (a page that helps the user find information on other sites) is an example of the second type of transaction. The Web server normally provides some type of feedback for the user by transmitting a new page of information once the CGI application is complete. This could be as simple as an acknowledgment for data entry or a list of Internet sites for a data query.

Common Language Runtime (CLR)   The engine used to interpret managed applications within the .NET Framework. All Visual Studio .NET languages that produce managed applications can use the same runtime engine. The major advantages of this approach include extensibility (you can add other languages) and reduced code size (you don't need a separate runtime for each language).

Common Object Request Broker Architecture (CORBA)   This protocol describes data and application code in the form of an object. This is the Object Management Group's (OMG) alternative to Microsoft's Component Object Model (COM). Although CORBA is incompatible with COM, it uses many of the same techniques as COM to create, manage, and define objects. CORBA was originally designed by IBM for inclusion with OS/2.

Compiler   A program that converts English-like statements into machine instructions in an executable or intermediate form. In some cases, the executable code can run without assistance on the host machine (called a native executable). In other cases, the intermediate code requires compilation into an executable form. This secondary form can rely on an interpreter (BASIC) or runtime engine (Java), or it can use a secondary compiler or linker to change an object format into a standard native executable (C).

Component Object Model (COM)   A Microsoft specification for a binary-based, object-oriented

code and data encapsulation method and transference technique. It's the basis for technologies such as OLE (Object Linking and Embedding) and ActiveX (components and controls). COM is limited to local connections.

Computer Investment Program (CIP)   A special buying program for German computer users who meet specific requirements.

Computer-Aided Drafting (CAD)   A special type of graphics program used for creating, printing, storing, and editing architectural, electrical, mechanical, or other forms of engineering drawings. CAD programs normally provide precise measuring capabilities and libraries of predefined objects, such as sinks, desks, resistors, and gears.

Connectivity   A measure of the interactions between clients and servers. In many cases, connectivity begins with the local machine and the interactions between applications and components. Local Area Networks (LANs) introduce another level of connectivity with machine-to-machine communications. Finally, Wide Area Networks (WANs), Metro Area Networks (MANs), intranets, and the Internet all introduce further levels of connectivity concerns.

Container   In programming terms, an object used to hold other objects. For example, when working with XML, the container is the parent node of the current node. The root node is the container of all nodes within the XML document except for the processing instruction that defines the file type. When viewed from an Object Linking and Embedding (OLE) perspective, the container is a drive, file, or other resource used to hold objects. The container is normally referenced as an object itself.

CORBA See Common Object Request Broker Architecture

Cracker A hacker (computer expert) who uses their skills for misdeeds on computer systems where they have little or no authorized access. A cracker normally possesses specialty software that allows easier access to the target network. In most cases, crackers require extensive amounts of time to break the security for a system before they can enter it. Some sources call a cracker a black hat hacker.

CSS See Cascading Style Sheets

D

Data Mining The act of retrieving specific data from a data source. In most cases, the receiving application combines the data with data from other sources to create a composite that reflects a new use for the existing information. The data sources need not have any connection and the data need not be entered for the use intended by the data mining application.

Database A data collection that consists of one or more storage elements and any associated objects. The organization of the database depends on the features and functionality of the Database Management System (DBMS) used to maintain it. A database normally uses a hierarchical or tabular format. A hierarchical database relies on nodes connected in any of a number of ways, such as record pointers. The tabular format relies on rows (records) made up of columns (fields). A database can appear as a single file, as part of a collection with the DBMS, as part of a

worksheet for a spreadsheet, or any other organized disk format.

Database Management System (DBMS) A method for storing and retrieving data based on tables, forms, queries, reports, fields, and other data elements. Each field represents a specific piece of data, such as an employee's last name. Records are made up of one or more fields. Each record is one complete entry in a table. A table contains one type of data, such as the names and addresses of all the employees in a company. It's composed of records (rows) and fields (columns), just like the tables you see in books. A database may contain one or more related tables. It may include a list of employees in one table, for example, and the pay records for each of those employees in a second table. Sometimes also referred to as a Relational Database Management System (RDBMS) that includes products such as SQL Server and Oracle.

DBMS See Database Management System

DCOM See Distributed Component Object Model

Delimiter 1. A special symbol or symbols used to separate text. For example, many programming languages use the single (') or double (") quote to separate text elements. 2. A boundary between two different objects. The boundary normally consists of a special symbol or group of symbols. A delimited file contains variable length records. Each field normally uses a comma as a delimiter. Each record normally uses a carriage return as a delimiter.

Digital Subscriber Line (DSL) A term used to refer to any of a number of technologies that allow higher communication rates over standard telephone lines than normally allowed using standard modems. DSL is normally used between a remote location such as a home or office and the switching station or ISP. It isn't used between switching stations. Types of DSLs include asynchronous DSL (ADSL), symmetric DSL (SDSL), and high bit-rate DSL (HDSL). The technologies vary by their ability to pack data onto the copper line, distance from the switching station, and other characteristics. ADSL allows communication from 1.5Mbps to 9Mbps downstream (to the remote connection) and 16Kbps to 640Kbps upstream (from the remote connection). SDSL allows communication up to 3Mbps in both directions. HDSL allows communication up to 1.544Mbps in both directions.

Digital Video Disk (DVD)   A high capacity optical storage media with capacities of 4.7GB to 17GB and data transfer rates of 600KBps to 1.3GBps. A single DVD can hold the contents of an entire movie or approximate 7.4 CD-ROMs. DVDs come in several formats that allow read-only or read-write access. All DVD drives include a second laser assembly used to read existing CD-ROMs. Some magazines will also use the term *digital versatile disk* for this storage media.

Distributed Component Object Model (DCOM)   A transport protocol that works with the Component Object Model (COM), and is used for distributed application development. This protocol enables data transfers across the Internet or other nonlocal sources, but is usually limited to a Local Area Network (LAN) or Wide Area Network (WAN) environment. DCOM adds the capability to perform asynchronous, as well as synchronous, data transfers between machines. The use

of asynchronous transfers prevents the client application from becoming blocked as it waits for the server to respond.

DLL   See Dynamic Link Library

Document Type Definition (DTD)   A document that defines how an application should interpret markup tags within a HyperText Markup Language (HTML), eXtensible Markup Language (XML), or Standard Generalized Markup Language (SGML) document. In some cases, such as HTML, the DTD is an actual specification. In other cases, such as XML, the DTD is an external document supplied by the user or the vendor. A DTD can define every characteristic of a document as long as those characteristics are defined using standard tags and attributes.

DSL   See Digital Subscriber Line

DTD   See Document Type Definition

DVD   See Digital Video Disk

Dynamic Data   Information that changes regularly due to internal or external events, as a result of the nature of the data, or consistent with a systematic or mathematical progression. For example, an application can provide automatic updates as it detects changes in the underlying data used for presentation. Many research sources, such as the Internet, now rely on dynamic data to reduce the effects of data aging.

Dynamic Link Library (DLL)   A specific form of application code loaded into memory by request. It's not executable by itself like an EXE is. A DLL does contain one or more discrete routines that an application may use to provide specific features. For example, a DLL could provide a common set of file dialogs used to access information on the hard drive. More than one application can use the functions provided by a DLL, reducing overall memory requirements when more than one application is running. DLLs have a number of purposes. For example, they can contain device-specific code in the form of a device driver. Some types of COM objects also rely on DLLs.

E

ECMA   See European Computer Manufacturer's Association

embedded Visual Basic (eVB)   A specialized form of Visual Basic designed for use with mobile devices. This product has fewer features than standard Visual Basic and produces native code files that run on the host mobile device. Many developers now rely on newer alternatives to this programming environment such as the .NET Compact Framework.

Emulator   A specialized application that provides the same features and functionality as the target device. The device on which the emulator runs is normally more capable than the emulated device. For example, emulators commonly enable a developer to test applications designed for use on Personal Digital Assistants (PDAs) using the standard PC.

Encryption   The act of making data unreadable using a mathematical conversion. The data remains unreadable unless the reader provides a password or other key value. Encryption makes data safe for transport in unsecured environments like the Internet.

Error Trapping   The additional code required to detect, analyze, repair, report, and overcome errors in an application. An error trapping routine normally locates the precise origin of the error, determines the error type, and defines a course of action for repairing the error when possible. If the application can't recover, the error trapping routine helps the application fail gracefully after reporting the source and cause of the error to the application user.

European Computer Manufacturer's Association (ECMA)   A standards committee originally founded in 1961. ECMA is dedicated to standardizing information and communication systems. For example, it created the ECMAScript standard used for many Web page designs today. You can also find ECMA standards for product safety, security, networks, and storage media.

eVB   See embedded Visual Basic

eXtensible Hypertext Markup Language (XHTML)   A cross between eXtensible Markup Language (XML) and HyperText Markup Language (HTML) specifically designed for Internet devices such as Personal Digital Assistants (PDAs) and cellular telephones, but also usable with desktop machine browsers. Since this language relies on XML, most developers classify it as an XML application builder. The language relies on several standardized namespaces to provide common data type and interface definitions. XHTML creates modules that are interpreted based on a specific platform's requirements. This means that a single document can serve the needs of many display devices.

eXtensible Markup Language (XML) 1. A method used to store information in an organized manner. The storage technique relies on hierarchical organization and uses special statements called tags to separate each storage element. Each tag defines a data attribute and can contain properties that further define each data element. 2. A standardized Web page design language used to incorporate data structuring within standard HTML documents. For example, you could use XML to display database information using something other than forms or tables. It's actually a lightweight version of Standard Generalized Markup Language (SGML) and is supported by the SGML community. XML also supports tag extensions that allow various parts of a Web-based application to exchange information. For example, once a user makes a choice within a catalog, that information could be added to an order entry form with a minimum of effort on the part of the developer. Since XML is easy to extend, some developers look at it as more of a base specification for other languages, rather than a complete language.

eXtensible Style Language (XSL) This term is also listed as eXtensible Stylesheet Language by some sources. XSL is a technology that separates the method of presentation from the actual content of either an eXtensible Markup Language (XML) or HyperText Markup Language (HTML) page. The XSL document contains all of the required formatting information so that the content remains in pure form. This is the second style language submitted to the World Wide Web Consortium (W3C) for consideration. The first specification was for Cascading Style Sheets (CSS). XSL documents use an XML-like format.

eXtensible Style Language Transformation (XSLT) The language used within the eXtensible Style Language (XSL) to transform the content provided in an eXtensible Markup Language (XML) file into a form for display on screen or printing. An XSL processor combines XML content with the formatting instructions provided by XSLT and outputs a new document or document fragment. XSLT is a World Wide Web Consortium (W3C) standard.

F

Fault Tolerance The ability of an object (application, device, or other entity) to recover from an error. For example, the fault tolerance provided by a transaction server allows a network to recover from potential data loss induced by a system or use failure. Another example of fault tolerance is the ability of a Redundant Array of Inexpensive Disks (RAID) system to recover from a hard drive failure.

G

Graphical User Interface (GUI) 1. A method of displaying information that depends on both hardware capabilities and software instructions. A GUI uses the graphics capability of a display adapter to improve communication between the computer and its user. Using a GUI involves a large investment in both programming and hardware resources. 2. A system of icons and graphic images that replaces the character-mode menu system used by many older machines including "green screen" terminals that are connected to mainframes and sometimes to cash registers. The GUI can ride on top of another operating system (such as DOS, Linux, and Unix) or reside as part of the operating system itself (such as the Macintosh and Windows). Advantages of a GUI are ease of use and high-resolution graphics. Disadvantages include cost, higher workstation hardware requirements, and lower performance over a similar system using a character mode interface.

GUI   See Graphical User Interface

H

Hacker   An individual who works with computers at a low level (hardware or software), especially in the area of security. A hacker normally possesses specialty software or other tools that allows easier access to the target hardware or software application or network. The media defines two types of hackers that include those that break into systems for ethical purposes and those that do it to damage the system in some way. The proper term for the second group is *crackers* (see Cracker for details). Some people have started to call the first group *ethical hackers* or *white hat hackers* to prevent confusion. Ethical hackers normally work for security firms that specialize in finding holes in a company's security. However, hackers work in a wide range of computer arenas. For example, a person who writes low-level code (like that found in a device driver) after reverse engineering an existing driver is technically a hacker. The main emphasis of a hacker is to work for the benefit of others in the computer industry.

Handheld Device Markup Language (HDML)   A technology that predates most standardized efforts, such as the Wireless Access Protocol (WAP), for transmitting Internet content to cellular telephones. It's a proprietary language that users can only view using Openwave browsers. The associated transport protocol is the Handheld Device Transport Protocol (HDTP). A user types a request into the phone, which is transferred to a gateway server using HDTP. The gateway server translates the request to HTTP, which it sends to the Web server. The Web server provides specialized HDML content, which the gateway server transfers to the cellular telephone using HDTP. To use this protocol, the Web server must understand the `text/x-hdml` Multipurpose Internet Mail Extensions (MIME) type.

HDML   See Handheld Device Markup Language

Hierarchical   1. A method of arranging data within a database that relies on a tree-like node structure, rather than a relational structure. 2. A method of displaying information on screen that relies on an indeterminate number of nodes connected to a root node. 3. A chart or graph in which the elements are arranged in ranks. The ranks usually follow an order of simple to complex or higher to lower.

HTML   See HyperText Markup Language

HTTP   See HyperText Transfer Protocol

HTTPS   See HyperText Transfer Protocol Secure sockets

HyperText Markup Language (HTML)   1. A data presentation and description (markup) language for the Internet that depends on the use of tags (keywords within angle brackets <>) to display formatted information on screen in a non-platform-specific manner. The non-platform-specific nature of this markup language makes it difficult to perform some basic tasks such as placement of a screen element at a specific location. However, the language does provide for the use of fonts, color, and various other enhancements on screen. There are also tags for displaying graphic images. Scripting tags for using scripting languages such as VBScript and JavaScript are available, although not all browsers support this addition. The <OBJECT> tag addition allows the use of ActiveX controls. 2. One method of displaying text, graphics, and sound on the Internet. HTML provides an ASCII-formatted page of information read by a special application called a browser. Depending on the browser's capabilities, some key words are translated into graphics elements, sounds, or text with special characteristics, such as color, font, or other attributes. Most browsers discard any keywords they don't understand, allowing browsers of various capabilities to explore the same page without problem. Obviously, there's a loss of capability if a browser doesn't support a specific keyword.

HyperText Transfer Protocol (HTTP)   One of several common data transfer protocols for the Internet. HTTP normally transfers textual data of some type. For example, the HyperText Markup Language (HTML) relies on HTTP to transfer the Web pages it defines from the server to the client. The eXtensible Markup Language and Simple Object Access Protocol (SOAP) also commonly rely on HTTP to transfer data between client and server. It's important to note that HTTP is separate from the data it transfers. For example, it's possible for SOAP to use the Simple Mail Transfer Protocol (SMTP) to perform data transfers between client and server.

HyperText Transfer Protocol Secure sockets (HTTPS)   A secure form of HTTP that relies on the secure sockets encryption technology to transfer data.

I

IDE   See Integrated Development Environment

IETF   See Internet Engineering Task Force

IIS   See Internet Information Server

Infrastructure   The underlying base of an organization or system. One way to view infrastructure is a foundation on which all other elements of a system or organization are attached. Many vendors use this term to indicate the compatibility of their product with existing installations.

Integrated Development Environment (IDE)   A programming language front end that provides all the tools you need to write an application through a single editor. The IDE normally includes support for development language help, access to any tools required to support the language, a compiler, and a debugger. Some IDEs include support for advanced features such as automatic completion of language statements and balloon help showing the syntax for functions and other language elements. Many IDEs also use color or highlighting to emphasize specific language elements or constructs. Older DOS programming language products provided several utilities—one for each of the main programming tasks. Most (if not all) Windows programming languages provide some kind of IDE support.

Internet Engineering Task Force (IETF)   The standards group tasked with finding solutions to pressing technology problems on the Internet. This group can approve standards created both within the organization itself and outside the organization as part of other group efforts. For example, Microsoft has requested the approval of several new Internet technologies through this group. If approved, the technologies would become Internet-wide standards for performing data transfer and other specific kinds of tasks.

Internet Information Server (IIS)   Microsoft's full-fledged Web server that normally runs under the Windows Server operating system. IIS includes all the features that you'd normally expect with a Web server: FTP and HTTP protocols along with both mail and news services. Older versions of IIS also support the Gopher protocol; newer versions don't provide this support because most Web sites no longer need it.

Internet Protocol (IP)   The information exchange portion of the TCP/IP protocol used by the Internet. IP is an actual data transfer protocol that defines how the sender places information into packets and transmits from one place to another. TCP (Transmission Control Protocol) is the protocol that defines how the actual data transfer takes place.

Internet Server Application Programming Interface (ISAPI)   A set of function calls and interface elements designed to help developers create

applications for Microsoft's Internet Information Server (IIS). Essentially, this set of API calls provides the programmer with access to the server itself. This technology makes it easier to provide full application access to the Internet server so the developer can perform tasks such as Web page redirection, security checks, and incoming data parsing. There are two forms of ISAPI: filters and extensions. An extension replaces script-based technologies like CGI. Its main purpose is to provide dynamic content to the user. A filter can extend the server itself by monitoring various events like user requests for access in the background. You can use a filter to create various types of new services like extended logging or specialized security schemes. Most developers use technologies such as Active Server Pages (ASP) in place of ISAPI because these technologies are easier to use. For example, ASP makes it easy to modify a file without the need to recompile it. However, ISAPI is still used for speed critical applications such as the Simple Object Access Protocol (SOAP) listener used by some SOAP implementations.

Internet Service Provider (ISP)   A vendor that provides one or more Internet-related services through a dial-up, Digital Subscriber Line (DSL), Integrated Services Digital Network (ISDN), or other outside connection. Normal services include email, newsgroup access, full Internet Web site access, and personal Web page hosting.

IP   See Internet Protocol

ISAPI   See Internet Server Application Programming Interface

ISP   See Internet Service Provider

J

JACOB   See Java Component Object Model Bridge

Java Component Object Model Bridge (JACOB)   A special DLL used to create a connection between Java applications and the Component Object Model (COM) technology provided on Windows machine. This DLL lets Java developers use COM objects within their application.

Java Development Kit (JDK)   A special set of application development tools, resources, example code, help files, and other resources designed to help a programmer create Java applications. The JDK normally contains a full set of development tools and a copy of the Java Runtime Enviroment (JRE). However, most developers will require one or more third party solutions to create a complex Java application. For example, unlike many languages today, Java doesn't provide SOAP support, so the developer would require a third party library to create an application that relies on SOAP.

Java Runtime Environment (JRE)   Another name for the Java Virtual Machine (JVM). This set of files provides Java support on the host machine allowing it to run Java applications.

Java Virtual Machine (JVM)   The application used to interpret the Java language originally developed by Sun Microsystems. This includes both text and byte code .CLASS files containing common routines. Java is similar to C++, but eliminates many of the complex programming constructs and uses a more restrictive security scheme. Many operating systems have a Java Virtual Machine including most versions of Windows, Mac OS, and Unix. The use of text files means that Java applets can run on any number of operating system platforms without modifications, but the use of an interpreter implies slower execution speed.

JDK   See Java Development Kit

JRE   See Java Runtime Environment

JVM   See Java Virtual Machine

L

LAN   See Local Area Network

Local Area Network (LAN)   Two or more devices located in a relatively small physical area connected together using a combination of hardware and software. The devices, normally computers and peripheral equipment such as printers, are called nodes. A NIC (network interface card) provides the hardware communication between nodes through an appropriate medium (cable or microwave transmission). The actual connection is provided through cables, in many cases, but can also rely on radio waves, infrared, and other technologies. There are two common types of LANs (also called networks). Peer-to-peer networks allow each node to connect to any other node on the network with shareable resources. This is a distributed method of files and peripheral devices. A client-server network uses one or more servers to share resources. This is a centralized method of sharing files and peripheral devices. A server provides resources to clients (usually workstations).

M

Microsoft Database Engine (MSDE)   This term also appears as Microsoft Desktop Engine and Microsoft Data Engine in various publications. MSDE is a miniature form of SQL Server that enables developers to create test database applications. Microsoft designed this engine for use by one person, usually the developer, although you can potentially use it for up to five people. The developer accesses MSDE through a programming language Integrated Development Environment (IDE) or using command line utilities. In some cases, MSDE is also used to provide access to a remote copy of SQL Server. Some third party products, such as MSDE Query, provide a Graphical User Interface (GUI) for MSDE.

Microsoft eXtensible Markup Language Core Services (MSXML)   The executable code, special packaging, help files, and other resources used to provide the Microsoft XML support on Windows.

MSDE   See Microsoft Database Engine

MSXML   See Microsoft eXtensible Markup Language Core Services

N

Node   1. A single element in a file that might contain a number of leaf elements. The file normally couples nodes into a hierarchical structure, such as the structure used by the eXtensible Markup Language (XML). Some database systems also use the hierarchical structure of nodes and leaves to make data easier or faster to locate. 2. A single element in a network. In most cases, the term *node* refers to a single workstation connected to the network. It can also refer to a bridge, router, or file server. It doesn't refer to cabling, passive, or active elements that don't directly interface with the network at the logical level.

Non-connected Mode   A state in which the client can't communicate with the server. Most applications don't provide support for a non-connected mode unless they also provide some type of caching. For example, an application that normally communicates with a database over a network usually needs to maintain a connection to the database to operate. In some cases, applications support non-connected mode by establishing a local cache of data found at a remote resource, such as a Web service, by storing common data in a local database.

O

Object-Oriented Programming (OOP)   A method of programming that relies on objects. An object is one fully described section of code that includes properties (object values), methods (techniques for interacting with the object), and events (the means the object uses to communicate with the outside world). Unlike procedural code, everything needed to describe a particular task is included in one object. OOP encourages code reuse and reduces interaction-type programming errors since each object is self-contained.

OOP   See Object-Oriented Programming

P

P3P   See Platform for Privacy Preferences

Palm   A mobile, proprietary, handheld device produced by Palm Computing, Inc., which is normally associated with office tasks such as maintaining an address list or appointment calendar. The Palm uses the Palm operating system. Although this device lacks the processing power of higher end devices such as the Pocket PC, most office workers prefer its small size and long battery life.

Parameter   A value received by a function or procedure from another function or procedure, the command line, or some other source.

Parse   The act of reducing a string or other data structure to its constituent parts. For example, spreadsheets normally break words and numbers apart using the spaces between them as the break point. Developers use a multitude of application programming techniques to perform data element parsing and some object technology even includes a `Parse()` method.

PDA   See Personal Digital Assistant

PERL   See Practical Extraction and Report Language

Personal Digital Assistant (PDA)   A small handheld device such as a Palm Pilot or Pocket PC. These devices are normally used for personal tasks such as taking notes and maintaining an itinerary during business trips. Some PDAs rely on special operating systems and lack any standard application support. However, newer PDAs include some level of standard application support, because vendors are supplying specialized compilers for them. In addition, you'll find common applications included, such as browsers and application office suites, that include word processing and spreadsheet support.

Personal Web Server (PWS)   A less capable version of Internet Information Server (IIS) that's designed to provided limited Web access on an intranet. PWS isn't designed to provide the same level of services as IIS, but it does provide enough capability for a small company intranet or for a developer's test setup.

PHP   PHP Hypertext Processor

Platform   A description of the combination of software and hardware used to create a computing system. For example, many users use a combination of the Windows operating system and an Intel processor. The combination often appears as the Wintel platform. In some cases, a discussion will only use the operating system as the basis for a platform. A developer might create applications only for the Windows platform. The use of the term *platform* is often ambiguous and requires the actual platform type to make the meaning clear.

Platform for Privacy Preferences (P3P)   A Worldwide Web Consortium (W3C) sponsored technique for ensuring privacy through specialized programming techniques. The specification defines methods of communicating information requests, use, storage technique, and requirements to the requestor. The requestor then decides whether the requirements are acceptable and optionally transfers the necessary information.

Point of Presence (POP)   An access point to the Internet normally associated with physical access such as a modem connection.

Pocket PC   A mobile, handheld device used to perform any of a number of computing tasks. A Pocket PC normally runs some form or advanced mobile operating system such as Windows CE or Windows XP. Most developers differentiate a Pocket PC from a Palm handheld device by the enhanced processing power, greater number of features, and larger display of the Pocket PC. A Pocket PC is also bulkier than a Palm, making it less suitable for some applications.

POP   See Point of Presence

Practical Extraction and Report Language (PERL) Originally designed as a report generation language for the Internet, PERL has found other uses, as well, for more general Internet programming needs. PERL is normally an interpreted scripting language.

PWS   See Personal Web Server

Q

Query   A request or question made by a user of an application program using an interface. The query can appear as part of a form or other type of input, or the user can make the query as part of a script when using automation. Common queries include search requests for documents or a request to perform a task such as checking the status of the computer hardware.

R

RAID   See Redundant Array of Independent (or Inexpensive) Disks

Recordset   The result of a query on one or more tables of a database. A recordset contains a single result set consisting of a single table. The recordset relies on a connection with the DBMS in order to perform data exchanges and updates.

Redundant Array of Independent (or Inexpensive) Disks (RAID)   A set of interconnected drives that reside outside the server in many cases, but are connected to the server through cabling. Workstation RAID setups tend to reside in the workstation cabinet. There are several levels of RAID. Each level defines precisely how the data is placed on each of the drives. In all cases, all the drives in a group share responsibility for storing the data. They act in parallel to both read and write the data. In addition, there is a special drive in most of these systems devoted to helping the network recover when one drive fails. In most cases the user never even knows that anything happened, the "spare drive" takes over for the failed drive without any noticeable degradation in network operation. RAID systems increase network reliability and throughput.

Remote Procedure Call (RPC)   One of several methods for accessing data within another application. RPC is designed to look for the application first on the local workstation, and then across the network at the applications stored on other workstations.

REpresentational State Transfer (REST)   A technique for passing data to a Web service using one or more arguments as part of an URL. Each argument represents an XML node that the client would normally pass as an XML document. This technique is also known as XML-over-HTTP. The input to the Web server is a standard URL with arguments, while the output is an XML document. Some developers use this technique to reduce the coding required to obtain Web service output on less capable devices or on Web sites.

REST   See REpresentational State Transfer

RPC   See Remote Procedure Call

S

Sandbox   1. A special environment for application execution that prevents access to other areas of the system. The application is cut off from any resources it doesn't need. Many application execution environments rely on this technique to improve overall system security and reliability. 2. An alternative execution environment that mimics a production environment. The two environments offer the same features and functionality. In most cases, the sandbox environment also offers test data, which is based on the production environment data. The application developer uses the sandbox for application testing and demonstration purposes.

Schema   A formal method for describing the structure of a database, storage technology, or data transfer technique such as XML. The schema defines the requirements for constructing the object in question. For example, a schema for a relational database would include information on the structure of tables, fields, and relations within the database.

Screen Scraping   A technique for removing data from a Web page. The goal is to remove the data without damaging it in any way and without removing any tags or formatting information with the data. In many cases, the developer uses this technique to interact with the Web site through an application program.

Script   Usually associated with an interpreted macro language used to create simple applications, productivity enhancers, or automated data manipulators. Most operating systems support at least one scripting language. You'll also find scripting capability in many higher end applications such as Web browsers and word processors. Scripts are normally used to write small utility-type applications rather than large-scale applications that require the use of a compiled language. In addition, many scripting languages are limited in their access of the full set of operating system features.

SDK   See Software Development Kit

Secure Socket Layer (SSL)   A digital signature technology used for exchanging information between a client and a server. Essentially an SSL-compliant server will request a digital certificate from the client machine. The client can likewise request a digital certificate from the server. Companies or individuals obtain these digital certificates from a third party vendor like VeriSign or other trusted source that can vouch for the identity of both parties.

Serializer   Specialized software used to convert data chunks, such as a string or a file, into individual bits for transmission to a remote location. The act of serializing data makes it possible to transfer large quantities of data as individualized bits and then reconstruct the original form at the remote location.

Simple Mail Transfer Protocol (SMTP)   One of the most commonly used protocols to transfer text (commonly mail) messages between clients and servers. This is a stream-based protocol designed to allow query, retrieval, posting, and distribution of mail messages. Normally, this protocol is used in conjunction with other mail retrieval protocols like point of presence (POP). However, not all uses of SMTP involve email data transfer. Some Simple Object Access Protocol (SOAP) applications have also relied on SMTP to transfer application data.

Simple Object Access Protocol (SOAP)   A Microsoft-sponsored protocol that provides the means for exchanging data between COM and foreign component technologies like Common Object Request Broker Architecture (CORBA) using XML as an intermediary. SOAP is often used as the basis for Web services communication. However, a developer could also use SOAP on a LAN or in any other environment where machine-to-machine communication is required and the two target machines provide the required infrastructure.

SLN   See Solution File

Smartphone   A special form of the cellular telephone that normally includes a larger display, better processing capabilities, and more memory. The Smartphone makes some types of advanced development possible. However, a Smartphone doesn't posses the same capabilities of some handheld devices such as the Pocket PC or Palm. Some programming environments, such as Visual Studio .NET, provide special support for the Smartphone.

SMTP   See Simple Mail Transfer Protocol

SOAP   See Simple Object Access Protocol

Software Development Kit (SDK)   A special add-on to an operating system or an application that describes how to access its internal features. For example, an SDK for Windows would show how to create a File Open dialog box. Programmers use an SDK to learn how to access special Windows components such as the Component Object Model (COM) or the Media Player.

Solution File (SLN)   The file used by Visual Studio and other development environments to store application settings such as special file views and a list of the files contained within the application. The solution file is the central storage location for application-specific information that doesn't affect the actual application code.

SQL   See Structured Query Language

SSL   See Secure Socket Layer

Static Data   Information that doesn't change. For example, many Web sites provide static data output; the information remains the same from visit to visit.

Structured Query Language (SQL)   Most Database Management Systems (DBMSs) use this language to exchange information. Some also use it as their native language. SQL provides a method for manipulating data controlled by the DBMS. It defines which table or tables to use, what information to get from the table, and how to sort the information. A typical request will include the name of the database, table, and columns needed for display or editing purposes. SQL can filter a request and limit the number of rows using special features. Developers also use SQL to manipulate database information by adding, deleting, modifying, or searching records. IBM research center designed SQL between 1974 and 1975. Oracle introduced the first product to use SQL in 1979. SQL originally appeared on mainframe and minicomputers. Today it's a favorite language for most PC DBMSs as well. There are many versions of SQL.

T

Tag   A generic term that refers to the specialized combination of keywords and punctuation used in a markup language such as HyperText Markup Language (HTML) or eXtensible Markup Language (XML). In many cases, the tag appears as a tag pair. For example, `<H1>My Header</H1>` contains a tag pair, `<H1>`, and associated text. The `<H1>` tag designates a level 1 header.

TCP/IP   See Transmission Control Protocol/Internet Protocol

Transmission Control Protocol/Internet Protocol (TCP/IP)   A standard communication line protocol (set of rules) developed by the U.S. Department of Defense. The protocol defines how two devices talk to each other. TCP defines a communication methodology where it guarantees packet delivery and also ensures the packets

appear at the recipient in the same order they were sent. IP defines the packet characteristics.

U

UI   See User Interface

Unicode Transformation Format (UTF)   A standardized method of representing characters both printed and abstract using codes. Other forms of character representation include ASCII. Some sources also abbreviate this term as Universal Character Set (UCS) Transformation Format.

Uniform Resource Identifier (URI)   A generic term for all names and addresses that reference objects on the Internet. An URL is a specific type of URI. See Uniform Resource Locator (URL).

Uniform Resource Locator (URL)   A text representation of a specific location on the Internet. URLs normally include the protocol (`http://` for example), the target location (World Wide Web or `www`), the domain or server name (`mycompany`), and a domain type (`com` for commercial). It can also include a hierarchical location within that Web site. The URL usually specifies a particular file on the Web server, although there are some situations when a Web server will use a default filename. For example, asking the browser to find `http://www.mycompany.com`, would probably display the `DEFAULT.HTM` or `INDEX.HTM` file at that location. The actual default filename depends on the Web server used. In some cases, the default filename is configurable and could be any of a number of files. For example, Internet

Information Server (IIS) offers this feature, so the developer can use anything from an HTM, to an ASP, to an XML file as the default.

URI   See Uniform Resource Identifier

User Authentication Token   A secure means of identifying the user using a long string of characters of any value (the string can contain non-alphanumeric characters). Using a long character string makes it difficult for someone to guess the character sequence. However, the lack of user information in the string also keeps the user's identity secure from anyone who does manage to see the string.

User Interface (UI)   The portion of an application that contains user accessible controls and data manipulation elements. The user interface for a Windows application is commonly comprised of buttons, text boxes, static text, graphics, and other design elements.

URL   See Uniform Resource Locator

UTF   See Unicode Transformation Format

V

VBA   See Visual Basic for Applications

Visual Basic for Applications (VBA)   A true subset of the Visual Basic language. This form of Visual Basic is normally used within applications in place of a standard macro language. Normally, you can't create stand-alone applications using this language in its native environment; however, you could move a VBA program to Visual Basic and compile it there.

W

W3C   See World Wide Web Consortium

Web Services Description Language (WSDL)   A method for describing a Web-based application that's accessible through an Internet connection, also known as a service. The file associated with this description contains the service description, port type, interface description, individual method names, and parameter types. A WSDL relies on namespace support to provide descriptions of common elements such as data types. Most WSDL files include references to two or more resources maintained by standards organizations to ensure compatibility across implementations.

Wireless Markup Language (WML)   An XML-based language used to communicate with Wireless Access Protocol (WAP) devices such as cellular telephones or personal digital assistants (PDAs). Most cellular telephones provide support for WML. The pages are served in a manner similar to the used by the Handheld Device Markup Language (HDML).

WML   See Wireless Markup Language

World Wide Web Consortium (W3C)   A standards organization essentially devoted to Internet security issues, but also involved in other issues such as the special <OBJECT> tag required by Microsoft to implement ActiveX technology. The W3C also defines a wealth of other HTML and XML standards. The W3C first appeared on the scene in December 1994, when it endorsed SSL (Secure Socket Layer). In February 1995, it also endorsed application-level security for the Internet. Its current project is the Digital Signatures Initiative—W3C presented it in May 1996 in Paris.

WSDL   See Web Services Description Language

X

XHTML   See eXtensible Hypertext Markup Language

XML   See eXtensible Markup Language

XML Schema Definition (XSD)   The portion of the eXtensible Markup Language (XML) specification that defines data types and other data elements. Most browsers and other applications use XSD to verify the XML document. XSD is also related to a Web site containing such information by use of XML parsers. A designer can create a custom XSD for use with a particular application.

XSD   See XML Schema Definition

XSL   See eXtensible Style Language

XSLT   See eXtensible Style Language Transformation

Z

Zip   A file that acts as a container for other files. The Zip normally provides some level of data compression to make the resulting package smaller than the individual files. Some operating systems such as Windows XP provide built-in support for the Zip file. However, in many cases, you need to buy or download an application that provides the Zip file functionality.

Index

Note to the Reader: Throughout this index, page references in **bold** indicate principal discussions or definitions of a topic. Illustrations are indicated in italics.

Y

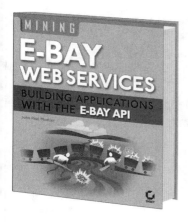